handbook of
ADMINISTRATIVE HISTORY

handbook of

ADMINISTRATIVE HISTORY

Jos C.N. Raadschelders

Transaction Publishers
New Brunswick (U.S.A.) and London (U.K.)

Library of Congress Catalog Number: 97-26144
ISBN: 1-56000-315-4
Printed in the United States of America

Library of Congress Cataloging-in-Publication Data

Raadschelders, J. C. N.
  Handbook of administrative history / Jos C.N. Raadschelders.
    p. cm.
  Includes bibliographical references (p.   ) and index.
  ISBN 1-56000-315-4 (alk. paper)
  1. Public administration—History. I. Title.
JF1351.R25 1997
351'.09—dc21
                                                       97-26144
                                                        CIP

Contents

Preface

Public administration is assumed to be a young discipline based on and exempted from inter alia law and political science. Scholars of public administration succumb to an old question always asked of a new discipline in the social sciences: what is your contribution to the understanding and, better still, the solution of some of the current problems. Public administration in academic teaching has come to provide a professional degree, with students graduating who have little knowledge of the past because what is being studied ought to be useful. Students are presented with knowledge and skills directly applicable in the career they envisage. Scholars also appear to be in search of usable knowledge, striving to provide guidelines, if not prescriptions, for the future. Although most administrative scientists would acknowledge *The Presence of the Administrative Past* (Fesler 1982), their time horizon is limited to the recent past. Indeed, much of our understanding of the present is collected on the rationale of how it can be turned into use for the future.

This book was written for a number of reasons. First, public administration has a long-standing tradition, both in practice as well as in writing. Proper administration, in whatever terms, has been an issue ever since human beings recognized the need to organize themselves in order to protect the environment where they lived. Human beings thrive in a predictable and stable environment and one of the conditions for such a stable environment is leadership. Tribal chiefs, god-kings, sovereign princes, and the like organized their leadership. Their leadership was allowed or even accepted as long as they provided stability and predictability through the protection of the land, the provision of food, and the building of places of worship. No matter how "primitive," some organization was needed. Many of the characteristics of "modern" government were established in ancient and medieval government. From a trivial point of view, several characteristics of government are timeless, such as the territorial and functional division of administration, a hierarchical structure of administration, legitimacy of government, and citizen participation. The time- and context-specific manifestation of structure and functioning of governments, however, make a universal administrative history impossible and calls for comparative research.

Leaders not only required organization but also ideas. Most of the earlier writings on public administration and leadership dealt with the elites in society, and more specifically with the relationship between ruler and ruled. As a practitioners' science, administrative science found its roots in the descriptions of how rulers ought to behave toward their subjects. With the growth of government in early modern times, the attention to governance was extended to the administrative organization proper. The first handbooks of public administration appeared in the seventeenth century, starting a tradition traveling from cameralism, via administrative law and/or political science, back to public administration proper.

Second, students of public administration (future leaders in the civil service, politics, etc.) and citizens ought to be aware of the importance and contemporary impact of past decisions and old traditions. In chapter 1, I discuss in some detail why administrative history is important in the study of public administration. This importance is not limited to scholars and practitioners only. Indeed, these professionals have an obligation to explain to the citizenry time and again why certain measures are necessary, why certain procedures exist, and how certain structures and procedures developed. The relevance of administrative history to society is demonstrated when it helps us understand the delicate balance between the citizen and his/her government.

Whether we like it or not, government is the largest single actor in most states, which is more than enough reason for a willingness to understand how this came about. It is human nature to leave or transfer responsibility and authority (and blame) to a few. Especially in Western nations, the population-at-large to a great degree has come to depend upon government for its welfare. In some welfare states (Netherlands, Sweden) more then in others (United States), but in general, government is held responsible for our collective welfare. What is perceived as "collective and public responsibility" has slowly emerged in the last five or six centuries. It is almost a paradox that people nowadays complain about government when that same government provides more services than ever before. Administrative history may help us understand and, indeed, accept the "Leviathan" we have created. Criticism of government is good for reasons of accountability and democracy, but we should do so on the basis of knowledge about how government in its contemporary manifestation has come about. After all, government size, bureaucracy, and the like are a consequence of what we ourselves desired: the transfer of individual risk to the collective. Impersonal government is the modern equivalent of the tribal chief: its rule is legitimized as long as protection and services are provided.

Third, administrative history is a topic of academic interest and the research which has been done so far ought to be more accessible to scholars and practitioners. With this book I hope to provide an entry into contemporary literature on administrative history. The examples of a general administrative history proper (Gladden 1972) and of an administrative history in the broader sense (Jacoby 1976, 2d ed.) are still important but dated, as well as limited in the amount of literature used. Much research has been done in the 1970s, 1980s, and 1990s. In general, so much literature is available that a bibliography is surely needed. From the literature it becomes evident that administrative history is pursued both for reasons of utility as well as for *savoir pour savoir*. Too much emphasis on administrative science as a problem solving and future-oriented study, however, will impoverish the potential cognitive richness of this field of research. Instead of being swayed from the one fashion to the other, public administration should find a balance between professional and academic interest. Indeed, the search for lawlike generalizations will profit from research that unravels long-term trends in the development of administration and government. Thus, administrative history is an indispensable part of administrative science which, in turn, is the core-field for the understanding of today's government-run world.

Fourth, being a historian by training and an administrative scientist by profession, I have had an opportunity to familiarize myself with both worlds. Historians of administration have enriched their understanding of the past by using inter alia administrative science concepts, models, and theories. Administrative scientists have come to search for the origins of the phenomena they study and, in the process, enlivened their analyses. This book is an attempt to bring what has been done together. It does not provide a general theory in the style of Berman, Tilly, and Weber, but it is a guide to social and administrative science perspectives on administrative history. As such it is intended to stimulate cross-disciplinary research.

Administrative history not only satisfies our curiosity about the past, but it can illuminate trends and patterns in the development of administration. It makes for better understanding of contemporary government, not just through knowing the "roots" but through realizing that our "system" is no better or worse then earlier systems. The norms and values of today determine our ideas on what was good or bad in the past. It is human to think we have done better than our ancestors, just as it is human to think that the generation after us is not as good as we were (as in, for example, education: "...in my time we had to study a lot harder..."). In other words, we enjoy being king as long as it lasts. Herein may lie my deeper reason for pursuing administrative history. It teaches the administrative scientist to be cautious and realistic with what is prescribed, and it teaches the historian that individual and unique phenomena acquire meaning in a more interpretative and, perhaps, pattern-seeking framework.

This book is the outcome of several years of research and thinking about the development of government. Some chapters in this book are based on articles and chapters I have published elsewhere. Thus, an article in the *International Review of the Administrative Sciences* (1994) served as the basis for chapter 1. A review of Dutch literature on this topic was published in the *Yearbook of European Administrative History* (1992). Part of chapter 7 (the development of the civil service) is based on an extensive chapter in a book (1996). Insofar as illustrations to the main argument in chapters 5–7 are concerned, the more elaborate discussion of the Dutch case was published earlier in *Administration and Society* (1994). Chapter 8 is based in part on an article published in *Public Administration* (U.K.) (1995) while another part is based on a chapter I co-authored which was published in the *History of Administration* series of the International Institute of Administrative Sciences (1991).

The structure of this book was developed between 1988–1994 when I taught a course called "Institutional Development in Western Nations", first at the School for Public and Environmental Affairs (Indiana University, Bloomington 1988), and in the following years in the International Program of Public Administration at Leiden University. I am grateful for the opportunity provided both by SPEA and SPEA's Director of International Programs, Randall Baker, and my own department for developing and teaching a class that does not fit the mainstream curriculum in public administration. A class with a historical perspective for students of administrative science challenges the teacher to walk a fine line between general outline and illustrative detail, and between the more theoretical and applied approaches of the administrative sciences and the more chronological and factual approach of the classical historical discipline.

In the first part of this book, the field of administrative history is layed out. The first and second chapters provide an introduction to this field of research and to general and introductory literature. Methods and problems of research are discussed in chapter 3. In chapter 4, I explore what theories on the development of administration exist, and discuss them in the background of evolutionary theories in the social sciences. In this part of the book I will refer to literature regarding all five continents.

Parts 2 and 3 of the book cover what I have labeled administrative history proper and administrative history in a broader sense. They are somewhat different from part 1 in the sense that I will basically refer to literature about the Western world, being the "area" I am most familiar with. Administrative history proper (part 2) deals with administration itself: tasks, organization and functioning, and actors (chapters 5–7). Each of these three chapters will open with (Western-based) theoretical considerations, covering such issues as concepts, definitions, and theories in administrative science regarding the topic of each chapter. Chapters 8 through 10 (part 3) focus on administrative history in the broader sense, providing the wider background against which administrative developments proper ought, at least, to be understood. Thus the relationship between citizen and government, the processes of state-making and nation building, and developments in international relations are discussed. As a conclusion to parts 2 and 3 the position of administrative history within public administration and the contribution of administrative history to understanding the complexities of today's and tomorrow's challenges is discussed in chapter 11.

Literature on administrative history is opened for the reader in two ways. The main part of each of the chapters 5 to 10 provides information about the "development of..." (public tasks, public organization, civil service, etc.), and is concluded with an annotated bibliography on the literature regarding the topic of that chapter. This provides a thematic entry into the literature mentioned in the bibliography. Part 4 provides the bibliography of administrative history organized by continent and country. It is preceded by some notes on the collection of the literature. A variety of authors is mentioned in the chapters. Whenever a reference concerns administrative history proper or broader, the full citation can be found in the bibliography. Other literature (political science, public administration, law, and so forth) referred to in a chapter is listed at the end of each chapter. This is especially the case with literature on comparative research and explanation (chapter 3), evolution studies (chapter 4), theories from (Western) public administration (chapters 5–7) and legal history, church history, the history of ideas, political theory, international relations, military history, the history of colonialism, and the welfare state (chapters 8–11).

Bouncing ideas off students as well as on colleagues has proved very fruitful. The continuous discussions with some of my colleagues at the University of Leiden have helped shape my ideas, among them especially Frits M. van der Meer, Mark R. Rutgers, Renk J. Roborgh, and Theo A.J. Toonen. Over the years their comments as partners in research, and even more as friends, have been and will remain challenging, provocative, and constructive. I also would like to thank Walter J.M. Kickert (Erasmus University, Rotterdam) and Romke van der Veen (University of Twente) for their comments. Of fundamental importance has been the influence of Professor Emeritus Aris van Braam with whom I took my first classes in public administration. As his research assistant he guided me in my initial steps in administrative history. Together with Uriel Rosenthal, Van Braam founded the Interuniversity Department of Public Administration (based in Leiden and Rotterdam Universities) in 1984. Especially through the efforts of Rosenthal and Toonen, this department has opened up to the world. Our faculty has benefitted from international contacts established at conferences and from the many visiting professors we have hosted.

Among those whom I have met in the past few years I especially would like to thank Peter Bogason (University of Rosskilde), Jan-Erik Lane (University of Oslo), Edward C. Page (University of Hull), Cynthia J. McSwain (George Washington University), Richard J. Stillman II (University of Colorado), Orion F. White (Virginia Polytechnic), and Vincent Wright (University of Oxford). I am very honored by the attention Dwight Waldo gave the earlier version of this book. His comments and those of the others mentioned above led me to write chapter 11, in which I pull the various lines of argument of the whole book together. Other comments concerned the structure and content of the book. I hope I have done justice to the various remarks.

Others have commented upon parts of this book that were based on earlier publications. I am thankful for the comments of Louis C. Gawthrop (Yale Gordon University) on the article that was the foundation for the present first chapter, and for the comments of James L. Perry (Indiana University) on the chapter about the history of the civil service that I co-authored with Mark Rutgers and was published in Bekke/Perry/Toonen (1996). I have also gained much insight from the meetings of the Working Group on the History of Administration (chaired by Vincent Wright, University of Oxford) of the International Institute of Administrative Sciences. I am indebted to the Steering Committee of the research project on Civil Service Systems in Comparative Perspective (a project coordinated by SPEA in Bloomington and the Leiden Department of PA) for giving me the opportunity to do research and complete the bibliography during a stay in Bloomington in the summer of 1994. For the second phase of this project, area- and topic studies are envisaged. This study is a topic study building on the historical perspective developed in the first phase of this joint project.

In the end it is genuine curiosity about each other's work and honest scholarship (calling for straightforward, and sometimes painful, commenting upon each other's work) combined with friendship and passion that results in solid studies. The combined forces of curiosity, scholarship, friendship, and passion of the colleagues mentioned above have been enthusiastic and very supportive. The shortcomings of this study, however, are entirely mine. I am indebted to Wendy Kooistra who adapted the bibliographic references according to the APA style and who helped to collect the data I needed for tables two to four in chapter two. I owe most to Julie Bivin Raadschelders, the least of which is taking the time to correct my text, both for errors of reasoning and of grammar. As for the rest, a simple thank you is all she would want.

This is a compact book, and was thus intended. It is a handbook for anyone who is interested in administrative history. It is a guide to literature and methods, as well as an attempt to present this field of research through topics of interest. For the student it provides a stepping stone to further study. For the administrative scientist it offers entries into the type of development he/she is interested in. The close reader and specialist in the administrative history of his/her own country may find omissions in the bibliography, but given the enormous amount of secondary sources already available, such is unavoidable. Therefore I would welcome information on any related literature which is not mentioned.

Jos C.N. Raadschelders
Department of Public Administration
University of Leiden, May 1997

Acknowledgments

1. Chapter 1 adapted from J.C.N. Raadschelders, "Administrative History: Contents, Meaning and Usefulness" in *International Review of the Administrative Sciences*, vol. 60, no. 1 (1994) pp. 117–29. Reprinted by permission of Sage Publications.

2. Chapter 3, section 1 (The use of models), adapted reprint of J.C.N. Raadschelders, "The Use of Models in Administrative History. A Reply to Thuillier," in Bernd Wunder (ed.) *The Influences of the Napoleonic "Model" of Administration on the Administrative Organization of Other Countries* (Brussles: IIAS, 1995), pp. 263–66. Reprinted by permission of the International Institute of Administrative Sciences.

3. Chapter 3, figure 3.1 from J.C.N. Raadschelders, M.R. Rutgers, "Verklaring en Bureaucratie," in *Beleidsanalyse*, vol. 18, no. 2 (1989) p. 76. Reprinted by permission of Staats Drukkerij en Uitgeverij.

4. Chapter 4, table 4.2, adapted from Anthony Giddens, *The Constitution of Society* (1989, reprint), p. 244. Reprinted by permission of Blackwell Publishers.

5. Chapter 4, table 4.3, from Gilbert Rozman, "Urban Networks and Historical Stages," reprinted from *The Journal of Interdisciplinary History*, IX (1978, 79) with the permission of the editors of *The Journal of Interdisciplinary History* and the MIT Press, Cambridge, Massachusetts, © 1978 by the Massachusetts Institute of Technology and the editors of *The Journal of Interdisciplinary History*.

6. Chapter 4, table 4.4, from Gudmund Hernes, "Structural Change in Social Processes," in *American Journal of Sociology*, vol. 82, no. 3 (1976–77), p. 79. Reprinted by permission of the University of Chicago Press.

7. Chapter 4, appendix, table from H.J.M. Claesen and P. Skalnik (eds.), *The Early State* (The Hague, Paris, New York: Mouton Publishers), pp. 640–41. Reprinted by permission of Mouton de Gruyter Publishers.

8. Chapter 4, appendix; and chapter 7, figure 7.1 and table 7.3, from J.C.N. Raadschelders, "Understanding the Development of Local Government: Theory and Evidence from the Dutch Case," in *Administra-*

tion & Society, vol. 25, no. 4 (1994), pp. 418, 419 and 432. Reprinted by permission of Sage Publications.

9. Chapter 4, appendix, table from Stein Rokkan, *Citizens. Elections. Parties* (Oslo: Oslo Universitetsforlaget, 1970), pp.61–62. Reprinted by permission of Oslo Universitetsforlaget.

10. Chapter 6, figure 6.2, from J.C.N. Raadschelders, "Organisatiedifferentiatie bij de rijksoverheid in historisch perspectief," in *Bestuurswetenschappen*, vol. 48, no.6 (1994), p. 491. Reprinted by permission of VNG Uitgeverij.

11. Chapter 6, appendix 1, figure from Jos C.N. Raadschelders, Mark R. Rutgers (1996), "The Evolution of Civil Service Systems." Reprinted from *Civil Service Systems in Comparative Perspective*, edited by Hans A.G.M. Bekke, James L. Perry and Theo A.J. Toonen. Bloomington: Indiana University Press, 1996.

12. Chapter 7, table 7.1, from Richard Rose, *Public Employment in Western Nations* (Cambridge: Cambridge University Press, 1987), p.9. Reprinted by permission of Cambridge University Press.

13. Chapter 7, table 7.2, from F.M. van der Meer, L.J. Roborgh, *Ambtenaren en Bureaucratie in Nederland* (Alphen aan den Rijn: Samsom H.D. Tjeenk Willink, 1993), p. 109. Reprinted by permission of Samsom H.D. Tjeenk Willink.

14. Chapter 8 adapted from J.C.N. Raadschelders, "Rediscovering Citizenship: Historical and Contemporary Reflections," in *Public Administration (UK)*, vol. 73, no. 4 (1995), pp. 611–25. Reprinted by permission of Blackwell Publishers.

15. Chapter 10, figure 10.1 from Michael Wallace and J. David Singer, "Intergovernmental Organization in the Global System, 1815–1964," in *International Organization*, 24:2 (Spring 1970), pp. 239–77, © 1970 by the World Peace Foundation. Figure 10.2 from Joseph S. Nye Jr. and Robert O. Keohane, "Transnational Relations and World Politics: An Introduction," in *International Organization*, 25:2 (Spring 1971), pp. 329–49, © by the World Peace Foundation. Reprinted by permission of the World Peace Foundation.

Part One

Scope and Methods
of Administrative History

1

The Study of Administrative History

Administrative history is indispensable to administrative science research as well as the training of (future) civil servants and politicians. Given the contemporary challenges governments face it is all the more important to acquire an understanding of how government developed and what limits that development places upon reform. Administrative history is an exciting venture in itself, but gains meaning when we realize how "path-dependent" reform proposals can be. In this chapter I discuss the development of administrative history (section 1.1), what it is (section 1.2), why it is scientifically interesting (section 1.3), and how it has practical applications (section 1.4).

1.1 The Development of Administrative History in Brief

Administration is of all times, but it did not receive separate attention until the early modern era (1600s). The relationship between ruler and people had received more attention. With Kautilya (third century B.C.) a tradition of advisory literature started. The common denominator in Kautilya's *Artha-sāstra* (Shamasastry 1961), the medieval *Fürstenspiegel*, and Machiavelli's *The Prince* is that they all present the ruler whom they served with guidelines on how to rule. Old too is the tradition of reflecting upon "administrative man," upon the ideal society, upon the interaction between citizens and their government. Authors in this tradition were political theorists, and names such as Plato, Aristotle, Cicero, Dante, Montesquieu, Mill, and Marx come to mind. Up to this day, political theory is a practiced field of thought.

Attention for the position of the ruler came to an end in the seventeenth century, when it was no longer the person of the ruler but the abstraction of the state and the organization of government that required thought. A different group of authors emerged such as Ludwig Von Seckendorf (seventeenth century), M. de la Mare (eighteenth cen-

3

tury), and Lorenz Von Stein (nineteenth century). These and others established administrative science. At first, attention was focused on understanding contemporary administrative structures and processes in order to improve them. Once administrative science acquired an independent place in the specter of disciplines (eighteenth century), the interest for a historical and comparative approach increased. This development came to an end when administrative science was incorporated in administrative law (early-nineteenth century onward) under the influence of the constitutionalism inspired by the Atlantic Revolutions. Administrative history then fell under the guise of constitutional history/legal history, and political history. Indeed, administrative and legal history are still often intertwined, especially in German literature.

While in earlier approaches to (administrative) history the past was searched for lessons (Tocqueville 1955), researchers in the late-nineteenth century sought to produce complete and factual descriptions of the past. It was under the aegis of a more sociological approach that historic-comparative research began again with Max Weber and, in Weber's slipstream, Otto Hintze—its most illustrious representatives (Weber 1980–86; Page 1990). At the same time, various scholars in the now mature *national states* began research on administrative history of their own countries. Recent bibliographic articles on, for example, Australia (Caiden 1963), Czechoslovakia (Maly 1993), Denmark (Dübeck and Tamm 1991), England (Pellew 1991), Finland (Tiihonen 1995), France (Church 1974), Germany and Austria (Schulze 1985), Italy (Melis 1989), the Netherlands (Van der Meer and Raadschelders 1992), Poland (Izdebski 1990), and Spain (García Madaría 1980) testify to the advent of administrative history in the first half of the twentieth century. It is characteristic of this period (1880–1940) that the historical and often legalistic research is conducted without addressing the question of whether it is useful. Meanwhile, enthusiasm resulted in impressive output, sometimes comparative in nature (Barker 1944). In the *Yearbook of European Administrative History* one can get an idea of the number of publications available in various Western European countries. France, Germany, Great Britain, and Italy clearly took the initiative.

After the Second World War a meaningful shift occurred. Administrative scientists felt the need to prove that public administration was able to analyze administrative structures and processes and suggest improvements in terms of efficiency and efficacy. Furthermore, they attempted to advocate public administration as a *body of knowledge* requiring independent study in addition to, not as part of, administrative law and/or political science. As a result of this renewed attention for current issues, administrative-historical research disappeared into the background. This shift is clearly visible in E.N. Gladden's career. In the beginning he published a historical article. He then moved toward general public administration, and finally at the end of his career he returned to administrative history (Gladden 1937, 1949, 1972a, 1976). According to Mansfield, the list of publications of Leonard B. White (who wrote an administrative history of the United States covering the 1776–1901 period) in four volumes (1948–1958) reveals the same pattern (Mansfield 1959). Attempts to generate interest did not immediately increase research in this field. An exception must be made for Nash's *Perspectives on Administration: The Vistas of History* (1969), a monograph commissioned by Waldo. This publication inspired Gladden to write his two-volume *A History of Public Administration* (1972a) (Waldo 1984: ix, 13).

Continued empirical research on national developments is characteristic of postwar administrative history in Europe and the United States. Cross-national comparisons between some countries are also published (Armstrong 1973; Mosher 1968; Rose 1987, 2d ed.). Since this historical research effort does not interlock with the mainstream of administrative science research, it has hardly been noticed. On both sides of the ocean, administrative scientists regard administrative history as the necessary start, if that, for the analysis of a contemporary issue. Ashford thinks that administrative histories are regaining legitimacy after having been cast aside in the 1950s, and he says that "studies of this kind are common in Europe, which has a less hostile environment..." (Ashford 1992: 31). The bibliography shows that this is not entirely true; U.S. scholars have produced many historical-administrative studies.

Even though hundreds of historical-administrative articles and books have been published in the last forty years, they are but a drop in a bucket when compared to the total output of administrative science. In addition to empirical studies, some articles have been published in the United States and Europe regarding the contents, meaning and usefulness of administrative history as part of the field of public administration (In the United States: Mansfield 1951; Fesler 1982; Karl 1976; Nash 1969. In Latin America: Cárdenas 1983; Dana Montaño 1975. In Europe: Gladden 1972b; Jeserich 1978; Molitor 1983; Tiihonen 1989. In Australia: Hume 1980; Wettenhall 1968, 1984). This, however, has not led to *systematic* research efforts. It is most likely that the endeavor to write a truly comparative administrative history is beyond what any individual researcher can do. In Europe the nationally oriented administrative history research dominates, based on detailed and intimate knowledge of a country. It has now been complemented with a (modest) systematic-comparative dimension. Molitor took the initiative for a working group on administrative history within the International Institute of Administrative Sciences. This working group regularly reports on its activities (for example, Wright 1991; Wunder 1995). In addition, the yearbooks already mentioned specifically provide a comparative perspective. In the United States the interest for administrative history has found a forum in the *Public Administration Theory Network* (annual meetings since 1987) which is coordinated by the Department of Public Administration of California State University in Hayward. Researchers in this network also aspire to a comparative perspective (Argyle 1994; Chandler 1994).

1.2 Definition of Administrative History

In the literature regarding administrative history as a research topic, definitions are rarely given. Caldwell provided one such definition in a somewhat older but still relevant article. He describes the focus of administrative history as *the study of the origins or evolution of administrative ideas, institutions and practices* (1955: 455). This definition contains both descriptive as well as normative issues, but it is incomplete and not entirely clear. What exactly is the focus of administrative history? Most authors provide a short historical overview of the developments in the topic they have researched. This hardly provides us with an idea of the focus of administrative history. Several authors categorized themes in this field. Gladden presented the following six topics: leadership and top management, functions and organizations, personnel, administrative techniques, biography, and theory (1972a: viii–x). Some years later Molitor presented the same type of list: doctrine, structure, functionaries, services, methods and techniques, and process of decision making (1983: 2). Yet other lists can be found in García Madaría (1980: 36–38; law, institutions, organizations, ideas, practices, customs, and relations with society) and Tiihonen (1989: 132, 148; structure, officials, activities, tasks, expenditures, process, ideology, and type of domination).

García Madaría, Gladden, Molitor, and Tiihonen present a useful but eclectic list of topics, which neither constitute nor define a field.

And yet, administrative history is not a discipline, but a topic within a range of disciplines as Jeserich (1978: 361) and Tiihonen (1989: 149) correctly remark. Thus, a definition of administrative history should emphasize the locus (public administration) and not the focus (the approach) of the field (the multidisciplinary approach of administrative science, or the more monodisciplinary approaches of inter alia history and legal history).

A definition of administrative history can be constructed from the basic concepts of public administration: structure (particularly organization), functioning (particularly processes) and functionaries (Van Braam 1986: 4). With these three concepts one can analyze developments in any organization or policy field. They result in descriptive questions, but normative questions are also possible. What was regarded as the ideal organization in a certain period? The ideal civil servant? The ideal decision-making process? In addition to the ideas, institutions, and practices mentioned by Caldwell, public functionaries are an important topic of research. The historian Strayer once wrote that most attention is reared to the *glamorous institutions* (such as sovereignty, kingship, nation-state, judiciary, high councils of state) while too little attention is paid to the details of the recruitment, training, career patterns and financial rewards of the people who make the institutions work (1975: 504). Dwight Waldo would agree with that observation as he remarked that a genuine administrative history (*proper*, as defined below) has yet to be written (1987: 111; see also García Madaría 1980: 35; Gladden, 1976: 338; Jeserich, 1978: 361), and that the history of government as such-its functions, institutions, and operations-is a nonsubject (Waldo, 1990: 80). Waldo states that Gladden came closest to such an administrative history (1987: 111; 1990: 80). In this respect I consider Webber and Wildavsky's history of public finance to be very much an administrative history proper as well as in the broader sense (1986).

The aspects of structure, functioning, and functionaries concern *government*: the administration and management of and by public institutions (Van der Meer and Raadschelders 1992). This is administrative history proper, and is understood as such by, for instance, Gladden, Molitor, and Waldo. I define administrative history proper as *the study of structures and processes in and ideas about government as they have existed or have been desired in the past and the actual and ideal place of public functionaries therein*. In this type of administrative history national studies dominate. Sometimes a comparative inquiry is presented: the theme of bureaucracy and bureaucratization, for instance. Heady states that *bureaucracy* is a key concept since it is one of the most dominant types of large-scale organizations in the contemporary world. Bureaucracy is crucial in every type of empire or state (1991: 150–155; Eisenstadt 1958; Kamenka 1989). Occasionally "administrative history" is used to refer to bureaucratic procedure as is clear in the following:

> As a state commission, the Gates have an administrative history which is much more thoroughly documented than their aesthetic evolution, since every financial and bureaucratic transaction was duly recorded by the scribes of the Subsecretariat of Fine Arts. (Grunfeld 1987: 176)

In this sense, however, administrative history encompasses only part of what I have labeled administrative history proper.

Administrative history should also have an eye for the legitimacy of government, the societal context in which it is embedded, as well as the balance between public and private institutions. Many authors would agree with the idea that the development of administration can not be understood without attention for the society in which it is embedded. Indeed "if administrative history is to mean anything at all, it must always be related to the society from which it springs" (Cromwell 1966: 254–255). The same is true of course for the context in which theories have been developed. Weber's theory on bureaucratization makes more sense when presented in relation to his theory of the rationalization process (Weber 1980). Therefore questions about the function of administration/government and politics in society in various ages are important, as are questions about the relationship and interaction between government and citizen and between public and private actors in its consequences for the structure and functioning of government. This relationship between society and citizen relates more to *public administration*, which is a more encompassing concept referring to all public (including politics), semi-public and private actors involved in the provision of public services (education, health care, etc.). This is administrative history in a broader sense: the interplay between government and society at large. Research on the development of political systems, of the state and of the welfare state are examples. The number of comparative studies in this approach is much larger (e.g., Bruce 1961; Eisenstadt, 1958; Flora and Heidenheimer 1984; Jacoby 1973; Mommsen 1981; De Swaan 1988; Tilly 1990).

1.3 Meaning of Administrative History

Most authors would describe the meaning of *administrative history* in terms of (a) enhancing insight in the meaning of human behavior in relation to (b) the contextuality of human action to circumstances of space and time (Mansfield 1951: 152; Nash 1969: 60; Castles 1989: 12). For a proper understanding of contemporary structures and relations in public administration, a geographical and historical setting is of great importance. Such a context does not only provide identity to individuals but also to institutions (understood both in terms of values and norms as well as in terms of organizations). Without knowledge of the geographical and historical context, we are not able to assess the uniqueness nor the comparability of societal phenomena.

Knowledge of the past enlarges and sharpens our insights in the how and why of contemporary administrative structures and processes and their origin. Thus Strayer displayed astonishment about the number of people that assumed that European administrative systems had grown out of military needs and were modelled after the military organization (Strayer 1975: 504; Miller 1983). Administrative history may contribute to the notion that all *innovations* in administration are relative. Administration nowadays is not necessarily better than it was in the past. Besides, many structures, habits, and the like are hardly of recent origin. Nigro points out how modern notions about the civil service, public duty and ethics of civil servants were already present in the writings of Plato and Aristotle (1960; see also Waldo 1987: 96–99; Gawthrop 1993: 5–6). It would be interesting to see what impact the rediscovery of Greek ideas about government and administration had on Western countries, for that is not limited to democracy. It would be equally interesting to see if, how, and when certain administrative ideas and practices penetrated Western countries. Creel for instance suggested that medical and civil service exams originated in China and—via Baghdad—were introduced and implemented at the court of King Roger II of Sicily (1105–1154). Furthermore, he suggests that several Chinese administrative techniques found their way to the West, especially in the area of financial management. Again Roger II must be mentioned, as he in turn influenced his grandson Holy Roman Emperor Frederick II (1210–1250, author of the *Constitution of Melfi*, 1231), King Philip II of France (1180–1223) and, likely, King Henry II of England (1154–1189, creator of the chancery, exchequer and judiciary in England) (Creel 1964: 162–163; 1970: 9–27; 1982: 95, 116–117; Teng 1943). In early modern Europe, civil service exams appeared for the first time in late-seventeenth-century Prussia. The most famous, however, are those introduced by the Northcote-Trevelyan Report (1853) whose findings were based on experience in the Indian Civil Service.

Government in Western countries may have been influenced by administrative developments and innovations elsewhere, but Western governments surely have influenced the rest of the world (Braibanti 1966; Burke 1969; Davidson 1992; Martin 1987; Miewald 1984; Quah 1978; Sarfatti 1966; Wettenhall 1977). Administrative historical research must both assess the impact of colonization on indigenous administrative systems as well the inheritance of colonial systems in the "New States." Naturally the dissemination of administrative practices and theories within the Western world requires attention as well. Several examples of such copying behavior are mentioned in the next chapters. However, it is equally interesting to see that sometimes attempts were made to prevent such copying. Deutsch (1966: 15) mentions in this respect Ernest Barker's (1951) analysis of how Edmund Burke succesfully tried to keep the rationalistic individuals such as Thomas Paine and Dr. Joseph Priestley (who both went to the United States) separated from the "...disadvantaged chapel groups like the Presbyterians, Baptists, and Methodists." He did so in an attempt to prevent the possibility of a powerful alliance between the two groups. Such a coalition could have generated pressure for change in England in light of the French Revolution.

As already mentioned, much historical research in public administration is concentrated on one country. It is, however, in comparative studies that administrative history may provide the most important contributions (see also section 1.4). National studies provide the building blocks for research on similarities and differences in administrative developments, both in terms of contents as well as in terms of speed (Skocpol and Ikenberry 1983: 89). This might result in generalizations about administrative developments that hitherto could not be made since systematic comparison has not yet been attempted.

It is especially true for Anglo-American literature that insight, but above all the level and quality of generalization on which justification of administrative historical research should be based. This can be contested.

1.4 Usefulness of Administrative History

It is remarkable that the question of whether administrative history is a useful pursuit is only raised in Anglo-American literature. American, and to a lesser extent English and Australian administrative scientists, feel the need to justify such research more on utilitarian rather then scholarly (*savoir pour savoir*) grounds. In the eyes of Caldwell and Nash the success of administrative history depends upon the level of generalization achieved. Caldwell assumes that the highest level is to be found in the study of social evolution and the role of government in the evolution (1955: 454). Nash points out that things and circumstances at different levels can be connected with one another. He distinguishes among *low theory*, *middle-range theory* and *grand theory*, even though he does not elaborate on what they are in the field of administrative history (1969: 63). I assume that Nash's *grand theory* is comparable to what Caldwell calls *highest level of generalization*. In this respect Skocpol and Somers speak of macrocausal analysis (1980: 175–180; see also ch. 3).

Some would argue that the higher the level of generalization, the more insights about development can be used for application in the present and, above all, the future. The reverse, however, is just as plausible: the higher the level of generalization, the more limited its practical use. After all, such *general "laws"* are not specific enough for a concrete problem in a policy area, or a concrete problem in an organization. A specific historical study may provide more insight in the situation as it exists or unfolds. Understanding of the present in administrative science is too often determined by its utility for the future.

Something else needs to be kept in mind in our pursuit and use of theory. Theories such as those of Eisenstadt (1963), Tilly (1990), Weber (1980), or Wittfogel (1957) represents the accumulation of knowledge and development of ideas of one author. Testing such a theory in its entirety presumes digestion of at least the same primary and secondary sources. Often, therefore, only *parts of a theory* are subject to analysis and rethinking, and are thus interpreted *out of context*. This has been the fate of Weber's bureaucratization theory, attacked on rather detailed elements instead of on its function in understanding the rationalization process as a whole (Mayntz 1965). What is more, someone else's interpretation of *facts* may lead to slightly or quite different conclusions given the fact that we ourselves (*homo gubernatio*) are subject *and* object of research.

According to some, the use of administrative history (and thus the legitimacy of research efforts in that field) is only shown when its usefulness for the present and the future is clear. Different approaches and remarks in literature combined help us to clarify why administrative history is likely to be useful. This can be done in three steps:

1. Acquiring knowledge for itself to serve (better) understanding of the present;
2. Listing practical lessons from this knowledge about developments; and
3. Contributing to the solution of current problems and the shaping of society in the future.

Fesler strengthened the case for administrative history by arguing that its relevance operates in two time dimensions. Attention for the *distant past* rests on its enrichment of our understanding, not in the discovery of lessons for present and future practice. It is a civilizing and liberating influence, reminding us of the profession's roots and its development, identifying the major innovations that led to much that we take for granted, and highlighting problems unsolved then and unsolved now (Fesler 1982: 2). An example of a question regarding historical knowledge for understanding of the present is: to which degree is the historical and geographical context wherein an organization is *born* of influence on its structure and functioning in the present? (Meyer and Brown 1977: 366; see also Meyer et al. 1985). This question is an example of a concrete question as meant above. It is not only interesting for an administrative history proper. In general the present circumstances in which we govern and are governed are the result of choices made in the past (Rose 1987: xiii). It is why Fesler calls for attention of the *recent past* since it may prevent us from making the same mistake twice and can result in altering the conditions accounting for earlier failures. Interest in the recent past serves *institutional memory* and helps to assess the *impact of (past) decision making* (Fesler 1982: 19–20).

It might be important for civil servants and politicians to realize that certain issues appear on the public agenda over and over again (Legendre 1972: 361), to know why certain choices had been made, and what arguments were used at the time. It is in this respect interesting to note that, at least once, a class has been taught concerning the uses of history for decision-makers (at the Kennedy School of Government in Harvard: see Neustadt and May 1986). Knowledge of the past is especially important for *new* policy areas. Decision making about metropolitan governance in the Netherlands could profit from knowledge about comparable plans earlier (Van der Meer and Raadschelders 1988). Civil servants and politicians, but citizens and students just as much, will at least have to have an idea as to why social functions were slowly incorporated within governments' responsibility. The citizen does not only complain, but also demands protection, equal rights, and special support. Understanding of bureaucracy will not have to mean that one accepts it without criticism, but constructive criticism of bureaucracy is only possible when having an understanding of the reasons for its development in the welfare state. In general this requires knowledge of administrative history in a broader sense. The student of public administration should be acquainted with administrative history proper as well, since they will be the decision makers of tomorrow. They need to understand and assess the possible impact of their decisions on structure, functioning, and functionaries. What is more, they need to appreciate that their present scope of options is set by the limits and the opportunities of past decisions.

Understanding of the present through administrative history is enhanced when approached by means of comparative analysis. Administrative history in this sense is comparison over time, enabling us to see through the political and administrative fads and fashions of the day and getting a perspective on more fundamental differences and similarities between present and obsolete structures, operations, and policies. To speak with Alexis de Tocqueville: "There are far more ways of structuring society than man, living in a specific country, is able to envisage" (in Jacoby 1976: 222). Our perception of reality is bound by both time and place, and comparative administrative history holds the promise that it can break through these boundaries.

The assessment of practical lessons for the present is motivated by the idea that certain facts will repeat themselves and one does not have to re-invent what already exists (Caldwell 1955: 454). Jeserich suggests a motivation for the practical and political meaning of administrative history by pointing to its contribution to reform of public organizations, its contribution to general education of politicians and civil servants, and in its contribution to strengthening the relationship between those who govern and those who are governed (1978: 363). Mansfield cautions against the idea that we can construct lessons from the past since circumstances, persons, and environments change constantly.

Based on steps one and two it ought to be possible to solve current administrative problems and help shape future society. According to Caldwell and Hume, that is the most important source of legitimacy for administrative history (Caldwell 1955: 458; Hume 1980: 436). Maybe this indeed is possible, but then only when it regards historical research in a specific area. Maybe we can then derive ideas about how to shape government and society. Our expectations should be realistic though. The most innovative courses, reforms, and techniques are obsolete at the moment of their implementation/use (Strayer 1975: 508). Furthermore, we should not underestimate the influence of tradition and public opinion.

Most researchers will not dispute the scientific relevance of administrative history. It becomes more difficult to indicate what its relevance might be for society-at-large and for policy-making. Relevance for society can be found in *historical sensitivity* toward how government is influenced by its environment and how it might enhance the ability to both appreciate more as well as criticize adequately the government of one's own era. This may be considered important, but it seldom finds its way into the public administration curricula as Scott and Wettenhall remarked (1980: 494). Relevance for policy-making is difficult to show, let alone prove—that is, if we think in terms of practical lessons and solutions for the future. This is so in all of the social sciences. Few will dispute that knowledge and insight in administrative development might be important for the day-to-day actions and behavior of politicians, civil servants, and citizens.

1.5 Final Remarks

Administrative history is a rich field of research. Realizing how large the number of potential topics is, it is as demanding and time-consuming as any field of research. Several authors can be mentioned whose expertise in administrative science is uncontested and who have contributed to administrative history with either research in a particular topic or through articles regarding the field of administrative history. As remarked in section 1.4 it is in the special topics that administrative scientists can make their best contributions. Based on this, some among them should, in cooperation with historians, work on systematic and comparative studies. Considering the amount of publications, it is possible to write such an administrative history proper as well as one in the broader sense, at least at the level of a middle-range theory. Administrative history is stimulated through systematic and comparative research and teaching.

With regard to research, knowledge from such disciplines and/or fields as public administration, political science, organization sociology, history, legal history, church history, military history, the history of international relations, and the history of ideas about governing need to be combined. The very fact that students will seldom major in both history and public administration inhibits the study of administrative history. And if one does major in both fields the "...student is left to his or her own devices in acquiring interest and skill in exploring and developing the connections between the two disciplines" (Wettenhall 1984: 3). Wettenhall calls for cooperation across disciplines. Few will claim to have adequate knowledge in all of these areas. Cooperation among researchers of different disciplines is a necessity if only to achieve that:

> history of administrative institutions and processes [can be] treated both more broadly (through time and across circumstances) and more clearly (with the use of concepts that more sharply define the phenomena). (Waldo 1984: xxiii)

With regard to education, it is astonishing to see that students of public administration hardly have an idea of the historical development of their own governments and societies. Would it serve their understanding if they knew what administrative ideas and practices constituted their government?

One final remark: administrative history is an important field of research and education within public administration, but it is as incorrect to deduct prescriptions from the past as it is to understand the present and shape the future without knowledge of the past.

References

A different and shorter version of this chapter was published in the *International Review of the Administrative Sciences* 60, no.1 (1994): 117–129.

Argyle, Nolan J. 1994. "Origins of the Career Bureaucracy: Church-State Conflict and the Emergence of the Secular Civil Servant." Paper presented at the Seventh Annual Symposium of the Public Administration Theory Network at University of Ohio, Akron.

Barker, Ernest. 1951. *Essays on Government*. Oxford: Clarendon Press.

Braam, A. van and M.L. Bemelmans-Videc. 1986. *Leerboek Bestuurskunde*. Muiderberg: Coutinho.

Chandler, Ralph Clark. 1994. "Public Administration in the Ancient World: Variations in Theory from the Huang to the Tiber." Paper presented at the Seventh Annual Symposium of the Public Administration Theory Network at University of Ohio, Akron.

Deutsch, Karl W. 1966. "External Influences on the Internal Behavior of States." In *Approaches to Comparative and International Politics*, edited by R. Barry Farrel, 5–26. Evanston, IL: Northwestern University Press.

Gladden, E.N. 1949. *An Introduction to Public Administration*. London: Staples Press.

Mayntz, Renate. 1965. "Max Webers Idealtypus der Bürokratie und die Organizationssoziologie." In *Kölner Zeitschrift für Soziologie und Sozialpsychologie*, 493–502.

Meyer, Marshall W. and M. Craig Brown. 1977. "The Process of Bureaucratization." *American Journal of Sociology* 83 no.2: 364–385.

Meyer, Marshall W., W. Stevenson, and S. Webster. 1985. *Limits to Bureaucratic Growth*. New York and Berlin: Walter de Gruyter.

Waldo, Dwight. 1984. *The Administrative State: A Study of the Political Theory of American Public Administration*. 2d ed. New York and London: Holmes & Meier Publishers.

————. 1990. "A Theory of Public Administration Means in Our Time a Theory of Politics Also." In *Public Administration: The State of the Discipline*, edited by Naomi B. Lynn and Aaaron Wildavsky, 73–83. Chatham, NJ: Chatham House Publishers, Inc.

Weber, Max. 1980. *Wirtschaft und Gesellschaft*. Tübingen: J.C.B. Mohr.

2

Countries, Authors, and Sources:
General and Introductory Literature

The bibliographic articles of administrative-historical studies mentioned in the first chapter present a state of the art. Ideally, such an article should contain literature covering all three aspects of administrative history proper (structure, functioning, and actors) as well as administrative history in the broader sense. The same can be said about national administrative histories. In this chapter I confine myself to general and introductory literature. Specialized, country-specific literature will be discussed in chapters 5–10. The studies in this chapter are mentioned by way of example, and more references can be found in the bibliography.

2.1 General Administrative Histories

General, that is, global or regional introductions to the history of administration and government are scarce. They are usually limited in time and space. Barker's study (1944) of the development of public services in Western Europe is an example of a regional introduction covering the 1660–1930 period. Comparative literature on the development of the welfare state provides another example of studies limited to a particular time period. The studies by Wittfogel (1957), Eisenstadt (1963), Tilly (1990), and Greenfeld (1992) cover a variety of eras and areas, but the scope of time is limited. There are two studies that are both global as well as unlimited in time. The first was published by the American writer Duganne in 1860. His narrative consists of statements about types of government and their organization over a wide range of civilizations and periods. Duganne provides a compilation of what was known about the development of government at the time. Almost 40 percent of his book deals with the ancient and medieval governments (in Asia, Africa, and Europe). A large section is devoted to the development of government in the monarchies and republics of the nineteenth century (with attention for Western as well as Asian and American states). There is, however, no reference to studies he may have used. The second global (and first) scholarly study is Gladden's *History of Public Administration* (1972). That study, too, has its limitations, at least according to Strayer:

> The author set himself an impossible task; no one could cover the subject in 700 pages, especially since Chinese, Indian, Middle Eastern, Mayan, and Aztec systems were included. About all he could do was to summarize a few books, and he did not always find the best books. (1975: 506)

It is true that Gladden did not make adequate use of the extensive literature that was already available at the time, but that does not devalue his attempt to present an overview. It is, however, possible to adequately cover a variety of civilizations, as the studies of Eisenstadt, Tilly, and Wittfogel show. The strength of those studies is the ordering of material around concepts derived from theory. I know of one study unlimited in time and based on one topic, and that is Kamenka's study of the development of bureaucracy (1989).

In general, a systematic study that goes beyond a fragmented and chronicle-type description of the development of administration and government is best served by a set of explicit and consistent concepts (see also ch. 3). In the case of comparative studies also, time and geographical area limits may be called for. Not only is it physically and geographically impossible for one author to master all the primary sources, as Eisenstadt remarked (1963: viii), it is just as impossible to master all the secondary sources. Secondary sources may be more accessible but the sheer abundance of them makes it difficult for anyone to claim to have read everything. Indeed, adequate interpretation of the literature presupposes not only detailed knowledge of eras and areas, but also familiarity with the larger environment within which administration and government develop(ed). One usually has such familiarity with the country where one was born and raised, and it provides the contextual understanding to the detail of the empirical analysis. The greater the number of countries covered, the less likely the chance that the rich empirical detail "...can be marshalled to explain what is observed" (Rose 1991: 456).

2.2 Region- and Country-Specific Administrative Histories

The discussion of general and introductory literature will be done by region (Africa, Asia, Australia, Europe, and Latin and North America), distinguishing among ancient/early states, medieval states (Europe), pre-modern, and modern states. With respect to Africa, Asia, and Latin and North America, attention will be given to the periods of colonization and independence.

Africa

There are no general introductions to the administrative history of Africa. There is, however, an edited study by Eisenstadt et al. (1988) on the early state in Africa, containing several references. A personal view on the development of the African state in the last 150 years is provided by Davidson (1992). Claesen and Geschiere conducted a study of state formation in Africa (1984). As to be expected, much attention is focused on the impact of colonization in general (Davidson 1992; Hartmann 1957), as well as on specific countries (Nicolson 1969 on Nigeria; Lewin 1978 on Ghana; McCarthy 1983 on Ghana). Some studies are also available on the legacy of colonial administration in general (Burke 1969) as well as for specific countries (Kooperman and Rosenberg 1977 on Kenya and Ghana). While literature on the general administrative history of Africa appears to be limited, much information is likely to be found in historical studies on Africa and African countries.

Asia

As with Africa, there are no general administrative histories of Asia. There are several early state studies (Quaritch 1934 on Thailand; see also for China and India below). Braibanti's collection of studies on the legacy of the British imperial tradition, published shortly after the independence surge in Asia, is required literature for all who are interested in administrative developments in recent decades (Braibanti 1966). In this respect Quah's article on the origins of bureaucracy in ASEAN (Association of Southeast Asian Nations) countries is also worthwhile reading (1978). With respect to country-specific studies China, India, and—to a lesser extent Indonesia and Japan—have attracted much attention. I will limit myself here to a brief discussion of the literature on China and India.

China's influence in Asia is large. China is one of the oldest states in the world, and has a continuous history of at least 3500 years. China provides a case of a succession of extremely self-conscious governments, recording the administration's business for generations to follow (Balasz 1957). These histories testify to the continuity of Chinese bureaucracy, but what attracted most attention are the periods of change and innovation, most notably during the Ch'in dynasty (221–206 B.C.), the western Han dynasty (206 B.C.–A.D. 9), the northern Sung dynasty (960–1127), the Ming dynasty (1368–1644) and the Ch'ing or Manchu dynasty (1644–1911).

During the Ch'in, a centralized unitary state was established (Creel 1964, 1982). The following western Han is known for the establishment of a civil service and an examination system (Bielenstein 1980; Loewe 1967; Wang 1949). A substantial amount of research has been done on the reforms during the Sung dynasty. Some general studies on the Sung are available (Davies 1986; Kracke 1953; Sariti 1970), as well as special studies on the civil service reforms (1068–1085) when civil and military administration were separated. Most of these special studies center around the person of Wang An Shih (1021–1086, chancellor 1069–1086), although some of his reforms were revoked after 1086. The Ming era was important for the expulsion of Mongol rule (1264–1368) and the reestablishment of China as an independent centralized state based on strong territorial (provinces) and functional (government departments) differentiation (Hucker 1958, 1966; Liang 1956). Under the Ch'ing, or Manchu, dynasty, China reached its ultimate, largest size—a territory ruled through a police-state system (Ho 1952; Hsieh 1925; Metzger 1973; Michael 1942). There is no general administrative history of China encompassing the entire range of dynasties, but it ought to be possible to write one considering the literature available.

Contrary to China, the early history of India is one of invasions. The first time that a large part of this subcontinent was brought under one rule was during the Maurya dynasty (321–185 B.C.) (Altekar 1955, 2d ed.; Shamasastry, 1961). Of all the invasions that followed (Parthians, Huns, Arabs, Mongols, and Moghuls), the Moghul invasion and empire (1526–1757) attracted the most attention, not so much for its administrative innovation but for its splendor (Taj Mahal). The Moghul empire was constantly under external (Afghans) and internal (Muslim versus Hindu) pressure (Hasan 1936; Lybyer 1913; Mishra 1989; Moreland 1957; Sakkar 1920; Smith 1926, 2d ed.; Srivastava 1979). The last 100 years of Moghul rule coincided with the establishment of European trade posts on India's coasts. The English presence would be lasting. Especially the Indian Civil Service, model for the Northcote and Trevelyan Reform Proposal of 1853, has received much attention (Cohn 1966; Ghosal 1944; Mishra 1977; O'Mally 1965–2; Spangenberg 1976). A general administrative history of the period of English domination is available (Puri 1968).

Australia

Australia was drawn in the annals of history when the English started to develop it as a prison colony (1788). A general administrative history is available (Finn 1987), as well as various, more specific studies.

Europe

In the literature that is to be regarded, more or less, as administrative history, the studies on Europe and North America clearly dominate (see also section 2.6).

There are various studies on Greek and Roman government, as well as on medieval European polities. Both antiquity and the Middle Ages are the playgrounds of historians and legal historians (Arnold 1906; Berman 1983; Burn 1952; Jones 1960; Loewenstein 1973; Strayer 1970; Ullmann 1966). Several studies have been published on the Byzantine Empire (Franzius 1967; Bréhier 1949) and England (Lyon 1980; Tout 1916).

The early modern and modern periods have been studied extensively by administrative scientists, legal historians, and historians. A fair number of comparative studies covering Western Europe, usually focused on a particular topic, is available (Armstrong 1973; Barker 1944; Blockmans and Tilly 1994; Tilly 1975, 1990; Torstendahl 1991; Williams 1970). There are several administrative histories for individual countries: Austria (Helbling 1974–2), Denmark (Frandsen 1984), Finland (Tiihonen 1989), France (Fougère 1972; Sautel 1971), Germany (Jeserich et al. 1983, 1988), Norway (Benum, Debes, Maurseth, Tönnerson), Poland (Kutrzeba 1920), and Sweden (Tarschys 1978).

As can be expected, the number of studies of a particular period and/or area is much larger. The Napoleonic period often serves as the end (early modern developments, 1600–1800) or the beginning (modern developments, 1800–present) of a study. Several regions in the Austrian-Habsburg and Holy Roman Empires have separate administrative histories. Prussia in particular attracted much attention since the Prussian model of administration has been highly influential in Europe. Among the European countries most intensively studied are France, Germany, Great Britain, and Italy, and to a lesser extent, the

Netherlands, Poland, Russia, and Turkey (including the Ottoman Empire). Given the interchange of ideas in Europe, a variety of comparative (specific) studies involving two or three countries have been published: the Germanies and Russia (Raeff 1980), England and Germany (Mommsen 1981; Schmidt 1932; Supple 1985, 2d. ed.), Austria and Prussia (Hintze 1901), Britain, France, and the Netherlands (Fritschy 1990), Britain and France (Mathias and O'Brien 1976), France, Prussia, and Russia (Armstrong 1972), and France, Russia, and China (Skocpol 1983).

Latin America

Most information on early states/empires in Latin and Central America will be found in histories of civilizations such as the Inca, the Maya, the Aztec, and other (smaller and older) Pre-Columbian states. A lot of research has been done on the impact of Spanish colonization. General introductions to this period are available (Haring 1947; Roscher 1944; Sarfatti 1966), sometimes restricted to a particular period (Lynch 1958). Also several country studies can be found, often on a particular topic, such as bureaucratic change in Bolivia during decolonization (Lofstrom 1973), the growth of bureaucracy in Brazil during the struggle for independence (Manchester 1972), the town council in Spanish Peru (Moore 1954), and on Spanish rule in the Kingdom of Quito (later: Ecuador) (Phelan 1967). Studies about administrative development after independence can be found in the (comparative) political science literature (Heper 1991; Wiarda 1974, 1981).

North America

There is a tradition of administrative history in Canada, as is clear from studies on Quebec (Gow 1971, 1979, 1986). A statewide study concerning the 1841–1867 period is available (Hodgetts 1955). There are, however, many more studies available on the United States. White's four-volume study (1948–1958) provides an indispensable introduction to the 1776–1901 period. The lack of a comprehensive study of American administrative history in the twentieth century is made up for by various topical studies on for example the civil service (Van Riper 1958; Nelson 1982), public works (Armstrong 1976, local government (Griffith 1974; Schiesl 1977), and specific offices (Corwin 1970; Hatch 1934; Mansfield 1939; Williams 1956). The volume on historical perspectives in American public administration edited by Fesler (1982) contains contributions about the United States as well as about other Western countries. Also informative is a collection of earlier published papers concerning specific topics brought together in a volume edited by Chandler (1987).

Summary

General, though tentative, conclusions on a state of the art of administrative history can be drawn on the basis of the overview in this chapter and the bibliography (see ch. 12).

1. General administrative histories of the world will prove to be very difficult to produce. Only a group of scholars is able to succeed in such an endeavor, though they may find it necessary to limit the study to particular aspects.

2. General administrative histories focusing on a particular region are scarce, especially for Africa, Asia, Australia, and the Americas. Most comparative studies deal with a number of countries that share a common heritage.

3. The study of administrative history is deeply rooted in European public administration. France, Germany, Great Britain, and Italy have been studied extensively because of the influence these state and administrative systems have had on Europe as well as the world. Outside the European region, China, India, and the United States are the most studied countries.

4. The amount of literature available on the Netherlands makes us aware of what might be available in various countries. Articles discussing the state of the art in individual countries (such as those mentioned in ch. 1) will be very welcome.

5. In general there are five themes that have attracted much attention. For administrative history-proper these are bureaucracy in terms of civil service (including size of the civil service and recruitment and selection procedures and career patterns), bureaucracy in terms of institution and organization (including hierarchy, government departments, territorial administration), and careers of important administrators. The analysis of policy development is slowly becoming more important. Administrative history in the broader sense appears to focus on development of the early state, and the development of the welfare state.

6. The early and medieval history of government and administration is dominated by historians and legal historians. The early modern and modern periods have been of interest to historians, legal historians, as well as administrative scientists. Given the abundance of literature on Europe (in general and for specific countries), it should be possible to write a comprehensive administrative history. Again this is probably best done as a cooperative undertaking for which an analytical framework should be developed.

2.3 Statistical and Contemporary Sources

Statistical information is usually available on the nineteenth and twentieth centuries, since that is the period that Western governments began collecting information on a systematic basis. National census bureaus provide large data sets, often annually collected and published on various topics. Examples are the publications of the Dutch Central Bureau of Statistics (among which a volume on 1899–1989 statistics, 1989) and of the U.S. Census Bureau (among which a volume in historical statistics on government finance and employment, 1964). Historical statistics on Europe are available covering the 1750–1970 period (Mitchell 1980). Flora et al. (1983) published a volume covering Western Europe for the 1815–1975 period.

The State Almanacs are an indispensable source of information, since they provide an (often annually revised) overview of the most important officials in government departments, field agencies, and subnational governments. They can be used to generate an overview of the development of administrative differentiation. Other sources of information are the annual *Stateman's Yearbook* (London: MacMillan) and the *Almanach de Gotha* (Justhus Perthus). How they can be used to obtain information has been shown by Rose (1976). Some studies are available on the use of statistics by governments in general (Woolf 1991), and for some specific countries (Hoock 1989, on France and Germany). Finally, studies about size and composition of the civil service often provide tables with data collected from primary (archives) or secondary (census bureaus, etc.) sources.

While available statistics make it easier to get a perspective on developments in size, and secondary literature can be used as a source for tentative comparisons, contemporary documents of whatever kind are indispensable for any in-depth study. A distinction can be made between:

1. documents compiled as a record of the administration's business (for instance tax records, minutes of meetings, statistical records such as the Doomesday Book and the Napoleonic inventories);
2. documents conveying the intention of the administration to the public (legislation, regulations, announcements);
3. documents serving as a contract between government and (part of) the public (Magna Carta, Bill of Rights, constitutions, and so forth);
4. documents displaying a dominant or antagonistic political theory (advice literature, instructions for office holders, ideas on proper administration, pamphlets, newspapers).

Many (Western) countries have made their public records accessible through storage in libraries and archives (Public Record Office in London; Library of Congress in Washington; Algemeen Rijksarchief in The Hague) and through publication series of important documents. One will find that central government documents have been opened up more then local government documents. These type of documents can be used to generate data on tax returns, size of public employment, and so forth. Several studies are available. The records of Chinese dynasties have already been mentioned (Balasz 1957). Breasted (1906–07) published a study on ancient records of Egypt. Barker's 1956 study deserves to be mentioned since it concerns documents and ideas about society and politics in antiquity. It helps us understand the roots of political and administrative development in Europe. Although he does not discuss documents pertaining to administration, he does refer to them (Barker 1956: 87). Clanchy (1979) investigated the increasing use of written documents in medieval England for the 1066–1347 period. Bell (1953) produced a study on the history and records of the Court of Wards and Liveries in England. Ledgers of the royal treasurers in sixteenth-century Spanish America were subject of a study by Haring (1922).

Legislation and regulations provide a second source of information. Study of the Poor Laws in Great Britain and America, for instance, will show that state intervention in poor relief–however simple it may seem for a twentieth-century observer–has a long-standing tradition, and shows changes in government motivation and goals.

A third source is provided by so-called constituting documents, often representing a benchmark in the relations of an old with a new power elite at the time. Poole's (1951) study about developments from the Doomesday Book to the Magna Carta (covering the years 1087–1226) provides an idea of how these documents can be investigated. Griffiths (1968) compiled sixteenth-century documents and wrote commentaries to these resulting in a comparative constitutional history of several European states. Compilations of documents regarded as important to a country's administrative history serve an educational purpose as well, and may include a variety of documents. Mosher (1983, 2d ed.) brought documents together on the U.S. administrative history including constituting documents (such as Declaration of Independence, the Constitution), legislation, government reports or excerpts thereof (such as Eaton's famous report on the civil service in Britain, the Brownlow Committee), and organization and reorganization measures.

The last type of document can be used to develop a notion on prevailing ideas about proper administration. Studying instructions of office holders over a period of time reveals information about what was expected of candidates and incumbents of public offices. With the term *advice literature* I refer to all those publications (books or pamphlets) that were written on assignment or as personal outcry concerning proper conduct of a ruler towards the citizenry. Kautilya's *Artha-sa˘stra* or Machiavelli's *The Prince* are prime examples of such, but there are also pamphlets written by individual citizens as a *j'accuse* of existing practices in government. Examples of these are the *Cahiers de Doléances* in France or the *To the People of the Netherlands* by the Dutch patriot Joan Derk van de Capellen tot den Pol. The grand literature of political theory belongs also to this category of sources (for example Plato, Aristotle, Thomas Aquinas, Jean Bodin, Johann Althusius, Thomas Hobbes, John Locke, Montesquieu, Jeremy Bentham, John Stuart Mill). And, last but not least, the early handbooks on public administration ought to be considered (von Seckendorff, de la Mare, von Stein). The history of public administration as a separate field of research (coming next to the older tradition of advice to rulers) advanced at the time that public employment and functional differentiation was rapidly increasing (seventeenth century). This is seldom a topic of research (Rutgers 1993).

2.4 Bibliographic Sources

There is a large number of journals and periodicals in which administrative history articles can be found. Most prominent among these are the *International Review of the Administrative Sciences* and the *Comparative Studies on Society and History*. The *Yearbook of European Administrative History* is an interesting and exemplary new development in comparative studies in Europe. In comparison to the attention for the rise of the state, however, the history of government as a general enterprise and in terms of its role in civilization is not well documented. To quote Waldo: "Why should there be a *History of Political Thought* journal and not a *History of Government* journal?" (Waldo 1990: 80). Several studies provide detailed bibliographies such as those by Bendix (1977), Claesen and Skalnik (1978), Claesen and Van der Velde (1987), Eisenstadt (1963), Eisenstadt and Rokkan (1973), Eisenstadt (1986), Flora and Heidenheimer (1981), Tilly (1975), Tilly (1990), Webber and Wildavsky (1986), and Wittfogel (1957). It goes without saying that the various national studies provide a substantial amount of literature.

An analysis of articles in the 1975–1984 period of two of the leading American journals, *Public Administration Review* and *Administration & Society*, showed only a few articles involving a longitudinal perspective. The problem-oriented approach dominated (Perry and Kraemer 1990: 359). Rugge (1993: 369–380) scanned a number of administrative science journals for the 1986–1990 period on the historical nature of their contents. His findings are presented in table 2.1.

TABLE 2.1
Articles and Reviews on Administrative History in Percentages of
the Total Amount of Articles and Reviews

	Historical	Articles Partially Historical	Historical	Reviews Partially Historical
1	2.10	2.10	5.35	4.28
2	3.87	3.44	1.45	5.80
3	1.32	0.88	5.40	1.66
4	14.03	—	15.81	4.59
5	0.98	—	1.42	2.85
6	8.08	1.01	—	—
7	5.93	1.69	2.06	1.23

Source: Rugge 1993: 369–380

Legend: 1 = *Public Administration* (UK); 2 = *Public Administration Review*; 3 = *Öffentliche Verwaltung*; 4 = *Die Verwaltung*; 5 = *Revista trimestale de scienza dell'amministrazione*; 6 = *Amministrare*; 7 = *Administrative Science Quarterly*

This table illustrates the somewhat isolated nature of administrative history in the field of public administration. One could argue, however, that the selection of journals is not quite representative for the field. Journals like the *International Review of Administrative Sciences* and *Administration & Society* have a declared interest in administrative history. *Administration & Society* even has an associate editor to cover this topic. At first sight, it appears that administrative history is not a high priority in historical journals, but when looking through the volumes of the *Comparative Studies in Society and History*, one can frequently find administrative history articles. I have compared a number of journals over the period 1973–1993 on their attention for administrative history. Given that as a topic it is of interest to various disciplines, I have selected some journals in the field of public administration, political science, and (one) in history. The results are presented in table 2.2.

TABLE 2.2
Percentage of Articles on Administrative History, 1973–1992

	1973–76	1977–80	1981–84	1985–89	1989–92
1	3.5	5.0	10.0	6.9	6.9
2	5.0	2.9	5.1	5.5	6.3
3	11.6	7.4	21.1	3.7	10.4
4	10.8	18.2	15.4	18.2	33.0
5	2.2	1.8	1.7	3.4	3.8
6	2.8	2.3	3.6	10.4	6.8
7	0.9	4.8	2.4	1.4	1.2
8	4.1	10.2	7.4	10.2	6.9
9	*	*	24.2	10.6	18.6

Legend: 1 = *Administration & Society*; 2 = *Political Studies* (UK); 3 = *Public Administration* (UK); 4 = *Comparative Studies in Society and History*; 5 = *Die Öffentliche Verwaltung*; 6 = *Public Administration Review*; 7 = *Bestuurswetenschappen* (Dutch); 8 = *International Review of Administrative Sciences*; 9 = *Revue Française de Science Politique*. * data unavailable

In general the figures in table 2.2 confirm the findings of Rugge in that the field of public administration does not devote much attention to the past. My findings suggest, however, that the interest for the topic is slowly increasing. In terms of interest for administrative history, the Netherlands lags behind other Western countries. Public administration and political science in France and Great Britain appear to have more of a historical orientation than comparable journals in the United States, or the Netherlands. The one historical journal (CSSH) has a marked interest for this topic.

Articles concerning administrative history proper are less in number than articles on administrative history in the broader sense (see table 2.3; see for this distinction the definitions in ch. 1). The difference, though, is not large. The fact that the broader perspective somewhat dominates can be explained in that most administrative history articles in political science journals are concerned with that broader perspective.

TABLE 2.3
Number of Articles on Administrative History Proper and Broader in
Comparison to the Total Number of Articles

	Total	Proper	Broader
1	367	4	23
2	514	24	5
3	434	39	7
4	491	15	75
5	1742	9	34
6	974	28	25
7	669	4	10
8	546	5	38
9	382	47	19
Total	6119	175	236

Legend: see table 2.2.

Given the lack of systematic comparative literature in this field
(see ch. 1), the articles found were divided according to whether
they dealt with a national topic or a comparative perspective (see
table 2.4). In this sense the difference is striking, since the number
of nationally oriented articles totals up to three-quarters of all articles. In a way this is to be expected. First, with the exception of
IRAS and CSSH, most journals are naturally oriented toward the
domestic peer group. In all journals articles were published concerning a particular development in one other country. Second, and
more important, scholars are most acquainted with the developments
in their own country. Third, it is obvious that comparative research
in primary sources is difficult for reasons of time and money. Comparative research on administrative history will to a large extent
depend upon secondary sources.

The findings in table 2.4 are in line with what has been remarked
about comparative research in other areas. In the case of administrative history, only 26.5 percent of the articles are comparative,
which is not much of a difference with the one-fifth to two-fifths of
journal articles of a comparative nature in political science journals
(Page 1990: 444–446; see also Rose 1991: 453). It appears that real
comparative studies call for book-length exercises (see Page 1990:
445).

TABLE 2.4
Number of Articles on Administrative History from a National
and a Comparative Perspective

	National	Comparative
1	24	3
2	19	10
3	40	6
4	53	37
5	43	—
6	38	15
7	14	—
8	36	7
9	58	8
Total	325	86

Legend: see table 2.2.

2.5 Authors, Countries, and Topics

As mentioned in chapter 1, France, Germany, Great Britain, and Italy have developed a great tradition in the study of administrative history. As Tiihonen has shown, students of administrative history can draw upon a large variety of histories (for instance on church, army, politics, 1989: 139–142). He also mentions cultural history as a source because of its attention for inter alia symbols and semiotics (Tiihonen 1989: 141). This issue has not been pursued much in administrative history. There is, however, a volume of the *Yearbook of European Administrative History* in preparation on this topic.

In his overview of administrative history Tiihonen discusses the roots in France, Germany, Great Britain, and Sweden. The discussion below is summarized from his chapter (1989: 107–131) unless otherwise indicated.

Germany has the oldest tradition. Authors such as Schmoller and Hintze laid the foundations for constitutional history. Schmoller published his extensive studies in the *Acta Borussica* (edited by Hintze; Page 1990) that included both studies of Germany as well as international comparisons. Weber added a theoretical perspective. More recently authors such as Hattenhauer, Heyen, Jeserich, Rosenberg, and Wunder have followed in that tradition, combining a historical approach with a social scientific and/or legal perspective. Indeed administrative history in Germany is reported to be a truly interdisciplinary affair, especially since the 1960s (Schulze 1985: 373). Main topics of interest are the civil service, and the meaning of Prussian administration for German government.

In Great Britain the foundations for administrative history were laid by Tout and Maitland and mainly focused on constitutional history. This inspired a great number of institutional histories of which the "Whitehall series" on government departments in the first half of the twentieth century is the most prominent (MacLeod 1973: 1387). Dicey laid the foundations for the history of the ideas behind the changes, summarizing the major developments in administration in terms of the change from laissez-faire individualism to collectivism (MacLeod 1973: 1388). After the Second World War researchers such as Aylmer focussed on civil service, while others such as Barker, Cohen, and Swart pursued change and/or sales of offices.

In France two approaches can be distinguished: attention for the *ancien régime* and administrative change, and the *ancien régime* in relation to social and economic history. In addition to attention for sales of office, a Europe-wide problem in the seventeenth and eighteenth centuries when governments frantically looked for financial resources, and organization of the state (Mousnier, 1971), the French have paid special attention to the development of high councils of state and regional administration. The fourth classic country in administrative history is Italy, with much attention for the Roman Empire and for regional administration in early modern and modern times. The fact that Italian universities have five chairs in administrative history underlines the importance of this topic in that country.

Swedish research in the early-twentieth century as inspired by Carlsson was much influenced by a Weberian perspective. After the Second World War scholars like Bucholz drew more attention to the social context of administration. In general the research output in administrative history (including administrative reform) is quite large in the Nordic countries, and averages about 21 percent of a total of 323 articles in Denmark, Norway, and Sweden in the 1979–1993 period (Jörgenson 1996: 95). In Finland the government created the Finnish Commission for the History of Administration in 1986. Their work has recently ended (1996). Over the years twenty-three studies have been published, representing the largest single research project in administrative history. Since most studies were written in Finnish, it is fortunate that an overview of the results of this project have become available in English (Seluvuori 1996).

In the Netherlands (Van der Meer and Raadschelders 1992) administrative history before the Second World War was mainly studied by legal historians and historians. After the Second World War a few social scientists displayed attention (Van Braam 1957; Brasz 1960). The interest of administrative scientists for the past is of relatively recent origin (the 1980s), and a result of the fact that public administration became a separate discipline recruiting its faculty from among various disciplines.

The United States' tradition in administrative history goes back to Eaton's report (1880) on the civil service in Great Britain. Research on the development of the civil service was continued after the Second World War (Van Riper 1958; Mosher 1968). In the early-twentieth century attention was concentrated on colonial government in America (Andrews 1904, 1908; Dickerson 1912), and this remained a declared interest (Karraker 1930; Merritt 1966; Griffith 1972). In the aftermath of the local and state reforms, attention went to the development of state administration (Coleman 1935; Shambaugh 1938; Garnett 1980) and local administration (Fesler 1967; Schiesl 1977). Leonard B. White's four-volume administrative history (1948–1958) stands out and deserves a sequel that covers the twentieth century.

Other countries with a tradition in administrative history have been mentioned in section 2.2 above. The discussion in this section serves to illustrate that the advent of administrative history in general dates back to the turn of this century. It thus coincides with the period that government is growing both in terms of expenditure as well as in terms of personnel (see chs. 5–7). This sudden growth of government must have baffled contemporaries and created a need to understand how it had come about. Given the current state of the welfare state in many Western countries, and especially considering cutbacks, research on the development of the welfare state since the Second World War has increased.

References

Jörgenson, Torben Beck. 1996. "From Continental Law to Anglo-Saxon Behaviorism: Scandinavian Public Administration." *Public Administration Review* 56 no. 1: 94–103.

Page, Edward C. 1990. "British Political Science and Comparative Politics." *Political Studies* 38 no. 3: 438–452.

Perry, James L. and Kenneth L. Kraemer. 1990. "Research Methodology in Public Administration: Issues and Patterns." In *Public Administration: The State of the*

Discipline, edited by Naomi B. Lynn and Aaron Wildavsky, 347–372. Chatham: Chatham House Publishers, Inc.

Rose, Richard. 1991. "Comparing Forms of Comparative Analysis." *Political Studies* 39 no. 3: 446–462.

Rugge, Fabio. 1993. "Eine Wissenschaft ohne Vergangenheit—eine Geschichte ohne Zukunft? Ein kleiner Streifung durch verwaltungswissenschafliche Zeitschriften." *Jahrbuch für Europäische Verwaltungsgeschichte* 5: 369–380.

Rutgers, M.R. 1993. *Tussen Fragmentatie en Integratie: De bestuurs kunde als kennisintegrerende wetenschap.* Delft: Eburon.

Waldo, Dwight. 1990. "A Theory of Public Administration Means in Our Time a Theory of Politics Also." In *Public Administration: The State of the Discipline*, edited Naomi B. Lynn and Aaron Wildavsky, 73–83. Chatham: Chatham House Publishers, Inc.

3

Methods and Problems of Research

Like any object of study, administrative history can be approached from various angles which are determined by the methodology employed and/or the disciplinary point of departure. Most of the methods of administrative history discussed below are characteristic of social science research in general, and so are the problems confronting the researcher. The purpose of this chapter is therefore not to identify specific methods and problems of administrative history (which is not possible since it is a research-object rooted in many disciplines: see ch. 1), but to identify the variety of approaches and problems to be tackled. One could even argue that problems of research can never be tackled satisfactorily—but we should at least be aware of what we are up against. In this overview I merely scratch the surface, because the literature on research methods and problems is abundant. The references at the end of this chapter should provide adequate introductions into that literature.

Each researcher faces choices regarding what is to be investigated and how to investigate. Ideally these choices are made explicit at the outset of the study and consist of observations concerning:

- The use of models. Are models helpful in the reconstruction of the past?
- The descriptive and/or explanatory nature of the study. Is knowledge pursued through description and understanding or, more daring, through explanation and generalization?
- The qualitative and/or quantitative nature of the study. How and why is a choice made for or against a qualitative analysis, a statistical analysis? Why is a certain method of qualitative and/or quantitative research employed? What is the nature of the collected (statistical) data (for instance: nominal data, data from primary or secondary sources).
- The singular or the comparative nature of the study. How and why is a choice made between a case study or a comparative study?
- The disciplinary rationale of the study. Is a study rooted in a particular discipline or does it attempt an interdisciplinary approach?

- The knowledge-integrative nature of the study. Given the variety of disciplinary backgrounds, how is integration of knowledge achieved? Why are what concepts and definitions employed?

In the following sections each of these issues and related problem(s) will be discussed. Wherever possible, relevant examples will be given from the body of literature collected in the bibliography.

3.1 The Use of Models

The use of models has been a hotly debated issue in the historical sciences. The classical position is repeatedly presented, for instance:

> ...by trade, the historian is skeptical, and shies away from grand principles, from doctrinal or juridical constructions, from "general views" disconnected from the archives, by experience he knows how much effort it takes to understand the searching, the hesitations, the tensions, and the counterpressures: all this goes directly against the use of models.... (Thuillier 1995: 33)

These arguments address the issue of whether *models* are useful. Thuillier's argument is one of a classical Rankean historian. How history became an academic discipline in the early nineteenth century is well known. Textbooks on the development of the discipline invariably refer to Leopold von Ranke as the man who gave history its scholarly foundation. At the time, history was badly in need of undisputed facts (separating fact from fiction) through document analysis and interpretation (*Kritische Philologie*) and meticulous archive research. The historian's goal was to establish *Wie es eigentlich gewesen ist* and create understanding through displaying the events in their *Zusammenhang* (Tholfsen 1967: 173).

In the second half of the nineteenth century Weber made clear that facts are interpreted in the framework of the observer and are thus not objective. Therefore our interpretative framework needs to be presented explicitely. At that time the search for *Warum es eigentlich passiert ist* had become full-blown. Many historians and social scientists in the twentieth century have taken up the habit of explicitly outlining their framework and their search for *why*. And not only that, for after the Second World War many historians pursued research along social scientific lines using theories and models, and many a social scientist entered the realms of history by searching in primary sources for support or refutation of theories and models (Kammen 1987: 3–63). In its twentieth-century variety, however, the Rankean historian is weary and even suspicious of the social sciences' methods when penetrating the past. *Nota bene*, I admit that the expression *Rankean historian* does not do justice to Ranke. Maybe I should speak of a *Buryan historian* after J.B. Bury who, in his inaugural lecture as Regius Professor of Modern History at Cambridge (1902), presented *wie es eigentlich gewesen ist* as a "...warning against transgressing the province of facts" (Tholfsen 1967: 218).

The opposition of the traditional historian appears to gravitate around the use of models. In the natural sciences a *model* is a formal representation of reality phrased in universal language. In the social sciences models are of quite a different nature. Sometimes they seem to be used as a straitjacket within which the facts are made to fit. This is, for instance, argued by G.R. Elton:

> Sociologists establish models which they test by supposedly empirical evidence. To a historian this seems a very dangerous procedure: far too often the model seems to dictate the selection of facts used to confirm it. (Elton 1984: 55)

He continues:

> Saving the social scientist from himself (and society from the social scientist) may be a worthy reason for studying history. (Elton 1984: 56)

In the field of history the use of models is sometimes considered quasi-scientific and a risk, allegedly leading to anachronism and present-mindedness. The correct use of a model in the social and historical sciences is the comparison of that model to reality. A model of this kind is known as an *ideal type*, a concept developed by Weber. In his exploration of history through the use of ideal types, Weber is extremely cautious and goes to great length to explain the proper use of ideal types (Weber 1985: 146–214). His ideal type of bureaucracy (see ch. 6) did not, does not, and never will exist, but combines various elements from ancient, medieval, and early modern administrative practices and ideas. Despite Weber's warnings, the notion of ideal type was frequently misunderstood, and required constant reminders of its function (Mayntz 1965: 493–502).

Why are models used? First, they help to interpret facts instead of just piling them up in the belief that through chronology and *Zusammenhang* the understanding will emerge of its own accord. Second, a model is meant to simplify, but does not necessarily mutilate (past) reality as, for instance, Elton and Thuillier suggest. Through the use of models we can understand how things came about and, more importantly, maybe even why. The mechanisms behind events may never be revealed, but models bring us closer to the "why." Third the use of models may help to raise new questions. Such trivial facts as dates of birth and death, ancestry, the publication of a charter, or a military battle may, in principle, not change, but our interest in the past changes and with it our interpretation of the past. The use of a model redirects and channels our interests into unexplored topics (economic history; the history of homosexuality; the history of women; the history of labor) which help us understand our own times. The fourth reason is perhaps the most important, for it is through the use of a model that *systematic comparisons* (cross-time, cross-national, cross-level, cross-policy) are possible. In comparative research we do not seek to force the facts into a framework, as Thuillier and Elton fear and warn against; we seek to uncover similarities *and* differences between systems. Indeed, it helps to positively identify the peculiarities of a particular system. From a normative point of view comparative research helps us to be both more appreciative and more critical of the society wherein we were raised. From an empirical point of view systematic comparison reveals both common traits as well as indigenous adaptations. Thuillier warns that the use of models does not allow for disorder. I would argue that in their comparative relation to reality the proper use of models presupposes disorder.

Some researchers will favor staying close to the facts, like Thuillier. Others embark upon a search for mechanisms and trends. The one cannot do without the other. How impoverished would historical research be if it was not supported by data from primary, archival sources. And, how lifeless would historical research be if no attempt was made to develop a more generalized framework built upon and arising from the very same archives Thuillier cherishes—and upon the gathering of a mass of information from secondary sources (cf. Tilly 1990). A model in general is definitely not *"une commodité de langage"* as Thuillier has argued (1995: 32) To be sure:

> This is not a plea for writing history backwards, for structuring history in the light of current preoccupations. It is merely a reminder that, perhaps, social scientists and historians...are locked into interdependency, and that inherent tensions should not prevent interaction. (Wright 1990: 280)

The nature of this interdependency has been aptly phrased by Mouzelis. Writing about organization theory he argued that it is often ahistorical, and that generalizations about organizational behavior ought to depart from historically specific social structures and cultures. At the same time the "...ocean of details" provided in the more descriptive and particularistic historical studies would gain in depth when "...handled in a more analytic and theoretical manner" (Mouzelis 1971: 175).

I would like to rephrase Thuillier's remark with which I opened this section: "by trade the historian and the social scientist (and so the student of administrative history) is sceptical, he searches for facts as well as grand principles, and attempts to develop generalized views based on archival work, from experience he knows both the risks and the attractiveness of the use of models, and therefore does not need to hesitate when using them: all this argues directly in favor of the use of models."

3.2 Explanation, Understanding, and Generalization

The first goal of any research is description, but what distinguishes scholarly pursuit from chronicle-type listings of events is that scientific knowledge needs to be presented in an explicit frame of reference (theory). That framework consists of an unambiguous research question, clear concepts and definitions, adequately operationalized dependent and independent variables, a discussion of relevant theoretical considerations pertaining to the object of research, a discussion of what knowledge is lacking in literature as well as what approaches have and have not been employed in research so far, and a discussion of how the researcher arrived at the choices made. Thus the research is not only linked to previous literature and firmly embedded (to be judged) within the limits set out by the author, but more importantly, the research is linked to and embedded in a larger (explanatory) context. The degree to which a piece of research is related to phenomena in a wider context determines to a large degree whether it adds to existing knowledge in intersubjective terms. That link between events to be explained (dependent variables) and explanatory events (independent variables) can be constructed on the basis of *explanation* or *understanding*, but it depends on the rigor with which these events are pursued and whether or not the explanation/understanding is impressionistic.

Explanation and understanding are presented as different ways to link object and context. Some consider explanation to be one step ahead of understanding in the sense of it being less descriptive (see also section 3.3). Thus, according to some, a phenomenon is explained when it can be logically deducted from a law or theory. An empirical law is then explained when deducted from theoretical laws (deductive explanation). This most rigorous approach to explanation qualifies any other explanation as more or less descriptive, and suggests a one-to-one relationship between cause and effect (monocausality, causal explanation). In this approach explanation is most adequate when it can predict the occurence of certain events. That social reality is not that simple is universally recognized by social scientists. Weber wondered

> how is causal explanation of even an individual event possible?... The number and nature of causes that have determined an individual outcome is always infinite (Weber 1985: 177)

Thus explanation would be served by a set of independent variables that is as broad as possible. Writing about urban policy processes, Cole argued that:

> attempts to construct an explanatory model based upon a single gross phenomenon...is destined to be a simplistic, inadequate, and, at best, only partial model of such a process. (1974: 94)

In an attempt to do justice to the richness of the past,

> Different and unique sets of explanatory variables are required almost from function to function, time to time, and place to place. One reason for this is the diversity of contexts which are called urban: every city is in some respects unique, and to understand its policies requires an idiosyncratic (configurative) set of explanatory variables. (Fried 1975: 324)

Cole's and Fried's comments were made within the context of urban studies but are relevant to social science research in general. The factor of *time* in administrative history will make explanation even more difficult.

A more cautious and realistic approach to explanation is when *meaningful* relation(s) between observed (new, so far unknown) facts and known facts are established. This can be done in various ways (Bottomore 1970; Dore 1973; Lessnoff 1974; Silvers 1987; Watkins 1973). But whatever type of explanation is pursued in the social sciences (functional, structural, classifying, genetic, teleological, ideal typical, etc.), it usually attempts to identify regularities. And even that is sometimes approached with caution, as is the case when identifying regularities take the form of clarifying phenomena through *understanding* (or *Verstehen*). The most prominent representative of this approach is Max Weber:

> For a science focused on the meaning of action an explanation is: the display of how everything was linked together, considering the subjectively intended meaning, in an actual intelligeble action. (1985, 6th ed.: 4)

This is the type of explanation Skocpol and Ikenberry have in mind when they observe in the introduction of their study of the development of the American Welfare State that

> This is not a rigorous explanatory exercise, either in historical or comparative terms. Its ambition, at once more limited and fundamental, is to offer an analytic-descriptive overview..." (1983: 92)

Many studies in administrative history provide such an analytic-descriptive overview aimed at understanding.

Whatever their nature, explanations are usually based on generalizations of reality in which the search for regularities of and/or between certain phenomena is central. A classical distinction is made between three types of generalization, depending on the scope (McCullagh 1984; Silvers 1987). The first type is the *universal law*, considered to be valid under all circumstances (unlimited in time and space). It cannot be deducted from other laws. The assumption of universality, though, may be challenged in new research. Thus the laws of Newton are still universal but, since quantum mechanics and relativity theory, in a more limited domain. *Lawlike generalizations* are limited in space, but not necessarily in time. An example of this type is Tilly's explanation of state development in terms of varying configurations of the interplay between capital accumulation in the cities and the coercive capabilities of governments (Tilly 1990). There are no temporal limits in his analysis, but the spatial ones are clear. Generalizations are valid for each of the particular areas since not all areas analyzed show the same configuration. Third, the *accidental generalization* is limited both in time and space. Thus the statement that "The *cahiers de doléances* of 1789 are strong evidence of at least one historical instance of widespread, numerous, and varied demands from below for bureaucratization" is limited both in time (1789) and in space (France) (Markoff 1975: 498). Also McDonagh's analysis of administrative development is limited in time (1825–1875) and in space (Victorian England), and even in terms of case studies (Parris 1960; Cromwell 1966). However, such generalizations are often followed by a call for more research, since a particular phenomenon is suspected of occurring in other instances. This is clearly the objective of the following statement:

> the patterns described here need not be peculiar to finance agencies or to the history of the civil service movement in the United States. Effects of origins and the environment and the discontinuous pattern of change should be evident for diverse institutional sectors. (Meyer and Brown 1977: 384)

If confirmed that certain phenomena are more *universal,* we move from accidental to lawlike generalizations. In the social sciences lawlike and accidental generalizations are what can be achieved.

Much of the research in administrative history faces the problem of overcoming what Laslett (1980: 219) called the seeming contradiction between uniqueness of place and time and the effort to develop generalizations. This goes back to Windelband's distinction between the nomothetic natural sciences and the idiographic historical sciences, but is now considered obsolete if not misleading (McCullagh 1984: 130). In specifying the types of generalization in sociohistorical studies, Laslett argues that those emphasizing *outcomes of change* are dominant (Laslett 1980: 219). Whether or not they are dominant in administrative history as well I cannot say, but this generalization is concerned with showing how, from different historical backgrounds, one outcome emerges. An example would be the process of bureaucratization, as in: "no matter how different the route, all Western countries have developed highly bureaucratized governments." This is a rather trivial statement, though, for it disregards the contemporary differences in structure and functioning of national bureaucracies. And so, Laslett then argues that a generalization that denotes *causes* instead of *outcomes* might be just as fruitful: showing how multiple outcomes result from a more limited set of causes. An example of that would be that the pursuit of control over the territory affected the structure and functioning of administration everywhere, but the outcome in each area was different. The fashionable concept of "path-dependency" applies here.

Explanation, understanding, and generalization are closely linked. Generalization provides the wider context in which explanation or understanding is attempted. Explanation and understanding can be pursued in qualitative and/or quantitative terms.

3.3 Qualitative and Quantitative Research

As a sweeping generalization one could say that in the social sciences explanation is considered stronger when based on quantitative-statistical analysis. With respect to administrative science this is especially so in the United States. The pursuit of *harder knowledge* has resulted in elaborate and inventive statistical methods and techniques. As this type of research gained momentum, historians were quick to point out that our knowledge of the past is extremely patchy, and not adaquate enough to warrant a statistical approach (Elton 1967: 41–42; McCullagh 1984: 154). This is especially true when one studies a more distant past—for the nineteenth and twentieth centuries there is literally tons of recorded material in censuses, school records, and tax returns for instance (McCullagh 1984: 142). Another observation was that no matter how advanced a technique, personal judgement always slips in—both when the original research problem is defined and operationalized *and* when the result is interpreted (Kitson-Clark 1970: 187). Thus completeness of data-series, research design, and interpretation are general stumbling blocks on the road of quantitative research.

In quantitative research, however, a statistical and a descriptive type can be distinguished. Specific problems for *quantitative-statistical research* are representativeness of the sample, the sampling method, and the reliability of indicators (Laslett 1980: 217; McCullagh 1984: 144–149). Combined with the general problems (completeness of data, research design, interpretation) we can conclude that this type of research is almost impossible in administrative history. Most quantitative research in administrative history is descriptive in nature. *Quantitative-descriptive research* can be done in two ways. First through the collection and aggregation of elementary data from primary (archival) sources. Historians are accustomed to the use of primary sources in order to supplement incomplete documentation. This is time-consuming work and requires skill both in archive research as well as in, for instance, palaeography (García Madaría 1980: 38–39).

Very seldom will administrative scientists generate data from primary sources. Given their focus on middle-range and grand theory (see below), they rely on time-series that have already been made available, such as through national census bureaus. Using existing data (for instance from census bureaus) is less time consuming, but in that case we need to know the collection-rationale before the data can be used. In order to produce a consistent time-series, rearrangement of these original statistical data may be called for. Sometimes various time-series are collected and made available to a large audience (Flora et al. 1983; Mitchel 1975). Although this may result in little more than descriptive data, as Anderson reminds us (1973: 286), the accumulation of time-series (whether based on primary or secondary data-sources) on selected indicators is indispensable to administrative history. With respect to administrative history, the use of secondary data is most common, especially in the analysis of developments in public employment in general (Rose 1987) and civil service studies in particular (see ch. 6).

More often than not, understanding in administrative history is provided through a qualitative-descriptive analysis, based on the study of contemporary documents, archival records, and secondary literature. Description takes a specific form within the social sciences, as Eisenstadt indicates in the preface to his study:

> This analysis does not purport to be a historical analysis or description,...a description of the unfolding of a given society or polity in time, nor an application of sociological tools to the analysis of such a history...Its main objective is the comparative analysis of a certain common type of political systems. (1963: vii–viii)

What is specific is the systematic analysis used in conjunction with sociological concepts in order to get a different perspective on the past. It represents a rearrangement of available knowledge.

What we consider *contemporary documents* ranges from such epoch-making documents as the Magna Carta, the Bill of Rights, or the Rights of Man, to laws, dictionaries, fictional novels (*Gulliver's Travels*; *Lettres Persanes*), to newspapers, and pamphlets. In her excellent study, Greenfeld (1992) showed how changes in the language of legal texts, dictionaries, books, and pamphlets are instructive in the understanding of how nationalism came about. Milward's study of archival records and secondary statistical data resulted in an impressive volume on the making of the European Community (1992). And, finally, on the basis of earlier research by himself and others, Wittfogel wrote a study on hydraulic societies (1957), Eisenstadt analyzed the political systems of empires (1963), and Tilly (1990) produced a challenging study of the development of national states. The studies of Eisenstadt, Greenfeld, Milward, and Tilly are examples of qualitative-descriptive analysis in the best tradition. The vision they present is not ideological nor impressionistic, for it is embedded and presented in a rigorous, explicit, and consistent manner. Wittfogel's study, though, has serious ideological undercurrents and was met with severe criticism (O'Leary 1989: 236, 250–261).

Because of the limits inherent in social science research in general, general theories (broad, cross-cultural, all-encompassing formulations of social phenomena) are considered difficult, if not impossible to achieve. Increasingly, attention has shifted to *middle-range theories* (more modest and restrictive, but intensively studied segments of reality) (Heady 1991: 15–16). Many such studies are based on comparative research.

3.4 Comparative Research

The oldest examples of systematic attention for comparative government are found in the writings of Herodotus, Aristotle, and Ibn Khaldun (Blondel 1990: 5; Warwick and Oakerson 1973: 4). Comparative research is pursued for cultural, methodological/theoretical, and utilitarian reasons. Comparison not only helps us to understand and appreciate the system within which we were raised, it also makes us look more critically at that system. It is thus an antidote for narrow perspectives developed from the study of a single system (Peters 1988: 4), and provides us with context (Blondel 1990: 5; Hague et al. 1973: 24). The theoretical value of comparative analysis has been argued thus: "...(it) is integral to theory development and testing. It is necessary for the identification of key concepts, relations among concepts, and the underlying logic or dynamic for the associations" (Bekke et al. 1993: 207; also Hague et al. 1973: 25). With respect to public administration, Dahl observed that "no science of public administration is possible unless there is a body of comparative studies from which it may be possible to discover principles and generalities that transcend national and peculiar historical experiences" (1947: 11). Two decades later Lasswell (in Collier, 1991: 7) and more than thirty years later Bekke et al. (1993: 208) argued along the same lines.

Establishing general patterns and uniformities in development had been inspired by a naturalistic ideal in the social sciences. For a long time it was considered necessary to prove that cultural characteristics were a consequence of human nature and that they developed independently from foreign cultures. Only that would guarantee the validity of lawlike generalizations. More than a century ago the British statistician Galton pointed to the problem that one could only conclude functional correlations if and when the possibility of historical diffusion was controled. In other words: when certain developments in different cultures are comparable, but resulted from common origin, then there is no functional relationship between culture and society (Narroll 1970: 975; Scheuch 1990: 28; Sztompka 1990: 53). However, in the internationalizing society that we live in, diffusion is an even larger factor in cultural exchange than it once was. The search for lawlike generalizations may just as well be abandoned, as is illustrated in an antinaturalist countermovement that searches for uniqueness among (superficial) uniformities. That, in turn, invokes a historical perspective—for how are we to otherwise understand divergence (Sztompka

1990: 55–56)? Since the 1960s comparative historical analysis has gained momentum (Collier 1991: 24). Another objective Bekke et al. mention (1993: 208) is utilitarian in nature. Comparative analysis "...may enhance the policymaker's capacity to design..." which no doubt refers to the learning effect of comparisons. This element is also mentioned by Cassese and Pellew (1987: 15) who argued that comparative analysis is interesting because it brings to light the interweaving of parallel developments in different countries as well as the diffusion of certain experiences through imitation. Although not often mentioned, but certainly utilitarian, is the idea that predictions can be made based on comparisons (Hague et al. 1973: 25).

However promising comparative analysis may appear, the problems are enormous. At the level of conceptualization there are linguistic and methodological problems. Sometimes different concepts are used for the same phenomenon (such as decentralization and devolution); often one phenomenon is defined in various ways to suit the type of research. Another issue is whether knowledge generated in one frame of reference can be transferred to another framework. Popper argues that this is possible (*myth of the framework*), whereas Kuhn and Feyerabend consider it impossible (*incommensurability*) (see also section 3.6). Peters's observation that it is difficult to generate and analyze comparative data, because of the absence of useful theoretical language (1988: 22) should therefore be amended: it is the absence of a useful *universal* theoretical language that boggles the mind of the social scientist. Recently Rutgers (1994) convincingly argued that comparison is not primarily a methodological but rather an epistemological and semantical problem. He sketches these problems as a *trilemma*, for in the study of public administration we have to deal with different natural languages, divergent administrative cultures, and different scientific languages. This distinction carries the fairly common understanding of semantical problems in comparative research beyond the search for concepts in different languages that have the same meaning (see for instance Smith, 1985: 84). Rutgers advocates a distinction between *authentic meaning* of a concept in a specific place and time, and a *meaning ratio* as a yardstick for interpretation and comparison (like Weber's ideal type of bureaucracy). In the context of comparative research, this constitutes an explicit choice for either *authentic meaning* or *meaning ratio*: "...if we pursue *authentic meaning*, we may have a better understanding of local phenomena, but actual comparison remains open to interpretation, while in the case of *meaning ratio* we may distort our observations in a way that affects our conclusions. Put differently, according to the rules of (syllogistic) logic, *authentic meaning* will provide strong premises, but we cannot be certain that these are of the same order. In the case of the use of *meaning ratio*, the conclusions follow with 'logical necessity' from its premises, but we cannot be certain about the validity of the premises" (Rutgers 1994: 25).

The shortage of (reliable *and* comparable) indicators (Peters 1988: 23) is another more mundane problem. The third problem Peters mentions concerns the minute and subtle differences between systems (1988: 23), recognized by every researcher and referring to cultural peculiarity. It is important, for one, to acknowledge that national administrative systems are linked to national political systems (Heady 1991: 6). But then, how does one select and appraise what is important in the administrative heritage of each country? (ibid.: 150). In more general terms, how does one prevent a *selection bias*? (Hague et al. 1973: 38). One solution to this dilemma may be *focused comparison*. Cassese and Pellew argued that the choice for a compact topic (like theirs: the development of merit systems) is preferable, but that at the same time that topic should be sufficiently representative of the selected countries (1987: 15). Rose draws attention to another aspect of systematic and focused comparison. Single-country studies, he argues, are often cast in ideographic, system-specific terms, whereas a comparative study ought to depart from a framework of generic concepts allowing comparison of functionally equivalent units of analysis (Rose 1991: 448–449, 462). In general it may be true that in Western Europe the Napoleonic era and the years 1880–1920 represent a crucial threshold in the development of contemporary government, but this does not mean that the administrative development in each country was the same or that the independent variables explaining that development are valid everywhere to the same degree. Comparative administrative history proper cannot disregard comparative political history.

A problem of a different order is that in comparative studies the researcher is never able to master all relevant primary sources, and is thus bound to rely on available literature with which he has to become acquainted (Eisenstadt 1963: viii). A final problem in comparative studies appears sometimes in the explanation and conclusions of findings as the *fallacy of the wrong level*. This can occur in two ways. First, data concerning an individual level (for example: one organization) are aggregated to a higher level (a group of organizations, for example), and related to one another, but the conclusions can only pertain to the individual level. This is sometimes the case in quantitative-statistical research. Second, in qualitative-descriptive research a theory can be developed encompassing an entire phenomenon but based on empirical study of a limited number of cases. How far can one go with generalization?

Peters distinguished among cross-national, cross-time, cross-level, and cross-policy comparisons (Peters 1988: 3–7). When using these types of comparative research as starting point then, obviously, most research in administrative history is comparative by nature. Examples of administrative history that do not make a comparison in one or more of these ways are rare (an example: Markoff 1975). Most administrative histories of one country provide a combination of cross-time, cross-level, and cross-policy comparisons. Cross-national comparisons often include the other three types. In national and cross-national overviews, cross-level comparisons (local up to central government) are not common, basically because most empirical research focuses on the central government level. We can, however, find cross-level comparisons in studies on the development of public employment (Van der Meer and Roborgh 1993; Rose 1987, 1989). Cross-level comparison can also be approached in terms of macro- down to micro-level studies, moving between the constitutional and political framework within which decision-making takes place, down to the motives, intentions, and perceptions of the individuals involved (Ashford 1992: 35).

Dominant in many *national* studies are the cross-time comparisons of one topic, such as the development of a particular office (e.g.,: secretaries of state and regional administrators), the development of an organizational unit (e.g., government departments), the development of a specific policy (e.g., police, poor relief, welfare), or the development of regional administration (e.g., *départements* in France, counties in England). The bibliography provides many titles in this respect. Like cross-level comparison, cross-policy comparisons are rare. Closest to cross-policy comparisons are studies of the development of various welfare policies (for instance health insurance, unemployment benefits, pension). The Flora and Heidenheimer study on the development of the welfare state in Western nations is a good example of this. With an eye on the Dunn (1981), Castles (1989), and Ashford (1992) studies, it appears that historical studies in comparative public policy are on the rise. Hume believes that administrative scientists ought to focus primarily on the development of administrative arrangements and processes. In his view, historical research in one specific policy area requires a detail of knowledge that administrative scientists usually do not have (1980: 423; see also Gladden, 1976: 338; Nash 1969: 61). I disagree with this. Could it be that the study of administrative arrangements and processes is only interesting in relation to a specific policy field or organization? To put it differently: are there similarities and differences between policy areas with regard to the development of administrative arrangements and processes?

Comparative studies can not only be classified according to *what* is being compared (Peters 1988) but also according to *how* the comparison is done. A methodological distinction is the one between *case studies*, *statistical analysis*, and *focused comparison* (Hague et al. 1973: 37–39). Skocpol and Somers (1980) provide a more theoretical distinction. They identified three logics-in-use. Comparison as a *parallel demonstration of theory* is the first type and provides comparison by repeatedly demonstrating the fruitfulness of an explicitly delineated hypothesis or theory, showing that a theory holds up from case to case. The problem with this approach is that cases can only illustrate a theory, not validate it, since cases are selected in terms of the given theory. As example of this type they discuss Eisenstadt (1963) (Skocpol and Somers 1980: 176, 191).

The second type is comparison *as contrast of contexts*. This is done in order to bring out the unique features of each particular case and to show how these features affected the general social process. The contrast is developed with the aid of broad themes, orienting questions, or ideal-type concepts. Without understanding the context, more detailed causal inferences are not possible. The example Skocpol and Somers discuss is the Bendix study of nation building (1977). Many such studies outline general issues and themes at the start of the book or of each major section. This approach is strong in displaying the chronology of unique events, but its inherent descriptive holism precludes the development of explanatory theory. Theoretical explanations are implicitly presented as self-evident truths, or else as neutral tools (Skocpol and Somers 1980: 178–181, 192–193).

The last type they discuss is comparison as *macrocausal analysis*. Skocpol and Somers argue that this approach resembles statistical (multivariate) analysis, since it attempts to set up approximations to controlled comparisons by means of selecting or referring to aspects of historical cases. Barrington Moore's study (1966) is discussed as prime example. Skocpol and Somers claim that this type of comparison is the only way to validate causal hypothesis about macro phenomena, although they realize that perfectly controlled comparisons are not feasible. This approach breaks through the unity of time and place in order to clarify and solve explanatory problems, thus providing generalizations at middle-range level with a wink at general theory. It appears that many of the studies in administrative history combine the second and third type of comparison, with maybe a slight preference for contrasting contexts.

In general, I conclude from the body of literature provided in the bibliography that there are numerous comparative studies available. Indeed, there are many *national* studies that could serve as a basis for comparative research (such as on the development of the police, of a government department, of a particular office). The problems inherent to comparative research are not simple, but that should not prevent us from pursuing such (cross-national) comparisons. It would be ideal, though difficult, to try for *systematic* comparisons, based on an explicit (and agreed upon) set of concepts and definitions. Adequate comparison would also be served when scholars from various disciplines join hands, for one of the basic problems in comparative research is the fact that one scholar cannot possibly oversee (let alone judge) the entire body of literature relevant to his object of study.

3.5 Disciplinary Traditions

In 1969, Nash could write that historians were more oriented to the uniqueness of phenomena, whereas social scientists were looking more for patterns. With the achievements of economic and social history as well as the French *Annales* in mind, we can safely claim that distinction between both traditions to be obsolete. Indeed since the 1960s, sociologists and historians have frequently roamed in each others' realms with considerable success as is shown by Kammen (1987: 3–63, especially 13–35). Again, some caution is called for. Ashford reminds us that linking history to macrotheory should not be selective, nor should the interpretation of the historian be cast aside. Furthermore, the detail in pure historical studies (both in terms of information as well as in terms of controversies) cannot be reworked in a social science framework (Ashford 1992: 33).

Hume believes that historians have been doing more and more research about the development of government because of its increasing importance in society. This importance is also recognized by administrative scientists but in general they are mainly interested in the present and future (Hume 1980: 432–435; see also Nash, op. cit. 61; Gladden, op. cit. 1976: 347). There are, however, some basic differences between both traditions. In the Netherlands at least, historians focus on the medieval and early modern period. Studies that focus on the last two centuries are not as common (Van der Meer and Raadschelders 1992). This is less the case in countries such as France, Germany, and Great Britain. Social scientists in general have mainly focussed on the nineteenth and twentieth centuries, being the period in which the welfare state developed. Administrative scientists pay primary attention to the last 100 years in the belief that it was the formative period for understanding contemporary government. Indeed, when it comes to the development of the welfare state, the 1880s and after have been most important. But many characteristics of contemporary government go back much further (see chs. 5–7).

Administrative history can build upon the knowledge and approaches generated in at least three different traditions: social sciences (public administration, political science, historical sociology, anthropology), history (church, army, international relations, economic and social history, etc.), and legal history. When combined they provide a prism through which a particular phenomenon can be studied from different angles. I know of no study where one topic was studied from different disciplines departing from the same interdisciplinary framework. Triangulation within a discipline (especially in the social sciences) is becoming popular, but *across* disciplines it is yet a dream. As already mentioned above, systematic studies in a multidisciplinary setting would require consensus about the framework. The first step in that process is to learn from one another's traditions. The second step would then consist of developing an interdisciplinary framework (see next section), but seldom happens. Unless they occur through personal cross-disciplinary contacts, there is hardly any *systematic* cross-fertilization.

There are various reasons that help us understand why systematic cross-fertilization is not pursued or is difficult. A *practical reason* has to do with the enormous amount of studies within each discipline and/or field of interest. Keeping up with that literature is already quite a task, let alone trying to monitor publications in other fields. A social reason might be the *esprit de corps*, verbalized or not, among researchers of one discipline/field. Research of the same topics in another field might be looked upon with *dédain*, jealousy, or even as a threat, more so between closely related disciplines such as administrative and political science than between legal history and administrative science. A social reason of a different order (and certainly pertaining to public administration) is the pressure to legitimize one's endeavors. Could it be that social scientists believe that curiosity for the past needs to be justified by claiming lessons for the present and providing solutions to today's and tomorrow's problems? The past is then looked upon in an instrumental way. The familiarity with a discipline provides a *psychological reason*, in the sense that one might feel less secure and confident when *entering* another realm. Having been educated in a particular perception of reality may result in professional deformation, the inability to recognize, appreciate, and work with different theories and methods. This is more of an *intellectual reason* why cross-fertilization may be difficult. It is not easy to familiarize oneself with different methods and techniques of research, nor with different bodies of knowledge when having worked in one discipline for years. And finally the question as to whether or not it is possible to transfer knowledge and the framework in which it was generated to another discipline, provides a more *philosophical reason*.

3.6 Integration of Knowledge: Concepts and Definitions

In an academic climate where knowledge is generated in ever increasing fragmented disciplines and fields, the matter of integrating that knowledge becomes a challenge in itself. Especially in the twentieth century, social sciences' fragmentation has been a notable development. The abundance of research in a particular field resulted in segregation of such fields from a mother discipline (assuming that indeed such had existed). Thus political science, anthropology, and administrative science have become fields with an identifiable object, clearly demarcated from sociology in general. The need to legitimize the distinctness of a field, usually in organizational terms, strengthened fragmentation. Meanwhile, this fragmentation inhibits integration of knowledge.

The various fields and frameworks ultimately refer to different principles. A *principle* is comprised of an *object of cognition or knowledge* and an *ideal of cognition or knowledge* embedded in a whole of explicit or implicit assumptions and norms. That principle is not subject to debate within one scientific community, since it is viewed as unproblematic. The object of knowledge, first, concerns the phenomena in reality to which the collection of knowledge is reared. We will, however, never know the ultimate reality, independent of the observer, and thus this aspect of the object of knowledge could be called the *material object* (or *locus*). The object of knowledge may also refer to the specific way in which reality is perceived and analyzed, and concerns the concepts and definitions, the relations between these, the *cut* from total reality analyzed, as well as the (dependent and independent) variables studied. This could be labelled the *formal object* (or *focus*), our formal, linguistic representation of reality in scientific statements.

The ideal of knowledge also consists of a two-fold distinction. First, the *type of knowledge* generates concerns about choices as between description or prescription, type of explanation, level of generalization, etc. Second, the *form of knowledge* concerns the way in which it is presented (quantitative, qualitative). It is obvious that a close interdependence exists between object and ideal of cognition. These elements of a scientific principle are summarized in the figure below.

The various positions with regard to integration of knowledge can be placed into this figure. Popper believes that the object and ideal of cognition can easily be transferred from one framework to the other since they are always expressed in a scientific language. This standpoint has become less self-evident. In this respect Kuhn and Feyerabend developed the theory of *incommensurability*, which basically states that concepts developed in a particular theoretical framework derive their meaning from that framework. The meaning of a concept is constituted by its relation with other concepts within that framework. As a consequence, copying certain concepts from one framework into another results in an alteration of meaning and would make integration of knowledge illusory. Incommensurability is not simply a conceptual

FIGURE 3.1
Elements of a Scientific Principle

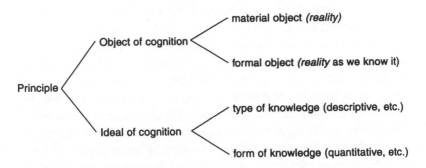

Source: Raadschelders and Rutgers (1989a: 76); Rutgers (1993: 35).

and theoretical issue, though, since concepts and theories emerge in a particular cultural framework. It has been argued, however, that incommensurability is less and less a problem in the social sciences, simply because of a historical tendency toward convergence and commensurability of societal and sociological concepts. Society globalizes, and sociological concepts internationalize. Thus, historical forces eliminate the problem of incommensurability (Sztompka 1990: 50–53). This line of reasoning, however, is not entirely satisfactory, since definition and interpretation of social phenomena still may and do vary across cultures. Solving the problem of incommensurability by pointing at globalization is too big a leap.

Integration of knowledge is a methodological and philosophical problem for every discipline/field that is defined by one object of cognition but by varying cognitive ideals. Thus *administration* and *government* constitute one object of cognition, but can be and are studied in a variety of ways (historical, legal-historical, social-scientific, etc.). Furthermore, even within a field different approaches are employed while the object is the same. This is the case with administrative science, which in sociological terms is an independent discipline, but builds upon knowledge and insight from law (codification of values and norms), economics (distribution of scarcity), political science (use of power), sociology (human interaction), history (continuity, diversity, and change), and so forth. An adequate administrative history would at least attempt to take notice of that variety of knowledge, but *integration* requires more.

Given the variety of approaches to a cognitive object a researcher needs to establish how far integration can and ought to be carried. *Strong integration* is based on the idea that various approaches can merge and consolidate into one overarching discipline. Thus administrative science could be considered a synthesis of sociology, economics, political science and the like, when it seeks to be the integrative discipline for the study of *administration* and *government*. This would probably require a second Einstein. A more modest approach is when various approaches embrace knowledge and frameworks from one another, without *losing* identity. This *weak integration* allows disciplines/fields to exist separately while profiting from cross-fertilization. In this point of view administrative science is not a monodiscipline, but merely refers to different disciplines/fields with varying principles that share one object of cognition (administration and government). This results in a multidisciplinary approach, in which the various bodies of knowledge and frameworks are related to each other and weighed in that process (Raadschelders and Rutgers 1989a: 77).

Administrative history can only profit from a multidisciplinary approach, indeed, will only then acquire more stature within the scientific community both in scholarly as well as practical terms. Weak integration of knowledge may very well carry administrative history beyond mere description and chronology, as well as beyond the obligatory chapter on *what went on before*. What is more, weak integration may convince students that administrative history is useful for the understanding of contemporary structures and processes in public administration. Intellectually, the challenge is enormous. Within the social sciences joint ventures have become quite common and resulted in a large variety of edited volumes. Especially when comparative, the editor(s) is/are aware of the analytical limits of the enterprise, since many a volume is presented in terms of *mapping-the-field* and hold a promise of further, more analytical and systematic comparisons. This is one type of research that administrative history could not do without. What ought to be pursued though, is more joint ventures between social scientists, historians, and legal historians. Impressive as such joint ventures are, the monograph written by one author that presents a vision on a particular development backed by empirical research ought to be yet another road to follow.

References

Parts of this chapter are based on two earlier publications (Raadschelders and Rutgers 1989a, 1989b). Section 3.2 was published earlier in *The Influences of the Napoleonic "Model" of Administration on the Administrative Organization of Other Countries*, edited by Bernd Wunder (Brussels:IIAS, 1995) 263–266.

Anderson, James G. 1973. "Causal Models and Social Indicators: Toward the Development of Social Systems Models." *Administrative Science Review* 38, no. 3: 285–301.

Atkinson, R.F. 1978. *Knowledge and Explanation in History. An Introduction to the Philosphy of History*. London: The MacMillan Press Ltd.

Bekke, Hans, James L. Perry, and Theo Toonen. 1993. "Comparing Civil Service Systems." In *Research in Public Administration*, edited by James L. Perry, 191–211. Greenwich, CT and London: Jai Press Inc.

Blondel, Jean. 1990. *Comparative Government: An Introduction*. New York: Philip Allen.

Bottomore, T.B. 1972. *Sociology: A Guide to Problems and Literature*. London: George Allen & Unwin/ New York: Random House.

Cole, R.C. 1974. "The Urban Policy Process: A Note on Structural and Regional Influences." In *Quantitative Analysis of Political Data*, edited by S.A. Kirkpatrick. Columbus, OH: Charles E. Merit Publishing Co.

Collier, David. 1991. "The Comparative Method: Two Decades of Change." In *Comparative Political Dynamics: Global Research Perspectives*, edited by Dankwart A. Rustow and Kenneth Paul Erickson. New York: Harper Collins Publishers.

Dahl, Robert A. 1947. "The Science of Public Administration: Three Problems." *Public Administration Review* 7 no. 1: 1–11.

Dore, R.P. 1973. "Function and Cause." In *The Philosophy of Social Explanation*, edited by A. Ryan, 65–81. Oxford: Oxford University Press.

Dunn, William N. 1981. *Public Policy Analysis: An Introduction*. Englewood Cliffs, NJ: Prentice-Hall.

Elton, G.R. 1984. *The Practice of History*. Bungay: Suffolk.

Fried, R.C. 1975. "Comparative Urban Policy and Performance." In *Handbook of Political Science: Policies and Policymaking* 6, edited by F. I. Greeenstein and N.W. Polsby, 305–379. Reading, MA: Addison Wesley Publishing Company.

Garfinkel, A. 1981. *Forms of Explanation: Rethinking the questions in Social Theory*. New Haven, CT:Yale University Press.

Hague, Rod, Martin Harrop, and Shuan Bresling. 1992. *Comparative Government and Politics: An Introduction*, 3d ed. London: The MacMillan Press.

Kammen, Michael. 1987. "Historical Knowledge and Understanding." In *Selvages and Biases: The Fabric of History in American Culture* 3d ed., 3–63. Ithaca, NY: Cornell University Press.

Kitson Clark, G. 1970. *The Critical Historian*, 2d ed. London: Heine mann.

Laslett, Barbara. 1989. "Beyond Methodology: The Place of Theory in Quantitative Historical Research." *American Sociological Review* 45, no.2: 214–228.

Lesnoff, M. 1974. *The Structure of Social Science: A Philosophical Introduction*. London: Allen Unwin.

Mayntz, Renate. 1965. "Max Webers Idealtypus der Bürokratie und die Organisationssoziologie." *Kölner Zeitschrift für soziologie und Sozialpsychologie*, 493–502.

McCullagh, C. Behan. 1984. *Justifying Historical Descriptions*. Cambridge: Cambridge University Press.

Meyer, Marshall W. and M. Craig Brown. 1977. "The Process of Bureaucratization." *American Journal of Sociology* 83 no.2: 364–385.

Mouzelis, Nico P. 1971. *Organisation and Bureaucracy: An Analysis of Modern Theories*. London: Routledge & Kegan Paul.

Naroll, Raoul. 1970. Galton's Problem. In *A Handbook of Method in Cultural Anthropology* edited by Raoul Naroll and Ronald Cohen, 974–989. New York: The Natural History Press.

O'Leary, Brendan. 1989. *The Asiatic Mode of Production: Oriental Despotism, Historical Materialism and Indian History*. Oxford: Basil Blackwell Ltd.

Peters, B. Guy. 1988. *Comparing Public Bureaucracies: Problems of Theory and Method*. Tuscaloosa, AL : University of Alabama Press.

Raadschelders, J.C.N. and M.R. Rutgers. 1989a. Grondslagen en grondvragen van de bestuurskunde: Over de methodologische funda menten van de bestuurskunde. *Bestuurswetenschappen* 43, no. 2: 72–81.

———. 1989b. "Verklaring en bureaucratie: Verklaren als methodologisch probleem voor de bestuurskunde geïllustreerd aan de hand van bureaucratie-onderzoek." *Beleidsanalyse* 18 no. 2: 22–29.

Rose, Richard. 1991. "Comparing Forms of Comparative Analysis." *Political Studies* 39, no.3: 446–462.

Rutgers, M.R. 1993. *Tussen Fragmentatie en Integratie: De bestuurs kunde als kennisintegrerende wetenschap*. Delft: Eburon.

———. 1994. Learning across the Borders: Some Philosophical Problems of Comparason and Translation. Paper presented at the Leiden-Wroclaw Conference on Administrative Systems in Tran sition, 22–25 May, University of Wroclaw, Poland.

Scheuch, Erwin K. 1990. "The Development of Comparative Research: Towards Causal Explanation." In *Comparative Methodology: Theory and Practice in International Social Research*, 19–37. London: SAGE Publications Ltd.

Silvers, S. 1987. "On Cause, Explanation, and Causal Explanation." In *Methodology and Science* 20, no.2: 120–135.

Smith, B.C. 1985. *Decentralization: The Territorial Dimension of the State*. London: George Allen & Unwin.

Sztompka, Piotr. 1990. "Conceptual Frameworks in Comparative Inquiry: Divergent or Convergent." In *Globalization, Knowledge, and Society: Readings from International Sociology*, edited by Martin Albrow and Elizabeth King, 47–58. London: SAGE Publications Ltd.

Tholfsen, T.R. 1967. *Historical Thinking: An Introduction*. New York: Harper and Row.

Warwick, D.P. and S. Osherson. 1973. *Comparative Research Meth ods*. Englewood Cliffs, NJ: Prentice-Hall.

Watkins, J.W.N. 1973. "Idealtypes and Historical Explanation." In *The Philosophy of Social Explanation*, edited by A. Ryan, 83–104. Oxford: Oxford University Press.

Weber, Max. 1980. *Wirtschaft und Gesellschaft: Grundriss der Verste henden Soziologie*, 5th ed. Edited by J. Winckelman. Tübingen: J.C.B. Mohr.

———. 1985. "Objektive Möglichkeit und adequate Verursachung in der historischen kausalbetrachtung." In *Gesammelte Aufsätze zur Wissenschaftslehre*, 6th ed. Edited by J. Winckelman. Tübingen: J.C.B. Mohr.

4

Era, Area, and Evolution:
Stage Models, Administrative History,
and the Social Sciences

Development over time is central to administrative history. In the attempt to understand processes in time, we link short and long-term variations (Meyer 1979: 34). Well-known is the distinction Braudel made between developments at the surface such as political and military events (*du temps court*), cyclical developments such as price and wage development (*du conjoncture*), and structural developments like demographic changes and changes in the geographical environment (*la longue durée*) (Braudel 1958). The development of explanatory models that connect such a variety of developments is a challenge in itself, bearing in mind what Cole, Fried, and Weber said about explanation (see ch. 3). The complexities to be embraced in time-models require complex explanatory models. Such models (that could be called *general theories*), however, do not (yet) exist. What is available, at best, are generalizations of the types Bottomore listed as:

a. Generalizations asserting rhythmical recurrences or phase sequences of various kinds (e.g., attempts to distinguish the *stages* of economic development, Bücher, Schmoller and others);

b. Generalizations describing the main trends in the evolution of humanity as a whole (e.g., Comte's law of the three stages, the Marxist theory of development from primitive society to communist society, Hobhouse's theory of social development" (after Ginsberg, Bottomore 1972: 34).

Bottomore recognizes that these two types are not theoretical generalizations (in the sense discussed in ch. 3), but are compounds of descriptive-historical statements and interpretations.

In this chapter I focus on the first of these two types, since the second type has mainly been in vogue in the nineteenth century as part of the general belief in progress. A few words, though, need to be said about this second type. The nineteenth century stage models were constructed in the belief that it brought understanding as to what happened in history. Hence, the long range evolutionary trends were presented with an implicit notion about the mechanisms that fueled those major changes. Nowadays it is generally believed that stage models represent a static view of development (diachronic approach), and serve as a means of providing some order to the mash of events. They present a succession of changes characterized by their overall direction. This has been labelled an *evolutionist* perspective (Van Parijs 1981: 51). By no means are they explanatory, for an explanatory model would consist of a theory of *evolutionary mechanisms* (synchronic model) (Döbert 1981: 74–75, 81; Giddens 1991: 232–233; Van Parijs 1981: 51). If the underlying mechanism is not specified, an explanation is merely a *black-box explanation*, consisting of mere *accusations* (Van Parijs 1981: 13). As it stands there are few, if any, such evolutionary models of social change. The use of a concept or concepts as an explanatory mechanism comes closest to that ideal. Thus in Greenfeld's study of nationalism (1992) *ressentiment* captures something of a mechanism, much as in Tilly's study of nation-state development (1990) the interplay between capital and coercion provide a glimpse of an explanatory mechanism. In both cases, however, the *operator* is not specified.

4.1 The Notion of Evolution in the Social Sciences

The notion of evolution within the social sciences developed side by side with biology (Nisbet 1969: ch.5; Giddens 1991: 228). The theory of evolution in biology, however, consists of specifying evolutionary mechanisms (mutation, selection, stabilization/retention), whereas in the social sciences the emphasis is dominantly on stage models referring to orderly processes of change passing through discernible phases (Giddens 1991: 229). Yet there are areas of social life where an evolutionary analysis is helpful and useful in the sense that "...society has learned to solve given problems in a better or more efficient way" (Döbert 1981: 73–74). Furthermore the reflexive nature of human beings "...subverts the explication of social change in terms of any simple set of causal mechanisms" (Giddens 1991: 237). The learning capability of human beings leads us to another difference between biological and social systems. In biological systems changes in the *genetic code* are brought about by chemical devices with a small chance of mutation (errors in the process of self-reproduction), whereas in social systems, changes in the *cultural code* are generated by the human mind which is focused on systems of meaning (non-genetic transmission of information: Hannan and Freeman 1978: 140). What differentiates cultural from organic evolution is that "...the gene has been replaced by the symbol as the basic structural element" (Parsons 1966: 30).

This concept of cultural code can be explored further using Van Parijs's analysis. With respect to the evolutionary perspective Van Parijs analyzed two patterns. The *Natural Selection evolutionary pattern* (NS-pattern), he argues, is hardly, if at all, relevant for the social sciences (1981: 93). The *Reinforcement evolutionary pattern* (R-pattern) is more promising. The NS-pattern differs from the R-pattern in three important ways. First, *NS* is restricted to entities capable of dying and reproducing, whereas *R* is restricted to entities capable of *registering, reflecting, feeling*, and *evaluating*. Second, in an R-pattern the presence of a feature is no longer explained through the selection of entities which they characterize, but rather directly *within* those entities. From this it follows, thirdly, that in an R-pattern an entity does not require a population of entities in order to change (Van Parijs 1981:94–97). An example of such a change within one entity is provided by the Pavlovian reaction: the repetitive use of a particular stimulant in order to alter the behavior (*individual reinforcement*). In a group, modified behavior may be imitated by other individuals (*inter-individual imitation*).

The development of new cultural (for instance administrative) habits is often a combination of individual reinforcement and inter-individual imitation. It is necessary for a change of behavior to be embedded in a social structure so that its consequences are recognized by some at least. Some, or many, individuals may simply pick up on a habit by imitation without realizing the consequences. This means that most people experience a time of change as a ride on something akin to a rollercoaster. They are carried toward something unknown, reinforcing the direction by imitating the behavior of others and, meanwhile, feel as if things are out of hand. A good example would be the decade or decades preceding a violent revolution, characterized by mounting social unrest and a great desire to restore social stability (in terms of *reaction* or a new equilibrium). Another example is provided by changes in the social and economic structure of a society. Thus the process of industrialization constituted a major upheaval in Western societies. The shift from agricultural-based economies with limited technology and low-surplus production to mass-production economies with advanced technology, occurred after a few decades of large migrations from rural to urban areas. People poured into cities in imitation of others and thus reinforced individual as well as societal behavior.

By opting for more, or different, *meaningful* possibilities we do not replace older systems of meaning. Thus the debate as to whether Weber suggested too much of a contrast between patrimonial and bureaucratic administration; or, that he suggested an evolution from one to the other *state*, as for instance Rudolph and Rudolph (1979: 197, 226) argued, is somewhat artificial. Comparison of ideal types with reality implies co-existence of older and newer forms (see also chapters 6 and 7 for further discussion of ideal types). In social reality it is likely that the new and the old co-exist, yes—for practical reasons it is smart for a ruler to allow older next to newer systems of meaning especially in case of conquest. Even regression is conceivable, as is suggested by the use of such phrases as *the rise and fall of...* or *the Carolingian Renaissance as interlude*. In many cases, however, it may be more appropriate to speak of *restoration*, the conscious effort to (partially) preserve older patterns of governance next to administrative innovations as happened after 1813 in most of the territories that had been occupied by Napoleon.

4.2 Adaptation and Selection

Organizational theory is flooded with concepts derived from biology. This is especially so with studies that relate (the development of) organization to (the development of) environment. Attention for the analysis of the organization in society gained momentum since the mid-1960s (Emery and Trist 1965; Lawrence and Lorsch 1967; Jurkovich 1974; Hannan and Freeman 1978; Aldrich 1979) and adopted such concepts as adaptation (contingency-studies) and selection (population-ecology studies) (for an overview see Lammers and Hickson, 1979; and Lammers 1987).

Adaptation and selection can be considered as two sides of a coin, but as organizing concepts can only carry weight when referring to specific interaction between organization and environment. If adaptation encompasses all phenomena that have proven or are assumed to have influence on an organization, the concept not only becomes diffuse (Giddens 1991: 234) but is even pseudo-science. Social scientists can do without jargon. There are plenty of concepts that have proven to be useful in the analysis of the social world (such as role, position, culture, structure, interaction). However, it is not easy to dispense with *adaptation* since it is assumed to provide one of the very few opportunities for discovering mechanisms in the social sciences. The search for a mechanism, though, is not only driven by a thirst for knowledge and a craving for the truth. If, indeed, we are to find the "...generalized motivational impulse for human beings to adapt more efficiently to their material environments...." (ibid., 236) we basically hold the ultimate trigger that may help vaporize some of life's uncertainties. Downgrading expectations somewhat we can attempt to specify adaptation, for instance in terms of (1) co-existence, (2) collective memory, and (3) learning through copying.

I have mentioned earlier that the history of an organization may have a bearing upon its present functioning, and that newer features can *co-exist* with older. Proper understanding of the more fundamental changes in organization is served by a long-term perspective. Only a long-term analysis will clarify how structural certain features are, indeed may corroborate assumptions about the importance of time of origin of certain features. By way of example, the modern bureaucracy in the Western world did not surface between, say 1880–1920, but is rather the outcome of an accumulative process that took centuries to unfold.

The environment of an organization comprises both the society in which it functions as well as the *collective memory*. Collective memory in turn can be understood both as the accumulated experience within one organization as well as the accumulated experience of other organizations in one society and in different societies at the same time and at different times. Cultural diffusion from one generation to the other, and even between societies, is crucial for understanding, in Parsons's phrase, the generalized adaptive capacity "...as the directional factor..." in social evolution (Parsons 1966: 21, 26, 111). History provides ample evidence of direct and indirect transmission of ideas, practices, and structures on the basis of records. Administration relies heavily on records, for purposes of taxation, adjudication, but also for learning. Balasz (1957: 211) reports how in China an office of historiographers has been maintained since the Qin and Han dynasties to register the Emperor's acts, the actions of government, to collect documents and maintain an archive, thus passing information from one generation of civil servants to the next. And so there exist numerous monographs, encyclopedias, collections of legislation, and local monographs (Balasz 1957: 214) covering every Chinese dynasty from the unification of the empire under the Qin dynasty (221–201 B.C.) up to the Qing or Manchu dynasty. Indeed, so influential were the principles of administration formulated under the Qin- and Han dynasties (206 B.C.–A.D. 220) that they were still cited in eighteenth and nineteenth-century China (Creel 1970: 113; Kamenka 1989: 38). Thus experience was handed down from generation to generation within one area, and is an example of direct transmission of experience over time in one society.

Trade and travel stimulated diffusion of ideas between areas. In some cases certain ideas about and practices of administration were consciously adopted, while in other cases they were more incorporated by chance. Kamenka reports several such instances. Through the conquests of Media (549 B.C.), Lydia (546), Babylonia (538), and Egypt (525) the Persians inherited significant bureaucratic traditions and arrangements (Kamenka 1989: 54). Imperial Rome adopted certain organizational principles from Egypt and the East (ibid., 68), and Frederick II (1212–1250) could build upon the bureaucratic system of administration developed by the Norman rulers of Sicily and their Greek and Arab predecessors (ibid., 89). Another example is provided by Miewald (1984) and Martin (1987) who testified to the German and French influences respectively on the study of public administration in the United States. An example of direct transmission in one time frame across organizations and societies is the advent of comparative journals in the nineteenth century (immediate and interindividual reinforcement) (Mestre 1990; Heyen 1990). Borrowing from other (much older) cultures is possible, without a discernable direct link through intermediate instantiations, "In record-keeping societies the rules and conventions which were obtained in the past are still available for copying in the remote future" (Harré 1981: 175; see also Giddens, 1991: 261 on information storage). An example of such indirect transmission is provided by the medieval church in its adoption of ideas and organizational techniques from the Roman Empire, in turn influencing changes in secular government (Miller 1983: 282, 288; ch. 9). Thus explanations of adaptation are possible without assuming a positive causal relationship between environment and practices. An example would be the introduction of civil service examinations in the West (late seventeenth century) as (maybe) influenced by the Chinese precedent (Creel 1964: 162; Teng 1943: 276–279). The most important reason to be cautious with the concept of influence is that no evolutionary model is free of ethnocentrism (Giddens 1991: 238). Much as scholars of Chinese history may wish to point to Eastern origins of Western practices, Western scholars may wish to believe it was the West that modernized the world. It is one of the four dangers of evolutionary thought (normative illusion: see table 4.1 below).

TABLE 4.1
Dangers of Evolutionary Thought

1. *Unilineal compression*: for instance, when feudalism is presented as the necessary condition for the advent of capitalism.
2. *Homological compression*: the development of complexity in societal organization is assumed to be matched by development of the ability of the individual to grasp complexity.
3. *Normative illusion*: the inclination to identify superiority.
4. *Temporal distortion*: the idea that history is change and that the passing of time equals change.

Source: Giddens 1991: 239

Unilineal compression comes close to causal explanation. Recognizing societal complexity, homological compression is a more common phenomenon in social science literature. Much as human beings like to believe they are increasingly able to grasp complexity, the opposite may just as much be true. Could it be that the very notion of "complexity" betrays our inability to grasp complexity? The normative illusion is very common, for instance in notions of the Western world being industrialized and fairly wealthy and thus superior to the developing world. Normative illusion is also apparent in the idea that human development proceeds from a lower to a higher stage. Examples of temporal distortions are found in the grand models of the nineteenth century social scientists (for instance Comte). When, however, history is seen in terms of continuity, diversity, and change, temporal distortions are more or less impossible.

4.3 Variations in Time and Place: Stage Models

After all of these limitations to and warnings against the use of evolutionary models, it almost seems as if there is nothing left for administrative history but mere description. Döbert, Van Parijs, and Giddens show that much still remains. Social change can be analyzed in terms of Giddens's five dimensions, together providing a theoretical framework (table 4.2).

TABLE 4.2
Dimensions and Examples of Social Change

1. *Structural principles*: the analysis of modes of institutional articulation (organizations, rules).

2. *Episodic characterization*: delineation of modes of institutional change of comparable form (e.g., thresholds in development).

3. *Intersocietal systems*: specification of relations between societal totalities (e.g., the exchange of practices).

4. *Time-space edges*: indication of connections between societies of differing structural type (e.g., the Carolingian and Arabic societies around A.D. 800).

5 *World time*: examination of conjunctures in the light of reflexively *monitored* history (as in "the time is right"; compare to the notion of *"policy windows"* in administrative science).

Source: Giddens 1991: 244.

In these we recognize some of the options for research mentioned earlier. Giddens's discussion of these dimensions (244–255) provides worthwhile, if not mandatory, reading since the examples he presents on the nature of change and of power are of direct relevance to administrative history.

Stage models are a means to organize an otherwise chaotic sequence of events, although they are limited usually to the first three dimensions in table two. "Stages" as a handy and convenient device for classification need to be distinguished from the notion of a "stage" as a condition containing the seeds of the next stage (Blanksten 1966: 129) (unilineal compression, see table 4.1). The most simple model is a chronology that identifies major eras in history, such as the distinction in European historiography between Antiquity, the Middle Ages, the Early Modern period, and the Modern Era. It represents a very rough periodization, but as soon as we start to analyze one or a few aspects of development rough generalizations become elusive. Especially in comparative research the chronology of particular developments may differ from area to area and from time to time. Thus, in retrospect, the unification—and at least advent—of a continuous territory into an independent state started earlier for England and France (thirteenth to sixteenth centuries), then for Spain (fifteenth to sixteenth century), the Netherlands (sixteenth to seventeenth century), Russia (seventeenth century), the United States (eighteenth century), Latin America (early-nineteenth century), Germany and Italy (nineteenth century), and most of the Asian and African states in the twentieth century (in both continents states existed before colonization). Likewise, the chronology of urban development is suggested to differ from country to country (see table 4.3 below).

TABLE 4.3
The Stages of Urban Development in Five Countries
(century estimated when each stage was reached)

Stage	China	Japan	Russia	England	France
A					
B	18th B.C.	7th	9th	2d B.C.	2d B.C.
C	8th B.C.	—	—	—	—
D	3rd B.C.	8th	11th	1st	1st
E	8th	13th	15th	10th	10th
F	11th	15th	16th	12th	12th
G	16th	17th	18th	16–17th	16–17th

Source: Rozman 1978: 79

Legend: A = pre-urban; B = beginning of urban development; C = established hierarchy of urban centers and appearance of a formal administrative hierarchy; D = increase of centralization; E = commercial centralization; F = development of intermediate market centers; G = establishment of national markets.

One of the tasks for administrative history is to unravel differences and similarities in the patterns of development. In doing so we need to be aware of at least two pitfalls. First, we may find that despite different roads there is a remarkable convergence to modernity (however defined). One could argue that all territories in the world converged to a system of governance characterized by some degree of centralization within a (national) state setting. To suggest convergence is one pitfall, and betrays *anachronism* (interpreting the past in terms of a contemporary model and set of meanings) and *present-mindedness* (interpreting the past in terms of a contemporary outcome). Now, we cannot dissociate ourselves from the time and context in which we live, and so in analyzing a development up to the present time we cannot but treat the present as the culminating point. We should not, however, suggest that the end of a development is reached, which is a notion to be found in most of the end-of-ideology (Bell 1960) and end-of-history literature (e.g., Fukuyama 1991). The awareness that developments do not end is visible in the increased use of such prefixes as *post-* or *neo-* (post-industrial, post-modern, neo-liberalism) when attempting to demarcate the present from a recent or more distant past (e.g., Bell 1973). This pitfall has therefore to do with the interpretation of time.

The second pitfall concerns the interpretation of context. Much of (administrative) history is dominated by Western, if not European, thought, just as much as the social sciences are dominated by Western concepts. Analyzing modernity in terms of the advent of the independent (national) state is equal to forcing developments in different parts of the world into a Eurocentric framework, and disregards the fact that independent states existed before Europeans even set foot in the region. This is the case with Africa (Davidson 1992), Asia, and Latin America. For instance, if we define modernity in terms of the advent of welfare systems, then Western Europe (1880s–1930s), North America (1930s–1960s), Australia (1940s–1970s), and Japan (1950s–1970s) have reached that happy state, with the rest of the world yet to follow. In this respect administrative history can learn from anthropology in revealing the indigenous manifestation of more general patterns in the development of human society through *thick description* (Geertz 1973: 27). In essence, administrative history should pierce beyond a teleological interpretation of development, and review processes of growth and contraction beyond a Eurocentric interpretation.

Eras of significant change in administration and government differ from area to area and time to time. One truly global change occurred during the first and second period of colonization (fifteenth through seventeenth centuries, and 1850s–1900) and the first and second period of decolonization (1770s–1820s, 1950s–1970s). The change itself varied, but the outcome was everywhere the same: the establishment of the state. But for the rest, change in administration and government shows varying timetables. Wherever disjointed territories in one region merged into a larger whole (through coercion and marital or military alliance), a period of change in governance was at hand. Not so much in terms of changes in functioning, practices, and habits of governance (although it was not uncommon to adopt certain practices of the newly acquired territory, see section 4.2 above), but more so in terms of structure, hierarchy, and (secret) control. Many of the stage models discussed in section 4.4 depart from changes in structure, hierarchy, and control. Models dominantly concerned with the development in functioning of administration and government are less common. Weber's typology of traditional, patrimonial, and bureaucratic administration (which is *not* a stage model: Silberman 1993: 6) is an obvious example.

Once we have adequately allowed for variance in time and place in general, we also need to take variety in the influence of certain variables into consideration as Fried (1975: 359) reminds us, "In sum, just as no variable is guaranteed to be decisive in all or most instances none is guaranteed to be of no effect," and that includes variance in time and place.

4.4 Approaches to Stage Models

Most of the stage models are based on, and therefore limited to, the experience of the Western world (see this chapter's appendix). Sometimes these models are presented as (prescriptive) frameworks of development, as was the case with Rostow's application of his theory of industrial development to the development of states (Rostow 1971). The current popularity of indigenous structures and practices is but a first step in the recognition that the Western world does not necessarily provide a model for the world. Indeed, this makes a case for the incommensurability of frameworks (see ch. 3), in the sense that not only philosophical and methodological but also cultural contexts need to be taken into consideration (Rutgers's "authentic meaning," see ch 3.6).

I propose to make a distinction between stage models approached from empirical facts and those approached from a theory.

There are at least four types of stage models that show an empirical approach. A stage model may come in the guise of a *classification* such as on a typology of the development of the early state (Claesen and Skalnik 1978). A second type could be called *periodization models*. They delineate stages by means of approximate start and end dates. It is not always clear whether each stage was necessary for a next one. Examples are Berman's analysis of the development of justice systems (1983), Grimm's development of state functions (1986), Mosher's development of the public service in the United States (1968), Tilly's development of states (1990), and Torstendahl's development of industrial capitalism (1991). *Functional models* do not provide an explicit periodization, allowing for variance over time and place, for example the development of states (Rokkan 1970), of urban areas (Rozman 1978), of the civil service (Raadschelders and Rutgers 1996), and of politics (Rostow 1971). *Interaction models* are the last type. They assume an interplay, a congruence between two compound variables, and allows for jumps from the one to a much later stage. The interplay between the development of ideas and the socioeconomic environment as explanation for local government development is one example (Raadschelders 1994).

These distinctions between empirical stage-models are based more on differences of emphasis in the presentation. Most of these stage models classify, provide a periodization, present an end state, and suggest an interplay between the world of ideas and the world of events. What many stage models have in common is that they present a suggestion of empirically observed sequences (as for instance Rozman claims, 1978: 81), while they first of all constitute a chrono-logical framework within which particular events can be positioned. Stage models are, above all, descriptive and are constructed on the basis of events itself. Major events serve as caesuras between stages. Such a chronology, though, does not provide an explanation. Dis-cussing the misuse of Weber's ideal types of authority, Silberman (1993: 9) argued that scholars have been tempted to read backward along the Weberian scalar indices. In doing so they committed—in Silberman's words—the "scalar fallacy" presenting the present as a function of the past.

Another feature that empirical stage models have in common is that they tend to address the macrostructure (the hierarchy, the reward sys-tem, the legal rules, the welfare provisions, the urban area, the state, etc.) rather than to provide a combined macro- and micro-level analy-sis. Examples to illustrate the model serve as but do not provide micro-level analysis. In studying constancies and change we should ideally pay attention to how they result from human motivation, to establish whether changes came about as intended or unintended consequences of purposive action (Hernes 1976–77: 544). It is here that research of historical developments runs into a major problem, for we cannot but rely on an interpretation of written texts and assume that they convey what went really on in the mind of its *auctor intellectualis*. The use of written (and concocted, designed) texts for strategic and tactical rea-sons is standard custom in twentieth-century government and is well-documented. It was no different in earlier times as the famous case of the *Donatio Constantini* shows (Elton 1982: 98; see also ch. 9).

The third feature empirical stage models have in common is that they are usually the outcome of a research, or the outcome of a lifetime of thinking about a particular development (e.g., Berman 1983; Tilly 1990). Seen in this light, a stage model is the intelligible summary of someone's knowledge about particular developments. They are not necessarily a summary of what really happened.

Fourth, most empirical stage models provide an indication of how the one stage is linked to the other. The linkage may not be completely explicit. Thus Berman does not clarify *how* the new justice system built upon a former one, since his analysis is basically devoted to the *Papal revolution*.

Finally, empirical stage models present an implicit or explicit assumption that social processes are characterized by *enlargement of scale and intensity* and/or by a *sense of progress* (such as increased penetration of society by the state; increased share of government in the GNP in a welfare state; enlargement of territory, law-as-order replaced by law-as-justice). The last stage appears to represent an end stage from which regression is hard to imagine.

It is possible to depart from a more *theoretical basis* when constructing stage models. Thus in the study of the development of organization in relation to the environment, the population-ecology approach (based on biology) suggest five units of analysis for organizations: members, subunits, individual organizations, population of organizations, communities of (populations of) organizations (Hannan and Freeman 1978: 136). These units can be taken as individual levels of analysis, and, making use of the biological analogies involved, could provide the framework of a study on the development of a government department or a field agency. However, these units could also be used as stages of development. Thus the specialization processes that characterized the development of governmental organization in Western Europe could well be analyzed in terms of the transformation of an individual organization (the *curia regis*), to a population of organizations (government departments), to a community of (populations of) organizations (government departments, advisory boards, interest groups). I have, though, no knowledge of whether that was ever done (see ch. 6).

It would also be possible to analyze developments in terms of types of change. Thus Eisenstadt has distinguished *accommodable change*, *total change*, and *marginal change* (1963: 313). The intensity of change is captured better in Hernes's (1976–77: 523–532) distinction between simple reproduction, extended reproduction, transition, and transformation since they are linked with a characterization of type of structure. The *output structure* represents the distribution of results; the *process structure* specifies the logical form of the process that generated these results; and the *parameter structure* constitutes the configuration within which these processes and outputs occur. How type of change and type of structure are linked in terms of the assumed impact of change in society is depicted in table 4.4.

TABLE 4.4
Institutional Change and Stability at Three Levels: The Extent of Reform

| Change in | Type of Change | | | |
	Simple	Extended	Transition	Transformation
Output structure?	no	yes	yes	yes
Parameter values?	no	no	yes	yes
Process structure?	no	no	no	yes

Source: adapted from Hernes, 1976–77: 524

When we apply this to administrative development, simple reproduction represents a static situation, the system functions and there is no need for change. An example of extended reproduction would be the growth of welfare provisions *after* the welfare state has already been established. The output structure changes (new welfare provisions added), but neither the process that generates that output (for instance, increased demands from citizens) nor the parameter values change (for instance, what is held important in society-at-large). The incorporation of a territorial unit into a larger whole may involve transition, when both output structure (new tasks, territorial division) and parameter structure (new values: liberty, equality) are altered. The Napoleonic reforms represent a case of transformation, since output structure (new tasks for government, changes in organization), parameter structure (new values) and process structure (formal hierarchy, pension system, use of statistics, codification) changed. Types of change can be helpful in the construction of stage models, in terms of providing a theoretical framework. In essence they do not constitute stages.

4.5 Types of Reinforcement in Stage Models

In a model of development the stages are linked. At first sight all models in the appendix of this chapter are evolutionist models, characterizing history in terms of progress, the one stage a necessary prerequisite for the next. Given the discussion of stage models so far, though, there are ample reasons to assume that they can be understood as R-evolutionary patterns. Elaborating on the difficulties of that approach,

Van Parijs introduces five distinctions that refer to time span of consequences (*immediate* versus *mediate reinforcement*), the nature of the
stimuli (*gratification* versus *penalization*), the types of selection (*selective retention through fixation* versus *selective modification through
correction*), the level of awareness (*collective* versus *societal reinforcement*), and the reaction to deviation (*attraction* versus *repulsion*)
(Van Parijs 1981: 140–155).

The first distinction concerns the possibility of whether individuals
can recognize the consequences of their behavior during the action. A
case of mediate reinforcement is at hand when consequences can only
be recognized after a (considerable) period of time. Thus the implications and long-term consequences of the change from a God-centered
to a human-centered universe during the Italian Renaissance (such as
the revolution in physics in the seventeenth century) could hardly have
been foreseen. Mediate consequences may never materialize though.
Thus the consequences of a policy may be functional in the long term,
but dysfunctional in the short term. People who have come to regard
the benefits of the welfare state as rights, may resist infringements of
those "rights", even when it may be clear that in the longer run a society can no longer afford a high level of welfare arrangements under
government responsibility (see also chs. 8 and 11). The consequences
may never be actualized because the deviation is corrected before the
policy has had time to produce the long-term effects.

A second distinction is one between *gratification* and *penalization*:
a practice evolves through positive or negative sanctions. Third, a practice may be retained selectively through a process of *fixation* or modified selectively through a process of *correction*. This distinction comes
close to a distinction between natural selection and reinforcement, but
as Van Parijs shows, is not so clearcut (1981: 148). More important,
fourth, is the distinction he makes between *collective reinforcement*
and *societal reinforcement*. In the case of collective reinforcement a
social practice evolves as an aggregation of individual R-evolutionary
processes. In societal reinforcement the evolution of a social practice
necessarily involves a society as a whole. Thus, a change of ideas, of
mentality, of moral rules can be widespread without individuals being
aware of it. In general, hindsight is needed to assess the importance of
particular *changes*. A perceptive contemporary can act as an agent conscious of the change. Tocqueville's observations about "...democracy
loosening social ties..." is an excellent example (1990: 233). The fifth
distinction Van Parijs makes is one between evolutionary *attraction*

and *repulsion*. R-evolutionary attractors correspond to practices which maximize the dominant side's chances of satisfaction. In case of real conflict the outcome is in between the two sides' optima (the example of Van Parijs illustrating this: capitalists' refusal to meet with the workers' refusal to work, stalemate).

He does not explicitly indicate whether we are to understand these *distinctions* as mechanisms, even though the notion of reinforcement is conceptualized as evolutionary and thus presupposes an underlying mechanism. And yet in some instances he speaks of these distinctions as *mechanisms* (1981: 129, 150), while in other instances the distinctions are used to indicate what type of mechanism (for instance mechanism of fixation, mechanism of attraction) we are looking for (1981: 146, 156). Instead he mentions these five distinctions because of the limits to an evolutionary approach (first and fourth distinction), the features of a *deviant* type of evolutionary mechanism (second and fifth distinction), and for the misleading resemblance between natural selection and fixation on the one and between reinforcement and correction on the other hand (third distinction) (1981: 129). Assuming that we are able to conceptualize the type of mechanism involved, we are still left with the task of identifying what underlying mechanism ("operator") of fixation, of attraction, etc. explains a particular evolution.

The question can also be raised as to whether these distinctions are somehow logically connected. The idea of immediate reinforcement suggests awareness by at least some individuals that the consequences of their behavior are satisfactory and thus ought to be reinforced. Such an awareness opens the door to selective modification (evolutionary correction) and collective reinforcement. Mediate reinforcement on the other hand involves a much longer time span, going beyond one generation at least. The chances that individuals develop an awareness of the consequences of changes in behavior are considerably less and thus selective retention (evolutionary fixation) and societal reinforcement come into play. The two types of stimuli (reward or punishment) and the types of reaction to deviation (attraction or repulsion) are not so easily linked with either one of the types in the other three distinctions. It seems that a social practice evolves through the use of both gratifiers and penalizers, and that the reaction to deviation usually displays a mix of attractors and repellors.

How does all this apply to stage models? Can they be characterized through these distinctions and better still, do these distinctions enhance our understanding of evolutionary processes?

Of the twelve stage models in the appendix, those that cover a relatively short period of time—say one to two centuries—(Grimm, Mosher, Rokkan, Rostow, Torstendahl) could be understood in terms of immediate reinforcement, evolutionary correction, and collective reinforcement. In order to do so we need to stretch Van Parijs's concept of immediate reinforcement somewhat. While Van Parijs defines immediate reinforcement in terms of individual or group reaction at the spur of the moment, I propose to include intergenerational transfer of behavior. In as short a time span as fifty years, an older generation can pass their interpretation of a particular development (their experience) in their time to a younger generation. Indeed, the collective memory of the suppression by the Napoleonic (secret) police organization in the Netherlands, prevented adequate reorganization of the police in the 1850s. The time gap between Van Parijs's immediate and mediate reinforcement is simply too large. Stretching the time span of the immediate reinforcement notion to cover inter-individual imitation over time through directly linked generations (parent/child/grandchild) will be helpful.

This interpretation also helps us to better fit in a mechanism of collective aggregation since a social practice can be enforced from above and spread like an oil spill but may also trickle down from one to the other generation. What is more, selective modification, interpreted as conscious effort, will only be pursued when some experience has been built up with (a change in) a particular social (for instance organizational) practice. Handing down experience is immediate reinforcement and quite normal in private and public organizations (an unbroken line of family members as owners of a company; a succession of government rulers in an unbroken line of sovereignty over roughly the same territory such as a dynasty or a succession of elected political leaders).

R-patterns are more difficult to pinpoint when the time span covered by a model moves beyond three to six generations. Four models in the appendix encompass at least four to eight centuries and three even a timespan of 1000 to 3000 years (Claesen and Skalnik, Rozman, Tilly). By definition truly long-term changes are examples of mediate and societal reinforcement wherein social practices are selectively retained through evolutionary fixation. We have to realize, though, that this qualification of the nature of long-term evolutionary processes is only given for lack of knowledge about how the N-number of possible explanatory variables constituted a particular result in a time far ahead. I believe this is why Van Parijs said that an R-evolutionary approach is limited. The same line of reasoning can be found among those who characterize evolutionary change in terms of *punctuated equilibrium*, a "...process in which long periods of stasis are broken by short, in geologic time, episodes of rapid speciation" (Krasner 1988: 77, after Gould and Eldridge). After all, an institution developed for a specific reason may later be put to different uses. An example would be the original and new roles of the United Nations in the global political order (see ch. 10). Such changes are unpredictable, and so "...explanation rather than prediction ought to be the primary objective of science" (Krasner 1988: 78). We simply are not able to specify the *modus operandi* on a longer term, let alone predict from them, and therefore withdraw into the type of empirical-descriptive stage models found in appendix 4.1.

An R-evolutionary approach may help the understanding of the relatively short-term changes, and we may even be able to determine the direct operator(s). The long-term changes, on the other hand, may only become intelligible at the high levels of abstraction provided by, for instance, chaos theory (Loye and Eisler, 1987) and autopoieses theory (Morgan 1986). The chances of falsifying these theories in a context of social change are slim if not absent, at least in our present state of knowledge. Assuming that in social systems order comes from chaos and that systems are self-referential is a long way away from observable facts and social realities. We can go one step further. The longer the time span we review, the less *history* makes sense, the more chaotic history appears and the more it seems that events are propelled by mere chance. It is only human that we search for structure, order, and regularity for it makes life a little more predictable. Thus viewed, *understanding* is not much more than *insecurity reduction*. While explicitly declaring that I do not adhere to methodological individualism (social phenomena are explained in terms of goals, beliefs, and actions of individuals), we should realize that all stage models relevant for administrative history have one more feature in common: they portray developments as something beyond the human grip. The notion of *insecurity reduction* understood at individual level might help balance that bias. We may even be able to intelligibly link short, medium, and long-term variations (Braudel 1958). After all, it is not the middle and long-term developments themselves that generate change, but rather our reaction to them in the short term within the institutional structures in which we are embedded. That reaction can be understood in terms of insecurity reduction and, when studied, constitutes a combined micro- and macro-level analysis.

4.6 Stages or Configurations?

I can not refrain from making one final remark. It seems that some social scientists still suffer from the fact that their field does not (yet) measure up to the natural sciences. The search for universal models and theories is indicative of this inferiority complex. Implicitly (sometimes explicitly: Loye and Eisler 1987: 56) they characterize the social sciences in terms of a stage the natural sciences have left behind. That betrays a limited, if not dead wrong, perception of the nature of the social sciences and what it has achieved. Social scientists have learned to handle *interpretation* and the *reflexive nature* of human beings to an extent the natural scientists are only about to discover. A social scientist who compares the state of the art of his field with that of a natural scientist, has not progressed beyond the stage of comparing apples with oranges. The fruit of science comes in different flavors and each deserves to be digested and appreciated in its own right. And so, being aware of the limitations of stage models, they do represent an intelligent interpretation of social configurations.

There may be yet another reason why social scientists use stage models to organize their data. For a while the natural scientists' community was able to create and internalize as well as externalize the idea (or should I say belief?) that objectivity—in terms of event and observation being separated—did exist (the logic of experiment). The natural scientist has the advantage of a universal language. But despite that, the natural scientist has now to come to terms with the fact that observation influences event, and that observation even creates ends, or changes facts (Zukav 1979). How to interpret this constitutes a whole new ballgame. The social scientist does not have a universal language but has stages and configurations. Human beings cannot grasp reality in retrospect or prospect without breaking it down into portions, as much as they cannot grasp reality without the idea that they have some control. The idea of stages and of configurations provide us with as much control as the idea of a universal language (the logic of interpretation). Using and combining knowledge from various disciplines "...to order structural types and relate them sequentially is a *first* (emphasis added) order of business which cannot be bypassed" (Parsons 1966: 111). Given the plurality of viewpoints about the nature of the world that surrounds us, whether physical or social, it is time to conclude that ultimately we do not know and thus sail with whatever sails we have. Now it is time to descend to the nitty-gritty of administrative history.

78   Handbook of Administrative History

References

Aldrich, H.E. 1979. *Organization and Environment*. Englewood Cliffs, NJ: Prentice-Hall Inc.

Blanksten, George I. 1966. "International Politics and Foreign Policy in Developing Systems." In *Approaches to Comparative and International Politics*, edited by R. Barry Farrell, 120–130. Evanston, IL: Northwestern University Press.

Bottomore, T.B. 1972. *Sociology: A Guide to Problems and Literature*. London: George Allen & Unwin, Vintage Books ed.

Bell, Daniel, ed. 1960. *The End of Ideology*. New York: Free Press.

———. 1973. *The Coming of Post-Industrial Society: A Venture in Social Forecasting*. New York: Basic Books.

Braudel, F. 1958. "Histoire et sciences sociales: La longue durée." *Annales* 13: 725–753.

Döbert, R. 1981. "The role of stage models within a theory of social evolution, illustrated by the European witch craze." In *The Philosophy of Evolution*, edited by U.J. Jensen and R. Harré Jensen, 71–119. Brighton: The Harvester Press.

Elton, G.R. 1984. *The Practice of History*, 10th ed. London: Fontana Paperbacks.

Emery, F.E. and E.L. Trist. 1965. "The causal texture of organizational environments." *Human Relations* 18, no.1: 21–32.

Fukuyama, Francis. 1991. *The End of History and the Last Man*. New York: Free Press.

Geertz, Clifford. 1973. "Thick Description: Toward an Interpretive Theory of Culture." In *The Interpretation of Cultures*. New York: Basic Books, Inc.

Giddens, Anthony. 1991. *The Constitution of Society: Outline of the Theory of Structuration*, 5th ed. Cambridge: Polity Press.

Hannan, Michael T. and John H. Freeman. 1978. "The Population Ecology of Organizations." In *Environments and Organizations: Theoretical and Empirical Perspectives*, edited by Marshall W. Meyer and Associates. San Francisco and London: Jossey-Bass, Inc.

Harré, R. 1981. "The Evolutionary Analogy in Social Explanation." In *The Philosophy of Evolution*, edited by U.J. Jensen and R. Harré, 161–175. Brighton: The Harvester Press.

Hernes, Gudmund. 1976–77. "Structural Change in Social Processes." *American Journal of Sociology* 82, no.3: 513–547.

Heyen, Erk Volkmar. 1990. Ausländisches Verwaltungsrecht im "Archiv für öffentliches Recht" und in der "Revue du droit public" vor dem Ersten Weltkrieg. *Jahrbuch für Europäische Verwal tungsgeschichte* 2: 213–234.

Jurkovich, R. 1974. "A Core Typology of Organizational Environments." *Administrative Science Quarterly* 19, no.3: 380–394.

Krasner, Stephen D. 1988. "Sovereignty: An Institutional Perspective." *Comparative Political Studies* 21, no.1: 66–94.

Lammers, Cornelis J. and David J. Hickson, eds. 1979. *Organizations Alike and Unlike: International and Interinstitutional Studies in the Sociology of Organizations*. London: Routledge & Kegan Paul.

Lammers, C.J. 1987. *Organisaties Vergelijkenderwijs*, 3d ed. Utrecht and Wijnegem: Het Spectrum B.V.

Lawrence, P.R. and J.W. Lorsch. 1967. *Organization and Environment: Managing Differentiation and Integration*. Cambridge, MA: Harvard University Press.

Loye, David and Riane Eisler. 1987. "Chaos and Transformation, Implications of Nonequilibrium Theory for Social Sciences and Society." *Behavorial Science* 32, no.1: 53–65.

Mestre, Jean-Louis. 1990. *La connaissance des droits administratifs allemands en France entre 1830 et 1869 à partir de la "Revue étrangère" de Foelix. Jahrbuch für Europäische Verwaltungsges chichte* 2: 193–212.

Meyer, Marshall W. 1979. *Change in Public Bureaucracies*. Cambridge: Cambridge University Press.

Morgan, Gareth. 1986. *Images of Organizations*. Beverly Hills, CA: SAGE Publications.

Nisbet, A. 1969. *Social Change and History*. London: Oxford University Press.

Parijs, Philippe van. 1981. *Evolutionary Explanation in the Social Sciences: An Emerging Paradigm*. Totowa, NJ: Rowman & Littlefield.

Parsons, Talcott. 1966. *Societies: Evolutionary and Comparative Perspectives*. Foundations of Modern Sociology Series. Englewood Cliffs, NJ: Prentice-Hall Inc.

Rokkan, Stein. 1975. "Dimensions of State-Formation and Nation-Building: A Possible Paradigm for Research on Variations within Europe." In *The Formation of National States in Western Europe*, edited by Charles Tilly, 562–584. Princeton, NJ: Princeton University Press.

Rose, Richard. 1976. "On the Priorities of Government: A Developmental Analysis of Public Policies." *European Journal of Political Research* 4, no.1: 247–289.

Rostow, Walt W. 1971. *Politics and the Stages of Growth*. Cambridge: Cambridge University Press.

Rozman, Gilbert. 1978. "Urban Networks and Historical Stages." *Journal of Interdisciplinary History* 9, no.1: 65–91.

Rudolph, Lloyd I. and Susanne Hoeber Rudolph. 1979. "Authority and Power in Bureaucratic and Patrimonial Administration: A Revisionist Interpretation of Weber on Bureaucracy." *World Politics* 31, no.2: 195–227.

Tocqueville, Alexis de. 1990. *Democracy in America*. Edited by Phillips Bradley. New York: Random House.

Weber, Max. 1980. *Wirtschaft und Gesellschaft: Grundrisz zur Ver stehenden Soziologie*, 5th ed. Edited by J. Winckelman. Tübingen: J.C.B. Mohr.

Wickwar, W. Hardy. 1970. *The Political Theory of Local Government*. Columbia, SC: University of South Carolina Press.

Zukav, Gary. 1979. *The Dancing Wu-Li Masters: An Overview of the New Physics*. New York: Williman Morrow and Company.

Appendix 4.1 Examples of Stage Models

A. Berman on the *development of the Western legal tradition* (1983: 18–21)

1   *The Papal Revolution, 1050–1200*: The Gregorian reform of the church resulting in an organizational demarcation of ecclesiastical and secular spheres of influence; adoption of Roman law as model for development of Canon law; justice associated with the Last Judgement and the Kingdom of God.

2   *The Protestant Reformation, 1517–1555*: Separation from the influence of Rome; justice associated with Christian conscience.

3   *The Glorious Revolution, 1688–1689*: Development of the King-in-Parliament notion; justice associated with public spirit, fairness, and the traditions of the past.

4   *The American Revolution, 1776–1789*: The first decolonization; justice associated with public opinion, reason, and the rights of man.

5   *The French Revolution, 1789–1792*: The advent of the people as a nation; justice associated with public opinion, reason, and the rights of man.

6   *The Russian Revolution, 1917*: The people as a source of power and authority; justice associated with collectivism, planned economy, and social equality.

B. Claesen and Skalnik and the *typology of the early state* (1978: 640–641)

	Inchoate	Typical	Transitional
degree of development of trade and markets	trade and markets of only limited (local) importance	trade and markets develop at supra-local level	trade and markets are of great importance
mode of succession to ownership of land	succession to high office is mostly hereditary	heredity balanced by appointment is dominant	appointment of functionaries
occurrence of private ownership of land	communal ownership and possession dominate	limited private ownership; state ownership gradually more importance	private ownership of increased importance for aristocracy and commoners
method of remuneration of functionaries	only remunerations (often in kind)	salaried as well as remunerated functionaries	salaried functionaries; naries; governmental apparatus becomes a relatively independent force
degree of development of judicial system	no codification of laws and punishment; special formal judges	start toward codification; formal judges besides general functionaries	codification complete; justice in hands of formal judges
degree of development of taxation	most by voluntary tributary gifts and occasional labor for state; neither is very regular or accurately defined	regular tribute in kind and services, major-works undertaken by compulsory labor - organized by government functionaries	well-defined system; complex apparatus to ensure regular flow of taxes

C. Elias on the *development of the state* (1982: part 2)
Central features: centripetal (integrative) and centrifugal (desintegrative) forces.
1. Belligerent and expansive phase: centripetal forces
2. Conservative rulers, increase of centrifugal forces
3. Complete desintegration
4. Establishment of monopoly over violence and taxes in an territory:
    (a) first within one region: battle between territorial lords, competition, a monopoly is established at the level of a county and duchy; and
    (b) second between regions: monopoly established at the level of a country
5. Functional differentiation in society: development of a sustained and specialized administrative apparatus for maintenance of monopoly over coercion and taxes. Decline of independent social units
6. Private monopolies become public, monopoly moves from one (the ruler) to a group (estates, Parliament)
7. The estates disappear, the civil service becomes an independent instrument of state power
8. The advent of the welfare state: the development of entitlements
9. Federative integration of sovereign units into a larger whole

D. Grimm on the *development of state functions* since the late nineteenth century (1986: 103).

1. The state corrects the most evident and flagrant abuses of economic freedom; legislation is used to correct laissez-faire; provisions in labor relations and social security. The First World War sets off phase 2.
2. The state helps to survive crisis; development of social services to help overcome poverty, unemployment, accidents, sickness. Increased complexity and interdependence lead to phase 3.
3. The state is expected to anticipate developments in the environment and to act accordingly; the state assumes responsibilities for economic, infrastructural, and technological progress.

E. Mosher on the *development of the public service* in the United States (1968: 54–55).
1. Government by gentleman: the guardian period, 1789–1829;
2. Government by the common man: the spoils period, 1829–1883;
3. Government by the good: the reform period, 1883–1906;
4. Government by the efficient: the scientific management period, 1906–1937;
5. Government by administrators: the management period, 1937–1955;
6. Government by the professional: the scientific period, 1955–

F. Raadschelders on the *development of local government* in the Netherlands (1994: 432)

Socio-economic structure	Orientation			
	A	B	C	D
	local	regional	national	international
1. Agrarian				
2. Trade and manufacture				
3. Industrial				
4. Technological				

When a local community changes from a 1.A to 2.B (or 2.B to 3.C and 3.C to 4.D) extra-proportional administrative development occurs when the size of local government (in terms of personnel employed) increases more rapidly than the size of the population.

G. Raadschelders and Rutgers on the *development of the civil service* (in Bekke, Perry, and Toonen 1996: 71–86)
1. Civil servants as personal servants: functionaries are very much personal servants to a ruler, no strict demarcation of public and private spheres;
2. Civil servants as state servants: personal and state household become separated, functionaries are either in state or in personal employ;
3. Civil servants as public servants: civil servants increasingly serve the public, administration becomes an independent source of state power;
4. Civil service as protected service: just as legislation has protected private property against the state, it now protects the civil servants against the political officeholder;
5. Civil service as professional service: civil servants become highly specialized functionaries.

H. Rokkan on six *development crisis* (1970: 61–62)
1. *Penetration*: Establishment of a rational field administration for resource mobilization (taxes, manpower), creation of public order, and the coordination of collective efforts (infrastructure development, emergency action, defense);

2. *Integration*: Establishment of allocation rules equalizing the shares of offices, benefits, resources among all cultural and/or politically distinct sectors of the national community;
3. *Participation*: Extension of the suffrage to hitherto underprivileged strata of population, protection of the rights of the organized opposition;
4. *Identity*: Development of media and agencies for the socialization of future citizens into the national community: schools, literary media, institutionalized rituals, and symbols (myths, flags, songs);
5. *Legitimacy*: Any effort to create loyalty to and confidence in the established structure of political institutions in the given system and to ensure regular conformity to rules and regulations issued by the agencies authorized within the system;
6. *Distribution*: Establishment of social services and social security measures, income equalization through progressive taxation and transfer between poorer and richer localities;

I. Rostow on the *development of politics* (1971).
1. *Take off*: quick creation of political, social, and institutional network for economic growth. Origin of the bureaucratic organization, the state claims more of the gross national product;
2 *Self-sustained growth* and
3 *Drive to maturity*: advent of labor unions and political parties; increasing demand for government intervention; the share of government in the gross national product increases rapidly;
4 *Mass consumption*: continuance of developments in 2d and 3d phase;
5 *Search for equality*: redistribution against the background of declining economic growth; expenses for administration and defense hardly rise in relative terms, while expenses for social services and (public) education increases rapidly.

J. Rozman on the *development of urban networks* (1978: 74–77)
1. Pre-urban
2. Beginning of urban development
3. Established hierarchy of urban centers and appearance of a formal administrative hierarchy
4. Increase of centralization
5. Commercial centralization
6. Development of intermediate market centers
7. Establishment of national markets

K. Tilly on the *development of warfare and state organization* (1990:29)
1. *Patrimonialism*, up to fifteenth century: tribute taking and feudal society;
2. *Brokerage*, 1400–1700: use of mercenaries, state dependence on private persons for loans and for the collection of taxes (tax-farming);
3. *Nationalization*, 1700–1850: development of standing armies, direct operation by the state of the fiscal apparatus;
4. *Specialization*, 1850–recent past: division of labor, increased influence of representative institutions.

L. Torstendahl on the *development of industrial capitalism* (1911:44–46)
1. *Classical capitalism*, up to 1870/90: liberal economy relying on market forces and a low degree of connection between industry and state;
2. *Organized capitalism*, 1890–1935/45: liberal economy in principle combined with a growing sphere of common and competing interests between industry and state. Growth of liberal democratic intervention;

3. *Participatory capitalism*, 1935/45–1970: interventionism and distributive welfare policy result in strong growth of the public sector;
4. *Corporative capitalism*, 1970–: the state takes over companies, provides subsidies; political power, bureaucracy, and interest organizations grow together.

Part Two

Administrative History Proper

5

Public Services and Public Finance: From Small to Big Government

In retrospect, the role of government in every day life has increased enormously since the time that the foundations were laid for government as we know it today. Medieval and early modern central governments were mainly occupied with effective control over the territory. In the localities, central government merely performed extractive (finance) and monitoring (legislative, judicial) functions. The provision and production of public services was mainly left to local government. The situation nowadays is quite different. Most Western countries have developed elaborate systems of public service delivery operating through a division of labor between central and local governments. Central government still performs its extractive and monitoring functions, but it produces services as well. There is, however, no such thing as a linear development toward modern government.

One could argue that in all Western national states the general pattern of government development has been one of differentiation and specialization (of tasks, of organizational structure, of personnel) resulting in ever increasing complexity (in terms of number of personnel, interdependence among organizational units, interdependence of policies). That, however, is about the only general statement one could make, and it is quite trivial and useless for, as soon as detail is applied, no general pattern exists.

In principle there are as many routes to modern government as there are countries. A grand theory of government development cannot but scratch the surface. It can serve as a framework enabling us to get a grip on the variety of events. Middle-range theories are more promising, limited as they are to a particular period and/or a particular topic. In this and the following chapters I will present such middle-range theories as can be found in literature on the development of tasks and finance (this chapter), on the development of organization (ch. 6), on the development of the civil service (ch. 7), on the development of participation and representation (ch. 8), on the development of the state (ch. 9), and on the development of international relations (ch. 10). First and foremost these middle-range theories are descriptive by nature and basically constitute a chronology of events.

Not surprisingly, once these chronologies are compared, a pattern of development emerges. Periods of formative transformation were followed by periods of relative tranquility. As we will see throughout this and the following chapters, Western society and government experienced major changes during the periods of 1120–1300, 1400–1600, 1780–1820, and 1880–1930. The centuries and decades in between witnessed variations on the theme set in the previous period of transformation. Transformation, however, was never complete in the sense that the one structure was replaced by an altogether different one. In the words of Tholfsen:

> The cardinal features of historical thinking, then, reflect an interest in the dimension of time in human life. The historian approaches the past through categories of diversity, change, and continuity. (1967:6–7)

Rather, older and newer forms of administration and government co-existed (see also ch. 4).

In chapter 1 I defined the focus of administrative history proper as the structure, functioning, and functionaries of government over time. Organizational structuring, work processes, and employees serve one basic goal: at least an effective and efficient management of public tasks, at best also a democratic service delivery. In this chapter I will focus on what governments did and how it was financed. Chapter 6 focuses on the *how* in terms of organization and functioning, while chapter 7 is devoted to *who* was employed in government. Sections 5.1–5.4 provide a general background, while in sections 5.5 and 5.6 a discussion of the literature is presented.

5.1 Tasks of Government: Definitions and Task Areas

Government performs tasks. A task is a related set of activities performed by one or more functionaries. A distinction can be made between tasks of an external nature and tasks of an internal nature. External tasks are all those that have to do with direct service delivery to the citizen, such as education, sanitation, public utilities, and so forth. These tasks are often organized in separate organizational units, constituting systems of line management. Internal or management tasks pertain to the operation of an organization, such as personnel, finance, organization, and information services. These are the staff units within an organization.

In the analysis of the development of governmental tasks, it is useful to distinguish among task areas. In my own research of the development of local government in the Netherlands (Raadschelders 1990, 1994) eight functional categories were defined. Those categories can also be used to analyze developments at central government level. In the following discussion of these task areas I will provide examples of both central and local government.

The first area is that of *general government and finance* and includes political functionaries (see ch. 7) and the general administrative units. These units perform tasks in the field of finance, record keeping, registration, and so forth. Examples of such units at central level are the Ministries of Home Affairs and Finance and general advisory boards like a Council of State and a Chamber of Accounts. At local level the town clerk's office and the treasurer's office are examples.

Public order and safety is the second task area concerned with the external protection of the territory and the internal monitoring of stability in the territory. Protecting the territory from outside threats has always been the responsibility of central government. The high politics of foreign affairs and defense became organized from the sixteenth and seventeenth centuries onward (diplomacy, standing army) and go hand in hand. Internal stability concerns tasks in the fields of preventive and repressive policing. Police is understood in its contemporary meaning of uniformed officials who maintain public order and safety through the arrest and prosecution of those who violate the law. In earlier days, police referred to government activity in general. Many of these public order and safety tasks were organized at local or regional level. The firewatch and nightwatch in many localities in Europe is an example of preventive policing. The presence of a representative of central government (bailiff, sheriff, prefect) guaranteed some degree of supervision. The judicial system is more repressive by nature, organized locally in a Bench of Magistrates and often presided by the bailiff or sheriff. Appeal was possible in regional (bailiwick) and central courts (High Court of Justice). The judicial apparatus came to be coordinated by a Ministry of Justice.

The third area, that of *health and societal care*, was for a long time a local government matter and encompassed tasks in the field of public health (municipal doctors and midwives; public hospitals), elderly care (elderly homes), social services, poor relief, care for orphans, labor mediation, and the like. Many of the typical welfare state functions belong to this category.

Education is the fourth area and included public schools and teachers, again basically a local task unto the late eighteenth century. Through legislation for public education, central governments increasingly became involved, especially where education became the main instrument of socializing citizens into the state. Statehood in the United States was only possible when a territory could prove it had organized a system of public education.

The fifth category, that of *trade and traffic*, was also a local government affair and comprised the supervision and regulation of markets and commerce.

Public works has been both a local as well as a central concern. At the local level it concerned the maintenance of municipal real estate (for instance the city hall, the public hospital), and of public areas such as streets, parks, squares, waterways, and roads. Central government has always been more involved in construction and maintenance of major infrastructural works such as interregional roads (Department of Public Works), large waterways (Department of Water Management), and the like.

The task areas mentioned so far have been a public concern ever since the Middle Ages. Depending upon the nature of the task it was a central and/or local concern. A whole new governmental task area was opened up in the nineteenth century with the creation of *public utilities*, the seventh category. This category includes gas and electricity factories, telephone companies, and slaughter houses.

A task area in which government no longer provides any services is *religious and church matters*. In a time that the Catholic or the Protestant faith was a state religion (for instance in England, France, and Sweden) or at least a state-affiliated religion (for instance in the Dutch Republic), government was also involved in terms of tasks and personnel. Even though the separation of church and state goes back as far as the Investiture Struggle (see ch. 9), the formal (legal) separation of the two did not occur until the late-eighteenth century. Thus in the Dutch Republic local government employed a church singer and reader and a sexton. A board of overseers of the church supervised the financial management. Once church and state were separated in the Netherlands (1796), these public tasks were abolished. Well into the nineteenth century, however, Dutch central government did have separate organizational units (Department of Catholic Affairs, Department of Protestant Affairs).

5.2 A Theory on the Development of Local Public Services in the Netherlands

For several reasons it is impossible to present a general theory on the development of public services. First, the present state of knowledge is quite limited in the sense that most research has been done on the nineteenth and twentieth century with an emphasis on central government. Second, a distinction needs to be made between local and central government if only because from early on the former provided a different and larger array of services then the latter. Third, there is great variety among countries as to how public services developed. Fourth, there is a practical limit. No matter how much one reads up on the development of administration and government, there is always more. Even a middle-range theory requires detail that is not always available. What is more, the process of collecting and working through literature never stops. It is quite common that one is not aware of the existence of particular studies until much later, stumbling across it by accident when looking for something different or when brought to one's attention by a colleague. Furthermore, based on an always limited set of studies, we should be cautious of generalizing. The development of local and central governments has not been uniform, and it is easy to fall into fallacies of the wrong level (see ch. 3).

With these provisos in mind I can now present a theory of the development of local government in the Netherlands. I will discuss to what extent I suspect it is exemplary of the development of central government in the Netherlands and of the development of central and local governments in other Western countries.

In terms of administrative history proper the development of local services in the area that is presently the Netherlands can be subdivided into five phases (from the 1200s onward).

Tasks of Police and Justice

Tasks in the area of police and justice were the oldest in local communities. Law was common law and one was judged according to the law of the tribe to which one belonged. In general this meant that in Western Europe justice was passed on the basis of either Frankian, Frisian, or Saxon law. The presence of the Franks was very important. Under Charlemagne government was innovated along three lines. First the older local judges were replaced by a Bench of Magistrates (*scabini, échevins*). At the same time, and closely related to the first, the territory was divided into districts at regional (bailiwicks) and at local level (municipalities). Local boundaries were often based on parish boundaries. The importance of this was that the tribal law no longer served as the basis of justice. Henceforth one was tried according to the law of the territory where the crime was committed. A third consequence of the Carolingian renaissance was that the system of parish-churches became widespread. These innovations were mainly introduced in the Frankish part of Charlemagne's realm. Charlemagne's realm was subdivided among his grandsons at the Treaty of Verdun (843). The Low Countries became part of the Middle Kingdom. Only for a short while though, since at the Partition of Meersen (870) the Middle Kingdom was eliminated and the Low Countries were added to the Kingdom of Louis the German. And so it came about that a century later they were part of the Holy Roman Empire. The Low Countries were governed by counts as representatives of the Holy Roman Emperor.

By the end of the twelfth century the Carolingian innovations were introduced in the whole of the Low Countries upon initiative of the Holland counts who had successfully separated themselves from the Holy Roman Empire. In the course of the thirteenth century, they installed bailiffs both at local and at regional level in their territory, who acted as their representative. This was a general Western European phenomenon (Van den Arend 1993: 13). Characteristic of this first period is that local government is the business of a bailiff or a sheriff and a Bench of Magistrates (as respectively central and local representatives). Local tasks were mainly limited to police and justice. It is possible that there were local tax collectors working for the locality and/or for the Count's treasury. Other tasks developed on the basis of individual initiative, such as in the area of local water management.

Tasks of a "Political" and General Administrative Nature

The appointment of separate more or less "political" officials heralded a second phase of development, to be understood against the background of the introduction of town charters. The modern Western city as it emerged from the eleventh century onward had two attributes that could not be found in towns and villages before that time: a middle-class population and a municipal organization. Once a town had acquired a certain economic and social status it demanded legal exemption from the surrounding area through a town charter. The count could confer such a charter that provided for a certain degree of self government in exchange for financial and military support (excises, the city as a link in a chain of fortresses). Of this town charter "movement" three things are important. First, it confirmed a legal distinction between urban and rural communities allowing for even more differentiation in economic development. Also, the town charters were often preceded by a market charter (the right to have an annual or even weekly market). The market and town charters strengthened the monopoly of the guilds.

Second, towns often copied the charter from another town. Filiation of town charters was quite common so that a chain of mother- and daughter-cities emerged. Thus the charter of the town of Den Bosch (1185) in Brabant served as the model for other town charters in the Low Countries (Haarlem, 1245; Delft, 1246; Alkmaar, 1254). Den Bosch in turn had copied its charter from the Leuven town charter. And the one in Leuven was probably based on the first charter in Flanders granted upon the town of Saint Omer in 1127, which in turn was probably copied from the charter of Cambrai in 1122. This process of town charter filiation was common throughout (at least) Western Europe (Berman 1983: 357–380; Müthling 1966; Redlich and Hirst 1970; Webber and Wildavsky 1986: 183).

Third, town charters generated changes in local government. A town charter generally led to codification of local customs. Furthermore, administration of local finances was needed. To that effect a town clerk and a treasurer were appointed. Next to the sheriff and the *scabini*, citizen representatives in the town government were installed (mayor, Bürgemeister). Thus some sort of a division of labor occurred between judicial tasks (sheriff and *scabini*) and legislative tasks (mayors and *scabini*). The last innovation in the area of political functions had to do with the creation of local councils (municipal council) from the thirteenth century onward.

Economic and Social Tasks

Market and town charters provided the basis for further development of the local community. In the thirteenth to fifteenth centuries interregional trade reemerged, sometimes resulting in more or less formal economic alliances such as the Hanseatic League. Trade both extended and intensified, and in turn required government regulation through central and local ordinances. The initiative for such ordinances came both from interest groups as well as from government. Interest groups (guilds, merchants) appealed for measures securing the safety of trade as well protection of their monopoly (Kieser 1989). Government issued ordinances in order to regulate producer-consumer relations and to secure an adequate income through excises. The work involved in all this could not be done by the handful of functionaries that hitherto were employed at local level, and so supervisors as well as workmen were appointed. The larger towns in the Netherlands also operated a Public Works department from the fifteenth century onward. In smaller towns the appointment of a municipal carpenter was sufficient.

From the second half of the thirteenth century onward, but even more in the fourteenth and fifteenth centuries, local government assumed tasks in the field of health and social care. When private institutions (such as the church) indicated they were no longer able (willing or allowed, see ch. 8) to fulfill their tasks and requested subsidies of the municipality, local government often took over (part of) their responsibility. This was for instance the case with almshouses and orphanages. Supervision of these was assigned to boards of overseers (see also ch. 7), appointed by the local council. For the day to day management of these institutions local government appointed middle management supervisors. The building of plague houses and the appointment of town doctors and midwives in the fifteenth century was a local government initiative. Thus a public health system was created in order to supply services to the poor and the elderly. From the late-fourteenth century onward local governments also opened public schools. Larger towns could even afford a Latin School. Although data concerning the size of local government in the medieval period are not available, we can safely assume that it must have increased substantially. During the early modern period local government did not develop initiatives into new task areas. New tasks were assumed within the existing framework (fire brigades and street lighting, late-seventeenth century; supervision of municipal midwives, eighteenth century; formal recruitment and selection procedures for municipal doctors, midwives, and teachers, eighteenth century).

Local Government as Entrepreneur: Public Utilities

The first signs of true transformation occurred in the early-nineteenth century. The judicial system was centralized and subsequently deconcentrated; public education came to be regulated by central measures; church and state were formally separated so that poor relief became a private responsibility. For a brief period local government experimented with privatization (of public works) and contracting out of new tasks (like gas factories and slaughter houses). This is the period of the so-called *nightwatch state* (the French speak of *état gendarme*).

From the 1850s onward, however, local government took initiative in a variety of task areas. Existing services such as in health care, elderly care, police, and treasury were modernized. The almshouses that until then had housed both the sick and the elderly were separated into hospitals and elderly homes. The nightwatch was abolished and a state and municipal police created. Tax farmers disappeared and were replaced by public employees. Privatized services, such as public works, were again incorporated into the municipal organization, and often split into a sanitation department (street sweeping, maintenance of recreational areas) and a public works department (road maintenance, upkeep of municipal buildings, public housing). Entirely new were tasks in the area of public utilities. Dissatisfied with the price and quality of services delivered by contractors and irritated with usury, local governments *municipalized* these services (gas factories and public slaughter houses). Also local governments built and financed electricity factories, sewage systems, water-supply systems, and telephone companies. As a result of the First World War many local governments started to operate a labor mediation bureau in an attempt to coordinate unemployment policy.

Local Government and Public Welfare

From the late-nineteenth century onward local governments became more active in for instance the area of social security and labor provisions. This municipal activity gave rise to more central legislation in order to assure equal levels of service delivery throughout the country. It is during the emergence of the welfare state that central-local relations in the Netherlands went beyond financial and legal ties. In the 1930–1960 period, local governments in the Netherlands lost many of the technical tasks they had so recently assumed. Many of the public utilities were regionalized on a joint provision basis. Other tasks such as those in the field of labor mediation were centralized and organized on the basis of deconcentrated field services. After the Second World War local government kept growing in terms of both tasks as well as number of employees. Specialists were now employed formally within the civil services, whereas hitherto they had only been consulted.

The research I did in the Netherlands led to a theory of local government growth. It is based on the idea that the size of local government in terms of personnel will increase more rapidly than the size of the population at a time when a change of socio-economic structure (from agrarian, to trade and manufacturing, to industrial, and to technological society) coincides with a change in collective orientation (from local, to regional, to national, to international orientation) (see appendix 4.1). The theory predicts that towns with an agrarian economic base and a local orientation will have smaller local governments than for instance towns with an industrial economic base and a national orientation. An advanced locality (in terms of its structure and orientation) is hindered in its local government development when situated in a less developed region, while a less developed locality is not necessarily advanced because of the influence of the advanced region to which it belongs. Finally, when local government in a less developed locality grows, it is likely to be the result of central government regulation requiring local implementation. For more detail, I refer to an earlier publication (Raadschelders 1994).

5.3 Development of Local and Central Government Services in Western Countries

The theory outlined in the preceding section is based on extensive archival research and calls for corroboration or falsification through other case studies. As we will see in sections 5.5 and 5.6 below, literature with detailed and empirical accounts on local and central government development is dispersed. And yet some assumptions can be made about the development of tasks elsewhere (i.e., central government in the Netherlands and local and central government in other countries).

The development of local government in the Netherlands coincided with important periods in the development of society-at-large. There is no reason to assume that the impact was less elsewhere as indeed is testified in numerous studies. Development of public services at the local level in other Western European countries appears quite comparable to that of the Netherlands as is indicated by references in the preceding section.

At the central level in the Netherlands the development of tasks is somewhat different. During the High Middle Ages, central government performed tasks in the area of law enforcement, taxation, and the judiciary. Under Burgundian and Spanish-Habsburg rule (1377–1581) centralization occurred (creation of advisory councils, see also ch. 6) and the Estates were organized. In the area of economic and social tasks, central government was basically involved through legislation. In some areas it promoted the creation of specific purpose governments for water management (regional water boards). It was not until the late-eighteenth century that tasks at central level in the Netherlands were growing, mainly in the area of supervision of regional and local governments. Structure and functioning of central government (see ch. 6) was reorganized. From the late-nineteenth century onward central government assumed new tasks. Specialized government departments were created for example in the fields of water management (1877), education (1918), and social affairs (1932).

In view of the literature on developments in other Western European countries, a distinction needs to be made between the more general trends and country-specific developments. In general one could say that the High Middle Ages (1120–1300) was a period with increased attention for legislative activity. During the Renaissance (1400–1600) increased interdependence between central and local governments occurred, basically as a consequence of the process of state making. At the time of the Atlantic Revolutions (1780–1820) central government was restructured (see also chs. 6 and 7) on principles of constitutionalism and equality. Finally during the advent of the welfare state (1880–1930) both central and local governments experienced an intensification as well as an extension of tasks in response to citizens' needs as well as in need of more efficient administration. As remarked above, citizen needs were served primarily at the local level until the end of the nineteenth century. After that it became a mixed central-local responsibility.

Comparing country-specific developments, three patterns emerge. Page (1991) analyzed the position of local government over time through the development of central-local relations in seven countries. He recalls Hintze's distinction between two epochs in the history of local government. In the first epoch, from the Middle Ages to the early-1800s, local government institutions were shaped by "actual relationships" between central and local officials, while in the second epoch (the nineteenth century) the development of local government was based on a conscious planning of administrative reorganizations (Page 1991: 112).

For the early modern period Page distinguishes three patterns of territorial administration. The first pattern was a system of central supervision through appointed officials in the region as was the case in France (intendant), Piedmontese Italy (refendary and military governor), and Spain (royal governor). The second pattern was a system of local self-government reminiscent of the old Germanic forms of territorial administration and found in Denmark and Norway until the mid-seventeenth and late-eighteenth century respectively. In both these countries this was replaced by a system where local government was more a unit of central administration. The third pattern was a system with strong local government as found in England and—from the seventeenth century onward—in Sweden. Hintze's explanation of these patterns is based on the degree to which feudalism determined central-local relations. In the Carolingian heartland (France, Germany to the Elbe, Aragon, northern Italy) the feudal system of personal contracts between monarch and nobility destroyed the county level of government, while in the more peripheral areas (England, Scandinavia, Poland, Hungary, Bohemia) a petty (landed) nobility existed that developed local government without an eye on its use for obstructing or opposing the national government (Page 1991: 117). As a result local government in France, Piedmont, Denmark, Norway, and Spain entered the nineteenth century as an administrative extension of the center, while in Britain and Sweden central control was far less direct. This was also the case in the Dutch Republic.

The nineteenth century was an age of local government reform and expansion throughout Europe. In the centralized systems mentioned above, this reform happened through "...an administrative relationship of control according to which the approval of a state official was required to ensure the legality of local government" (Page 1991: 133). In France and Italy a system of hierarchically structured central-local relations persisted, because of clientelism and local patronage. It disappeared in the Scandinavian countries where local government functions were extended through amalgamations of local government units after the Second World War. Such consolidation of local government was blocked in Italy and France because of the importance of local power bases for national politics. A radically different situation could be found in Scandinavia and in England where, for more than a century, "...the conception of the role of local government has been that of an institution with sufficient financial and economic capacity to deliver major public services" (Page 1991: 136). Page applies his analysis also to other unitary states such as Belgium and the Netherlands. Belgium fits into his category of *legal centralism*, a situation where local politics is tied to central politics and the shape of local government is very much decided by central formal legal provisions (as in

France and Italy). The Netherlands on the other hand displays more *legal localism* (as England and Scandinavia) (Page 1991: 141). Page, however, overstresses the position of the prefectorial institution in the Netherlands (the Queens' Commissioner as the governor of the province). Although local government reorganization varies in terms of scope and measures, it has touched just about every Western country in the postwar era (Alsboek et al. 1996; Dente and Kjellberg 1988; Hesse 1991; Page and Goldsmith 1987).

What all this means for the development of tasks and services at local level at present is summarized by Page in calling the major distinction between northern and southern European countries to be the development of local government as a *welfare state bureaucracy*. The weakness of political localism "...made unproblematic the reorganization of local government to provide, from the center's perspective, more efficient units of service delivery" (Page 1991: 143). Indeed welfare state expansion also coincided with local government reorganization in federal systems such as Germany and the United States (Page 1991: 144–145).

As far as efficient administration is concerned the transformation with the most impact was the one during the Atlantic Revolutions. It was then that the basis was laid for modern bureaucratic administration (see chapter 6.3.3). The increase of public tasks at both central and local level from the 1880s onward heralded another period of reform in organization and in role and position of public functionaries. The bureaucratization of organization is discussed in chapter 6, while the bureaucratization in the functioning of public functionaries is discussed in chapter 7.

5.4 A Theory on the Development of Taxation and Expenditure

As soon as something like a government develops, financial resources are needed. Taxation systems are then set up in order to extract adequate revenue. In a barter economy taxation is an awkward business as long as no common standard for valuing different commodities is developed. A taxation system can be characterized by the type of taxes and by the type of tax collection involved.

In general, three types of taxes are distinguished:

1. taxes in kind: a direct tax, when part of the produce is set aside for the household of the sovereign and sometimes even consumed on the spot;

2. taxes in labor (*corvée*): also a direct tax, requiring the (male) population (the untaxable poor as Webber and Wildavsky call them (1986: 22)) to put in time for the construction of large public works (pyramids, canals, roads, etc.); and

3. taxes in money: direct taxes such as income tax, and indirect taxes such as customs, excise, stamp tax, sales tax, VAT, taxes on external manifestations of wealth.

There are also three types of tax collection systems:

1. direct collection by government using a network of supervisors and central and local tax collectors;

2. indirect collection by government through tax farmers, using contractors for the actual collection and government supervisors to monitor the turnout; and

3. a mixed system wherein both direct and indirect collection are used, the choice between the two depending upon the type of taxable product.

Over time, governments developed and refined the technique of tax collection in order to ensure adequate revenue. Innovations in taxation have been both the result of changes in the economy and changes in the technical ability to extract revenue. Examples of changes in the economy in medieval Europe are the increase of interregional trade and the reintroduction of coinage. Double-entry bookkeeping, as invented in northern Italy in the fourteenth century, was a technical innovation. Only governments that operate in heavily monetized economies can extract cash income, as is the case in industrialized countries. Thus taxes in kind, taxes in labor, and indirect taxes in money were the three types to be found in medieval and early modern Europe, often collected in a mixed system. Direct taxes in money is a nineteenth-century phenomenon, as is the disappearance of tax farmers.

Seligman (1895), once called the brightest fiscalist of all times (Grapperhaus 1993: 9), distinguished among seven stages in the development of how we have come to perceive taxation:

1. Tax as an individual's gift to government as is illustrated in the Latin *donum* and the English *benevolence* used as words deep into the Middle Ages.

2. Tax as a humble request by government for support (in Latin *precarium*, in German *Bede*).

3. Tax as help to the state as is testified in the use of concepts like the Latin *adjutorium*, the English *aid*, *subsidy*, and *contribution*, and the French *aide*.

4. Tax as an individual sacrifice for the state, see the German *Abgabe*, the French *gabelle*, and the Italian *dazio*.
5. Tax as a civic duty.
6. Tax can be levied on the basis of coercion as is signified in the use of such words as *impost* and *imposition* (English), *Auflage* and *Aufschlag* (German), *impôt* (French), and *imposta* (Italian).
7. Tax finally becomes synonymous with an estimated tax by government regardless of the taxpayers will. Words used are *taxare* (Latin), *Scot* (English), *Schoss* or *Schätzung* (German), *taxe* (French), and *tasse* (Italian).

The origins of our contemporary tax system can again be traced to the time that economy and society in Europe experienced the most major transformation since Roman times. True, during the reign of Charlemagne (768–814) interregional trade had flourished and government had become somewhat centralized. But after his death the empire dissolved and with it interregional trade declined. Government and administration came to rely on a system of personal services known as feudalism. Whether or not interregional trade is the main factor explaining the changes in Europe in the twelfth and thirteenth centuries is not so important. The fact is that once interregional trade revived, the Germanic type of rule through personal relations was dropped in favor of the more Roman type of territorial administration. The new territorial rulers came to rely less on their vassals and more on servants appointed to their household and administration. Feudal armies gave way to hired mercenaries, and kings faced the necessity to find new sources of (non-feudal) revenue. They found these for instance in the granting of town charters, borrowing to cover deficits, currency debasement, and public loans. Although there was no official separation between private and public finance, gradually an administrative distinction developed between costs of the king's household and other expenses.

If ever there was something of a common pattern in the development of public finance during the Middle Ages, it was feudal administration as the dominant form of public finance in Europe. In the late Middle Ages and the early modern period the development of public finance is strongly related to the type of governance that developed in a territory. France was the only European country to emerge from the Middle Ages with a strong, centralized government and so with a centralized fiscal system (Webber and Wildavsky 1986: 174). The English kings on the other hand struggled with the aristocracy about the royal authority to levy taxes. In fact, in many of the territories in Europe *central* powers clashed with local and regional lords. In some centralization proved to be more successful (Spain) than in others (the Low Countries). What was common, though, is that personal servants of the king increasingly became (technical) specialists especially in the fields of foreign affairs, defense, justice, and finance (see also next chapter). Governments began to borrow money to finance their policies, at first from wealthy merchants such as the Fugger family.

In the course of the seventeenth century, however, public banks emerged. The Bank of Amsterdam issuing bonds and notes to finance the wars and trade of the Dutch Republic served as a model for the Bank of England (1693) created by Sir George Downing (Webber and Wildavsky 1986: 242–43, 256–57). By the end of the eighteenth century most European sovereignties had a central state bank. During that century the idea that *budget* was synonymous with tax proposal was replaced by the notion that expenditure ought to be related to anticipated resources. Toward the end of the eighteenth century pressure mounted to reform financial administration which was still very much relying upon indirect, regressive taxes and tax farming.

The first half of the nineteenth century witnessed the advent of the *balanced budget* together with the creation of a single organization for tax collection and a parallel organization for spending instead of the medieval and early modern system of multiple officials and organizations. By the end of the century central governments assumed a more interventionist role as well as pursued more redistributive and collectivist policies. Financing these involved not only the introduction of new budget recording techniques (next to the more traditional line-item budgeting), but also more progressive types of taxation based on income tax as the prime source of revenue. Due to this shift from indirect to direct taxation governments were able to more efficiently allocate funds to particular policies and to subnational units. Indeed, central and subnational governments became intertwined in terms of financial relations. Another novelty in the first half of the twentieth century was the development of social insurance, financed through contributions from employees and employers. By now income tax and social insurance constitute the two financial pillars upon which the welfare state is maintained.

After the Second World War government spending rose higher then ever, which gave rise to a revival of indirect taxes (retail sales tax, turnover tax, VAT) on goods and services. This could only be possible in a highly centralized tax system where the surplus of economic pro-

TABLE 5.1
Introduction of Income Tax and Social Insurance in some Western Countries

	Germany	United States	England	France	Netherlands
Income Tax	1891	1862	1799	1909	1892
Accident Insurance	1884	1930	1911	1898	1901
Disabled Insurance	1889	1956	—	1930	1919
Sickness Insurance	1883	—	1911	1930	1913
Unemployment Insurance	1927	1935	1911	1958	1952
Pension Act	1889	1935	1908	1935	1919

Sources: De Swaan 1989: 183–192; Peters 1991: 230; Flora and Heidenheimer 1984: 59, 83.

duction could be partially skimmed and channeled into public funds, which in turn were used to finance transfer payments to the nonworking part of the population. At first these transfers occurred on a national basis, but since the Second World War they have assumed global proportions through Marshall aid and development aid. Most recently we also see transfers within world regions. Thus the European Union seeks to promote the economic and social cohesion of the Community through financing projects in less-developed regions out of funds filled by the member states. The general trend in the distribution of welfare in the nineteenth and twentieth century thus appears to be:

1. from private and local to public and national welfare in the nineteenth and early-twentieth century;
2. transfer of revenue from the affluent to the less affluent within one country in the first half of the twentieth century; and
3. transfer of revenue from the affluent countries to the less affluent countries between world regions and within world regions in the second half of the twentieth century.

This trend has been adequately illustrated by Flora and Heidenheimer (1984: 55, 85) and Kohl (1983). The shift from expenditure in traditional areas (defense, foreign affairs, police) to welfare areas (education, housing, health, social insurance) is best shown when we let figures speak for themselves. In Germany the proportion of social expenditures rose from 15 percent to 62 percent in the 1870–1960 period; in England from 20 percent to 47 percent in the 1890–1960 period; and in Sweden from 30 percent to 53 percent in the 1900–1960 period (Flora and Heidenheimer 1984: 49–50).

The growth of public expenditure in the twentieth century is of such magnitude that it has generated a substantial amount of empirical research seeking to explain that growth. Most theories in literature pertain to national governments, while little is done in the field of subnational government. One of the oldest theories is Wagner's Law of increasing state activity (1890). He claims that with rising real per capita income, government will consume more of the gross national product. This mechanism is explained by the idea that government intervention is desired to alleviate the social tension (inequality) that has resulted because of demographic growth and urbanization. In such a situation, government begins financing projects that go beyond what the individual can do, or for which there is no provision in the market. The same type of economic determinism can be found with Wilensky (1975), who states that the level of economic development is the cause for the emergence of the welfare state. After all, a growing national surplus makes it possible to finance social security programs (Webber and Wildavsky 1986: 569–574). The views of Wagner and Wilensky have been contested on a number of grounds.

First for its temporal limits. Crowley points to swings in the relative share of government expenditure over the last 900 years. He attempted to see whether Pirenne's hypothesis that periods of decreased government expenditure are followed by periods of increased expenditure holds up when empirically tested. He concluded that Wagner's Law and Peacock's and Wiseman's hypothesis (see below) have limited value because they apply to the period of 1850–1970. On the longer term, he argues, we should look into the incidence and influence of war as an explanatory factor: "During periods of *laissez-faire*, the incidence of wars appears to decline and it increases during periods classified as government control" (Crowley 1971: 41).

Second, there are theoretical objections to Wagner's Law. According to Peacock and Wiseman it is not the demand for government intervention (i.e., expenditure) but the supply of public turnover that decides growth. Expenditure is limited by available revenue. Only in times of crisis, like war, do citizens tolerate extraordinary tax increases. Public expenditure will rise up to the ceiling of available revenue. Once the crisis is over taxes will decrease but not to the level of before the crisis (1961: xxvi–xxviii, 93, 133). Others have made the correlation between war and government growth plausible (Eichenberg 1983: 144–147, 151).

Kau and Rubin also believe that it is not failure of the market (i.e., demand for government services) but the availability of tax revenue that explains government growth. They argue that through technological change (specialization and division of labor, economy of scale, market versus home productivity, urbanization) new types of organizations and behavior develop that make tax collection easier and less costly. The enlarged tax return is thus used to improve the quality and quantity of public services (Kau and Rubin 1981: 261–262, 265, 273). Technological change and industrialization are often considered the driving forces behind the growth of government and bureaucracy (Clarke 1983: 128). It is interesting that this growth is stronger in countries where the largest part of government revenue comes out of indirect taxes and social insurance. Public functionaries can spend larger sums of money when the real costs can be hidden (Downs 1957: 51–74; Downs 1960: 541–563; Buchanan and Wagner 1977: 69, 96–98, 129). McKenzie also considers technological development to be closely related to the growth of government, but contrary to Kau and Rubin he argues that market failure is the source of that growth. Technological and industrial development create externalities which cannot be countered in the private sector (free-rider behavior). In view of market failure it is government that is forced to step in. By way of example McKenzie mentions car insurance, agriculture, police and fire brigade, unemployment benefits, welfare, and education (McKenzie 1980: 247–248, 257). Cameron, however, regards the type of explanations above as insufficient. His research indicates that the growth of government varies to the degree with which an economy is sensitive to and dependent upon changes in the international economy. Open economies have the fastest growing public sectors (Cameron 1978).

5.5 Literature on the Development of Public Services

There is an abundance of literature on the development of public services, but there are few general introductions. Barker's 1944 study on the development of public services in Western Europe (1660–1930) concentrates on territorial organization, public finance, and central-local relations. The study by Knight and Wiltshire on the development of public services in Australia (1973) is an example of a nationally oriented study. Schneider published a study (1938) on the history of public welfare in New York state (1609–1866).

A variety of studies is available on the growth of the welfare state. The studies by Flora and Heidenheimer (1984) and De Swaan (1989) are informative, comparative, and wide-ranging. Mommsen (1981) wrote a study on the development of the welfare state in Britain and Germany. The study by Köhler, Zacher, and Partington (1982) deals with a specific aspect of welfare state development, the development of social insurance. Several studies have considered the development of the welfare state in a specific country. Roberts investigated the origins of the welfare state in Victorian England (1960).

Most studies of public services, however, are limited to a specific task area in one country. Not surprisingly this type of study does not dominate in the administrative sciences. Histories of particular public tasks are often written by people who have been professionally involved and have taken up an interest in the development of the field in which they are familiar with the contemporary structure and functioning. At this point Hume's remark comes to mind: historical research in one specific policy area requires a detail of knowledge administrative scientists usually do not have, and that they should concentrate on the development of administrative arrangements and processes (see section 2.3). When looking at the literature, he appears to be correct. Many administrative histories are about organization, processes, and functionaries. However, the fact remains that many of those administrative histories could not have been written without intimate knowledge of policy areas. Many of the studies about a particular organization or a specific level of government address the development of the service(s) provided. Indeed, a study would be meaningless if such was not done.

Hume's point of view is relevant, but in another respect. Comparative studies of specific task areas are rare, mainly because the nationally oriented studies which could serve as a foundation of such comparison are outside the range that would catch the administrative scientist's attention. Interesting examples of nationally-oriented studies are the ones by Reith (1948) on the British police, McConville (1981) on British prison administration, Buisson (1958) and Le Clère (1964) on the French police, Petot (1958) on public works (roads and bridges) in France, Armstrong (1976) on public works in the United States, and Callahan (1962) on public schools in the United States. Comparison of the development of public service delivery in a special area may reveal interesting differences and similarities between countries, both in terms of what it was exactly that government did in that area and why it was involved, as well as in terms of how they did it. A recent study of health politics in France, Sweden, and Switzerland is a good example (Immergut 1992).

5.6 Literature on the Development of Public Finance

There is also a wealth of literature in the social sciences (economics included) focused on the growth of public expenditure in the nineteenth and twentieth century. Some of it has been discussed in relation to explanations of government growth (section 5.4). In this section I address the literature regarding the development of public finance and expenditure. Webber and Wildavsky's *A History of Taxation and Public Expenditure* (1986) serves as an entry into this literature. It is monumental given the fact that it traces developments from the earliest times up to the present in a comparative perspective. After a discussion of developments in the ancient civilizations (Egypt, India, China, Mesopotamia, Greece, Rome) the book concentrates on the Western world. It provides much detail without loosing sight of the main argument. In his inaugural address, Grapperhaus (1993) discussed the development of proportional taxation in Western Europe in the 800–1800 period. There is a variety of comparative articles available as well. Most books, however, seem to be nationally oriented studies, especially on France, England, Canada, and the United States.

For France the history of public finance can be compiled from various publications such as those by Ardant (1972) on the history of the impost, Bonney (1981) on the king's debts in the 1589–1661 period, Bosher (1970) on bureaucratization of finance during the 1770–1795 revolutionary decades, and Wolfe (1972) on the fiscal system during the Renaissance.

The literature on England appears to be most complete. Dowell (1965, 3d. ed.) wrote a six-volume history of taxation and taxes from the early times to the present. Specialized studies have been published about the development of fiscal relations in 1871–1919 (Bellamy 1988), public finance in 1774–1792 (Binney 1958), public credit in 1688–1756 (Dickson 1967), public finance 1485–1641 (Dietz 1964, 2d ed.), and public finance in the 1558–1825 period (Hughes 1934). In the light of Seligman's theory of the development of the perception of taxes, Kennedy's (1964) study about the development of policy and opinion of English taxation is interesting.

As far as North America is concerned, Bates (1939) published a financial history of Canada. His findings are complemented with Canadian studies on the growth of public spending (Bird 1970) and the development of public expenditure in Ontario in the postwar period (Foot 1977). Borcherding (1977) analyzed the interplay of budgets and bureaucrats in relation to government growth in the United States in the twentieth century. Ferguson (1961) published a study on public finance in the 1776–1790 period. Benson et al. (1965) provided a study of the history, administration, and economic impact of the American property tax. In all of the above mentioned publications, it is striking to see that so little attention is paid to political responsibility in budgeting and expenditure. The one exception seems to be Wilmerding's (1943) study of the history of expenditure control by the U.S. Congress.

References

Alsboek, Erik, Lawrence Rose, Lars Strömberg, and Kristen Stohlberg 1996. *Nordic Local Government: Developmental Trends and Reform Activities in the Postwar Era*. Helsinki: The Association of Finnish Municipalities.

Buchanan, J.M. and R.E. Wagner. 1977. *Democracy in Deficit: The Political Legacy of Lord Keynes*. New York: Academic Press.

Cameron, D. 1978. "The Expansion of the Public Economy: A Comparative Analysis." *American Political Science Review* 72, no.4: 1243–1261.

Dente, Bruno and Francesco Kjellberg, eds. 1988. *The Dynamics of Institutional Change: Local Government Reorganization in Western Democracies*. London: SAGE Publications.

Downs, Anthony. 1957. *An Economic Theory of Democracy*. New York: Harper & Row.

———. 1960. "Why the Government Budget is too Small in a Democracy." *World Politics* 12, no.4: 541–563.

Eichenberg, R.C. 1983. "Problems in Using Public Employment Data." In *Why Governments Grow: Measuring Public Sector Size*, edited by C. L. Taylor, 136–154. Beverly Hills, CA and London: SAGE Publications.

Hesse, Joachim Jens, ed. 1990–91. *Local Government and Urban Affairs in International Perspective: Analysis of Twenty Western Industrialized Countries*. Baden-Baden: Nomos Verlagsgesellschaft.

Kau, James B. and Paul H. Rubin. 1981. "The Size of Government." In *Public Choice* 37, no.2: 261–274.

McKenzie, Richard B. 1980. "The Economic Justification for Government and Government Growth." *Journal of Social and Political Studies* 5, no.3: 245–257.

Meltzer, Allan H. and Scott F. Richard. 1981. "A Rational Theory of the Size of Government." *Journal of Political Economy* 89, no. 5: 914–927.

———. 1983. "Tests of a Rational Theory of the Size of Government. In *Public Choice* 41, no.3: 403–418.

Page, Edward C. 1991. *Localism and Centralism in Europe: The Political and Legal Bases of Local Self-Government*. Oxford and New York: Oxford University Press.

Page, Edward C. and Michael J. Goldsmith, eds. 1987. *Central and Local Government Relations: A Comparative Analysis of West-European Unitary States*. London: SAGE Publications.

Peacock, A.T. and J. Wiseman. 1961. *The Growth of Public Expenditure in the United Kingdom*. Princeton, NJ: Princeton University Press.

Tholfsen, T.R. 1967. *Historical Thinking: An Introduction*. New York: Harper & Row.

Wagner, A. 1890. *Finanzwissenschaft*, 3d ed. Leipzig: Deutscher Verlag.

6

The Structure and Functioning of Government: Organizational Differentiation and Bureaucratization

From early in history, rulers (and later governments) experimented with organization. As soon as tasks and territory grew beyond the ruler's capacity to control by means of his own household, functional and territorial (re)organizations were required. Thus in the vast ancient empires of China, Egypt, India and Rome, government departments were created which constituted a functional differentiation at the central level. Some of these had field services in the various parts of the empire (deconcentration). The territory was subdivided into smaller units (provinces, municipalities), governed by a representative of the overlord. Sometimes these representatives functioned next to functionaries appointed from amidst the local or regional population.

The last highly organized governmental system in the ancient world was that of Rome. After its desintegration, (Western) Europe fell apart into a patchwork of small communities that once again could be governed through the ruler's household alone. This would remain so until the eleventh/twelfth centuries. In terms of organization Charlemagne's (768–814) government displayed a mix of personal and delegated rule. He divided his empire into counties and markcounties at the regional level and built upon the existing local communities for the construction of a local government. This territorial division was not matched with a functional division. From the central down to the local level, administration was the business of the ruler's household. The *curia regis* was the center of government, and the success of governance depended much on the physical presence of the king/emperor. Charlemagne's court was itinerant, if only because the bulk of taxes were in kind and needed to be consumed on the spot.

In this chapter I will discuss literature on the development of government organization in the Western world from the moment that territorial and functional differentiation were reintroduced. The *curia regis* was the organization from which certain tasks separated and developed into specialized government departments. Before discussing the literature, though, we need to discuss the frameworks within which organization has been and can be studied. Thus, I will discuss modern ideas about organization (section 6.1), the bureaucratic ideal-type (section 6.2), differences and similarities between medieval, early modern, and modern organization (section 6.3). In section 6.4 I present a descriptive theory on the development of organization in the Western world. With the groundwork laid, we can discuss the literature on territorial (re)organization (local and regional government, section 6.5), functional (re)organization (government departments, bureaucracy, and bureaucratization: section 6.6), councils (section 6.7), work processes and techniques (section 6.8), and public policy-making (section 6.9). In the discussion of the literature, I do not always refer to the time period and/or area a study is concerned with.

6.1 Principles of Modern Organization

Traditional organizational theory focused on rather static characteristics of organization: *division of labor*, *span of administration*, *departmentation*, and *unity of command*. These four constitute the classical cornerstones of organization (Robbins 1980: 196). They are not identical with nor exclusive for bureaucratic organization. Indeed, it is easy to find them to a varying degree in all organizations at all times whether consciously applied or not. They are interrelated as well. Due to physical and intellectual limitations as well as for reasons of efficiency, specialization develops and materializes in more or less clearly defined competencies. Once the number of employees around a related set of tasks grows, functional differentiation might be necessary. Specialized organizations then separate from a mother organization. Parallel to this a clear structure is necessary consisting of subdivisions, so that from the workfloor up to the top of the organization each supervisor can adequately control his subordinates (span of administration) and has no doubts about to whom he is accountable (unity of command). The classical (bureaucratic) organizational chart resembles the shape of a pyramid and is a *line organization*.

Dominating as this view of organization is, its principles have only guided governments since the nineteenth century. As we will see governmental organization before, say, the 1800s was a little more complex than the relatively recent "classical" model. Even during the heyday of the classical line model its insufficiency was underlined with the introduction of internal management units (the *staff line model*). The usefulness of the classical model in turn has been challenged in recent decades through the development and introduction of for instance the *matrix organization* (a combination of a classical and a project organization) (Robbins 1980: 284–285), and the *linking-pin organization* (Likert 1961).

An organizational structure reflects the ideas the designers had as to how the objectives of the organization could best be attained. Thus tasks and activities can be organized on various principles: *function* (units for personnel administration, public relations), *clientele* (a department of agriculture), *geography* (deconcentrated field agencies of a government department, regional and local government), or *process* (organizing according to required skills: tax registration, tax collection, statistics collection) (Gulick 1937; Self 1977: 55–57; Robbins 1980: 204–205). Most contemporary organizational structures display a mix of these principles in order to deal with the complexity of the tasks they have been set to do.

When taking the classical model and principles of organization as point of departure for analysis of the development of organization, we would be tempted to conclude that no matter the path of development, organizational structure ultimately converged to the one sketched above. That, however, would ignore the fact that an organization is a product of its own time and context. For an adequate analysis of organizational development, a more dynamic view is needed that emphasizes the processes involved in organizing rather than the structures. It should also include small organizations. Barnard's definition of organization as a "...system of consciously coordinated activities or forces of two or more persons..." (Barnard 1948: 73; see also Denhardt 1984: 15) meets these requirements. Organizational activity takes place within a structure and functions according to specified and nonspecified rules. We will see how these rules become more explicit (codified, written) over time as a result of increasing activity. We will also see that ideas about proper organization evolved from practical suggestions at the work-floor level (clear instructions for the lower level functionaries; the higher up in the hierarchy the less clear) to intricate systems of organization (with clear competencies at each level). As the *classical* principles of organization are not only characteristic for bureaucracy, so is the fact that rules are used not exclusive for bureaucracy. Given that bureaucracy is the dominant characteristic of contemporary organization and given that bureaucratization is a dominant concept in the analysis of organizational development, we can use Weber's ideal type as a framework.

6.2 Idealtypes, Bureaucracy, and Bureaucratization

The variety of meanings in which the bureaucracy concept is used can be reduced to two main types (Van Braam 1986: 216–217):

1. bureaucracy as a type of organization in society (*Legal-rationale Herrschaft*); and
2. bureaucracy as *civil service*, a totality of civil servants (*Bürokratische Verwaltungsstab*).

When some speak of a bureaucratization of the world they point to a phenomenon that is not limited to public or private organizations but permeates society as such (Jacoby 1973). Identifying the consequences of legal-rational authority for organization Weber produced a list of seventeen characteristics in *Wirtschaft und Gesellschaft* (Weber 1980: 124–130), Albrow (1970: 43–45) lists eighteen characteristics, and Van Braam (1977: 459) subdivided the ideal-type into twenty characteristics. The *laundry list*, as Silberman (1993: 6) aptly called it, can be found in appendix 6.1. Weber claimed that bureaucracy was the most rational and efficient of all organizations. This claim met with critique.

Few concepts in the socio-scientific approach of public organization have received so much attention, met with so much misinterpretation, and thus met with so much (unfounded) criticism as Weber's ideal type of bureaucracy and the context of his theory about the development toward a legal-rational society (see appendix 6.2).

As one of the first, Merton (1940, 1952) drew attention to the inefficient aspects of bureaucracy. He emphasized the negative consequences of strict-rule application and argued that the individual goals of employees might easily lead to goal displacement. Some years later Selznick pointed out that public servants behaved themselves according to rules that were wider than what is stipulated in the formal civil service codes of conduct (1943). Administrative rationality was bound by culture. Bendix (1949) argued that both formal rules as well as how human beings experience them ought to be investigated when assessing the efficiency of an organization. Hendershot and Parsons (1947), and Gouldner (1954) after them, focused on the tension that existed between professional power (the power of knowledge) and bureaucratic power (the power of hierarchy). Blau (1955) concluded that efficiency was not served by strict application of rules, but by the ability of a bureaucratic organization to adapt to a changing environment. Stinchcombe (1959–1960) joined the chorus of critics when he argued that certain characteristics of bureaucracy were not suitable for some organizations. The meaning of rules in bureaucracies led Crozier to formulate his *vicious circle of bureaucracy.*

The critique thus far was reason for Mayntz to open a famous article with the following remark:

> The fate that *Max Weber's* understanding and theory of bureaucracy met in view of their reception by—mostly American—organizational sociologists, has certain characteristics in common. (Mayntz 1965: 493)

She categorized the critique in four groups (Mayntz 1965: 494–499):

1. The concept of bureaucracy did not adequately describe reality because of lack of attention for informal structures and dimensions.
2. The ideal-type lacked attention for notions about goal-decision processes and relations to the environment.
3. Inner inconsistencies could be found in the ideal-type through establishing whether the various characteristics of bureaucracy (see appendix 6.1) were positively correlated.
4. The ideal-type did not appreciate the possible antagonism between administration and authority.

Mayntz acknowledged that these misunderstandings, as she called them, had resulted in new directions of research, however. By way of summary her counterarguments ran as follows: the ideal-type is not at all intended as a description of reality; informal structures and relations (that Weber did recognize) do not logically belong to the ideal-type; goal-decision processes are not the issue but the assumption as to whether the ideal-typical bureaucratic organization is really maximally efficient; characteristics of bureaucracy do not have to occur simultaneously; Weber did not regard administration and authority as antagonistic forces but as principles existing at the same time in a tense relationship. In an excellent exposé of Weber's ideal type of bureaucracy Mouzelis (1971: 42–49) argued along the same lines as Mayntz. A fifth group of misunderstandings consists of those who view the ideal types of traditional, charismatic and bureaucratic authority as phases in an attempt to assess to what degree a structure can be labelled as rational (see also ch. 4). Rather they should be looked upon as a definition of role characteristics enabling us to assess whether or not an essential constellation of role characteristics is present (Silberman 1993: 9–10).

Despite Mayntz's convincing argument, the critique of the bureaucracy concept had a life of its own. Thus Rudolph and Rudolph presented a theoretical and historical reinterpretation of Weber's ideal types of bureaucratic and patrimonial administration, arguing that the defects of bureaucracy could be met with neopatrimonialism. Maintaining patrimonial elements in a bureaucratic organization would reduce and maybe even eliminate the risk of anomy and resistance against formal rationality (Rudolph and Rudolph 1979: 195–199). Etzioni-Halévy is also critical about bureaucracy, although not very original: it has limited conceptual power, it is not an adequate description of reality, it has no eye for internal battles for power, it runs the risk of inefficiency, and it inhibits creativity (Etzioni-Halévy 1983: 35–38).

To assess whether or not the ideal type is a useful instrument for analysis, we need to look at the relationship between it and reality. Most of the critique is justified if the ideal type was intended as a description of reality. Weber himself indicated that such was not the case:

> Nothing, however, is more dangerous than the confusion of theory and history, in the sense that some believe that in theoretical conceptualization the actual situation, the meaning of historical reality is captured, or in the sense that we use theory as a Procrustus bed, to which history is forcefully made to fit…(Weber 1985: 195)

Since ideal types serve as a comparison to reality, we need to distinguish the logical meaning of the ideal type in its comparative relation to reality from the judgement about reality by means of ideals. Much of the criticism of the bureaucratic ideal type comes from the (seldom explicit) conflict between one's own ideals (freedom for the individual) and actual developments (limitation of freedom, bureaucratization). Weber's somber expectations about the future ("inexorable march of bureaucratization") and his doubts ("How is Democracy possible even in this limited sense?") led generations of researchers to search for and formulate alternatives.

6.3 Characteristics of Medieval, Early Modern, and Modern Administration

With the advantage of hindsight we could say that the roots of modern administration in the Western world go back as far as the 1200s.

The emergence of cities and universities, the reestablishment of inter-regional trade, the discovery of Roman law, the advent of the state, and the struggle for power between clerical and secular rulers etcetera, all in their own way contributed to changes in government. In this section I will focus on the changes in the organization of government (the first eight dimensions of the bureaucratic idealtype, see appendix 6.1; the dimensions concerning the functionaries will be discussed in ch. 7).

At first sight there may be remarkable convergence in Western states in the development toward one type of government and administration: the rational-legal authority with bureaucracy. Closer inspection, however, reveals that there is no single administrative tradition nor is there one path toward modernity. Instead, the matter of how to explain that administrative systems in various countries have taken to different forms, and why there is so little convergence has puzzled scholars thirty years ago as much as now (Fesler 1962: 77; Silberman 1993: ix). In the following, however, I will present a general outline only.

Medieval Administration, 1200–1500: The Birth of Bureaucracy

Characteristic of medieval organization around the year 1000 is its simplicity in structure. The ruler is aided by a royal council, a collegial advisory body, consisting of members of the clergy and the aristocracy. Secular government in the various parts of the realm is put in the hands of feudal lords. For the strength of this system of territorial administration the ruler very much depends upon the strength and loyalty of his appointees in various regions. In the more or less unified territories such as England or France a system of field administration develops, partially building on the experiments during the Merovingian and Carolingian eras. Thus bailiffs were created in France as part of a strategy to weaken feudal lords, and the idea to use bailiffs was possibly copied from Henry II (Fesler 1962: 85). Once regional lords acquired certain autonomy, central government introduced a new type of official (Greenfeld 1992: 516, note 99). However, as long as cooptation was the basis for the recruitment of officials, central government would not achieve a stronghold in the regions (Dibble 1965: 884–885, 896).

As a consequence the relationship between officials was determined by the rewards one could distribute and the control one wielded. Some of these officials, powerful at a local or regional level, needed to constantly balance between the variety of demands of those above them. The English sheriff, for instance, was accountable to the justice of the peace, the lord lieutenant and his deputy, as well as to the Privy Council (Dibble 1965: 881). Lack of clarity in jurisdictions, little hierarchy of authority, and problems with concerted action resulted in a higgledy-piggledy organization of government (Meyer 1985: 196–199).

When administrative activity picked up in the course of the twelfth and thirteenth centuries, a need for functional differentiation arose. This expressed itself in the creation of separate departments in addition to the royal council. Chancery, treasury, and courts reflected what was most important to government at the time: the royal household, the taxes, and justice. The advisory function was organized separately as well. Between the thirteenth and sixteenth centuries, a variety of councils were created. Some, like the Parliament, merely as a means to appease the Estates (clergy, aristocracy, and merchants); others were intended to supply the ruler with advice on high politics (the Council of State) and finance (Chamber of Accounts). It is important to realize that through the creation of his own administrative apparatus, the ruler could afford to depend less on clergy (for functions that required literacy) and noblemen (for the defense of the territory) for the administration of his affairs. The ruler thus created central royal power, destroyed feudalism, and through codification and administrative regulations created a bureaucracy. Among the oldest temporal collections of legal and administrative regulations is *the Constitution of Melfi* (1231), also called the birth certificate of bureaucracy (Jacoby 1976: 21) of Emperor Frederick II of the Norman empire in Sicily and southern Italy.

Toward the end of the Middle Ages, government organization is characterized by *collegial administration*, *territorial division*, some *functional differentiation*, *cooptation*, and the *use of written records*.

The Early Modern Period, 1500–1780: Continuity and Change

In terms of territorial organization, the early modern period (1500–1780) displays diverging patterns. Government in France and Prussia became more centralized. In a situation where the legislative, judicial, and administrative control by the center was strengthened, there was little autonomy left for local government. Such administrative control was virtually lacking in England and the Netherlands. It should be mentioned that the Tudor period in Britain represented something of an exception given the attempt to build a police state. The degree of centralization can also be assessed by looking at the relationship between law and administration. It is striking to see that the more changes in instruments of governance or changes in local administration are regulated in detailed legislation, the more centralized a system is, for instance France and Prussia. New tasks were organized within the existing local or regional administrative organization. The same was done in the Dutch Republic, but unlike France and Prussia there was no detailed legislation, at least not in the most important province of Holland. In England on the other hand, legislation until the early-nineteenth century was often private (Private Bills), local, and nonbinding (Parris 1969: 160). Separate local administrative bodies were created to facilitate new tasks (Turnpike Trust, Paving and Lighting Commission, Poor House).

In terms of the organization of actors, the early modern period is much more a continuation of the Middle Ages. There was still no clear distinction between political and administrative officials. First, because much policy making was prepared by political functionaries, and clerks were merely hired for routine jobs and copying. Second, the work of political officials and high civil servants overlapped to a large extent (Armstrong 1973: 24; Parris 1969: 24). Collegial organization was the organizing principle when new tasks were taken up and could be found everywhere in Europe (Rosenberg 1958: 96). For a number of reasons collegial administration was ideal (Parris 1969: ch.3). First, in terms of balance of power, delegating a task to a body of people (a *collegium*) instead of to one official, reduced the risk that a functionary could develop too strong a position. Second, a collegial body guaranteed continuity since the death of one of its members would not inhibit its work. Third, it was believed that members kept a good eye on one another and thus costs were relatively low. Finally, collegial administration increased opportunities for patronage.

By way of conclusion one could say that early modern government differed little from medieval government as far as organizational principles are concerned.

The Modern Period, 1780–Present:
Bureaucratization of Functioning

The years 1780–1820 are formative for the creation of modern government organization (Raadschelders and Rutgers 1996). In France existing government departments were reorganized and new ones were created (Church 1981: 77, 89). In England reorganization was the most important method (Chester 1981: 138, 222). In the Netherlands the first government departments were created in 1798 (Raadschelders 1989). The reorganized and newly created departments were structured according to the *unity of command* principle, with a clear hierarchy and clear sets of competencies. Hence collegial administration gave way to bureau administration which in turn helped the distinction between elected and appointed officeholders to develop. It also facilitated the effectiveness of measures against sinecures, sale of offices, and corruption. Thus the separation of office from office holder, as had been advocated by Pope Leo I (A.D. 440–461) and Martin Luther, finally came into effect (Hattenhauer 1978: 151; Miller 1984: 284). Comparable developments occurred in the United States after the abolition of the spoils system and the advent of the reform movement (1880s) (Schiesl 1977).

This is the period in which bureaucracy reaches its modern appearance, at least in so far as characteristics of functioning are concerned. Of the eight dimensions mentioned in appendix 6.1, several had developed before 1780.

Continuous administrative activity is indicated by the formal presence of public functionaries in the local community and society at large, and can thus be traced back to the Middle Ages. But what happened in the nineteenth century was that various part-time jobs become full-time commitments. Furthermore a variety of tasks that had been performed by citizen functionaries and contractors (see ch. 7) were transferred to public officials. The *use of formal rules and procedures* is also something that can be traced to the Middle Ages, especially in the areas of social and economic relations and instructions (i.e., job descriptions) for public office. Research in the Netherlands has shown that the number of instructions for public offices increased in the eighteenth century. This was related to the development of formal recruitment and appointment procedures which occurred first in the public health and education sectors but spread to other sectors in the nineteenth century.

One could say that *specialized offices* also started to develop from the Middle Ages onward. Van Braam distinguished among three types of offices (Van Braam 1977). The *ad hoc office* was a one-time activity limited in amount of work and duration, such as the nightwatch and firewatch, laborers for season labor (public works), and *surnummeraires* and *volontairs* occasionaly hired by a clerk in busy times. A *sinecure* was an office occupied for a specific amount of time (rotation of public office) and involving frequently recurring but limited tasks. Chester (1981: 123) distinguished three types of sinecure: those without tasks or responsibilities, those with insignificant tasks, and those executed by deputies. Sinecure offices disappeared in the late-eighteenth and early-nineteenth century either through abolishment or through the acquisition of its tasks by public servants. This is another indication of the shift to bureaucratic administration.

Most governments in Western countries in the medieval and early modern period developed a *hierarchical organizational structure* that consisted of four levels. The highest level was that of the *political functionaries* (see ch. 7) to whom every other public official was subordinate. The second level consisted of the *higher citizen functionaries* who operated on the basis of delegation and fulfilled coordinating tasks in a particular area (see ch. 7). Office holders at this level were literally related to *political office holders*, in the sense that through the system of cooptation, people were appointed as a citizen functionary and from there could enter—after having acquired some experience—into the political offices. The third level consisted of all the *higher civil servants* such as treasurers and chancellors. The fourth level consisted of *lower civil servants and laborers*. This was not a hierarchy as we know it today, since there was no unity of command. The pyramid structure of organization characterized by unity of command and clear competencies is a late-eighteenth century, early-nineteenth century phenomenon.

The *use of written documents* is of profound importance in the development of administration. Gladden even remarked that "...without the written record administration would have lacked the one technique vital to its extension" (Gladden 1972: part 1, 19). Of all the characteristics of bureaucratic functioning the use of written records is the oldest. The development of a financial administration and of codified law in the High Middle Ages would not have been possible without it. Another increase in the use of written records occurred in the time of Atlantic Revolutions as has been reported for France, England, and the Netherlands (Chester 1981: 283, 300; Church 1981: 97, 272; Cohen 1941: 151; Raadschelders 1990: 171). The workflow increased through the use of dossiers, archives, registration (of incoming and outgoing correspondence), and statistics. This in turn resulted in more expenditure for the means with which the work needed to be done. In the medieval and early modern periods, it was quite common that office holders had to supply the means (office, desk, paper, ink) out of their own "private" income. This was especially the case for political functionaries, citizen functionaries, and higher civil servants. Indeed, it was not uncommon that a public deficit was supplemented out of private funds. From the early-nineteenth century onward, however, government supplied the means.

This was not all. This dimension of Weber could easily be expanded to encompass the *processing of information*. Quill pens, ink, and paper were slow in usage and the written texts not always clear (smudgy) or accurate (corrections in margins). The use of written documents was facilitated through a rapid series of inventions which, in turn, accelerated the processing, the collection and the dissemination of information. It would be difficult to underestimate the impact on office administration of such devices as the steel pen (from the 1830s onward), the typewriter and stenography (from the 1850s onward), and the pneumatic dispatch (from the 1860s onward). The combination of paper and electricity resulted in the punched card, convenient for the storage of data (1890s). With the invention of the mimeograph and carbon paper (1900s), the handwritten copying of texts became obsolete. The combination of electricity and photography resulted in the copying machine (1938), while some years later the computer entered the stage (1944). Linking computer systems and combining telephone and paper (fax machines) has resulted in an enormous acceleration of the exchange of information. As a result, public relations and information services came into existence. This, together with radio and television, has provided governments with almost unlimited opportunities to inform their citizens.

The seventh dimension in Weber's ideal type is *nonownership of office* that had become more and more common since the High Middle Ages (see also ch. 7). The bureaucratization of functioning in government organization thus appears to be completed around the 1800s and is apparent in *rational discipline and control*. Astley (1985: 216–217) has distinguished among two main types of control. The first type is irregular direct and personal control. The second type is structural control, subdivided into technical and bureaucratic control. Technical control concerns the physical and technological environment, whereas bureaucratic control constitutes a system of systematic and frequent supervision. Personal and technical control were characteristic of the medieval and early modern period and were repressive in nature. Bureaucratic and impersonal control replaced personal control through standardized control systems. The embodiment of this was the personnel file (performance file) that emerged in most countries in the course of the nineteenth century: in France around the 1840s (Church 1981: 131), in the Netherlands in the 1880s (Raadschelders 1990: 193). Prussia was very early (early-eighteenth century) in developing such personnel files (Hattenhauer 1978: 157). Personnel files became more and more the sole basis for promotion on merit instead of promotion through seniority and cooptation.

6.4 A Taxonomy of Organization Development

The development of government organization, described above in brief, basically concerns options available to subsequent governments.

FIGURE 6.1
Options for Structuring Government Organization

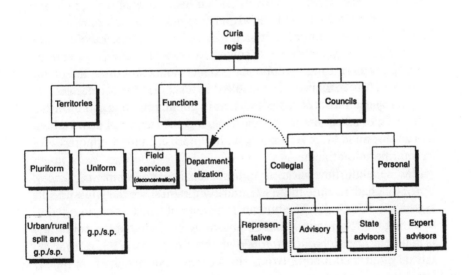

g.p. = general-purpose government
s.p. = specific-purpose government

Those options are depicted in figure 6.1 (see above). The choices an actual government made vary over time. Figure 6.1 should not be read as an outline of development since most reorganizations involved both the abolition and sometimes adaptation of existing structures as well as the introduction of new structures.

At first the ruler was aided by a *curia regis* (royal council). As governments' business increases both at central level as well as in the regions, organizational differentiation was called for. Differentiation is established in terms of territories, functions, and councils.

Territorial differentiation is hierarchical in nature, establishing tiers of government from the central down to the local level wherein two types of administrators function: a representative of the central government (for example the sheriff, bailiff, prefect) next to representatives of the subnational unit (mayor, alderman). Territorial administration in former days was often pluriform by nature since various types of local/ regional government existed side by side. After the 1200s the urban/ rural split was dominant. Towns that had been granted a charter were exempted from the law of the land and enjoyed a special status that the other villages did not enjoy. The urban and rural municipalities were types of general purpose government. There were, however, various specific purpose governments (such as the water boards in the urban areas in the Netherlands). In some countries a pluriform local and regional government still exists (such as in Great Britain and the United States). In other countries the pluriform type of territorial government was abolished in favor of a uniform type (such as in the Netherlands in the middle of the nineteenth century). Yet other countries were much earlier in making the change to uniform territorial government (France). Uniform territorial government is mostly general purpose government, existing in addition to specific purpose governments.

Functional differentiation has always been both vertical and horizontal in nature. In order to establish a better hold on the territories, central governments created field services (deconcentrated government) which also constituted a type of uniform government. The best example is the tax districts that most countries have as a regional/local branch of the Ministry of Finance. Field services are found in Europe from the 1200s onward. At the central level functional differentiation is apparent in the creation of government departments for specific tasks. The oldest departments date back to the high middle ages (chancery, treasure, judiciary). The reorganization of existing departments and the creation of new departments at the time of the Atlantic Revolutions

FIGURE 6.2
**The Development of Personnel Size and Organizational Differentiation
in Government Departments in the Netherlands, 1862–1992
(index 1992 = 100)**

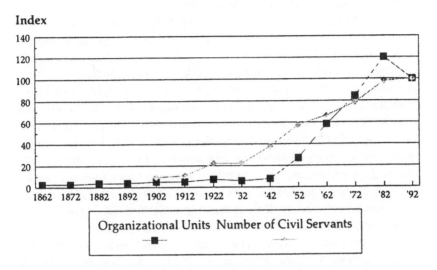

Sources: Personnel figures from Van der Meer and Roborgh (1993: 69); organizational units
from Carasso et al. (1994: 488); graph from Carasso et al. (1994: 491).

constitute a second phase of departmentalization (see also next section). A third phase occurs with the advent of the welfare state (1880–
1930), when parts of the functions of the Ministry of the Interior (or
Home Affairs) are organized into separate departments (for instance
for public health, public education). Up to the end of the nineteenth
century functional differentiation mainly occurred *between* complete
units of government (such as government departments). With the build
up of the welfare state and the increase of the number of public employees, functional differentiation also occurred *within* complete units.
Thus identifiable divisions and agencies were created within each department. In the 1862–1992 period the number of organizational units
within government departments in the Netherlands increased with a
factor-37 (Carasso et al., 1994; see figure 6.2). At around the same
time staff units enter the stage, in which internal functions (personnel
management, financial management, organizational management and
more recently, information management) came to be organized.

In the process of territorial and functional differentiation the *curia regis* lost its central importance. Indeed, as a council it was also split into two main types of councils: the collegial and the personal councils. The collegial councils in turn can be categorized according to their relation to the state. With the advent of monarchical power and the subsequent demise of the meaning of feudal relationships, the estates opted for more or less independent and representative councils. The creation of Parliaments (from the 1200s onward) is the prime example.

In the course of the seventeenth and eighteenth centuries some parliaments (Great Britain, the Dutch Republic) increasingly created special committees for specific areas (such foreign affairs, army, navy) to facilitate speedy decision making in the plenary sessions. These committees still exist, but part of their work since the late-eighteenth century has been taken over by newly created departments. This is another example of the organizational separation of political and bureau administration. It is only from the late-nineteenth century onward that parliaments, a political forum, became truly independent and representative.

The strengthening of royal power was achieved through the creation of specialized advisory bodies such as the Council of State and the Chamber of Accounts operating as collegial bodies. As time went by these became truly independent advisory bodies on the wings of the separation of powers movement. We have already seen how collegial bodies were created in early modern times whenever a new task was taken up by government. After the late-nineteenth century these collegial bodies disappeared and their function was taken over by a civil servant under supervision of a minister. For a long time government organization also functioned with the help of personal advisors. Some of these were state advisors, such as the *Raadspensionaris* (i.e., Council Pensionary) in the Dutch Republic—the highest advisor of the Estates of Holland on matters of law, justice, and governance. Sometimes a state advisor was also an independent advisory body. The *Ombudsman* in the Netherlands is a High Council of State (like the Parliament, the Council of State, and the Chamber of Accounts) but it is not a collegial body. A rather new phenomenon in government is the independent expert advisor. With the advent of the welfare state governments increasingly called upon experts from academia and the private sector for advice. Since the Second World War these experts (economists, educational scientists, biologists, political scientists, administrative scientists, and psychologists) have increasingly entered the public service as civil servants. Independent expert advice is still called upon especially for assistance in delicate reorganization processes of which there have been so many in most Western countries during the twentieth century. Often these outside experts are supervised and guided by an ad hoc committee of representatives from various public and societal organizations.

Not surprisingly policy making changed in nature. For a long time policy making referred to foreign and defense policy. In most other (domestic) areas, policy was considered in terms of "proper shopkeeping." The modernization of existing and the creation of new government departments and local services from the 1800s onward led to enhanced consciousness of planning for domestic affairs. This was even more so in the twentieth century, when "planning" became a standard phase in any type of public policy making, whether foreign or domestic.

6.5 Literature on Territorial Units

This section is concerned with the literature on the development of territorial units within a sovereignty. It should be clear that studies often touch upon several topics. A study of territorial units involves more than merely the development in the division of administrative jurisdictions. Thus many studies on the development of regional and local government deal with jurisdiction, tasks, and reform. The discussion of the literature cannot be exhaustive. Examples of studies will be given in the text, but there are more in the bibliography. Furthermore, only books will be mentioned, while the bibliography includes various articles as well.

General Literature

No introductory or comparative literature on the topic of territorial administration exists. The study of the development of territorial units and divisions should start with obtaining information from individual countries. Even that will prove time consuming, since the information is hidden in histories of central and subnational government. The one study that explicitly concerns territorial division is Frandsen's two volumes on the development of the Danish administrative division since 1660 (1984). Most studies provide a general overview of the development of a particular level of government in general.

The body of literature on functional units (such as public works, police, health, education, etc.) *within* regional or local government is probably very large, but seldom finds its way into more encompassing studies. An example I know well is the Netherlands. Many provinces and municipalities have their own history. Local and regional history thrives in the Netherlands, and many publications devote a chapter to the development of administration over time. In administrative science literature, attention for regional and local government is usually focused on such issues as reorganization. In general, regional and local government is a last chapter in a study on the development of government, of public services, and so forth (e.g., Barker 1944).

Regional Government

In this study regional government is understood as a territorial unit of general purpose government with a clearly defined boundary, and which operates as the governmental unit immediately above local government. In national states these regional governments come under a variety of names: for example *département* and *préfecture* in France, *county* in England and *state* in the United States, *Land* and *Kreis* in Germany, *provincie* in the Netherlands. In the past, these territorial units were in some cases more or less independent states. Thus the German *Länder* before the unification of 1871, the Italian provinces before the unification of 1859, and the Dutch provinces between 1581–1798 ought to be regarded as territorial units sovereign in themselves. For practical reasons I will, however, consider them as regional units. This discussion includes deconcentrated units of central government (field services).

There is a fair amount of literature on regional government, mostly about the early modern and modern periods. A general introduction is not available, let alone a comparative study. Most of the studies, though, are based on empirical research, and are thus a valuable sources of information.

In attention for regional government, France clearly leads the way, especially in the study of deconcentrated units. Michel (1910) and Strayer (1932) published studies about the administration of Beaucaire and Normandy in the Middle Ages. For the early modern and modern times there are a large number of studies on the *intendants* and the *préfectures*. General introductions on the intendants have been written by Gruder (1968) and Hanotaux (1884). A large number of studies is available on particular areas such as Aube (Arbois de Jubainville 1880), Provence (Ardashev 1909), and Bretagne (Fréville 1953). General introductions

on the prefects are provided by Bordes (1972), Chapman (1955), and
Pierre (1950). Sometimes a study focuses on a particular time period,
such as Richardson on 1814–1830 (1966), Savant about the Napoleonic
empire (1958), Siwek-Pouydesseau on the third and fourth Republics
(1969), and Wright and Le Clerc on the Second Empire (1973).

Interesting studies on regional units are available for other countries as well. There are two studies about Tirol in Austria (Bacher 1989;
Bundsmann 1961). Of all the German *länder*, Prussia has been studied
most extensively (Dorwart 1953, 1971; Ford 1922; Gillis 1971; Hintze
and Schmoller 1901; Muncy 1944; Rosenberg 1958). There are, however, also studies on other *länder*, such as Baden (Liebel 1955), Hanover
(Von Meler 1898–99), Bavaria and Würtemberg (Wunder 1978), and
Bavaria (Applegate 1990). As far as England is concerned there are
some studies about Welsh government: Morgan on the 1880–1980 period (1981), Richards on the Middle Ages up to modern times (1969),
and Williams during the reign of Elizabeth I (1958). Barnes's study of
Somerset 1625–1640 (1961) also needs to be mentioned. There is a
considerable amount of studies on the Dutch provinces at the time of
the Dutch Republic. Rijpperda Wierdsma's study of the province of
Holland is somewhat older but still important (1937). With regard to
Canada I refer to several studies about Quebec (for instance Gow, 1986).

Attention for specific-purpose government, either as deconcentrated
or as decentralized units, is not widespread. By way of example I mention Clinquart's studies of the customs in France during the revolution
and the 1848–1871 period (1983, 1989), Petot's study of the French
Ponts et Chaussées in the 1599–1815 period (1958), Hoon's Study of
the British custom system in the eighteenth century (1938), and Jacob's
study on field administration in Germany (1963). Dawson provides a
general introduction to local deconcentrated administration in France
(1969). In the Netherlands governments developed water-boards as
units of specific purpose because of amalgamations into units of regional government (nineteenth and twentieth centuries), while they used
to be local in terms of territory. In the western part of the Netherlands,
however, regional water-boards existed since the High Middle Ages
and early modern times (sixteenth century).

Local Government

As can perhaps be expected, the number of studies on local government is large, but often limited to one country. A comparative study

should be possible, given what is already available. There are various general introductions into the history of local government in early modern and modern times. Most of these concern histories of general-purpose governments, such as municipalities. By way of example: Australia (Larcombe 1978), Belgium (Gemeentekrediet 1984, 1986), Denmark (Jörgensen 1985), France (Bordes 1972; Dawson 1969), Germany (Heffter 1950; Müthling 1966), the Netherlands (Alberts 1966; Kocken 1973); on Scandinavia (Ericsson 1982), and the United States (Griffith 1972, 1974). Rare are introductions to both specific and general purpose local governments (on the Netherlands, Raadschelders 1992). Also several area studies are available, on local government in the province of Holland (Raadschelders 1990), for example, and on local government in Iowa (Shambaugh 1930).

However, Great Britain appears to have the most studies of local government. Cam (1963) and Jewell (1972) published studies on medieval local government. Thomson completed a research of Tudor local government (1923). There are some studies of local government in particular areas in early modern times: Skeel (1904) on Wales in the sixteenth and seventeenth century, and Willcox (1940) on Gloucestershire in the 1590–1640 period. Lucas and Richards (1978), Redlich and Hirst (1972, translated from German), and Smellie (1973) provide general introductions on the nineteenth and/or twentieth centuries.

Of particular interest to local government development is the period of growth and reform that occurred from the second half of the nineteenth century onward especially in countries with a strong local government tradition. On England the study by Borand is very useful (1974), and on the United States the studies by Schiesl (1977), Stewart (1929, 1950), and Teaford (1984) are informative. The studies about local government reform in Russia by Starr (1974) and Weismann (1981) are interesting in light of the movement toward a more liberal type of government during the last decades of the Tsarist autocracy.

Central-Local Relations

Many studies concerning territorial administration contain remarks about the development of central-local relations. There are few studies, however, that deal specifically with this issue. The one comparative study that comes to mind is Page's excellent analysis containing a large historical section (Page 1991: ch. 5). Worth mentioning is Bellamy's case study of the Local Government Board as an illustration of central-local relations in England during the 1871–1919 period (1988). One could argue that the study of center-periphery (imperial, colonial) relations are basically about central-local relations. In that case I should mention Burrough's study (1967) on relations between Britain and Australia with respect to crown-lands administration, and Dickerson's study (1912) on the British Board of Trade in the American colonies.

6.6 Literature on Functional Units

Functional units are understood as organizations structured around a particular set of related tasks. Departments (or Ministries) of central government are thus functional units, as are field agencies, and organizational units in regional and local government. In this section I will mainly discuss functional units at the central government level, since that is the level that has been studied most in the twentieth century.

General Literature

Searching for general and introductory literature on the development of government departments is fruitless; however, if you search with the keyword bureaucracy, the studies are abundant. Kamenka's *Bureaucracy* (1989) is a very lucid and attractive introduction to the development of bureaucracy. The title of the edited volume by Wertheim and Dalby (1971) is very promising, but the quality of the contributions differ. For studies on bureaucratization the reader ought to look at Jacoby (1973) and Torstendahl (1991), although they address bureaucratization of government in the context of the bureaucratization of society.

There is a range of nationally oriented general literature on the development of central government in, for example, Denmark (Jörgensen 1982; Sachs 1921), Finland (Tiihonen 1989), Germany (Ule 1961), England (Coleman and Starkey 1986; Cromwell 1978), the Netherlands (Fockema Andreae 1961; Raadschelders 1995), a complete history of Norway in the nineteenth and twentieth century is available (Benum 1979; Debes 1980; Maurseth 1979; Steffens 1914; Tönneson 1979), Russia (Yaney 1973), Spain (Carrasco Canals 1975), and the United States (White 1948–1958).

Central Government and Government Departments

There is a variety of nationally oriented studies around the theme of bureaucracy in terms of organization. Literature on bureaucracy in terms of personnel will be discussed in chapter 7 (see section 7.2 for the two types of definition of bureaucracy).

For Germany, Wunder's study (1986) is particularly instructive and encompassing. More limited in time-scope and/or area (geographic) but nonetheless very challenging are the studies by Fenske (1985), Heinrich and Jeserich (1992), Rosenberg (1958), and Süle (1988). On England the studies by Chester (1981) and Parris (1969) are valuable sources of information. Leading authors on the development of bureaucracy and central government administration in France are Fougère (1972), Légendre (1968), Sautel (1971), Thuillier (1980), and Thuillier and Tulard (1982). Church's study (1981) of the French ministerial bureaucracy in the 1770–1850 period provides much detail without loosing the quality of the main argument. Nelson's study (1982) on the roots of American bureaucracy in the nineteenth century is interesting and well written.

There is no nationally oriented general literature on the development of government departments. Most studies concern a particular department. Deane (1963) completed a study of the department of trade in Australia; Hyslop (1973) published a study of Australian naval administration. With respect to France, studies have been published about the ministry of justice (Durand-Barthez 1973), foreign affairs (Samoyault 1971), and home affairs (Tersen 1913). Good empirical studies of the home affairs department in the Netherlands were completed by Van Ijsselmuiden (1989) and Boels (1993). In the study of the development of government departments Great Britain, again, leads the pack: the Treasury (Baxter 1958; Heath 1927), the Colonial Office (Blakeley 1972; Fiddes 1926; Jeffries 1956; Young 1961), the Ministry of Works (Emmerson 1956), the War Office (Gordon 1935), the Foreign Office (Jones 1971; Steiner 1969; Strang 1955; Tilly 1933), the Board of Trade (Llewellyn-Smith 1928), the Home Office (Nelson 1969; Newsom 1954; Troup 1935), the Ministry of Health (Newsholme 1925), the Board of Education (Selby-Riggs 1927), the India Office (Seton 1926), and the Ministry of Housing and Local Government (Sharp 1969).

Reorganization

Reorganization is seldom a separate topic of study and is often discussed in the context of a history of a particular department. Again, the studies that are available are national studies, such as by Dorwart (1953),

Ford (1922) and Knemeyer (1970) on Germany, Prouty (1957) on England, Hassell (1967), Raeff (1966, 1983), and Weismann (1981) on Russia, and Karl (1963) on the United States. Studies concerning civil service reform will be discussed in chapter 7.

Deconcentrated Units

Field agencies and deconcentrated units of government are not studied as often as government departments, and then usually in the context of a specific department's history. The best examples that come to mind are the studies by Petot (1958) on the history of the administration of the bridges and roads and Clinquart (1983, 1989) on the administration of customs in France. The only general study I know of is also about France (Dawson 1969).

6.7 Literature on Councils

With the advantage of hindsight a distinction can be made between representative and advisory councils. The contemporary Parliament is a representative council with more powers than its medieval predecessor. In one respect, however, the medieval and early modern parliaments are similar to their current counterpart. They served as a link between the ruler and the society, even though that society was defined by a small number of people, the Estates. Being an institutional link between government and society, Parliaments belong to administrative history in the broader sense (see ch. 8).

As indicated above (section 3.1) advisory councils were first created in the fourteenth and fifteenth centuries. Their history is often dealt with in the context of a general history of governmental institutions. I have not found a general history of advisory councils—whether comparative or national. There are, however, some studies which focus on a specific institution: Boislisle (1884) and Antoine (1975) on the French *Conseil du Roi* (Royal Council), Bluche (1966) on the French *Cour des Monnaies* (Money Council), Richardson (1961) on the English Court of Augmentation, Whelan (1982) on the Russian State Council, De Schepper (1981) on the Dutch *Raad van State* (Council of State), and Van Soest et al. (1988) on the Dutch *Hoge Raad* (High Court of Justice). The studies by De Schepper and Van Soest et al. cover the entire period of existence, whereas the other studies are focused on a particular period.

Individual (expert) advisors have played an important role throughout the medieval, the early modern, and the modern period. Often, they were formally employed as state advisors. For centuries they were recruited for legal advice. In the light of history it is only recent that expertise other than juridical knowledge has been sought by government. With the advent of the welfare state, and especially in the mature welfare state since the Second World War, governments have made increasing use of expert knowledge in other areas such as economics, sociology, biology, political science, and administrative science. These experts serve as employees, as members of ad hoc advisory committees, and/or as independent advisors (consulting firms). To an increasing extent, governments have employed these experts. Despite the broadening of expertise inside government, governmental organizations and cabinets still use outside experts. Personal advisors will be discussed in chapter 7.

6.8 Literature on Work Processes and Techniques

In the discussion of the development of bureaucratic dimensions in government organizations, we can see that certain dimensions had emerged as early as the High Middle Ages. Central to bureaucratization was the development of standardized processes and techniques to handle the flow of information and human and financial resources. As a topic, the standardization of work processes is often studied in relation to a particular policy area or organization. There are very few studies about the increased use of written records. The one that comes to mind is Clanchy's (1979) study about medieval England.

Record keeping was the basis for institutional memory. Records could also be copied, that is to say it enabled others to inquire about particular new techniques (such as double-entry bookkeeping, the use of statistics), new types of offices (such as the bailiff), new types of organization, and new ideas about governance. There are some articles about the use of statistics in the modern state (Hoock 1989; Woolf 1991). The impact of technological innovations on office administration would be an interesting avenue of study, since it underlines the multifaceted nature of bureaucratization. In this respect a study about the collection and dissemination of information by governments would also be a profitable line of research. Separate studies about how governments influenced one another in their development are scarce. The Martin (1987) and Miewald (1984) articles about French respectively

German origins of U.S. public administration are examples of such studies. The *Yearbook of European Administrative History* (1989, 1990) provides other examples of copying behavior.

6.9 Literature on Public Policy-Making

The study about the development of policy-making is yet to be written. It appears that the interest for it is increasing, as shown by Dunn (1981) and two edited volumes (Ashford 1992; Castles 1989). The interest of authors, however, is understandably focused on the twentieth century. Information about developments in policy-making will have to be collected from studies concerning developments in particular policy areas (see ch. 5).

References

Albrow, Martin. 1970. *Bureaucracy*. London: Pall Mall Press Limited.
Astley, W.G. 1985. "Organizational Size and Bureaucratic Structure." *Organization Studies* 6, no.3: 210–228.
Barnard, Chester. 1948. *The Functions of the Executive*. Cambridge, MA: Harvard University Press.
Bendix, Reinhard. 1949. *Higher Civil Servants in American Society*. Boulder, CO: Universtiy of Colorado Press.
————. 1956. *Work and Authority in Industry: Ideologies of Management in the Course of Industrialization*. New York and London: John Wiley and Sons.
Blau, Peter M. 1955. *The Dynamics of Bureaucracy: A Study of Interpersonal Relations in Two Government Agencies*. Chicago, IL: The University of Chicago Press.
Braam, A. van. 1986. *Leerboek Bestuurskunde*. Muiderberg: Coutinho.
Denhardt, Robert B. 1984. *Theories of Public Organization*. Pacific Grove, CA: Brooks/Cole Publishing Company.
Etzioni-Halévy, E. 1983. *Bureaucracy and Democracy: A Political Dilemma*. London: Routledge & Kegan Paul.
Gouldner, Alvin W. 1954. *Patterns of Industrial Bureaucracy*. Glencoe, IL: The Free Press.
Gulick, Luther. 1937. Notes on the Theory of Organization. In *Papers on the Science of Administration*, edited by L. Gulick and L.F. Urwick. New York: Institute of Public Administration.
Hendershot, A.M., and Talcott Parsons. 1947. *The Theory of Social and Economic Organization*. New York: Oxford University Press.
Likert, Rensis. 1961. *New Patterns of Management*. New York: McGraw Hill.
Mayntz, Renate. 1965. "Max Webers Idealtypus der Bürokratie und die Organisationssoziologie." *Kölner Zeitschrift für Soziologie und Sozialpsychologie* 17, no.2: 493–502.
Merton, Robert K. 1952. "Bureaucratic Structure and Personality." In *Reader in Bureaucracy*, ibidem et al. Glencoe, IL: The Free Press.
Meyer, M.W., W. Stevenson, and S. Webster 1985. *Limits to Bureaucratic Growth*. Berlin and New York: Walter de Gruyter.

Mouzelis, Nicos P. 1971. *Organisation and Bureaucracy: An Analysis of Modern Theories.* London: Routledge & Kegan Paul.

Page, Edward C. 1991. *Localism and Centralism in Europe: The Political and Legal Bases of Local Self-Government.* Oxford and New York: Oxford University Press.

Robbins, Stephen P. 1980. *The Administrative Process,* 2d ed. Englewood Cliffs, NJ: Prentice-Hall, Inc.

Rudolph, L.I., and S.H. Rudolph 1979. "Authority and Power in Bureaucratic and Patrimonial Administration." *World Politics* 31, no.2: 195–227.

Self, Peter. 1980. *Administrative Theories and Politics: An Enquiry into the Structure and Processes of Modern Government,* 2d ed. London: George Allen & Unwin.

Selznick, P. 1943. "An Approach to a Theory of Bureaucracy." *American Sociological Review* 8, no.1: 47–54.

Stinchcombe, A.L. 1959–1960. "Bureaucratic and Craft Administration of Production." *Administrative Science Quarterly* 4, no.2: 168–187.

Weber, Max. 1985. *Gesammelte Aufsätze zur Wissenschaftslehre,* 6th ed., edited by J. Winckelmann. Tübingen: J.C.B. Mohr.

Appendix 6.1

Weber on characteristics of bureaucratic organization (with the additions by Van Braam, 1977: 459; and Raadschelders and Rutgers, 1996: 97).

A. *Characteristics of functioning (*Legal-rationale Herrschaft)
 1. continuous administrative activity,
 2. formal rules and procedures,
 3. clear and specialized offices (*Ambten*),
 4. hierarchical organization of offices,
 5. use of written documents,
 6. adequate supply of means (desk, paper, an office, etc.)
 7. nonownership of office,
 8. procedures of relational discipline and control.

B. *Characteristics of functionaries (*Bürokratische Verwaltungsstab)
 9. office held by individual functionaries,
 10. who are subordinate, and
 11. appointed, and
 12. are knowledgeable, have expertise,
 13. assigned by contractual agreement,
 14. in a tenured (secure) position,
 15. who fulfil their office as their main or only job, and
 16. work in a career system,
 17. are rewarded with a regular salary and pension in money,
 18. are rewarded according to rank,
 19. are promoted according to seniority, and
 20. work under formal protection of their office.

Appendix 6.2

Weber on *types of authority and administration* (1980–5: 130–134, 580–596).

1. *Traditional authority and administration*: the ruler has no personal administrative staff; lack of clearly defined competencies and of rational hierarchy; functionaries are not members of an administration but of traditional associations and of the

citizenry; authority of the ruler is based on the acceptance of it by traditional associations.

2. *Patrimonial authority and administration*: the ruler establishes a personal administrative and military staff; the ruler partially delegates rights and (financial) means to regional and local communities and/or individuals through appropriation; that delegated authority is sometimes personal, sometimes hereditary; the actions of the ruler limited by the privileges he has bestowed; knowledgeability comes to play a role in the selection of functionaries.

3. *Bureaucratic authority and administration*: authority and administration no longer bound to the person of the ruler but to the state; authority of administration no longer bound by estates or privileged communities, but by distribution over different bodies (legislative, executive, judiciary); specialization is the prime factor in recruitment of functionaries.

7

The Civil Service: Bureaucratization
of Administrative Officeholders

By way of simplification, one could argue that government in medieval and early modern times was primarily concerned with safeguard-
ing the internal and external order and stability in its territory through
policing and regulating relationships between citizens. To this end they
replaced feudal (and later mercenary) armies with standing armies,
developed a judicial system, refined a tax system, created more or less
specialized organizations, and issued series of charters and ordinances
that delineated the boundaries within which citizens were supposed to
act. As a result government grew in size, both in terms of spending as
well as in terms of the number of people directly involved in the business of government. We have seen how, at the local level, government
was also concerned with welfare given the provisions for the poor, the
orphans, the widows, the elderly, the sick, and handicapped in the medieval and early modern period. However, government was but one
actor among others providing welfare services. In most Western societies the church played an important role, especially in the provision of
welfare functions. Also in most Western societies private associations
other than the church, and even individuals provided welfare services.
In the course of the nineteenth and twentieth centuries the role and
position of government changed quite dramatically as a consequence
of individualization.

> The true problem of our times resembles a closed sphere. Centralization of all
> functions and accumulation of power are on the inside; isolation and impotence of
> the individual are on the outside. These opposites have consistently intensified
> each other. Thus the looser western interpersonal relations became, the more they
> depended on bureaucracy. As the feudal order—which had been both stable and
> protective—disappeared, people required increased guidance and assurance, ob-
> tainable only from organizations and central agencies staffed by professionals.
> The world became more individualistic, and as each individual assumed responsi-

bility for himself, he was less secure and had greater need of a strong state and a competent government. Once each man acquired greater faith in individualism, and swept only in front of his own door, so to speak, he found he had to rely on a centrally directed professional cleaning system for public streets. As society became modernized—that is to say industrialized, intricate, technologized, and interlocking—the modalities of control were shaped into one of their oldest forms: that of bureaucracy. (Jacoby 1976: 1–2)

This quote perfectly summarizes what happened in the last eight centuries: government slowly moving to center stage in the regulation of society, other actors slowly becoming restricted to an ever smaller sphere of influence. It also illustrates why I trace the roots of contemporary government in Western nations to the High Middle Ages. It was in the twelfth century that church and state became separated—at least in practice. The state—again in practice—and its sovereign were about to assume the ultimate authority, higher than the regional lords within that territory. Through the breakdown of the feudal system, state and sovereign segregated from the traditional authorities like clergy and aristocracy, and assumed tasks that hitherto had been provided by many. Public behavior became more and more codified and moved away from customary law. As a result government grew in size. This major transformation was followed by centuries of refining the principles of governance laid down in that twelfth century: further departmentalization, further separation of church and state, the establishment of the centralized state, the codification of common (public) practices, the incorporation of more tasks. The thirteenth up to the late-eighteenth century are very much an intermediate period.

The 1780–1820 decades experienced the second major transformation in Western government. It was then that the foundations laid in the twelfth century were expanded with new insights about the relationship between state and society, between government and citizen (see also ch. 9). Central government now was about to assume its role in the regulation of society and the protection of the individual to the full, since its laws and regulations covered more issues than ever and permeated down to the local level. A constitution would come to serve as the supreme framework within which government actors and citizens were to maneuver. Church and state were separated by law. The political functionary and the administrator were to be separated, the one invested with office through election, the other through appointment. The citizen was about to exercise rights instead of having only duties (see ch. 8). Contemporaries could not have seen that what was established during those four decades—if not in practice, then in idea—provided the structure that was needed for government to be able to assume so many new responsibilities from the 1880s onward. In the advent and blossoming of the welfare state, government again grew significantly in terms of size.

This growth of government from the late nineteenth century onward has attracted much scholarly attention. Indeed, government having become the prime actor in the public realm provided new momentum for the independent study of public administration. The fact that administrative science has become an important field within the social sciences is thus an illustration of how important government in contemporary society must be. Therefore those involved in the business of government attract much research: their sheer size, the civil service, the training and recruitment of administrators, the relationship between politicians and administrators, particular offices, the role of specialists, and the functioning of public servants. A variety of topics and approaches of the changes in size and training and recruitment of the civil service can only be fully appreciated when we see what went on before. If, however, we discuss those changes we first need to define exactly who we refer to as public functionaries.

7.1 Types of Public Functionaries

Changes in the size of government in the twentieth century are often operationalized in terms of government share in the gross national product. When investigating a longer period of time this is not an adequate indicator for the simple reason that data about the development of the GNP before 1850s are lacking. Size can also be measured through revenue and public expenditure, but for lack of consistent time-series before the 1850s/1900s this too is an inadequate indicator of government growth. The only indicator that remains is the number of public functionaries. Sometimes data have been collected, such as those by Aylmer on the size of the civil service in early-seventeenth-century England or the size of the civil service in the twentieth century. But it is more common that time-series will have to be collected through archival research. The number of public functionaries is generally believed to be a simple but adequate indicator of government development (Hinings et al. 1975: 170; Rose 1987). It is, however, important to distinguish public functionaries from other professionals that are somehow involved in the business of government.

Public functionaries are those who fulfill a public service/task, are appointed by and instructed on behalf of the authority of one or more of the decision-making public bodies in government and are compensated through a salary and/or payment in kind and/or an attendance fee (Raadschelders 1994). This definition covers a range of functionaries. Not only does it include administrative personnel and workmen, but also political appointees and citizens who (as part of their civic duty) were involved in the provision and/or production of public services. It also includes the functional categories (administration, education, post, transportation, and industrial) distinguished in the HIWED Project (Eichenberg 1983: 141).

Public functionaries can be classified into seven different categories. *Political functionaries* are those elected and/or appointed officials at the top of a public organization and responsible for the administration. All other functionaries are subordinate to them. Political functionaries can be elected through cooptation (as was usual before the 1800s) or through elections, such as members of a (municipal, county, provincial) council and members of parliament, members of the daily board of a council (aldermen), and of a bench of magistrates. Examples of appointed political functionaries are—in some countries—mayors and sheriffs (if appointed by the head of state as its representative at local level).

Citizen functionaries are those who have no labor contract or salary but are entitled to certain emoluments, are involved in the preparation, formulation, and/or execution of a task in a particular field on the basis of delegated authority of one or more boards of political functionaries. They are accountable to political functionaries. These tasks are fulfilled as a civic duty. The elites in a community had access to political office and to the higher citizen offices such as overseers of the nightwatch, overseers of the poor, overseers of the school, churchmasters, and so forth. The citizenry at large was required to participate in the nightwatch and the firewatch. Citizen functionaries could often be found in local government. When new tasks were taken up by government it was normal in the Western world up to the end of the nineteenth century that the council delegated responsibility to a board of citizen functionaries (collegial administration, ch. 6) (Raadschelders 1988).

Civil servants/administrative personnel are those that fulfill bureauwriting and administrative tasks. They work in an office and their work requires only intellectual ability. These are the white collar workers, such as a town clerk, a treasurer, a municipal engineer, the civil service (in its meaning of higher public officials), and so forth. *Workmen* mainly perform, sometimes heavy, manual labor, such as those employed in public works and public utilities (sanitation department, street cleaners). Adequate job performance sometimes requires special skills (e.g., workmen at a public gas or electricity factory). *Auxiliary personnel* fulfill lower administrative functions. Their work requires light manual labor and semi-administrative and/or policing tasks. They often perform their duties in uniform. Examples are beadles, doorkeepers, policemen, overseers of the markets, harbor masters, and supervisors in public utilities. They are neither white nor blue collar workers. *Medical and care personnel* fulfill tasks in the field of health and social care, such as public doctors, nurses, and midwives as well as personnel in public charities such as the public orphanages, poor houses, hospitals, and so forth. The last category is that of *teaching personnel* employed in public schools.

Next to these groups of public functionaries an additional workforce can be distinguished whose work had some relation to government but who were not employed and paid by government on a regular basis. They need to be mentioned since they were of some significance up to the middle of the nineteenth century, especially in local government. The first type of additional functionaries is the *admitted* or *authorized functionary* who had been given permission to work in office of a public nature. Among the *higher* authorized functionaries one can find notaries public, realtors, and schoolteachers in private schools. The *lower* functionaries consist of all laborers working on the market, the nightwatchmen, and the firewatchmen. Also at local level, the municipality could annually select people for delivering certain services to government such as the town baker (providing the charity homes with bread), and the town apothecary. These constitute a second type of additional functionaries. Finally there are the *contracted laborers*, the third type, hired for specific jobs for limited amounts of time (such as laborers in the public works departments hired as seasonal labor). Hardly any figures exist about the size of contract labor. The little that is known (see ch. 8) indicates that they could have been quite important. However, when discussing size of government, I limit myself here to public functionaries as defined above.

7.2 The Size and Composition of Government Employment

Literature concerning the size of government can be divided into two categories. The first is that which approaches size in subjective terms, the second approaches size in empirical terms.

The perception of the presence and size of government changed remarkably in the second half of the eighteenth century. Until then *political functionaries* were seen as a power factor from which the power of all other public functionaries was derived. Criticism of government was equal to criticism of individuals abusing their public office. After the second half of the eighteenth century, criticism of and resistance to government was directed to government in its entirety. And it was almost immediately stereotyped as *bureaucracy*, the concept attributed to Vincent de Gournay (1712–1759, merchant and *Intendant du Commerce*). Although he never put it into writing, he spoke about it. Thus according to a letter (1 July 1764) by the philosopher Baron de Grimm:

> The late M. de Gournay...sometimes used to say: "We have an illness in France which bids fair to play havoc with us; this illness is called bureaumania." Sometimes he used to invent a fourth or fifth form of government under the heading of bureaucracy. (Albrow 1970: 16; Kamenka 1989: 94)

And so de Gournay made his distinction between bureaucracy and bureaumania (nowadays referred to as bureaucratism) in analogy to the classical dichotomies between proper and degenerate forms of government (monarchy versus tyranny, aristocracy versus oligarchy, *poleis* versus democracy).

In this respect Albrow wrote about de Gournay:

> He is identifying a new group of rulers and a method of governing. The complaint against them is not that they are acting unlawfully, outside their proper authority, but that governing seems to have become an end in itself. (Albrow 1970: 17)

It is almost as if once the concept of bureaucracy is coined the reason for reform became visible. At the time of the Atlantic Revolutions, large scale reforms were undertaken in France and the territories occupied by the Napoleonic armies (Church 1981; Wunder 1994) and even as far as in Egypt (Otto 1987: 142) and the Dutch East Indies (Eymeret 1973). But reforms were also initiated in England (Chester 1981). Surprisingly, these reforms did not lead to a decline in the number of public functionaries. In France (Church 1981: 136) it resulted in growth.

Since bureaucracy was "discovered," citizens and political functionaries have displayed ambivalence, at the same time remarkable as well as understandable, toward bureaucrats. The growth of the administrative apparatus was frightening and had to be contained, then and now. Some despised bureaucrats, like Robert von Mohl (1799–1875, German cameralist) who in 1846 defined bureaucracy as:

the false understanding of state tasks, filled with many, partially very mediocre members, who wallow in purely formal gestures and function in an organization of professional civil servants with many personal lack of manners. (Kaltenbrunner 1976: 7)

Contempt is also visible in "...the Elephant disease called Bureaucracy..." (Eisermann 1976: 50) and in "...those civil servants multiply like rabbits." (Zehm 1976: 52). The stereotype that civil servants are mediocre, formal, not up to the job, and grow fast in numbers is widespread and deeply rooted. No matter how often arguments to the opposite are offered, the stereotype remains (Goodsell 1983). Kaufmann reveals this ambivalence when he writes:

> The rapid and unpopular growth of administration does not prove that our bureaucracies are uncontrolled; on the contrary, one could more persuasively contend that responsiveness of the system to the myriad demands on it [...] accounts for phenomena we all deplore. (Kaufmann 1981: 3)

And indeed, increasingly government has taken responsibilities and is held accountable for many affairs.

The second group of literature is concerned with questions about growth and its causes, mechanisms, and limits. Available analysis has been divided into internal, demand, and supply theories (Larkey, Stolp, and Winer 1981). Internal theories and explanations focus on mechanisms of growth within the bureaucracy itself. They present growth as inherent to bureaucracy. These mechanisms can relate to the structure of the organization (Dewar and Hage 1978; Beyer and Trice 1979; Astley 1985) or to characteristics of those who work in the organization (McDonagh 1958; Downs 1967; Niskanen 1971, 1973; Hannan and Freeman 1978). Research on the influence of internal factors basically concern bureaucratization of structure (see ch. 6) and of functionaries and functioning (see section 7.4 below). However, given the amount of literature in the 1970s and 1980s on the influence of the environment (supply and demand, push-and-pull factors) on size of organization most authors will agree with Downs's observation that,

> The major causes of growth, decline, and other large-scale changes in bureaus are exogenous factors in their environment, rather than any purely internal developments. (Downs 1967: 263)

Thus the growth of government has been understood as a function of demographic change (Aikin and Bachrach 1979), economic development (Peacock and Wiseman 1961; Kau and Rubin 1981; Clarke 1983; McKenzie 1980; Cameron 1978; Fried 1975, 1976), political developments (Aikin and Bachrach 1978; Peltzman 1980; Clarke 1969), war (Crowley 1971), and changes in ideology (Grimm 1986; Webber and Wildavsky 1986). The demand literature pays attention to citizens requesting certain public services, while the supply literature focuses on increased state intervention.

In general one can see two moments of major change. The first can be called *municipalization*—when local government takes over certain tasks from the private sector. This happened both at the end of the Middle Ages and at the end of the nineteenth century. The second can be called *nationalization* when local tasks are taken over by central government or brought into the central governments' sphere of influence through national legislation. This occurred at the end of the eighteenth century and throughout the twentieth century. Literature on the size of government is limited in both topic and time, concerning central government from the 1850s onward (for example the HIWED Project; Rose 1987). Local government is seldom an object of research (Van der Meer and Roborgh 1993; Raadschelders 1990, 1994). Comparative literature is almost always limited to central governments in the twentieth century.

The general impression to be gained from literature is that government (both central and local) grew slowly in size from the Middle Ages onward, and that growth gained momentum in the second half of the nineteenth century. The following graph from my own research in four Dutch municipalities covering a period of almost 400 years illustrates this pattern of slow growth followed by exponential growth.

The explosive increase of public employment after the 1880s can be found throughout the Western world. The following tables almost speak for themselves.

In the period between 1880–1940 government growth was one of public employment. In the postwar period government growth is more significant in terms of expenditure, given the increase of income-maintenance programs under the mature welfare state. The interesting difference between Britain and France on the one hand and Germany and Italy on the other in the early postwar period may be explained in that wartime mobilization in the first two countries influenced massive post-1945 nationalization of large basic industries and the expansion of welfare services (Rose 1987: 9). Overall, public employment more then doubled since the early-1950s.

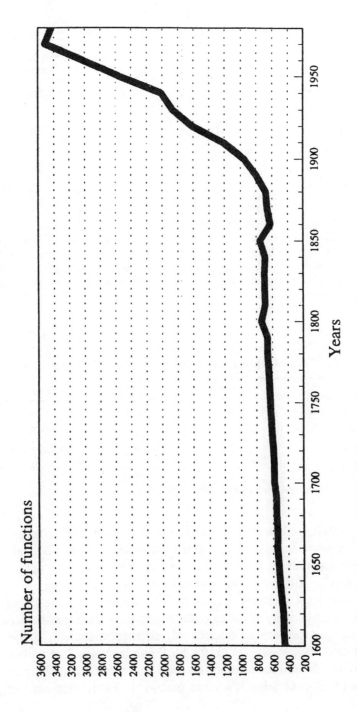

FIGURE 7.1

Total Number of Employees and Functions in the Four Municipalities, 1600–1980

Source: See table in appendix, Raadschelders, 1990, p. 104.

TABLE 7.1
A Century of Growth in Public Employment to 1951
(as percent of labor force)

	Mid 19c*	Pre-1914	1951**
Great Britain	2.4	7.1	26.6
France	5	7.1	16.0
Germany	7.2	10.6	11.9
Italy	2.2	4.7	9.9
Sweden***	3	2.0	7.0
United States****	0.8	1.4	11.8

Source: Rose (ed.) *Public Employment in Western Nations* (1987, 2d. ed.: 9)

* = First year for which suitable statistics are available;

** = to maintain consistency with the time series, figures for 1951 may differ slightly from those in this table, as it is taken from a time series including the prewar era;

*** = Swedish data not comparable to other countries as it is given as percentage of the total population. In 1950 public employment was 7.0 percent of the population and 15.2 percent of the workforce;

**** = federal employees only for 1871 and 1914.

TABLE 7.2
The Growth of Public Employment 1950-1988 (in millions)

	1950	1970	1988
United States	6.4	13.0	17.6
Germany	2.3	3.6	4.6
Netherlands	0.4	0.5	0.6
Sweden	0.5	0.8	1.5

Source: Van der Meer and Roborgh 1993: 109.

Both central and local governments have increased in terms of public employment in the past century, but since World War II local government accounts for a larger share in that growth. It appears that in terms of services offered to the public, local government is again becoming as important as it was before the 1880s. After all, the major social programs in todays welfare state (education, health, pensions, personal social services) are provided to "identifiable consumers," to use Rose's phrase (Rose 1987: 31), in the local communities. Even when taking differences into account between the United States and Western European countries there is a clear pattern of the development of public employment in the last four to five decades. Rose (1987: 47) came to the following conclusions:

1. In every country, nonmarket employment (income-maintenance grants and public employment to produce giveaway goods and services) has been growing more than market employment;
2. Employment in the private sector has been contracting in four out of five major European countries; in the United States private sector jobs have grown slowest of the four sources providing incomes;
3. Government has been exclusively responsible for the creation of additional jobs since 1951 in nearly every major European country.

Whatever the explanation (government taking over private firms, increased demand for services, continued operating of services where revenue does not match expenditure: Rose 1987: 48) it appears that government is becoming more and more the sole bearer of responsibility for communal welfare and the first—if not only—provider of social stability. The fact that government has moved to center stage with respect to communal welfare has had profound effects on the administrative apparatus both in terms of the role and position of those employed in the public service as well as in terms of their functioning.

The changes in the total size of public employment is but one indicator of the effect that changes in the environment have upon government. Another indicator that is just as significant is change in the composition of public employment. In my research of the development of local government in four Dutch municipalities it appeared that the largest categories of functionaries in the seventeenth and eighteenth centuries were political functionaries, citizen functionaries, auxiliary functionaries, and workmen. The largest categories nowadays are administrative functionaries (civil servants proper) and teachers. The number of civil servants has risen sharply everywhere in the Western world, especially in the twentieth century. The national patterns may differ in detail, but the overall nature of the change has been the same everywhere.

The need for reform of government was undeniably present from the 1880s onward, based on both reasons of democracy as well as efficiency. In the United States democratic considerations dominated in the movement to reform the top of the local administration, while efficiency dominated in the pursuit to modernize existing services according to principles of scientific management (Schiesl 1977). At the same time a comparable urge for (local government) reform is found in other

Western countries. The number of teaching personnel began to increase as soon as government recognized the need for a minimum standard level of education for the population-at-large in order to provide better qualified workers to the new enterprises (whether in industry or service sector). The growth of administrative and teaching personnel brought about major changes in the relative composition of the local public workforce as illustrated in table 7.3.

By no means can we say that this is a pattern to be found everywhere, but at the same time it would be surprising if developments elsewhere (in other local governments, at central level, in other countries) would be radically different. The growth of white collar workers in government, often described in terms of bureaucratization, has occurred everywhere.

7.3 The Development of the Civil Service

The development of a particular phenomenon begins to make sense only when it is related to specific circumstances of time and place. In the case of the administrative apparatus of government, its advent and evolution are to be understood in the context of ever-growing government responsibilities for communal welfare. As long as responsibility for communal welfare is shared by a number of institutions, and as long as that welfare is provided through charity, neighborly care, and

TABLE 7.3
Ranking of Categories of Functionaries of Four Municipalities
in the Netherlands, 1600–1980

Year	Largest	Functionaries				Smallest	
1600	D	A	E	B	C	G	F
1700	D	B	A	E	C	G	F
1800	B	D	E	A	C	G/F	
1900	G	E	D	B	A	C	F
1940	E	G	B	D	C	A	F
1970	G	E	C	D	F	A	B
1980	C	G	E	D	F	A	

Source: Raadschelders, Administration and Society 1994: 418;

Legend: A = political functionaries; B = citizen functionaries; C = administrative functionaries; D = auxiliary functionaries; E = workmen; F = nursing and caring personnel; G = school teachers.

civic duty the chances for the creation of an elaborate administrative apparatus for government are small. It is not just shared responsibility, though, that accounts for the small size of government in the early Western nations, because shared responsibility is based on dispersed power. Thus, in a situation where power, the right to use coercion, is fragmented, those who wield power will not have the opportunity—and maybe not even the need—to develop a strong and elaborate organized backup. Nowadays the right to use force is limited to the sovereign state and force itself is understood as physical violence. In medieval Europe physical and moral coercion both were experienced as forces to be reckoned with. Secular lords used the sword to protect the status quo, while religious lords could very convincingly threaten with excommunication in order to keep the flock in line.

For a long time during the Middle Ages the only uniting and universal authority (see ch. 9) was embodied in the church. This is true for Western Europe with the exception of the Carolingian Renaissance. In general the church had a balancing influence that was recognized and accepted by all upon the threat of eternal *Inferno*. Secular rule was dispersed among a multitude of territorial lords linked in a system of conciliary and auxiliary obligations known as feudalism. True, the lord-vassal relationship implied some sort of hierarchy drawn upon in times of need. But as long as one kept his feudal obligations, the autonomy to rule in ones own territory was not challenged. A king was first among equals, the highest feudal lord, first and foremost recognized as the top of the feudal pyramid and not so much as the highest secular authority. That would not have been possible anyway since the king did not control a well-defined and continuous territory. Europe was a Europe of the regions in which various actors shared power and responsibilities. The two main groups were clergy (Pope, bishops, priests) and aristocracy (Holy Roman Emperor, kings, princes, dukes, counts, barons), and each of those religious and secular lords had a small household menagerie to manage their affairs. In fact, the seat of their household (the castle) served as a center point in the local/regional community, the place where people rallied to in times of danger.

Arcadia (at least in the eyes of those in power) ceased somehow to exist in the twelfth century. There were at least three developments which brought down this feudal order: a move for autonomy by the church, a move for sovereignty by some secular lords, and the advent of interregional trade. If power was dispersed in the feudal age, it was also very much intertwined. Secular and religious lords had no clearly defined authority. Indeed the question as to who had authority over what gave rise to numerous conflicts among lords of various persuasion. Since this pursuit for autonomy is discussed in the next chapter, it will suffice for the moment to say that the origins of the contemporary civil service can be traced to that age. In the reshuffling of power between clergy, aristocrats, and kings the civil service was born. For a secular/temporal lord seeking dominance in a larger territory than what he possessed, it was impossible to further rely on the services of those who could potentially threaten his claim to dominance.

The literate clergy and the armed aristocracy slowly lost their functions to this new species: the civil servants, loyal—at least in principle—only to the one who monopolized sovereignty. The bid for sovereignty was based, at least in part, on the availability of an administrative apparatus independent of the traditional authorities. Furthermore, the advent of interregional trade provided lords who claimed universal authority with an extra source of power. The local communities who first profited from that trade, strived for some independence from the local/regional aristocracy. And so in exchange for revenue (tolls, excises) some local communities acquired town charters. The effect of this was twofold. At the local level the king had created allies supervised with varying success by royal representatives, and the chartered towns could operate independently from feudal lords. The central-local relationship based on royal power, together with an administrative apparatus at central level, provided the basis upon which the new authority was founded. Feudalism as a means of payment to royal representatives made for weak links between lord and vassal.

To be sure, this new political and administrative structure was not established overnight. For three centuries to come powerful regional lords contested the central royal authority. Also for three centuries the church remained an influential institution in public affairs. But as early as the twelfth and thirteenth centuries, the ingredients for a secular government based on a single authority, a structure of central-local relations, and an *independent* administrative apparatus operating in a well-defined sphere of competence were present. Of course it is only in retrospect that we can see this. Contemporaries went with the flow to the best of their abilities, not knowing where it all would end.

It is against the background of autonomous royal power and the authority that flowed from it that we can understand the emergence of the civil service. And it is against the background of the concentration of power in the state and changing ideas about governance that we can understand the evolution of the civil service. This background will be discussed in chapters eight and nine. For the purposes of this chapter, I only need to lay out the development of the civil service as outlined by Raadschelders and Rutgers (1996) into five phases. In this section I will limit myself to a general overview, while in the next section the development of the civil service will be analyzed in terms of the characteristics of functionaries (see appendix 6.1).

At first the civil servant was a *personal servant* of a lord. They were small in number and provided strictly personal and clerical services. In essence, the *seignorial household* was the lord's personal unit of direction and management (Gladden 1972(1): 3). Their numbers increased when secular lords sought to enhance their control over a territory through a monopoly over the use of violence and the imposition of taxes. Both kings (as first among equals) and powerful regional lords (dukes) built an administrative apparatus. Indeed the fact that some of these regional lords had larger administrations than their king, accounted for the fact that a sovereignty invested in a central state took centuries to develop.

It is the centralization of communal functions in government bodies (whether local or central: see ch. 5) together with the movement toward separation of public and private that a new type of civil servant emerged: the *state servant*. Even during the heyday of absolutist rule in the seventeenth and eighteenth centuries, wherein the king embodied sovereignty, the king could no longer say that the territory he ruled was his possession. Unlike the secular lords in the Middle Ages, the king of the early modern period increasingly had to recognize a private from a public realm. At this time political theory was moving away from the question of how to limit abuse of power by individuals (*tyrannus secundum titulum*) toward how to limit the abuse of power by the state. Increasingly, the power of the state was not perceived as invested in the king only but as grounded in the king and his administrative apparatus. Critique of government concerned less individual office holders and more and more the apparatus. In fact public discontent of government was directed to the highest office holders (the kings) and the system they had helped to create (the bureaucracy) and allowed to exist (abuse of office: venality of office, the development of commissary officials, hereditary office).

It is not until the late-eighteenth century that civil servants become *public servants*. Whether through peaceful or violent reorganization, bureaucracy underwent some serious changes between 1780–1820.

These are the decades in which some of the dichotomies we still struggle with are defined and have their organizational consequences: public versus private, politics versus administration, and ministerial responsibility versus civil servant's neutrality. The recognition of these dichotomies had profound implications for the structure and functioning of administration already discussed in chapter 6 (unity of command, hierarchy, organizational differentiation) as well as for those that populated the administration (see section 4 below). Henceforth, the civil servant functioned—ideally—in a constitutional state wherein elected and appointed officeholders were to prove, time and again, the legitimacy of their actions in the context of a constitutional framework. The civil servant became truly a public servant when not the state but the public, the citizenry, was to be served. A public servant served the *volonté générale*, the will of the public, in all matters that were not considered private.

For the larger part of the nineteenth century the public servant was still considered as one having duties, much like the citizen was assigned more duties than rights. But as citizens became aware of their power and the call for changes in the political system could no longer be ignored (extension of the suffrage, political parties, emancipation of the masses), so public servants became aware of their contribution to the build up and expansion of government. Like citizens, civil servants demanded rights, especially in the area of job security. After all, a neutral and loyal public service could only be guaranteed in exchange for security and protection. Up to the early-nineteenth century it had been normal to dismiss civil servants upon a change in power. At the same time, though, the higher office holders were part of the elite, held together by bonds of kinship and friendship. And it is here that we see the meaning of separation of politics and administration, because for some holders of public office, it meant loss of political power. At the same time it implied increased demand for professional administrative support. The development toward a civil service which was recruited through open competition and entry exams went hand in hand with legal protection of position.

One could reasonably argue that in the development outlined so far, the civil servant increasingly became a professional, and yet the fifth phase in the development of the civil service is the one in which the civil servant becomes a *professional servant*. Indeed, in the middle ages lords and kings hired students of law to replace the clergy. In the seventeenth and eighteenth century a higher office of a more or less administrative nature required legal training, and schools of public administration had been created in the eighteenth century (*Kameralwissenschaften*, *Science de la Police*). But most scholarly and practical activity was focused on the rules which public servants had to abide and on the position they had within the administrative system. This became even more pronounced in the nineteenth century when public administration was to become part of the study of law. With the exception of the French technical schools (Ecole des Ponts et Chaussées, 1747; Ecole du Génie, 1748; Ecole Polytechnique, 1795) there was no training available for specific public tasks. This came in the late-nineteenth and early-twentieth century onward when municipalization and nationalization of tasks, hitherto private, called for civil servants who had received specialized training in a particular field (such as education, medicine, architecture, economics, environmental science). The public demand for more and better services resulted in the employment of a wide array of professional servants. Table 7.3 showed what effect this had on the composition of the public service.

There is one specific phenomenon in table 7.3 I would like to draw attention to. In the four municipalities I investigated political functionaries were the second largest category in the year 1600. It is shown in table 7.3 how the relative size of that category gradually diminished over time, to become the smallest category in the late-twentieth century. In view of the development of public services and of the size and composition of the body of public functionaries it can be assumed that the relationship between political officeholders and civil servants changed. In general one could argue that before 1800 little if any demarcation existed between the political officeholders and the higher civil service. The fact that they belonged to the same elite separated them from middle and lower public functionaries. That the higher positions were filled with people from the elite did not change after the 1800, but now higher civil servants were formally subordinate to political officeholders. In practice, however, the growth of public services after the mid-nineteenth century, resulted in increased influence of higher civil servants on policymaking. Political-administrative relationships have received ample attention in political and administrative science, basically because of the idea that bureaucracy constitutes a fourth power that challenges the primacy of politics. Aberbach et al. (1981) and Peters (1985) presented typologies of interaction between politicians and civil servants, building on contemporary research by, for example, Dogan (1971), Heclo (1978), and Ridley (1968). The generally accepted idea that political-administrative relationships in the nineteenth and twentieth century developed from a situation where politics and administration were separated both formally and in practice, to a situation where politicians and higher civil servants are highly intertwined, has not been put to an empirical test. About the Aberbach et al. study, Page has recently remarked:

> The more novel of their conclusions, that there is a growing tendency for a convergence of political and bureaucratic roles, is ultimately less than convincingly supported by the data for the simple reason that cross-time hypotheses are notoriously difficult to substantiate through data that refer to a single point in time. Moreover the hypotheses itself would have had more significance if it had been more closely linked to the fact that in some countries, above all France and to a lesser extent Germany and Italy, institutional arrangements encourage the intermingling of political and bureaucratic careers. (Page 1995: 136)

Historical literature on this issue suggests that both groups were intertwined throughout the nineteenth and twentieth centuries. This intertwinement becomes visible in a social scientific framework. The idea of separation of political and administrative officeholders is more in line with a juridical-normative framework. An inquiry into the development of political-administrative relationships is under way in the working group on the "History of Administration" of the International Institute of Administrative Sciences. The results are expected to be published in 1997, and will contain country studies as well as more elaboration of the social-scientific versus the juridical-normative framework.

7.4 Bureaucratization of Functionaries

Changes in the size and composition of public functionaries and changes in their position can also be analyzed by means of the characteristics of functionaries in the Weberian ideal-type (appendix 6.1). Characteristics concerning the *Legal-rationale Herrschaft* have been discussed in section 6.3. In this section I will discuss the characteristics of the *Bürokratische Verwaltungsstab*. Since it is an ideal-type, the twenty dimensions are closely related to one another, but they are not correlated since they do not necessarily have to occur at the same time. A consequence of the fact that they are related is that certain phenomena described in this section could easily have been discussed under several of the characteristics. In the discussion of each of the characteristics, I will refer to its relation with other characteristics. Examples of how these characteristics developed have been taken from the Netherlands. I will, however, refer to other countries.

Weber distinguishes collegial administration through honorary and accumulated office from monocratic administration through educated and individual functionaries (Weber 1980: 562). He speaks of monocratic administration when the authority to rule is invested in one person or body (unity of command). However, collegial administration can very well be monocratic in the sense that the highest authority is invested in a body (parliament, council). Thus it is more useful to speak of monocratic versus polycratic administration where the authority to rule is dispersed over various bodies. The first of the characteristics of functionaries, *office held by individual functionaries*, is closely related to *clear and specialized offices* as discussed before. In early modern government, a mixture of monocratic and polycratic administration could often be found. For instance in the Dutch Republic where local government at the top was polycratic. Legislative authority was invested in three *political* bodies (the sheriff, the mayors, the aldermen). It also happened that the right to appoint certain officials was shared by these political bodies. This was especially the case with the more important administrative positions. Polycratic administration could also be found within the civil service, for instance when one office was held by two or more functionaries who together supervised a number of functionaries (for example, two or three town clerks supervising clerks). Finally, political bodies at the local level often delegated their authority in a number of areas to collegial bodies (such as the overseers). Within each of the services, administration was organized along monocratic lines. The development toward monocratic administration reached its conclusion in the nineteenth century when administrative organization came to rest on unity of command and collegial administration was limited to political functionaries only.

The next characteristic, *office held by subordinate functionaries*, is not only characteristic of bureaucracy. Public functionaries have always been subordinate to the highest authority. The degree to which functionaries were considered subordinate differed with the nature of the office. Thus citizen functionaries were chosen and received no salary. Their subordination must be evaluated in terms of *civic duty*. The elite could decline to fulfil such an office against the payment of a fee (Church 1981: 250; Raadschelders 1990: 175). In general, higher (citizen or administrative) functionaries enjoyed more independence because of their relationship with holders of political office. Lower functionaries were truly subordinate, illustrated by the fact that there were stern sanctions in cases of dysfunctioning. The difference between higher and lower functionaries still exists but they are nowadays treated according to a uniform standard and the position of lower functionaries no longer depends on the whim of those in power.

The appointment of officeholders is not an exclusive characteristic (*office held by appointed functionaries*) of bureaucratic organization. A large number of office holders always had been appointed. Only political and citizen functionaries were recruited on the basis of cooptation. In the course of the nineteenth century co-optation gave way to election of political functionaries and appointment of civil servants.

Weber regards the recruitment of *knowledgeable and expert functionaries in office*, assessed by an entry test and/or relevant education, a typical characteristic of bureaucracy. In medieval and early modern times one was recruited on the basis of different criteria. For higher offices (political and citizen functionaries), one was selected on grounds of wealth and wisdom. Experience in public office was required for the highest offices. Thus in the Dutch Republic one could not become a mayor unless one had occupied a *lower* office such as overseer. In general, the higher administrative offices required legal training, from the High Middle Ages onward. In early modern times, legal training also became a requisite for political offices, especially in bourgeois countries like the Dutch Republic. For most administrative offices some experience was required, often achieved through voluntary employment without pay (*volontair, surnuméraire*: Church, 1981: 179).

In the course of the sixteenth and seventeenth centuries school teachers, midwives, and town doctors in the Dutch Republic had to prove their ability through a test. It was not until the nineteenth century that pre-entry (secondary) education became a requirement for all positions. Formalized in-service training did not appear until the end of the nineteenth century, at least in the Netherlands where the newly created unions of local civil servants developed general and function-specific courses for civil servants. The selection of candidates changed accordingly. Up to the early-eighteenth century public servants could be recruited on the basis of volunteer experience and informal relations. From then on it became normal that one had to apply for an office and prove ability. The application procedure we use nowadays (publication in newspaper, application with letter, interview of candidates, selection of the best candidate) dates back to the early-eighteenth century and was developed for positions in education (school teachers) and health care (midwives, general practitioners). Open competition for all positions became normal in the nineteenth century, when formal education criteria were set. Also in the nineteenth century a period of probation was introduced as a means of selection after appointment.

The next characteristic, *appointment as contractual agreement*, was in fact characteristic for the post-feudal period. Most public offices since the late middle ages were based on voluntary and contractual agreement. For a limited number of positions, a system of duties existed until the middle of the nineteenth century (especially citizen functionaries: collegial boards).

In light of history it is only recently that public office is regarded *as a tenured (secured) position*. Most political and citizen functionaries were bound to terms of office and rules were in use for reappointment. In the course of the seventeenth (especially) and eighteenth centuries, terms of office were not met and some of these highest functionaries could hold a position for several consecutive terms. This is known as oligarchization. Most administrative and other functionaries were, in principle, appointed for life, meaning that only very old age, death, cutbacks, abolishment of office, or change of power holders would terminate employment. A public official was not entitled to a tenured position, but depended on the benevolence of those in power. The modern distinction between a tenured and a temporary position came about at the end of the nineteenth century, when a temporary position was offered and could be continued as a tenured appointment after a probation period. The term of office was set once the concept of retirement age had been introduced (see below).

Quite modern is also the fact that *public office is fulfilled as a main or only job*. Many political and citizen functionaries in the Middle Ages and the early modern times fulfilled their position next to other positions. In fact, the elite could afford to take up public office since they enjoyed income based on landed property. Lower administrative and other personnel often *collected* a number of positions in order to get a reasonable income or combined a public office with some other job (as for instance rural policemen in the nineteenth century in the Netherlands who were shopowners or craftsmen). When the workload increased in the nineteenth century, so did the working hours of public servants. In order to make sure that they were continuously available adequate payment had to be arranged (see below).

Up to the early-nineteenth century public servants did not *work in a career system*. Career used to be related to social status. We have already seen how experience in a position as citizen functionary opened the possibility to be recruited for more political functions. The distinction between these two highest hierarchical levels was rather vague, since recruitment for these offices was based on co-optation from among the elite. Within each of the collegial boards some *hierarchy* existed since one could be elected president-mayor or president-alderman on the basis of seniority in office. The distinction between these two and the other categories of functionaries was more difficult to break through, and then only if one was related to the elite. For most administrative and other positions, however, there were only limited career opportunities. It was common that one worked in one position during the entire period of employment. This changed with the introduction of a formal rank system in the early-nineteenth century. Promotion then became possible on the basis of merit (achievement) instead of birth (ascription).

One of the most remarkable characteristics of bureaucratization is an *adequate regular salary and pension in money*. Without it, neither full-time employment nor a ranking system are possible. Before the 1800s three types of payment existed. The first was *profit-in-office*. It was not uncommon that an office holder had to pay a certain amount of money prior to taking office. Once in office a certain percentage of the emoluments had to be paid to the public treasury, and costs attached to fulfillment of that office had to be carried by the office holder. The salary thus existed in the difference between costs of office and emoluments. This opened opportunities for usury and corruption. A second type of payment was *payment-per-action*. Many clerks were paid according to the number of pages they had copied. The third type was a *fixed salary* often paid per year or per three months. The salary level was based upon employment, and could be raised—upon request—after some (or many) years of satisfactory work. Salary increase was by no means automatic. Next to financial compensation, office holders enjoyed certain advantages, such as freedom of certain excises and partial or total compensation for housing and heating costs.

Decrease of salary was quite common, as a means of retrenchment or as a means of securing pension. There were three types of pension. The first involved a cutback in the salary of a successor. Only when the previous office holder had died, the salary could then increase to normal level. The second type were the so-called funeral funds, filled by a group of office holders out of their income in order to pay an annual amount of money to the widow of a former colleague. Finally, pensions could be given upon request. However, standardized arrangements for pension did not exist. Salary and pension (super-annuation) became standardized throughout the Western world in the early-nineteenth century, although the age of retirement was subject of much debate (Hattenhauer 113–114, 182–187; Church 1981: 189–192; Chester 1981: 129, 134; Cohen 1941: 60, 155; Van Ijsselmuiden, 1988: 100).

It follows that *rank determining salary and pension* is also a nineteenth-century phenomenon. Different categories of functionaries were treated according to different salary-scales. In the twentieth century most countries have established a more or less uniform salary system wherein each position is qualified according to level of requirements. A ranking system also facilitated *promotion through seniority and merit*. Seniority, however, never was really the only promotion criterion, and merit rapidly became standardized.

Together with salary and pension in money, the *formal protection of employment* is characteristic of the last phase of bureaucratization. During the Middle Ages and the early modern period protection of office was based on the relationship with those in power. As such, administrative and other positions were not protected against the whims of those in power. The idea that public servants not only had duties but also rights dates from around the 1900s as is indicated by the development of public pension funds, accident insurance, and full-time employment in exchange for adequate salary and career perspective. The variety of regulations concerning public employees came to be integrated in civil service acts, such as those in the United States (1883), the Netherlands (1929), and France (1946) (Church 1981: 288; Nelson 1982: 119; Raadschelders 1990: 184).

I have argued that the roots of contemporary bureaucracy can be traced back to the High Middle Ages (thirteenth century) when the ruler sought to strengthen his position against clergy and aristocracy. When comparing the development of characteristics of structure and functioning (ch. 6) with those of functionaries, it is clear that especially the latter developed during the nineteenth century. One could maybe even argue that bureaucratization of structure and functioning is a precondition for bureaucratization of functionaries. However, characteristics 9–13 (see appendix 6.1) had already become full-blown before the 1800s. The changes at the time of the Atlantic Revolutions (1780–1820) basically concerned the *Legal-rationale Herrschaft* especially at the central level. Changes in the *Bürokratische Verwaltungsstab*, more particularly the last four characteristics, around the

1800s were often limited to central government. Local governments followed as soon as they entered their era of expansion (1880–1930).

Does this mean that we have reached *full bureaucracy* and should explore possibilities of debureaucratization? For an answer we need to return to the discussion in chapter 6 of the Weberian ideal-type. In its ideal typical form (fully and completely realized) bureaucracy never existed and will never exist. We have seen how bureaucratization developed in terms of the twenty characteristics, but there is no room for an independent *bureaucracy* as highest authority in societies where politics decides. What is more, certain features of patrimonial administration still exist. How else are we to explain the "old boys' network" as recruiting ground for (higher) public office? Whether bureaucracy is the most rational and efficient type of organization, as Weber suggested, is therefore immaterial. The ideal-type does not relate to the real world, but is—nothing more, nothing less—a logically consistent abstraction. All things considered, Weber and his critics talk about two different things: ideal-type versus reality. What can be argued, though, is that the ideal-type itself can never be put to the test: it can only be compared with reality.

7.5 Literature on Actors in Government

The civil service, public functionaries, and the size of government have been extremely appealing avenues of research evidenced by the number of publications available.

The number of truly comparative books on the civil service in general is surprisingly small. Armstrong's *The European Administrative Elite* (1973) is an exception to the rule. Most studies are nationally oriented. Dominating countries in terms of amount of books are Germany (Hattenhauer 1978; Henning 1984; Lee 1980; Mommsen 1966; Rosenberg 1958; Süle 1988; Wunder 1978), England (Aylmer 1961, 1973; Cohen 1941; Craig 1955; Fry 1969; MacLeod 1988; Tout 1916; Wright 1969), and the United States (Aronson 1964; Hoogenboom 1968; Van Riper 1958, 1987; Stewart 1929). To a lesser extent literature is available on France (Sharp 1931; Wishnia 1977), the Netherlands (Van Braam 1957; Van der Meer and Roborgh 1993), Russia (Pintner 1980; Torke 1967), and Sweden (Tarschys 1978). The number of comparative articles is not much larger as inspection of the bibliography will show. It appears that in the Anglo-Saxon countries, there is more interest in the bureaucracy as a civil service, while on the European continent the emphasis is on bureaucracy as an organization. Studies of the civil service often involve an examination of the development of its size. A comparative overview of developments in size is provided by Rose (1984, 1987) and Taylor (1983). National figures can be drawn from such books as mentioned above.

Likewise, studies of the civil service will often pay attention to such issues as training, recruitment of and exams for public servants. The chapter by Fischer and Lundgreen (1975) in Tilly's edited volume on the development of national states is a must for those interested. There are few, if any, empirical studies on the development of pre- and post-entry training and then mostly in the form of an article: for France (Fisher 1977; Kessler 1977; Osborne 1983; Wright 1976), for Germany (Marx 1982), for England (Roach 1971).

Little explored, but extremely important is the impact of specialists (higher civil servants with a specialist/academic background) in policy-making. Given the fact that the number of administrative functionaries has increased tremendously and that this increase has everything to do with the incorporation of specialists within government, it is important to investigate their impact. It would be too early to hope for comparative studies, but there are some national studies that could lead the way, such as MacLeod's (1988) study on specialists in England in the 1860–1919 period, and Bemelmans-Videc's (1984) study on the influence of economists in government on policy making in the Netherlands in the 1945–1975 period. Equally important, but even less explored in a comparative framework, is the development of the relationship between political officeholders and civil servants. Information about that can be drawn from such national studies as mentioned above. At present the "History of Administration" working group of the IIAS conducts a comparative study titled "Administering the Summit," covering the nineteenth and twentieth centuries.

An interesting and profitable approach to the study of actors in government is a focus on one particular office. The number of studies using this approach is quite large. In France, substantial research has been done on such offices as the *intendants* and the prefects. An entry into the role and position of the *intendants* is available (Gruder 1968). There is not as much literature on one type of office in other countries. Rather, one will find an array of different, interesting studies, such as those on the lord lieutenants in Tudor England (G.S. Thomson 1923), the secretaries of state in eighteenth-century England (M.A. Thomson 1932), the sixteenth and seventeenth century justices of the peace in

England (Gleason, 1969), prefects in nineteenth and twentieth century Italy (Randeraad, 1992), queens' commissioners in the Netherlands from the early-nineteenth century onward (Janssens 1992), provincial governors in Tsarist Russia (Robbins 1987), the American presidency from 1787 to 1957 (Corwin 1970), the American vice presidency (Hatch 1934; Williams 1956), and the American Comptroller General (Mansfield 1939).

This short discussion of literature would not be complete if biographies were not mentioned. We will probably never be able to assess the impact of structural developments on individual behavior, or of individual behavior on structural developments. Some individuals, however, have left a mark in their times which sometimes made an impact for centuries. China's Wang-an-Shih as initiator of the Sung reforms (eleventh century) is an example. Many of the *intendant* studies in France are related to one particular office holder (e.g., Coulaudon 1932). The series of biographies of German political and administrative officeholders deserves to be mentioned (Jeserich and Neuhaus 1991). Research into the development of a particular office over a period of time taking the biographical angle would be very interesting. However, biography seem to be in the historians' realm. It might be, though, that the study of the influence of individuals in the framework of a study on the impact of specialists would provide interesting insights into the actual decision-making process. One could argue, for instance, that Lindblom's partisan analysis (1980) ultimately calls for such research effort.

References

Aberbach, Joel D., Robert D. Putnam, and Bert A. Rockman. 1981. *Bureaucrats and Politicians in Western Democracies*. Cambridge, MA: Harvard University Press.

Aiken, M. and S.B. Bachrach. 1978. "The Urban system, Politics, and Bureaucratic Structure: A Comparative Analysis of Forty-four Local Governments in Belgium." In *Organization and Environment: Theory, Issues, and Reality*, edited by L. Karpik, 199–250. London: SAGE Publications.

———. 1979. "Culture and Organizational Structure and Process: A Comparative Study of Local Government Administrative Bureaucracies in the Walloon and Flemish Regions of Belgium." In *Organizations Alike and Unlike*, edited by C.J. Lammers and D.J. Hickson. London: Routledge & Kegan Paul.

Astley, W.G. 1985. "Organizational Size and Bureaucratic Structure." *Organization Studies* 6, no.3: 201–228.

Beyer, J.M. and H.M. Trice. 1979. "A Reexamination of the Relations between Size and Various Components of Organizational Complexity." *Administrative Science Quarterly* 24, no.1: 48–64.

Cameron, David R. 1978. "The Expansion of the Public Economy: A Comparative Analysis." *The American Political Science Review* 72, no. 4: 1243–1261.

Clarke, C.J. 1983. "The End of Bureaucratization? Recent Trends in Cross-National Evidence." *Social Science Quarterly* 64, no.1: 127–135.

Clarke, J.W. 1969. "Environment, Process, and Policy: A Reconsideration." *American Political Science Review* 63, no.4: 1172–1182.

Dewar, R. and J. Hage. 1978. "Size Technology, Complexity, and Structural Differentiation." *Administrative Science Quarterly* 23, no.1, 111–136.

Dogan, Mattei, ed. 1971. *The Mandarins of Western Europe. The Political Role of Top Civil Servants.* Beverly Hills, CA: SAGE Publications.

Downs, Anthony 1967. *Inside Bureaucracy.* Boston, MA: Atlantic Little-Brown.

Eichenberg, R.C. 1983. "Problems in Using Public Employment Data." In *Why Governments Grow: Measuring the Public Sector Size,* edited by C. L. Taylor, 136–154. Beverly Hills and London: SAGE Publications.

Eisermann, G. 1976. "Auf dem Weg zur Parteibuch-Republik." In *Der Apparatschick die Inflation der Bürokratie in Ost und West,* edited by G.K. Kaltenbrunner. Freiburg/Basel/Wien: Hercler.

Fried, Robert C. 1975. "Comparative Urban Policy and Performance." In *Handbook of Political Science: Policies and Policymaking,* edited by F.I. Greenstein and N.W. Polsby, 305–379. Reading, MA: Addison Wesley Publishing Company.

———. 1976. "Party and Policy in West German Cities." *The American Political Science Review* 70 no.1, 11–24.

Hannan, Michael T and John H. Freeman. 1978. "Internal Politics of Growth and Decline." In *Environments and Organizations: Theoretical and Empirical Perspectives,* edited by Marshall W. Meyer et al., 173–199. London and San Francisco: Jossey-Bass.

Heclo, Hugh. 1978. "Issue Networks and the Executive Establishment." In *The New Political System,* edited by Anthony King, 87–124. Washington, D.C.: The American Enterprise Institute for Public Policy Research.

Hinings, C.R., R. Greenwood, and S. Ranson. 1975. "Contingency Theory and the Organization of Local Authorities: Contingencies and Structure." *Public Administration* (UK) 53, no.2: 169–190.

Kau, J.B. and P.H. Rubin 1981. "The Size of Government." *Public Choice* 37 no.2: 261–274.

Kaufmann, H. 1981. "Fear of Bureaucracy: A Raging Pandemic." *Public Administration Review* 41 no.1: 3–12.

Larkey, P.D., C. Stolp, and M. Winer. 1981. "Theorizing on the Growth of Government." *Journal of Public Policy* 11 no.2: 157–218.

Lindblom, Charles E. 1980. *The Policy-making Process,* 2d ed. Engle wood Cliffs, NJ: Prentice-Hall.

McKenzie, R.B. 1980. "The Economic Justification for Government and Government Growth." *Journal of Social and Political Studies* 5, no.3: 245–257.

Niskanen, W.A. 1971. *Bureaucracy and Representative Government.* Chicago, IL: Aldine-Atherton.

———. 1973. *Bureaucracy: Servant or Master? Lessons from America.* London: Institute of Economic Affairs.

Otto, J.M. 1987. *Aan de voet van de piramide: Overheidsinstellingen en plattelandsontwikkeling in Egypte—een onderzoek aan de basis.* Leiden: DSWO-Press.

Page, Edward C. 1995. "Comparative British Public Administration." *Public Administration* (UK) 73, no.2: 123–141.

Peltzman, S. 1980. The Growth of Government. *Journal of Law and Economics* 23, no.2: 209–287.

Peters, B. Guy. 1985. "Politicians and Bureaucrats in the Politics of Policy-making." In *Bureaucracy and Public Choice,* edited by Jan-Erik Lane, 256–282. London: SAGE Publications.

Ridley, F.F., ed. 1968. *Specialists and Generalists: A Comparative Study of the Professional Civil Service at Home and Abroad*. London: George Allen & Unwin.

Weber, Max. 1980. *Wirtschaft und Geselschaft: Grundriss der Verstehenden Soziologie* 5th ed., edited by J. Winckelmann. Tübingen: J.C.B. Mohr.

Zehm, G. 1976. "Die Hohle Staat und der dicke Apparat." In *Der Apparatschick*, edited by G. Kaltenbrunner. Freiburg/Basel/Wien: Hercler.

Part Three

Administration and Society

8

Citizens and Government:
Participation, Representation,
and Citizenship

Judging from what has been published recently, issues such as participation, representation, and citizenship are no longer unique to the realm of political science. Indeed, the administrative science angle deserves attention given the focus on the question of whether democracy and efficiency in public service delivery can be enhanced through the involvement of citizens and if so, how citizens could be more actively involved in the provision and production of public services. Most studies depart from the concept of citizenship, either in a more or less general political theoretical framework (Cooper 1991; Heater 1990; Jordan 1989; Meehan 1993) or from a more specific approach such as corporatism (Scholten 1987; Streeck and Schmitter 1985), coprovision and coproduction (Ferris 1984; Raadschelders 1986, 1988), the commons and self help (Lohmann 1992; E. Ostrom 1990) or paragovernmental and nongovernmental organization (Hood and Schuppert 1988). The issue of citizenship and participation has become timely since many authors perceive a crisis of confidence in public opinion and a breakdown of *civic culture*. The phenomenon that government cannot or can hardly handle the variety of demands from the public was labelled by Easton as *demand overload* (1965: 120–121) and Brittan spoke of *excessive expectations* (1977: 130). More recently Alford and Friedland remarked that,

> The capacity of political systems and political leadership to handle multiple and complex decisions simultaneously is sorely tested by the location of the state in the midst of competing, overlapping, inconsistent, and expensive demands for new programs and expenditures but seldom for the elimination of old ones. (1985: 157)

The crisis of confidence is not only visible in lack of faith in government's problem solving capability. There is no doubt that government is also mistrusted for its objectives. The question that is seldomly answered is whether this crisis of confidence is real. Reality is determined by perception and so it is the public perception that makes politicians and civil servants act. Lack of faith in government and mistrust of government's objectives are perceptions and have been observed in most Western countries. There is no empirical test for these perceptions but they seem to hold less when one goes from an aggregate level (the public) to an individual level. Individuals are usually more satisfied with what government does than the group/population perception would predict. But the breakdown in civic culture and the idea of dwindling citizen participation are not only perceptions, and they can be tested empirically.

In this chapter I will explore what the governed in the Western world since the twelfth century have gained and lost in the relationship with those who govern. The basic question for this chapter is how the citizen was incorporated in the body politic of his/her time. The relationship between citizen and government changed significantly, first in thought then in practice. I will concentrate for now on (changes in) role and position of the citizen. The wider perspective for understanding the citizens' role and position is offered in chapter 9 when I discuss the development of the notion of sovereignty against the background of state-making and nation-building. In section 8.1 I define concepts relevant to this topic. In section 8.2 I discuss the development of citizen participation and representation from the High Middle Ages up to Thomas Hobbes. This is followed by a section covering the era from John Locke to John Stuart Mill. Sections 8.2 and 8.3 are taken from political theory: the ideas existing at a given time concerning citizen involvement. In section 8.4 I present a theory on the development of citizenship that is helpful in acquiring a nuanced perspective on perception and reality of dwindling participation and citizenship. This section is based on empirical work.

8.1 Participation, Representation, and Citizenship in Concepts

Participation, representation, and citizenship are concepts which refer to citizen involvement in the public realm.

The concept of *participation* can be understood at two levels. First, citizens can partake in the actual delivery of public services. They are invited by government to help out, to cooperate to a smaller or larger extent. A distinction can be made between voluntary and compulsory participation (see below). Second, participation can be defined as citizens involved in the actual decision-making process. It is this second meaning of participation that dominates the modern world. Lane and Ersson distinguish direct participation through referenda from indirect participation via political parties and interest groups. According to them indirect participation has become the more common form (1987: 210–211). Alford and Friedland mention advisory boards, community action committees, task forces, and neighborhood elections as examples of indirect participation, although these generate little power in terms of the capacity to control resources and outcomes (1985: 158).

Increasingly these indirect forms of participation are perceived as a possible road toward overcoming the limits of the classical twentieth century social order of community, market, and state (Streeck and Schmitter 1985). The problem-solving capabilities of spontaneous solidarity (community), of dispersed competition (market), and of hierarchical control (state) are under stress (Streeck and Schmitter 1985:8). Private interest government as "arrangements under which an attempt is made to make associative, self-interested collective action contribute to the achievement of public policy objectives" is then assumed to be the solution to insufficient or lacking government initiative and, hence, to problems of dwindling participation (Streeck and Schmitter 1985: 17). This approach is supported by the idea that an active role of government is permitted only when private initiative is insufficient or lacking. The Catholic notion of *subsidiarity* (first formulated by Thomas Aquinas and restated in the papal encyclical *Rerum Novarum* 1892), and its secular variant of *self-help* (Samuel Smiles 1812–1904; Horatio Alger 1832–1899) embody this idea. Subsidiarity appears to enjoy new attention now that it has been adopted as official policy in the European Union and its meaning has not changed since Aquinas. Self-help, however, has changed in meaning. In the works of Smiles and Alger, self-help is the individual effort to reach a higher station in life ("from rags to riches") through zeal, virtue, and perseverance. Up to the late-eighteenth century (Cooper 1991: ch. 3) and nowadays self-help is defined in terms of communal organization (Hood and Schuppert 1988: 9). But, whatever the meaning of participation, in essence it refers to a citizen somehow involved in the preparation and/or implementation of governmental policy.

This brings us to the concept of *representation*. In Rousseau's idea, direct rule of the citizen ensured optimal involvement. Government literally defined as the will of the people constituted a state of direct democracy. However, even Rousseau realized that such was only possible in a small body politic. The larger the territory of a state, the less the opportunities for direct rule and the greater the need for representation. Representation can also be understood in two ways. First, there is the concept of *representative government*, a situation in which the composition of government in terms of political functionaries reflects the cleavages in society (gender, religion, education, social class, income, language, political affiliation). A representative government is considered legitimate since each segment in society is politically represented. Free elections are the vehicle that supposedly assure such representation. *Representative administration* is a second concept which refers to a situation in which the composition of the civil service is a close reflection of the different (cultural, linguistic, religious, racial) segments in society. Neither participation nor representation have ever existed in their ideal form. In historical perspective, it is only recently that these notions have actually influenced the relationship between the governed and those who govern. In fact, even as concepts, participation and representation are of relative recent origin.

The same cannot be said for *citizenship*. From early in history, citizenship was considered an important agent for realizing public services. The concept of citizenship could refer to different meanings (defined legal or social status, means of political identity, focus of loyalty, requirement of duties, expectations of rights, yardstick of good social behavior) defined and redefined in different contexts (Greek city-state, Roman Republic and Empire, medieval and Renaissance city, the nation-state) (Heater 1990: 161; Meehan 1993: 175–176).

In our time citizenship is regarded either as a set of rights enabling the individual to "...function relatively equally in private life or in exchange in civil society", or as a moral duty "...to take part in constructing and maintaining [the] community" (Meehan 1993: 177). The first notion is one of *liberal citizenship* and is of recent origin. The second notion is known as *republican citizenship* and dates back to Plato and Aristotle (Jordan 1989: 69). Citizenship nowadays is channelled into interest groups, consisting of (active) citizens and representing an institutionalized, segmented involvement aimed at influencing a specific policy through lobbying and pressure. The (active) citizen thus operates on the input side of policy-making. In the Western world the notion of citizenship has been researched not only at political-theoretical level, but also—although limited—at the level of organizational styles. Thus *coproduction* refers to the phenomenon of the voluntary or compulsory active conjunction of personally and/ or functionally involved citizens and government officials in the care-taking of common (mutual, public) interests whether it be policy-for-mulation, policy-implementation, or the production of goods and/or services (Raadschelders 1988: 268). This is close to *corporatism*, "…a resolution to the problem of social order (where) the state, rather than superimposing a structure of autocratic authority, tries to succeed by sharing its public order function with organized groups in civil soci-ety" (Hemerijck 1992: 77). Coproduction and corporatism are impor-tant social science concepts that can well be applied in the study of the development of relations between state and society.

8.2 From the Magna Carta to Hobbes

Around the year 1000 the administrative map of Europe consisted of a patchwork of more or less autonomous, very much self-reliant regions. At the local level many of the tasks we would now call public relied heavily on collective private initiative (for instance, water management in the Netherlands). Whatever government existed, it took part in the formulation and implementation of measures of collective interest. One of the few areas in which government participated and, in fact, took the lead was law enforcement. More than a thousand years ago Emperor Charlemagne created a simple local government system the main fea-ture of which was justice administered by a bench of (usually seven) magistrates chosen by and from among the villagers and presided by a centrally appointed sheriff. This, however, did not make for a coherent administration of justice. For centuries to come, local government oper-ated with a system of customary law, by nature highly fragmented.

At central level the situation was not very much different. The ruler had some sort of control over justice in his jurisdiction, and was not much involved in any other task but defending his own territory against outside threat. In order to pay for all his military and household needs, taxes were levied on a frequent basis. Often extraordinary taxes were imposed, especially when war was at hand. The subjects in his terri-tory were subordinate, either directly or indirectly through vassals. Individuals delivered their services on a compulsory basis, especially the serfs, the slaves and, up to a certain extent, the free peasants. The relationship between lord and vassal was more reciprocal. The vassal provided his lord with counsel (*consilium*) and military assistance (*auxilium*) in exchange for independence within his jurisdiction. Unlike the population at large, the vassal had the right to refuse services to his feudal lord in case when the lord had violated the terms of their mutual agreement (*diffidatio*).

The elite (nobility, clergy) participated in the business of government during the feudal era. As soon as some feudal lords attempted to usurp a higher authority, the nobility sought to protect its autonomy through charters such as the English *Magna Carta* (1215) and the Hungarian *Golden Bull* (1356). These charters limited the power of the prince through law and as such are prototypical for the development of a *Rechtsstaat*. We have already seen how at that time a new elite had formed: the merchants. They played an important role in the movement to acquire some degree of autonomy for their towns (the town charters) in exchange for an annual sum of money to the lord who granted that charter. We have also seen how the elites in chartered towns enhanced their control over the local community and against the central lord by the creation of mayors and councils of city fathers that were to serve as a counterweight to the bench of magistrates. These three bodies together constituted local government and were vested with an authority that was derived from its free citizens often organized in guilds. This bid for authority and self-government was strengthened by the employment of administrative officials. At the central level the claim for authority was backed by the creation of government departments.

The development of local, regional, and "national" representative institutions in late medieval Europe has been analyzed by Blockmans. He developed a typology of contexts within which popular representation developed. In *rural societies*, the first type, representation depended very much upon the ruler. Popular meetings were limited (France, Germany, Spain, Central Europe). The second type is that of *rural economies connected to interregional markets*. Here a higher frequency of popular meetings could be found (parts of France and England). In *urbanized societies*, the third type, privileged cities function within a system of Estates meetings (Brabant, Holland, Flanders). The *urban leagues*, such as the Hanse, constitute a fourth type. And finally there were the *autonomous cities*, especially in northern Italy (Blockmans 1978: 204–208). He concludes that what began as a "...spontaneous emanation from the commercial and entrepreneurial urban bourgeoisie [...], gradually became more an instrument of the centralized government..." (Blockmans 1978: 209) with the exception of the northern Low Countries (Blockmans 1978: 211).

Public officials were recruited from among the elite. For the highest local positions (mayors, councilmembers) it was expected that individuals took turns but it was voluntary by nature. The same was the case with offices of a supervisory nature (Overseer of the Poor, Fire Master). The subordinate tasks of a more compulsory nature were performed by the citizenry: nightwatch, firewatch. These tasks could be found mainly at local level. This situation would exist deep into the eighteenth century: the elites were represented in the local, regional or even national Estates; the populace served. There was one counterforce to this dispersement of authority. In regions where one lord successfully managed to be accepted as sovereign king, power gravitated around that person. In the vision of Thomas Hobbes (1588–1679) the sovereign represented all—"A multitude of men, are made One Person, when they are by one man, or one Person, representated." His views of how to organize public life, as did the earlier views of Jean Bodin (see next chapter for more detail), reflected the need to counter the consequences of civil war and anarchy.

8.3 From Locke to Mill

John Locke (1632–1704) rejected the Hobbesian *Leviathan* state. In the public realm, Locke argued, countervailing forces ought to be created against potential violence and oppression by an absolute ruler. Life, liberty, and estate (property) of the individual would best be protected through participation of the people, or their representatives, in the business of government. Government existed for and derived legitimacy from securing the rights of the individual. The *Legislative* was to act as the people's agent, and the *Executive* would enforce the legal system. The individual is able to satisfy his/her own needs and develop capabilities and opportunities in a process of free interaction with others. The political community is a burden that the individual must bear. In Locke's conception, like Spinoza (1632–1677) before him, self-maintenance is a positive force, while Hobbes had viewed it as *self-seeking* and thus a negative force. In the Lockean *political community*, state powers are restricted and the citizen has rights, duties, and powers. The citizen needs to devote part of his time to serving the communal, public interest. This constituted a radical change in thought and it paved the way for *representative government*.

Locke wrote his *Two Treatises of Government* (1689) in reflection and justification of the Glorious Revolution in which the sovereign was forced to step down and parliament won the battle for supremacy. The English Parliament was the only one that acted in ways we are accustomed to nowadays. The French Parliament followed the tails of the sovereign until the French Revolution. In time, Locke's ideas would prove to be very influential. When Charles de Sécondat, Baron de Montesquieu (1689–1755) visited England he acquainted himself with English government and Locke's ideas. In his *L'Esprit des Lois* (1748) the Lockean notion of a separation of powers was expanded with a *Judiciary*. Montesquieu's contemporary Voltaire (François Arouet, 1694–1778) advocated human rights and tolerance in his *Traité sur la tolérance* (1763). Voltaire, too, came to appreciate the relative freedom of speech in England during his years of exile.

The idea of citizen participation was carried the farthest by Jean-Jacques Rousseau (1712–1778). In *Discours sur l'égalité* (1755) and *Du contrat social* (1763) he laid down his ideas about the will of the people (*volonté générale*). In his view, the state needed to bridge the gap between rich and poor. Inequalities were not acceptable and in a real community people would take care for one another. His theory of direct or participatory democracy is based on self-regulation and self-government, which implied that transfer of sovereignty was not necessary: sovereignty originated in the people, that is, women and poor excluded.

For all practical purposes the idea of democratic government was very much a theory, in need of suggestions as to how it could be realized. Jeremy Bentham (1748–1832) and James Mill (1773–1836) addressed that issue with, by now, a well-known question: how can the people be protected against the despotic use of power? Their recipe was simple enough: through voting by secret ballot, competition between potential political leaders (representatives) in popular elections, a separation of powers, and the liberty of press, speech and public association. If, indeed, a government was to act on behalf of the people, then it should be directly accountable to an electorate who would be frequently consulted. The idea of elections on a recurring basis was born. It did not imply universal suffrage, for Bentham and Mill both believed that certain segments in society were to be excluded from the franchise, namely the labor class and women. On the other side of the Channel, Condorcet (1743–1794) pushed ahead of his times when in his theory about progress in history he advocated the abolishment of class differences, state education for all, equal rights for women, health insurance and care for the sick and elderly.

It was James Mill's son, John Stuart Mill (1806–1873), who became the great defender of individual development within a democratic framework. In his view representative government served not only to impose limits in the pursuit of individual satisfaction (*my freedom is limited by yours*), but it also was an aspect of the free development of the individual. Participation in political life (passive and active voting rights; local government as the school for democracy; jury duty) were of vital interest to government. In *On Liberty* (1859) he stated clearly that social and political intervention of the state was only justified when individual acts would harm others and when an individual was not able to provide for himself. This was the theoretical foundation of the *welfare state*. Mill came to favor universal franchise as is testified in the following,

> The principle which regulates the existing social relations between the two sexes—the legal subordination of one sex to another—is wrong in itself, and now one of the chief hindrances to human improvement; and...ought to be replaced by a principle of perfect equality.... (Mill 1869: ch. 1)

It appears that the principles upon which today's welfare state could develop surfaced gradually between 1690–1870.

8.4 A Theory on the Development of Citizenship

In the social sciences, and especially in historical and comparative sociology, the development of citizenship has been regarded as a process in which the working classes established some degree of equality within the capitalist system. In this approach the political and economic changes in society serve to explain the changing nature of citizenship. T.H. Marshall's analysis stands out as a prime and influential example (1965; see also Turner 1986: 25: 44–48). Marshall focused on the development of national citizenship, a process of geographical fusion of citizens and functional separation of civil, political, and social rights. Each of these rights were embedded in separate institutions (Marshall 1965: 78) (see table 8.1).

TABLE 8.1
The Development of Citizenship (after Marshall)

Right	Content	Institution(s)
Civil	Legal rights of individual	Courts
Political	Participation	Parliament, Local councils
Social	Welfare, Social Security	Educational system, Social services

The development of all three groups of rights can be traced back to the 1200s, and than especially at local level, but our modern interpretation of them does not come about until after the 1800s. Civic duties were replaced by civil rights, such as freedom of speech, and the right to own property. This was followed by an expansion of old political rights to new sections of the population through slowly expanding the franchise until it included the entire adult population. And, finally, the social rights had vanished in the eighteenth and early-nineteenth century, but experienced a revival from the second half of the nineteenth century onward. Education for literacy and social services for protection were intended to enhance equality and improve the exercise of civil and political rights (Marshall 1965: 79–91).

Marshall's theory can be complemented with a theory about the development of the relationship between citizen and government. Such a theory, in turn, may help to explain the phenomena described in chapters five through to seven. The elements for such a theory can be derived from literature and include at least five elements: type of rule, role of central government, nature of citizen participation, public expenditure, and role of the citizen.

Control over the population in order to extract sufficient human and financial resources motivated the development of central government in the early modern era. Central government needed these resources to continue an expansionist policy. State-making was the dominant process and, as a result, position and stability in the international sphere was of prime concern to rulers. Resources were used for warfare and the central states' policy was outwardly oriented in the sense that many internal policies served to strengthen the international position (Kohl 1983; Webber and Wildavsky 1986). The territory was governed through indirect rule using powerful intermediaries (clergy, urban oligarchies, landlords, professional warriors) who enjoyed significant autonomy in governance at the regional and local levels (Tilly 1990: 104). Time and again, such a system met its limits when these intermediaries gained too much power. In attempts to reestablish control over the various regions within a realm, rulers appointed new intermediaries (Greenfeld 1992: 516, note 99).

Citizen participation occurred mainly at the stages of policy implementation and execution. Participation at the policy-making stage was only open to the (local) elites. The population-at-large and elites were involved because of a civic *duty*. Too much success with an outwardly oriented policy could result in *imperial overstretch*, a situation in which the central state experiences increasing problems with effectively controlling the enlarged or enlarging territory. In the effort to maintain such control, the central state drew heavily upon internal resources, depleting them in the process. Kennedy argues along these lines in his study on the dynamics of the development of great powers (1988: xvi–xvii). The inexorable crumbling of an empire signifies imperial overstretch (Tilly 1990: 71) (see table 8.2 below).

By using the same characteristics as for the early modern period, and thinking about current notions of dwindling citizen participation, a new characterization for the present situation evolves. The argument would run as follows. The consequences of industrialization, urbanization, and social unification for government (nation-building, nineteenth century) were visible both in public expenditure as well as in the size of the bureaucracy. Central government shifted its attention to internally oriented policies. The increase of public expenditure for welfare functions such as health and education is amply documented (Cameron 1983; Kohl 1983; Flora and Heidenheimer 1981). In this respect, Tilly remarked that "the omnipresent state, the struggle over its rulers and policies, the formation of serious budgetary competitors to the armed forces..." emerged in the nineteenth century absorption of the general population into the state. European states converged into a model of bureaucratic intervention and control (Tilly 1990: 63). This constituted a system of *direct rule*: unmediated intervention (by the state) in the lives of local communities, households, and productive enterprises (Tilly 1990: 103). The vehicle for this intervention was legislation, with a dependence on local government for implementation. To meet growing citizen demand for more and better services, both central and local government grew in terms of number of public employees, increasingly recruited on the basis of professional skills. Professionalization of the public service resulted in declining opportunities for citizen participation. Insofar as citizens participated, it was more and more at the input side of the policy-making process through interest groups. The role of the citizenry (the population-at-large) came to be defined in terms of civil rights (Cooper 1991: 1). The consequence for government can be a situation of demand overload, or—to maintain consistency with the first characterization—a situation of administrative overstretch.

State-making preceded nation-building and during the phase of state-making, central governments were outward oriented, guarding external stability and position through the extraction of human and financial resources. This was possible because in a system of indirect rule, local

TABLE 8.2
Development of the Rlationship between Citizen and Government
from Early Modern to Modern Government:
A Characterization of Assumptions in Literature

Period	16th–18th centuries	19th–20th centuries
Characteristics	State-making	Nation-building
Type of rule	Indirect	Direct
Role central government	Outward	Inward
Citizen participation	Output oriented	Input oriented
Public expenditure	Warfare funds	Welfare funds
Citizen role	Civic duty	Civil rights
Possible effect	Imperial overstretch	Demand overload

Source: Raadschelders 1995: 615.

government provided most welfare functions through conscripted and voluntary civic duty. This changed over a period of some 160 years. The nation-building process compelled central government to increase intervention in the entire territory, guarding internal stability through redistributive measures in order to promote welfare. Civic duty/responsibility became obsolete and was replaced by civil rights. As the (local) public service grew in absolute terms, their numbers relative to population growth declined. The increase of governmentally provided communal services accompanied by a decline in citizen involvement and an increase in citizen demand inevitably results in a large bureaucracy and may enhance the perception of demand overload. This is the dominant theory at the moment, and it is supported by data clearly showing a shift from warfare to welfare functions by the state, and a shift from part-time citizen employment to full-time civil servants (Cameron 1983; Flora and Heidenheimer 1982; Kohl 1983; Raadschelders 1994).

It now remains to be seen whether the theoretical notions about declining citizen participation and the theoretical assumptions about the evolution of the relationship between citizen and government can be confirmed with facts.

The Citizen in the Early Modern Period (1500–1780)

In foreign affairs, the dominant concern of central governments in the early modern period revolved around wars on land or at sea aimed at protecting and often expanding territory and trade. Central governments' primary domestic concerns were with order and stability (justice), control of producer-consumer relations in order to extract adequate revenue through tolls and excises (finance, government intervention through regulation of the economy—the mercantilist state), and management of the rulers' household and domains (chancery). It is no coincidence that the first government departments (courts, exchequer, and chancery) were created in these areas. Besides these concerns, central government had only limited attention for domestic matters, most of which (for instance poor relief, education, health) were left to the discretion of local government.

The first attempts at public service delivery in the sphere of welfare (public education, public health, poor relief, firewatch and, much later, gas and electricity supply) started at the local level. In the early modern period, private effort in these areas (for instance by the church or by contractors) was superseded by public effort (Raadschelders 1994). There was, however, no demand overload. One reason is that, in retrospect, this municipalization of communal services probably was very gradual, but more importantly because local government in principle could tap into the largest human resource available to any organization—the entire (male) population within the town limits.

Corvée (a compulsory labor tax for the lower-income citizenry) and *liturgy* and *munera* (voluntary contribution of goods and/or services by the elite) (Webber and Wildavsky 1986: 44, 68, 102; Lohmann 1992: 83–126) were quite normal from the ancient civilizations up to the late-eighteenth and early-nineteenth century. Civic duty was an individual's moral obligation to the community. In early modern Europe the citizen was always called upon when new tasks were taken over from the private sector (Raeff 1975: 1227). Lohmann reports how in Amsterdam inter alia hospitals, orphanages, almshouses, and schools had been operated by religious orders but, as a consequence of the Protestant Reformation, came under control of the city council in the early-seventeenth century (1992: 118–119). During the early modern period, the lower citizenry in the Netherlands was conscripted for the dikewatch, the nightwatch, and the firewatch. A member of the local elite was expected to serve time in such political offices as lord mayor and council member, and civic offices such as nightwatch or firewatch commander, school board member, overseer of the poor, the sick, the elderly, the orphans, and (in a time of incomplete separation of church and state) even as church masters. Districtmasters or quartermasters monitored the demographic development (birth, death, migration) in a neighborhood, and thus operated as a system of social control (Raadschelders 1988). Comparable situations have been reported in most other Western nations, such as England (Aylmer 1961: 7; Kamenka 1989: 117), France (Kamenka 100), Germany (Rosenberg 1958: 7–8, 43), and the United States (Cooper 1991: 85–86; see also Wickwar 1970: 30–59, on Western Europe and the United States; and Raeff 1975, on Europe).

There are virtually no historical data available on the size of citizen involvement in public service delivery other than normative contemporary texts on the *desirable* public role of the citizen (Cooper 1991: ch.3; Greenfeld 1992: 36; Webber and Wildavsky 1986). The only figures come from research on local government development in the Netherlands (Raadschelders 1994) (see table 8.3). *Citizen functionaries* was one out of seven categories of public functionaries distinguished in this research. Citizen functionaries were defined as *Citizens involved in preparation, formulation, and implementation of a task in particular field, based on delegation, civic duty* and represent the elite in a community.

It is impossible to establish the number of citizen functionaries who did not belong to the elite. And yet it appears from scarce sources that citizen involvement was very important indeed. In the town of Alkmaar in the Netherlands, a document from 1795 indicates how approximately 40 percent of public offices (from manual labor up to policy-making and implementing responsibilities) was performed through citizen functionaries recruited from every stratum of the local society

TABLE 8.3
The Number of Citizen Functionaries as a Percentage of the Total Number of Local Public Functionaries in Four Municipalities in the Netherlands, 1600–1970

Year	Alkmaar	Beverwijk	Purmerend	Zaandam
1600	20	20	18	17
1700	17	25	19	42.8
1800	13	45	44	39.5
1900	15	16	32	9
1940	14	18	42	5
1970	1	—	6	—

Source: Raadschelders 1995: 618.

(Raadschelders 1990: 124; 1988). People from the lower strata of the local community were mainly involved in the execution side of public policy; the elites were also active on the policy-making side as part of the local oligarchy. Assuming that this is not an extraordinary phenomenon in early modern local government, it would be interesting to collect data in other countries. The hypothesis could then be tested that the expansion of tasks at local government level (in Western nations) was possible through both compulsory and voluntary participation of the citizenry.

So far the first characterization (imperial overstretch) holds up. But what of demand overload? There are indications that it did exist in early modern times. The frequent food and tax riots in early modern times (Tilly 1975: 380–455; Webber and Wildavsky 1986: 235, 263) represent public discontent and demand for changes. The frequent occurrence of such riots did not necessarily lead to changes in the administrative machinery or the tax system; a riot was simply met with sheer suppression. Elaborate systems for food storage such as existed in ancient Egypt and Rome were not maintained in early modern Europe. Public anger was directed to those who abused their public function. Especially in times of food shortages, the *tax farmers* were a logical target, suspected (often with reason) of usury.

The division of labor between central government (warfare) and local government (welfare) was broken down in two phases. During the period of the Enlightenment and the Atlantic Revolutions (the first phase) the idea evolved that the state should also be concerned with the welfare (*eudaimonia*) of its citizens, as is testified in contemporary texts from German cameralists and French *police-scientists* (Rutgers 1993: 63–64). The advent of nationalism resulted in a more *inward orientation* of the state (Greenfeld 1992: 185). However, such inward orientation could not materialize until, as a result of industrialization, a surplus was created that made redistributive policies a viable option (the second phase).

The Citizen During the Age of Transition (1780–1945) and the Mature Welfare State (1945–present)

It is not until the second half of the eighteenth century that public discontent shifted from particular, individual functionaries, such as tax farmers or members of the local oligarchy, to bureaucracy which was and is more of an abstraction. Growing awareness of the state as an administrative state (Albrow 1970) coincided with the advent of the idea that the state ought to provide welfare as well and thus protect the citizen in more areas than the territory or the citizens' property alone. Changes occurred both at central and local level. Chester observed that most changes in the 1780–1870 period at central level were induced by the need to improve the administrative machinery, whereas changes at the local level were a response to changing social and economic conditions (Chester 1981: 322).

These material changes were accompanied by changes in the ideology about the citizens' position in the polity. At first the notion of civil rights was interpreted in terms of equality before the law, more so in the United States than in Europe (Cooper 1991: 1; Greenfeld 1992: 450). But as the nineteenth century progressed, it became apparent that the social problems created by industrialization, urbanization, and threats to public health "…grew too big too quickly to be resolved by private philanthropy…" (Webber and Wildavsky 1986: 305) or private communal effort, and the notion of civil rights came to include public welfare provisions.

Parallel to and as important as economic and urban development was the cultural and social unification of a state into a national state, made possible through technical innovations (train, telegraph, newspapers, telephone). Citizens of an entire state learned about social and economic circumstances in other regions and came to organize their demands instead of falling into an uprising. Markoff spoke of an anomalous case when he presented the *Cahiers de Doléances* (late-eighteenth century) as an early example of bottom-up wishes for better services (Markoff 1975). A century later it had become quite normal for citizens to write their local (Van Dalen 1987) or, I assume, central government with requests for intervention in a particular sphere.

Social unification was visible in the creation of nationally oriented professional associations (such as for general practitioners pursuing a healthier environment) labor unions, and political parties. In Torstendahl's words, a gradual transition occurred from noninstitutional collectivities to institutions and nonbureaucratic administration was replaced by professional, full-time administration (Torstendahl 1990: 23, 65). In the late-nineteenth century the nightwatches in the Netherlands were replaced by regular police officers and overseers (of whatever) gave way to full-time civil servants. Wherever compulsory and voluntary citizen involvement existed, it was slowly replaced by full-time public functionaries, specialists (Clarke and Pavlov 1985: 268) and organized interest groups. Citizen participation came to rest on voluntary consent solely, and then only through organization (Hart 1972: 609–611).

That the social structure was changing was recognized remarkably early by Tocqueville: "Democracy loosens social ties, but tightens natural ones: it brings kindred more closely together, whilst it throws citizens more apart..." (Tocqueville 1990: 233). This especially occurred when families moved from rural to urban areas where they had no support other than the family and, later, the local and central government.

Although developments varied among countries with a more centralistic tradition and those with a tradition of self-government, the dominant trend on the whole was centralization of communal functions. The effect of this centralization on the size and composition of the public apparatus was enormous. In absolute terms, the number of public officials formally employed rose sharply from the 1880s onward, both at the central as well as the local level. But at the same time, the number of public servants per 1000 inhabitants dropped, at least at the local level. The development of the number of public functionaries per 1000 inhabitants (including citizen functionaries) of four towns in the Netherlands is shown in table 8.4.

The four towns in table 8.4 are all situated in the province of North Holland. Alkmaar and Purmerend were market towns where producers from a wide region brought their products. Both had a hospital; there were a total of four in that province. An increase of their regional importance led to an increase of the number of public functionaries. Many such towns had citizen committees for the poor, the elderly, and so forth (see above). Insofar as smaller towns, like Beverwijk, did not have such committees, they were installed after the occupation of the Netherlands by the French (1795). Zaandam profited from the proximity of Amsterdam and did not need to expand its local services. Furthermore, a fast-growing population in that town kept the number of public functionaries per 1000 low. From the 1850s onward a decline occurred. Only Purmerend maintained a fair number of public functionaries per 1000 because of its thriving weekly market. After World War II, however, the number of local public functionaries stabilized around 19 to 20 per 1000. We have already have seen from table 8.4 that the number of citizen functionaries in this period dropped significantly as well.

The fact that the number of publicly provided services grew and the number of public functionaries per 1000 inhabitants dropped might

TABLE 8.4
Total Number of Local Public Functionaries per 1000 Inhabitants in
Four Municipalities in the Netherlands, 1600–1970

Year	Alkmaar	Beverwijk	Purmerend	Zaandam
1622	21.7	*	37.9	*
1795	40	50.6	61.2	16.3
1851	37.5	20.2	32.2	15.8
1880	17.6	17.7	33.3	15.5
1900	18.7	16.2	33.5	15.7
1940	17.3	12.8	38.9	23.4
1970	19.1	17.3	22.6	19.4

Source: Raadschelders 1995: 620.

* no data available

suggest that government became more efficient in the governance, provision, and production of public services, but this would be a hasty
conclusion. Indeed, despite fast growing populations and two major
wars, government systematically enlarged the package of services; but
the parallel development toward a professional bureaucracy not only
entailed an improvement of administrative skills but also heralded a
shift from part-time to full-time employment. In early modern times,
public employment for many higher and lower offices was a part-time
job. In such a system *corvée* could be used. In a system of full-time
professional employment, *corvée* could not be used and became obsolete. Thus, while the number of public servants in absolute terms increased since the 1880s, so did the length of their work week.

Given this, have we now—a century later—reached a situation of
demand overload? According to public perception we have, and this is
confirmed by the fact that solutions for demand overload are sought
within political, administrative, and interest-group circles: bureaucracy
is *solved* through debureaucratization, rules diminished through de-
regulation, and government size dealt with through (neo-) corporatism
or privatization. The strength of the stereotype of bureaucracy as a
dysfunctioning phenomenon, and indirectly the strength of the idea of
demand overload, was debated by for instance Milward and Rainey
(1983) and was put to the test by Goodsell (1984). Goodsell's data
concern the United States and stipulate clearly how well government
continues to meet citizens' demands. His argument rests on the idea

that much of our perception is based on bizarre cases, and that the anti-bureaucratic sentiment is a handy vehicle for achieving one's own ends (Goodsell 1984: 4–5). In a recent study about the Dutch case, Ringeling argued that the negative judgment of government performance rests more on faulty criteria and biased evaluation models than on an analysis of the actual performance of government (Ringeling 1993).

As indicated above, the citizen organized and confronted government in order to influence policy-making. In less then a 100 years, some have come to believe that associations might be the solution to failing social mechanisms of community, market, and state (Streeck and Schmitter). This observation needs to be examined more closely. First, referring to union members Jacoby notices how "They do not want to be personally involved, but as long as no sacrifice is required, they are willing to benefit from their membership" (1976: 104). Democracy and welfare states apparently not only loosen social ties but transfer the responsibility for communal welfare to government and interest groups. In a gloomy mood, one could even say that democracy and welfare states have created a lazy citizen or at least—as for instance Fowler and Orenstein suggest—a citizen that feels uneasy about duty (1993: 109). The same was argued by C. Fred Alford (1989: 234–235) about the phenomenon of jury duty avoidance in the United States. That this lazy citizen does not quite exist is apparent from the growth of private interest government in the 1980s, for instance, in the Netherlands (Raadschelders 1986).

Second, Streeck and Schmitter at least imply that associations dwindled and were only recently rediscovered. This idea can be contested on two grounds. One is that there are in fact numerous examples of citizen participation and citizen functionaries in Western nations, among which in Europe the *sapeurs-pompiers* (fire fighters) in French communes and volunteer Special Constables in Britain. In the United States, citizen involvement is reported especially in the areas of cultural arts, recreation, health and human services, public safety programs (Ferris 1984: 330) and public schools (Chubb and Moe 1988). Another consideration is that the number of interest groups has increased enormously in the twentieth century (Lohmann 1992). Indeed, empirical evidence does not support the idea of dwindling citizen participation. Membership of voluntary associations in Western countries illustrates this, even when corrected for Church and Union memberships (Curtis et al. 1992: 143, 150). It might be that associations more actively involve the citizen in public service delivery than interest groups do, but beyond that, the differences are minor. No (comparative) research is available as to what extent public service delivery still rests on voluntary citizen involvement. In fact, an empirically sound argument about declining citizen participation in terms of involvement in public service delivery can only be made when we are able to compare a former with a recent situation. And there are clear signs that a "bringing-the-citizen-back-in" mood is no longer restricted to the conservative side of the political spectrum. In this respect King and Ward noticed how conservatives, liberals, and left-wing politicians alike have come to regard citizenship as a mutual responsibility. In relation to the so-called work-welfare programs in the United States and Great Britain they described this new attitude as follows:

> welfare recipients or unemployed persons, as citizens entitled to receive benefits, hold in turn obligations to the state and to their fellow citizens. (King and Ward 1992: 483)

This observation is of direct relevance to the issue of redefining citizen participation in general.

8.5 Literature

As indicated above literature on the development of participation, representation, and citizenship is often part of studies in political theory. Given the current popular and scholarly interest in these issues, and especially in its assumed potential for improving upon public service delivery, we may expect an increase in the number of studies that depart from an administrative science perspective. Some literature has already been mentioned in the introduction of this chapter.

Here I would like to point out that the study of the development of the interaction between citizen and government should start with the study of basic documents. Griffiths's 1968 volume is an excellent example. His annotated presentation of documents pertaining to representative government in Western Europe in the sixteenth century provides a framework for the kind of empirical analysis attempted in section 8.4 above. Tracing the developments in the administration of a country can be done successfully by presenting (parts of) original texts of important documents and providing them with a small introduction. The format of Frederick Mosher's collection (1983) of basic documents in American public administration (1776–1950) is unpretentious, attractive, and very instructive. This format could be used to present contemporary texts concerned with participation and representation. For the United States such a volume could include parts of political speeches, pamphlets and books such as, obviously, Tocqueville's *Democracy in America* (1839) and, less obvious, James Fennimore Cooper's *The American Democrat* (1832). However, one can find many collections of documents in the field of history. These documents, though, can and ought to be discussed in an administrative science framework as well.

Comparative empirical research on the development of participation and representation is scarce. The edited volume on the representativity of public administration (Wright 1991) published by the International Institute of Administrative Sciences may serve as an example.

Empirical studies concerning citizenship are numerous, especially in the field of coproduction, the commons, and self-help. The stereotypical notion of a crisis of legitimacy and lack of civic culture is proven one-sided at least when one looks at the myriad examples of citizen initiative in both Western and non-Western countries (Ferris 1984; Brudney 1983; Sharp 1980; Whitaker 1980). Furthermore, much of the coproduction literature is ahistorical and thus the perception is that coproduction is of fairly recent origin. The emphasis in research is on change. A historical perspective provides a more dynamic approach and reveals the interplay between continuity, diversity, and change. The same can be said about corporatism research which is highly oriented on the present. A combined historical and contemporary analysis (Hemerijck 1992: 69) enriches our understanding of this phenomenon and carries us beyond our own limited time-frame.

Recent empirical research has shown that citizen initiative and participation has a long-standing history and cannot be adequately appreciated in the traditional state-market dichotomy. Despite the powerful theoretical exegesis of collective inaction (Olson 1965), the tragedy of the commons (Hardin 1968; Hardin and Baden 1977), and the prisoners' dilemma, empirical research about the development of the commons has shown several convincing examples of a third way of organizing next to state or market. Indeed, both in the Western and non-Western world one can find organizations for common pool resource management several of which have a history of centuries (E. Ostrom 1990; Bromley 1992; Uphoff 1986; Raadschelders and Toonen 1993). An extensive bibliography is available (Martin 1989, 1992) and research efforts in this area are institutionalized in the International Association of the Study of Common Pool Resource Management.

References

Part of the introduction, part of section 8.1, and a large part of section 8.4 were published earlier in *Public Administration: An International Quarterly* (1995) 73, no. 4, pp. 611–625.

Albrow, Martin. 1970. *Bureaucracy*. London: MacMillan.
Alford, Robert R. and Roger Friedland. 1985. *Powers of Theory: Capitalism, the State, and Democracy*. Cambridge: Cambridge University Press.
Brittan, Samuel. 1977. *The Economic Consequences of Democracy*. London: Temple Smith.
Bromley, Daniel W. 1992. *Making the Commons Work: Theory, Practice, and Policy*. San Francisco, CA: ICS Press.
Brudney, J.L. and R.E. England. 1983. "Toward a Definition of the Coproduction Concept." *Public Administration Review* 43, no.1: 59–65.
Cameron, D. 1983. "The Expansion of the Public Economy; A Comparative Analysis." *American Political Science Review* 77, no.4: 1243–1261.
Chubb, John E. and Terry M. Moe. 1988. "Politics, Markets, and the Organization of Schools." *American Political Science Review* 82, no.4: 1065–1087.
Clarke, C.J. and V.L. Pavlov. 1985. "The Degree of Bureaucratization at the Societal Level and Political Democracy: Cross-National Evidence." *Journal of Political and Military Sociology* 13, no.2: 265–282.
Cooper, Terry L. 1991. *An Ethic of Citizenship for Public Administration*. Englewood Cliffs, NJ: Prentice-Hall.
Curtis, J.E., E.G. Grabb, and D.E. Baer. 1992. "Voluntary Association Membership in Fifteen Countries." *American Sociological Review* 47, no.1: 139–152.
Easton, David. 1965. *A Framework for Political Analysis*. Englewood Cliffs, NJ: Prentice-Hall.
Ferris, James M. 1984. "Coprovision: Citizen Time and Money Donations in Public Service Provision." *Public Administration Review* 44, no. 4, 324–333.
Fowler, Robert Booth and Jeffrey R. Orenstein. 1993. *An Introduction to Political Theory: Toward the Next Century*. New York: HarperCollins College Publishers.
Goodsell, Charles. 1984. *A Case for Bureaucracy: A Public Administration Polemic*. Chatham, NJ: Chatham House Publishers, Inc.
Hardin, G. 1968. "The Tragedy of the Commons." *Science* 162, no.4: 1243–1248.
Hardin, G. and J. Baden. 1977. *Managing the Commons*. San Francisco, CA: Freeman Press.
Hart, David K. 1972. "Theories of Government Related to Decentralization and Citizen Participation." *Public Administration Review* 32, no. 3: 603–621.
Heater, Derek. 1990. *Citizenship: The Civic Ideal in World History, Politics and Education*. London and New York: Longman.
Hood, Christopher and Gunnar Folke Schuppert. 1988. *Delivering Public Services in Western Europe: Sharing Western European Experience of Para-Governmental Organization*. Modern Politics Series vol.16. London: SAGE Publications.
Jordan, Bill. 1989. *The Common Good: Citizenship, Morality and Self-Interest*. Oxford: Basil Blackwell.
Kennedy, Paul. 1989. *The Rise and Fall of the Great Powers: Economic Change and Military Conflict from 1500–2000*. New York: Vintage Books.
King, Desmond S. and Hugh Ward. 1992. "Working for Benefits: Rational Choice and the Rise of Work-Welfare Programs." *Political Studies* 17, no. 2: 479–495.
Kohl, J. 1983. "The Functional Structure of Public Expenditures: Long-Term Changes." In *Why Governments Grow: Measuring the Public Sector Size*, edited by C.L. Taylor, 201–216. Beverly Hills, CA and London: SAGE Publications.

Lane, Jan-Erik and Svante O. Ersson. 1987. *Politics and Society in Western Europe*. Beverly Hills, CA and London: SAGE Publications.

Lohmann, Roger A. 1992. *The Commons: New Perspectives on Nonprofit Organizations and Voluntary Action*. San Francisco, CA: Jossey-Bass Publishers.

Marshall, T.H. 1965. *Class, Citizenship, and Social Development*. Garden City, NY: Anchor Books.

Martin, F. 1989. *Common Pool Resources and Collective Action: A Bibliography*, Part 1. Bloomington, IN: Workshop in Political Theory and Policy Analysis.

————. 1992. *Common Pool Resources and Collective Action: A Bibliography*, Part 2. Bloomington, IN: Workshop in Political Theory and Policy Analysis.

Meehan, Elizabeth. 1993. "Citizenship and the European Community." *The Political Quarterly* 64, no.2: 172–186.

Mill, J.S. 1970. *The Subjection of Women*, edited by Wendell Robert Carr. Cambridge, MA.: MIT Press.

Milward, H. Brinton and Hal G. Rainey. 1983. "Don't Blame the Bureaucracy." *Journal of Public Policy* 3, no.2: 149–168.

Olson, Mancur. 1965. *The Logic of Collective Action: Public Goods and the Theory of Groups*. Cambridge, MA: Harvard University Press.

Ostrom, Elinor. 1990. *Governing the Commons: The Evolution of Institutions for Collective Action*. Cambridge: Cambridge University Press.

Raadschelders, J.C.N. 1986. "Coproduction in the Fight Against Youth Unemployment: A Case for Autonomy." *Planning and Administration* 13, no.2: 14–24.

Raadschelders, J.C.N. and T.A.J. Toonen. 1993. *Waterschappen in Nederland: Een bestuurskundige verkenning van de institutionele ontwikkeling*. Hilversum: Verloren.

Ringeling, Arthur. 1993. *Het imago van de overheid*. Den Haag: VUGA.

Rutgers, M.R. 1993. *Tussen Fragmentatie en Integratie: De bestuurskunde als kennisintegrerende wetenschap*. Delft: Eburon.

Scholten, Ilja, ed. 1987. *Political Stability and Neo-Corporatism: Corporatist Integration and Societal Changes in Western Europe*. SAGE Series in Neo-Corporatism, vol. 3. London: SAGE Publications.

Sharp, E.B. 1980. "Toward a New Understanding of Urban Services and Citizen Participation: the Coproduction Concept." *Midwest Review of Public Administration* 14, no.1: 105–118.

Streeck, Wolfgang and Philippe C. Schmitter. 1985. *Private Interest Government*. SAGE Series in Neo-Corporatism, vol. 2. Beverly Hills, CA and London: SAGE Publications.

Tocqueville, A.C. de. 1990. *Democracy in America*, edited by P. Bradley New York: Vintage Books.

Turner, Bryan S. 1986. *Citizenship and Capitalism: The Debate Over Reformism*. London: Allen & Unwin.

Uphoff, N. 1986. *Local Institutional Development*. New York: Kumarian Press.

Wickwar, W. Hardy. 1970. *The Political Theory of Local Government*. Columbia, SC: University of South Carolina Press.

Whitaker, G.P. 1983. "Coproduction: Citizen Participation in Service Delivery." *Public Administration Review* 40, no.2: 240–246.

9

State-Making and Nation-Building: Sovereignty, Church, and Army

Human beings in every society create boundaries. In the earliest hunter-gatherer societies, there were no clear geographical boundaries and people traveled from the one to the other area. We can assume, however, the existence of boundaries of a social nature wherein each member of a group shared a sense of togetherness, *us* versus *them*: *tribes/nations*. In early sedentary societies, boundaries also demarcated the area belonging to one society and not the other: *states*. And soon internal boundaries are defined, mine and thine: *property*. Once such a society acquires a certain size and a government is created, the boundaries of government need to be established: *public and private*. Over the ages social, geographical, property, and public boundaries have been a source of constant dispute and have been resolved in a variety of ways. The major question is always: who or what is vested with the ultimate authority in a given society (whether socially and/or territorially defined) to decide upon matters of strife about area and property?

The first step in understanding the development of government is looking into the relationship between the governed and those who govern. What they want and expect from each other and how they shape those expectations (in other words, what internal boundaries are created) were discussed in chapter 8. In this chapter I will focus on the boundaries within which both the governing and the governed acted.

These boundaries can be defined in different ways, and usually in a combination of ways. First there are *geographical boundaries*, the territory within which government (whether embodied in a person, a group, or an entity) is invested with the highest authority. From this it follows, second, that *legal boundaries* are also defined. The highest authority is circumscribed in customary and/or written law. The ways to use this authority are also laid down in regulations. Once the actions of

191

a ruler go beyond what is commonly considered legitimate, a new ruler or group of rulers may bid for authority. From this it follows that "legal" in the above is not understood in its rather narrow modern and juridical sense, but interpreted in terms of legitimacy which is a social and legal concept at the same time. Legitimacy refers to acts in accordance with accepted standards (legality), that are reasonable and can be justified. Once the use of power by a person or a group in a community is earned, accepted, and maintained, it becomes legitimate authority and expresses a contract between those who govern and the governed. One could argue that power may be based on psychological (the threat of magic) or physical attributes (the threat of muscle), implying that sometimes there are no boundaries as to what the one or those in power may do. However, magic and muscle have their boundaries as well. Power is never absolute and presupposes a two-way relationship. Admittedly, the odds are not always balanced, but there is a point where magic and muscle are feared less then the loss of legitimacy.

In the Western world the context within which government developed was one of continuous refinement of legal and geographical boundaries. The development of legal boundaries is best summarized in the development of the concept of sovereignty (section 9.1), while the development of geographical boundaries draws attention to processes of, at first, state making and later nation building (section 9.2). It is generally believed that the church and army have played a significant role in the state-making process (sections 9.3 and 9.4) and had a bearing on the organizational development of government. In terms of administrative history the modern world starts around the 1800s. Most prominent in that period is the ideological fusion of state and nation into the nation-state, or in Tilly's phrase "the national state" (section 9.5). Given the rise of international associations and supranational organizations (see chapter 10), some argue that the nation-state has had its day. Others counter that the (nation) state is still the dominant focal point for (inter)governmental action. I briefly outline that debate in section 9.5 as well.

9.1 The Concept of Sovereignty and the Rule of Law

In stateless societies authority is based on psychological, moral, and/ or physical coercion. In principle authority emanates from and is part of the community. In situations where authority is monopolized and put to use for the interests of one person or group, the notion of community may come under the fire of that same authority it helped to create. In a situation where the concentration of power in one person or group is accepted by the people, one can speak of authority. In that sense authority is an accepted, legitimate power. In the Western world the notions of legitimacy and sovereignty are intertwined. Given that authority is based on a contract between ruler and ruled it follows that the state can never be the only source of power in a society.

In the High Middle Ages the temporal authority of kings was challenged by and depended upon (sometimes even shared by) representatives of the clergy and the nobility. In the late Middle Ages and the Renaissance, temporal authority of the king depended upon the willingness of the nobility and the merchant elite to cooperate. Even at the heyday of absolutism in seventeenth- and eighteenth-century Europe, when king and territory were perceived as synonymous, the king was never the only source of power in society, sharing it with peers. In modern times government too is the sole bearer of authority, but has to allow the influence of political parties, pressure groups, and interest groups. In all instances a source of sovereign power is identified, while at the same time that power is not absolute. Sovereignty can be understood in at least four ways:

- supremacy of authority to rule;
- royal rank, royal authority, royal power;
- complete independence and self-government (autonomy);
- final, absolute political authority in society.

Understanding institutional development in the Western world requires knowledge about the changing content of the concept of sovereignty.

In the ancient world a notion of sovereignty did not really exist. The ruler was identified with the gods and the law. Some would say that sovereignty was first conceptualized by Aristotle in his idea that some type of superiority should be invested in the law *above* the community, instead of in one person or a group from that community. He understood *polity* as *polis*, a political association encompassing both state and society. The polis concept would find its maximum extension in the Roman Republic: *imperium populi Romani*. The state was a corporation, a *res publica* (public cause), in which the citizen held authority. Public cause (society, community) and state were one and the same, like in Aristotle's notion. With the creation of the notion of *Princeps* (first citizen, 27 B.C., Emperor Augustus) the first stone was laid for a separation of state and society. The title of princeps was linked with that of *imperator* (caesar), a term so far only given to victorious generals. The emperor assumed divine characteristics and stood above the law. Sovereignty in the Roman Empire was equal to the rulers' imperium over the territory. However, in the Justinian compilation of Roman law, the *Corpus Uris Civilis* (A.D. 529), we can find the idea that the authority of the ruler originates in the people. But by then Christian influences had mingled in with the older traditions.

Medieval kingship is rooted in at least three traditions. There is the Greco-Roman tradition wherein the king is head of the commonwealth and strives for the well-being of the state independent of his own personal needs. In the Germanic tradition the king is seen as a body of and bound to the community. In the Christian tradition the king is the Lord's Anointed on earth and bound only by divine and natural law (much like pharao or many other rulers in the most ancient civilizations). St. Paul's observation is clear about the relationship between ruler and subjects:

> Let every soul be in subjection to the higher powers: for there is no power but of God; and the powers that be are ordained of God. Therefore he that resisteth the power, withstandeth the ordinance of God; and they that withstand shall receive to themselves judgement. (Rom. 13: 1–3)

The Germanic ideas about community and kingship were replaced completely by the Christian approach to kingship (at least in theory), as became clear in Alcuin of York (c. 735–804, advisor to Charlemagne):

> And those people should not be listened to who keep saying the voice of the people is the voice of God, since the riotousness of the crowd is always very close to madness. (Letter to Charlemagne, A.D. 800, *Works*, Epist. 127)

It is in this last sense that Carolingian kings from A.D. 769 on would assume the title of *Rex Dei Gratia* (king by the grace of God). On earth a king, however, could not be sovereign since ultimate and supreme authority was claimed by the Church and the Holy Roman Emperor (as the legal successor to the Roman Empire) in the West. For some time the battle for supreme authority raged between these two (see section 9.3 below), but while they were at odds, a third party emerged that was to usurp sovereignty and in the process curtail the supreme authority of church and emperor: the king and his state.

One of the consequences of the strife between spiritual (*sacerdotium*) and secular (*imperium*) authority was the establishment of clear boundaries in the law which in turn provided the basis upon which the modern concept of sovereignty could develop. In order to strengthen the idea that the church embodied the highest authority on earth, the monk Gratian, around the year A.D. 1149, developed a new conception of the law in which two types of law were recognized. Custom could no longer be the basis of law. *Natural law* (*ius*), the first type, was comprised of all principles according to which creation functions: the tendency to search for the good and avoid the evil, the tendency to self-sustenance, and the tendency to live in accordance with one's nature. Thomas Aquinas (see below) would distinguish among *eternal law* (which is known only to God) and *divine law* (revealed in the Old and New Testaments). He considered eternal and divine law the possession of Christians, supervised by the church. Natural law belonged to every human being, Christians and heathens alike. The second type, *positive law* (*lex*, enacted law), was the law of the community that sprang from reason and sociability. Natural law came before positive law. Given that the king was perceived as ruling on behalf of God, he could not be subject to positive law, and thus in essence, was above men's laws. The notion of sacral kingship was still defended in the *Norman Anonymous* of around 1100:

> If therefore the King and the Priest are both, by grace, Gods and Christs of the Lord, whatever they do by virtue of this grace is not done by a man but by a God and a Christ of the Lord. And when the King gives a bishopric or a Priest a kingdom, it is not a man who gives them but a God and a Christ of the Lord. (in Southern, 1975: 91)

Soon this theory would be crumbling. The rediscovery of Aristotle's work and of Roman Law was of great influence. In *Policrates* (1159) John of Salisbury (± 1180) reintroduced the idea of the state as a *res publica*, acting on behalf of the common interest. The true king obeys the wishes of his people, is a servant of the law and is bound to the principles of natural law. Once the king defies those principles and becomes a tyrant, the people can resist and denounce him (tyrant murder is even allowed; repeated in the early-fifteenth century by Jean Petit and the late-sixteenth century by Juan de Mariana). In this formulation the Germanic notion of *contract* and the feudal notion of *diffidatio* (the right to resist the lord in case of breach of contract and/or trust) were now incorporated in the idea of the state or—in Salisbury's words—*princeps* (defined by him as something above ruler and ruled).

The idea that the rulers' power is never absolute and bound by the law can also be found with Thomas Aquinas (1225–1274), probably the most influential of medieval theorists. Aquinas considers two authorities to be universal: the church (i.e, Pope) and the emperor, each with their own sphere of influence and complementary to one another. The emperor embodies the highest secular authority and as *dominus mundi* is called *Majesty*. There is no need for competition among lower temporal rulers. After all, they do not have sovereignty. How they reign is to be decided by the people themselves. Indeed, forms of state and forms of government can vary in Aquinas's opinion, since the oneness of humanity is best served through a plurality of overlapping authorities. This should not be understood in terms of pluralism or fragmented government. Overlapping authority with Aquinas merely refers to the fact that there were at least three authorities: the Pope, the emperor, and the local/regional rulers.

Ideas such as those by Salisbury and Aquinas were carried further. In *Defensor pacis* (1324) Marsilius of Padua (1275–1342) argued that popular consent is the basis for legitimate government. Formulated as such it is the first trace of a notion of people's sovereignty. Padua was very much against papal authority and thus presented a purely secular theory of the state. This befitted the times. Through the study of Roman Law the state was reinvented. The man-to-man system so characteristic of feudalism was replaced by the notion of the people being subjected to the state. The state was supposed to use, control, and regulate the moral power invested in the church. Spiritual power was now subjected to secular power, since all royal power directly came from God, not via the church. Such was argued, for instance, in the anonymous *Disputatio inter clericum et militens* ($\pm$ 1300). The opposite position, that royal power came forth from *sacerdotium* was defended as well as is clear from the papal bull *Unam Sanctam* (1302, see section 9.3). Whatever value faith may have for salvation, it had no business in worldy matters. The legislator, not natural law, was the source of the law, and the legislator was the people as a whole or as represented by the leading part.

The same idea can be found with the Dutchman Philips of Leyden (1325–1382). In his *De cura respublicae et sorte principantis* ($\pm$ 1355) he advocated the strengthening of royal power, not for the person of the king but for the benefit of the state. The church was a national institute and a voluntary organization of the faithful whose authority was restricted to the spiritual realm. The state could employ functionaries who served the interest of the state as servants of the king. And indeed, we have seen how the number of laymen functionaries in central (as well as local) government must have grown considerably from the thirteenth century onward.

With the advent of the state as prime actor in government the idea of universal authority disappeared (see also chapter 10). The Church had laid the foundation for being separated from secular government (see section 9.3 below), and regional lords were challenging the Emperor's authority. While the Emperor remained *dominus mundi* the king was said to possess *imperium* in his own territory: *rex imperator in regno suo*. This then was the moment that temporal authority became sovereign within the boundaries of the state and provided the theoretical basis for the state. Henceforth secular doctrines of the state serve to strengthen the idea that it ascends above individuals. The doctrine of the Two Bodies of the King (as person and as embodying the state) in France and England, the German *translatio imperii*, and the Polish *Corona regni Poloniae* provided the state an aura of invisibility, sustainability, and effectiveness (Pomian 1993: 40).

Now that the papal state had lost the battle for power from the secular lords, who in turn had effectively curtailed the influence of the Emperor in their territory, the most important problem became defining who is sovereign and how sovereignty could be limited. Niccolò Machiavelli (1469–1527) did not leave much room for doubt. In his view it was a principle of *raison d'état* that a prince should be allowed to do whatever he deemed necessary. In *Il Principe* (1512) (*The Prince*, originally *On Principalities*) the *raison d'être* is naked self-interest and pursuit of power. Maintaining and enlarging state power is the goal that sanctifies almost all means: treason, murder, intimidation, demagogy. Machiavelli's cynicism about the nature of men is clear:

> Men worry less about doing an injury to one who makes himself loved than to one who makes himself feared. The bond of love is one which men, wretched creatures that they are, break when it is to their advantage to do so; but fear is strengthened by a dread of punishment which is always effective. The prince must nonetheless make himself feared in such a way that, if he is not loved, at least he escapes being hated. For fear is quite compatible with an absence of hatred; and the prince can always avoid hatred if he abstains from the property of his subjects and citizens and from their women. (Machiavelli 1986: 96–97)

Machiavelli had been a high civil servant under the Medici family in the Florentine Republic, and wrote at a time when the Italian peninsula was fragmented into many principalities, each fighting the other ferociously. His ultimate aim was the unification of Italy, since it was only an absolute monarchy who could end chaos and anarchy. It is with Machiavelli that the idea takes root of a choice between anarchy and absolutism. The ruler as sovereign is completely separated from and the stabilizing and conserving force in the community. In this sense Machiavelli represented more the end-point of a development (defining characteristics of the ruler, a medieval effort) rather than the starting point of something new.

True innovation of thought about sovereignty came from the Frenchman Jean Bodin (1530–1596) whose *Six livres de la république* (1576) were published following a period of civil and religious wars in France. Bodin agreed with Machiavelli that chaos could only be ended when people would accept a central, unlimited, and absolute authority. Unlike Machiavelli, though, he believed that the king is not above the law. Bodin solved the natural tension between ruler and ruled by claiming that the *body politic* encompassed both. The state power is absolute, indivisible, inalienable (in other words, sovereign) and could be invested in one person, a group, or a people. Having thus defined sovereignty, a new problem arose. On the one hand the sovereign is above the law, being the source of law, while on the other hand the sovereign has to acknowledge the (property) rights of corporations. This exposes the major dilemma of absolutist theory: the sovereign as absolute power and source of law (like Machiavelli) versus the sovereign as bound to the rights of corporations (Grotius, Locke). The academic-legal theory of sovereignty had a complement in the popular ideology of *droit divin*. The *divine right* to rule was advocated by the English king James I (1566–1625) in his *Trew law of free monarchies* (1598) which played a role in France where the king became the symbol of national unity. In James's idea the king could not loose the right to rule, not even by a papal decree. This was also defended by William Barclay (*De regno et regali potestate*, 1600) and Bossuet; but resisted by for instance Suarez (see ch. 10). In England national sentiments aligned with parliament, as did the Dutch with the almighty Estates General. England and the Netherlands became strongholds of a constitutional tradition, while France became a centralist state. Bodin's book marks a threshold. Before 1576 sovereignty was seen as a stabilizing and conserving force; after 1576 it was considered a law-creating force. It also marks the transition from a *ständische Monarchie* (estates, feudalism) to absolute monarchy.

The importance of instability in society for the development of concepts also is apparent in England. Having experienced a vehement civil war (1640–1649), Thomas Hobbes (1588–1679) presented the English formulation of absolutism in *Leviathan* (1651). In the mind of Hobbes the sovereignty of the state was unlimited, omnipotent, and concentrated in one center. His line of reasoning is well-known. Initially individuals find themselves in a *state of nature* without a common power or state to enforce rules and restrain behavior. These individuals enjoy *natural rights* and use all means to protect their lives, to do whatever they wish, against whoever they like. The result is a struggle for survival: *bellum omnium contra omnes*. To avoid the risk of early death (through poverty, weakness, war against all) and ensure conditions of greater comfort certain *natural laws* or rules are required. The basic natural law is: "do to others as you would have them do to you" (Luke 6:31). But how can individuals strike a bargain with each other when it may be in the interest of one or some to break it? (the tragedy of the commons, the prisoners' dilemma). To avoid this, the individual surrenders his rights by transferring them to a powerful authority such as the state. The *social contract* consists of individuals handing over their rights of self-government to a single authority on the condition that every individual does the same. When this is the case, the state is formed and accepted by all as legitimate. With the civil war in mind, the choice between anarchy or absolutism did not seem difficult. With Bodin and Hobbes the period ended with the main problem of how to define sovereignty as an abstract principle. Now time had come to apply that principle in the practice of government.

Bodin and Hobbes both considered absolutism as the only possible safeguard against internal instability. Indeed an absolutist state could also provide the external stability so badly needed (see ch. 10), since the defense of the territory could be coordinated in one center. But shortly after Bodin a quite different theory was brought to attention.

In his *Politica methodice digesta* (1603) Althusius (1557–1638) criticized Bodin's royal absolutism and advocated the inalienability of sovereignty of the people. He argued that all relations in social and political life are based on contract. The *social contract* is the basis of every type of human society and is elaborated in custom and law. In the creation of a government by the people to serve the public interest a *political contract* is made. Higher associations develop from the ground up: family, tribe/corporation, local community, province, state. The state is formed through a contract between local communities and/or provinces. In this state the people are sovereign and the Estates serve as the natural representatives of the people. This theory justified the Dutch revolt against Spain. The absolute authority of King Philip II was denounced (1581) and sovereignty invested in the representatives of the United Provinces (1588), basically united in their fight against Spain. Internally each province was sovereign with the *stadholder* (the prince of Orange-Nassau) as unifying symbol. Provinces (backed by the merchant and city elites) and *stadholder* (backed by the nobility) embodied a double kind of sovereignty that in time would produce conflict. For the time being a mixed type of sovereignty of King, Lords, and Commons also existed in England.

In Althusius's theory we can already see a glimpse of the question which was to dominate political theory: how to limit the legitimate scope of state power and protect the individuals' natural rights? How to prevent state intervention in private life. John Locke (1632–1704) addressed this question in *Two Treatises of Government* (1690), written as a justification of the Glorious Revolution (1688). For Locke the individuals' rights and properties came before the authority of social and political organizations. The state was to guarantee the individual rights of life, liberty, and property through maintenance of public order and safety. This point of view provided the basis for the liberal concept of a police or nightwatch state.

The consequence of this line of thinking was the exclusive and omnipotent sovereignty of the people as voiced to the extreme by Jean-Jacques Rousseau (1712–1778) in *Du contrat social* (1762). In Rousseau's conception the state is equal to the body politic of the people and government is nothing but a *mere commission*. Rousseau's theory is characteristically French for its belief in the unity and indivisibility of sovereignty. It marks the transition from a monarchical to a national state in France. His concept of sovereignty is an example of monistic theory, in which sovereignty is invested in either people/electorate, parliament or legislator, or state.

The administrative systems in continental Europe are rooted in the *Roman Law tradition* which is characterized by codification of custom in general laws with detailed provisions, clarity about rules, and a strict separation of the public and the private spheres. The notion of *Rechtsstaat*, to which equality before the law is central, is rooted in Roman Law. This is the case in both unitary and federal systems and allows for differences between individual state-systems. The Dutch Republic was the living example of a more pluralistic theory of sovereignty in which the (con)federation and the states each had their own competence and their own sovereign political power. It inspired people like Hamilton, Madison, and Jay to advocate a pluralist system in the rebellious United States with checks and balances in order to avoid the problems (nepotism, oligarchy, slow decision making) of the Dutch Republic. In a Roman Law tradition, changes in society may call for a change of the text of the Constitution itself. The English and American experience is to be understood as a *Common Law tradition*, where constitutional rules are laid down and individuals propose rules on more specific issues within that constitutional framework. Once an individual's wish had been honored in court, and a ruling concerning that specific issue had been made, that ruling serves as precedent.

In comparison to the Roman Law tradition, this Common Law tradition leads to more juridification of society as illustrated by a higher number of lawsuits and lawyers. This is especially the case in the United States. Furthermore in the Common Law tradition, changes in society can be acknowledged through amending the set of constitutional rules, without actually changing the original text of the Constitution. A system with law based on precedence may lead to a situation that can be described as: *your freedom ends where mine begins* (compare with J.S. Mill's adage—*my freedom ends where yours begins*). When it comes to everyday government the Anglo-Saxon and continental European systems are different in degree but not so much in kind. The difference between a Roman Law and a Common Law tradition mainly concerns the relationship between government and society, and more particularly the role and position of the individual in determining that relationship.

The civil (Atlantic) revolutions of the eighteenth century not only marked the end of the classical *sovereignty debate* but also the end of the process of state-making. Even though few states (in a modern sense) existed at the advent of the nineteenth century the state had become the gravitating point of public life. From then on the state was molded in a constitutional framework that was to curtail the powers of the head of state. In countries where the head of state assumes office upon hereditary right, his/her powers are limited. This is the case in constitutional monarchies:

> The Sovereign has, under a constitutional monarchy such as ours (Great Britain, JR), three rights—the right to be consulted, the right to encourage, the right to warn (Walter Bagehot, *The Monarchy*, ch. 3).

In such a situation executive powers are invested in an independent head of government (a prime minister, as in Great Britain and the Netherlands). This is known as *bicéphalisme* (two heads). In countries where the head of state is elected, he/she may have extensive executive powers as well. That is known as *monocéphalisme* (one head) (Timsit 1976: 351) and found in republics (France, United States). However, there are republics where both head of state and head of government are elected, and the former only performs limited and mostly symbolic functions (Germany).

9.2 Patterns and Models of State-Making and Nation-Building

The concept of nation-state is somewhat ambiguous since in it two phenomena are fused in a manner seldom found in the real world. The concept of state is derived from the Latin *status*, defining a "...sound, prosperous community or a system of ranks or estates, each with its particular rights and duties" (Dyson 1980:25). In the Middle Ages it referred to positions of rank or power (estates: clergy, nobility, merchants). *State*, however, could also refer to a form of property, and so government was considered a form of property (nonseparation of public and private spheres). Under Dutch and French influence *state* in the seventeenth century came to denote authority, privileges and property of government (Dyson 1980: 26–27). Nations may coincide with states, but it is more common that a nation is not a state and a state not a nation. A definition of the *state* usually contains four elements: the control over a well-defined, continuous territory; a relatively centralized administration; differentiation from other societal organizations through the development of permanent and impersonal institutions; and a monopoly over the use of violence through the acceptance of a sovereign authority that can pass justice, and acceptance of the idea that this authority should receive loyalty of its subjects (Tilly 1975). *State-making* (or, *state formation*), then, is the process during which these elements emerge and solidify. *State* is basically a territorial unit. The last element is interesting since it reminds us of the fact that *loyalty* depends on the degree to which the population of a state is more or less homogeneous. That homogeneity is the result of a slow process of *nation-building*, a process of linguistic and cultural assimilation that forges a population into a people and then into a nation. Weilenmann described the elements which turn a population into a people and claims that only a people can become a nation. A population will become a people when a need is perceived to live in their own way (becoming apparent when outside forces limit the satisfaction of needs); when there is a need for and a recognition of a common, shared environment; when there is an interest in the common good; when there is a consciousness of belonging together; and, when common action is taken to maintain the status quo (Weilenmann 1966; Dyson 1980: 129).

A *nation-state* refers to a continuous territory whose sovereignty is recognized and respected both internally and externally and whose people share a strong linguistic, historical, and symbolic identity. Tilly and others argue that countries such as Sweden and Ireland approximated that ideal (Tilly 1990: 3), but that few European countries ever qualified as nation-states. He prefers to speak of *national states*: states governing multiple continuous regions and their cities by means of centralized, differentiated, and autonomous structures (Tilly 1975; 1990: 2). Examples of these are Great Britain, Germany, and France. Even these classic examples never were populated by a homogeneous people, which is what the concept of the "national state" presupposes. Therefore, Tilly recently considered the term *consolidated state* more appropriate and wishes to speak of *state transformation* rather than *state formation* (Tilly 1994: 5–6). He argues that national or consolidated states have only appeared rarely through most of history, most states being nonnational (e.g., empires, city-states) and many nations not being states (e.g., the Kurds, the Jews, the Basques, the Welsh, the Ibo). The introduction of the state as territorial unit of administration during the ages of colonization has done much harm. Especially so in Africa (Davidson 1992) and Asia for in the process of colonization, the local maps were redrawn to suit the European wish for demarcating empire, and disregarding territorial-tribal boundaries which already existed.

States and nations hardly ever appeared simultaneously with dynastic and territorial units built around an ethnic core. We have already seen how state making preceded nation building (ch. 8). The earliest example of a state becoming a nation as well is probably England.

Patterns of State-Making

A distinction can be made between exogenous and endogenous models. An exogenous model of state making describes this development in terms of state intervention in society and penetration of government by society. The external aspects (consequences) of political centralization is the core theme. In an endogenous model of state-making, the process is analyzed in terms of what happens within the state apparatus itself, the process being described in terms of administrative centralization. The focus here is on the internal aspects (consequences) of political centralization.

With the intertwinement of state and society being central to exogenous models, two patterns can be distinguished. First, the French-English pattern of state-making, characterized by early unification of the territory under one ruler and an expansion that starts from one center (Paris, London; twelfth through thirteenth century onward). Centralization is assumed to be fairly easy because of a relatively homogeneous landscape (for instance, well-defined in terms of physical boundaries: sea, mountains) and a certain level of technological development.

Speaking of the single-state pattern, however, Strayer made an important distinction between a unitary state and a mosaic state (Strayer 1966). In a unitary state, like England, central government need not worry about segregation movements of subnational units, nor does it create a large bureaucracy to coordinate and control these subnational units. It is in such a unitary state that a nation can be born, as happened in England in the fifteenth and sixteenth centuries (Greenfeld 1992: 30–87). In a mosaic state, on the other hand, central government is constantly aware of the risk that strong regional princes may strive for independence. Thus the powerful duchies of Burgundy and Brittany were a constant threat to the authority of the French king. It was not until the eighteenth century that France truly became a nation (Greenfeld 1992: 154–177).

Second, the German pattern of state-making characterized by the splintering of a *regnum* (the territory governed by a king) into many states, like happened in the German and Italian lands. It was only at a late stage in history that these lands became unified (nineteenth century), and then partially because of a sense of nationalism. Centralization in splintered territories was difficult because of great diversity in landscape and societies.

Examples of exogenous models of state making are those of Pomian (1993), Tilly (1975, 1990), Rokkan (based on Almond and Verba), and Rostow (1971) (see appendix 9.4). Pomian's study addresses the making of Europe from Roman times up to the present. It is an essayistic study written in the best of the descriptive tradition and analyzes how from the eleventh century onward three stages in the development of the state can be distinguished: the feudal state (eleventh through thirteenth centuries), the *Standenstaat* (the Estates: clergy, nobility, and gentry/merchants, thirteenth to eighteenth centuries) and the national state (nineteenth through the twentieth century).

Tilly, Rokkan, and Rostow discuss phases of development as a theoretical model. Tilly presents a long-term phase model that emphasizes how the political, economical, and cultural unification of the elite (up to the late-eighteenth century) was followed by incorporation of the citizenry at large into the state system through improvements in infrastructure and communications (canals, railroads, newspapers) and later, extension of suffrage, culminating into an unprecedented growth of public service delivery in the twentieth century. His model of understanding (or explanatory model) stresses the capital-raising capabilities of cities and how this funded states, and the concentration of coercion in the state and how this furthered a tightening of central-local relations. Tilly's phase model is based on a combined historical and social science perspective.

Rokkan's phase model (1970, 1975) also encompasses a large number of centuries but departs more from a political science perspective in which participation and representation are core issues. Rostow (1971) presents a short-term model (nineteenth and twentieth centuries) developed from his model of phases of industrialization. His analysis is constructed around the increase of the state's share in the gross national product—the state skimming off more and more of the productive surplus in order to finance public services demanded by a population which is more and more politically emancipated.

Two patterns are also distinguished in the endogenous models of state-making, central to which is the intertwinement and subsequent separation of politics and administration. The English model of state-making is characterized by a unified-decentralized structure with a strong but cooperative local government, a supposed tradition of amateur/semi-amateur self-government, relative restraint on the part of the central state on intervening in subnational government, and a low degree of bureaucratization since a truly separate class of civil servants did not exist. In addition to England (up to the nineteenth century) this was also characteristic for the Dutch Republic (up to 1795). The notion of amateur/semi-amateur government must be approached with caution, though. Fischer and Lundgreen (1975) pointed out how ahistorical and stereotypical this is. In the German-French pattern of state-making, we find a unified and centralized structure with a subordinate subnational government and much less restraint in central intervention. Selection and recruitment of a separate class of civil servants is partially based on prior training. A high degree of bureaucratization is established fairly early. The power of the center becomes apparent in the nature of central-local relations (for instance in France) and in the existence of a standing army (as in Prussia).

The only more or less endogenous model I know is the one developed by the sociologist Elias in part 2 of *The Civilizing Process* (1939, 1982) (see C in the appendix to chapter 4). His model is based on how the governmental apparatus developed between centripetal (centralizing) and centrifugal (dispersing) forces and he illustrates that elaborately with the developments in France.

Each of these authors presents phases of state-making in Western Europe and organizes the facts around a central theme. The general picture that emerges is that of the advent of the state (twelfth through thirteenth century), state-making (thirteenth through eighteenth centuries), and nation-building (nineteenth through twentieth century) with regional variations. States first emerge at the fringes of the European continent: France, England, the Scandinavian countries, and Poland. Spain and Portugal follow in the late-fifteenth century; Russia and the Dutch Republic in the sixteenth and seventeenth centuries. The middle of Europe consisted of myriad principalities all at one time or another belonging to a larger empire: the Habsburg Empire, the Ottoman Empire, and the Austrian-Habsburg Empire. These empires dissolved in the nineteenth and early-twentieth centuries, their territories divided in and among various states.

Patterns of Nation-Building

Nation-building very much strengthened the process of state-making for it provided the internal cohesion the state initially lacked. This internal cohesion is dependent upon an ethnic core. The notion of ethnic core is the one around which patterns of nation-building are constructed. In some Western European countries the state was built around an ethnic core, with other ethnic and regional groups being integrated through a combination of alliance, marriage, coercion, and administrative intervention (such as England and the annexations of Wales in the late-sixteenth century, Scotland in 1707, and Ireland in 1801; and France and its process of overpowering the regional duchies and counties). In such a historical state, a certain amount of autonomy can be possible for the incorporated regions (like the Frisians in the Dutch Republic and the Netherlands; the Catalans in Spain; the Scots in Great Britain; the Québecois in Canada). Twin loyalties do not have to conflict and ethnicity then is a situational phenomenon.

Four other patterns of nation-building have been identified. One can speak of an *immigrant pattern* when a relatively small ethnic group absorbs and assimilates waves of immigrants from various cultural backgrounds into what becomes a territorial state and a political community (examples: the United States, Canada, Australia, Argentina). One *ethnie* (i.e., the English, the Spanish creole) has an historical claim to cultural primacy even when the territory is not yet fully incorporated. In the *ethnic pattern* an ethnie exists prior to the advent of the state and nationalism. They transform into fully-fledged nations with their own territory, economy, and legal system (for instance many African and Asian states before the era of colonization). It might be that some nations are merged into a state (like Yugoslavia). In the *colonial pattern* of state-making, the modern state is imposed from above on an ethnically divided population. Nationalism is used to create a nation out of these divergent *ethnies* (as happened with the creation of African states in the nineteenth century). Sometimes a fifth (*semi-colonial*) pattern is distinguished in which a state is imposed on a population from above, but where that is followed by cultural unification (as happened in Latin America).

It is important to note that when state-making and nation-building are intertwined the result is a *strong state*, to use Migdal's expression (1988). It provides the basis upon which a welfare state can be built, and helps us partially understand that such is much more difficult in a situation where society and state have not merged into a nation or national state. Such mergers occurred in (Western) European countries in a combination of bottom-up and top-down forces, whereas in large parts of Africa and Asia, but also in parts of Europe (Czechoslovakia, U.S.S.R., Yugoslavia) merger was much more a top-down process.

9.3 Church and State in the Middle Ages and the Early Modern World

With the tentative definition of state in mind (see above) we can see how five centuries and more ago the territory of the state was contested, not well-defined, and considered the possession of the ruler; how government was generally not very centralized, with rival centers of power within one realm; how public and private organizations were not clearly separated from one another; and how the state had no monopoly over the use of violence. Around the turn of the millennium Europe consisted of hundreds, if not thousands, of jurisdictions, the Italian peninsula alone hosting between 200–300 city states around A.D.1200 (Tilly 1990: 40). It has been calculated that 500 years later

Europe was divided into at least "…500 states, would-be states, statelets, and statelike organizations" (Tilly 1990: 42). It was in this period that the basic loyalties of people transferred from the church to the secular state (Strayer 1966: 22) and, as I argued before, that the first step was made to separate church and state. While in Byzantium the church was subject to the state, in the West the church freed and even elevated itself above the state (cf. *Donatio Constantini*).

The initiative to define the realms of church and state were taken by Pope Gregory VII (1073–1085) who in a papal decree (1075) revived the Two Swords Theory of Pope Gelasius I (492–496: distinction between a spiritual-eternal sphere and a temporal-secular sphere of power with the spiritual one being superior) and declared that henceforth appointments in religious office were the sole prerogative of the Church of Rome. The fifty years that followed are known as the *Investiture struggle*, settled in the 1122 Concordat of Worms in which the rights Gregory VII had claimed were acknowledged. (Hoyt 1966: 42–43, 227–233). The church could then rely on the population to rally behind its cause, and with the threat of excommunication held a powerful instrument for subduing kings and princes. It would prove to be a Pyrrhic victory, though, since the state indeed would draw back into the temporal sphere and establish a secular government to which the population became accustomed and obedient. When Pope Boniface VIII (1294–1303) confronted Philip the Fair of France and Edward I of England on whether they had the right to tax clergy (without consent from Rome) and laity alike in a time of war, he—and so the church—discovered how far the power of the state had come to reach, and how much even the *local* clergy were unwilling to side against their king for fear of loss of influence. The papal bull *Unam Sanctam* (1302) made the highest claim to papal supremacy ever, but to no avail. Henceforth the state served as the focal point of public life (Hoyt 1966: 505–508). The formal separation of church and state in the law in the late-eighteenth century finalized a process that began more than six centuries earlier.

Meanwhile, the church had profound influence upon the development of the early modern state. To a large extent the innovations in government were modelled after the example of the church (territorial subdivisions from the sixth century on, but mostly since the eighth century; regular council (*curia*) meetings from the eleventh century on; the creation of government departments from the twelfth century on; recruitment of literates) and possibly because of the church. After all, the literate clergy had seen to the preservation of Roman legal thought and many a cleric played a major role in the rediscovery and remodelling of Roman law.

In his almost epic, and certainly seminal, study of the origins of the Western legal tradition, Berman refers to this period as the time of the Papal Revolution in which the new papal conception of *church* "...almost demanded the invention of the concept of the State" (1983: 23; Berman quotes Strayer, 1970: 22) and foreshadowing the Machiavellian *state* signifying a purely secular social order (Berman, 1983: 29). During the Lutheran Revolution the church came to be "...conceived as invisible, apolitical, alegal" and made a "...secularization of law and the emergence of a positivist theory of law..." possible (Berman 1983: 29). This is the background that helps us understand how and why in the protestant states of the sixteenth century (the Low Countries, the German territories, England) the responsibility for many of the social, health, and educational services (see ch. 5) transferred from the church to the state and local government as well as to private associations (see also ch. 8; and Lohmann 1992: 117–118). Education has especially been regarded as the area where state and church interests clashed (Rokkan 1970: 131; Archer 1979), much more so than with other local services. The state either removed control over education from the church as in France and Russia, or it set up a system of competitive nondenominational and vocational schools as in England and Denmark (the four countries analyzed by Archer, 1979: 127, 130). However, hospitals too were subject to strife between religious and secular powers.

> In Northern Europe, hospitals were taken over by public authorities through the seizure of church property during the Reformation or, as in France, during anti-clerical revolution. In Southern Europe, where the Catholic Church maintained a stronger role in hospitals, ownership was not transferred voluntarily to the state, as in Spain and Italy. (Immergut 1992: 56)

In the Netherlands, Germany, and Switzerland private and public hospitals co-existed as a consequence of religious pluralism (Immergut 1992: 56–57).

The extent to which church and state by the eighteenth century had become separate realms, is demonstrated in the following remark by Catherine the Great (1729–1796, Empress of Russia):

> Me, I am an autocrat; that is my trade. And the good Lord will forgive; that is his trade.

The Sovereign and God each had their own competence, indeed God was expected to forgive. Government, though, could play a role with regard to religion as Thomas Paine argued in one of his pamphlets:

> As to religion, I hold it to be the indispensable duty of government to protect all conscientious professors thereof, and I know of no other business which government hath to do therewith." (*Common Sense*, 1776, ch. 4)

9.4 Army and State in the Early Modern World

In chapter 1 I mentioned Strayers's astonishment with the fact that many researchers believe that early modern government was built after the example of the hierarchically organized standing army (Strayer 1975). His observation is correct, as became clear in the preceding section. The army, however, did play a significant role in the process of state-making. That is to say, the presence of a standing army required certain changes in structure and functioning of administration.

In a situation of highly dispersed authorities it was the reciprocal interaction between lord and vassal upon which the state depended. The aristocracy was the military branch of government, much like the judiciary, the chancery and the exchequer embodied the civilian branch of government. In the civilian branch the lord would find his strength, since with the military branch the relationship was rather ambivalent. It is understandable that the aristocracy eyed the growth of royal power with varying degrees of suspicion since it was their power that was under siege. The feudal army was an ad hoc army, difficult to control at times. Due to changes in technology (more firepower), organization (new techniques of laying siege), and finance (securing regular flow of money), lords slowly switched to using mercenary armies of which the fourteenth-century Italian *condottierri* are an excellent example. This example was copied by every European state from the fifteenth to the seventeenth centuries.

Why did European states not immediately turn to creating standing armies? In essence the answer lies with the power the aristocracy still had. Given the ongoing battle between king and nobility, and given that state power was not yet well established, the king would simply not have been able to build a professional army. On the other hand the aristocracy had to accept that it was no longer able to conduct modern warfare. So, while no longer having to rely on feudal support, the king could buy an ad hoc army. It made him a little more independent from the aristocracy, while at the same time it was the aristocracy that commanded those mercenary armies. For a while both parties, king and nobles, were satisfied. However, mercenary armies, too, were hard to control especially when a regular flow of wages was not guaranteed. What king in his right mind would like to have a mutinous and ravaging army on his hands?

Just as much as kings ruled their territory through intermediaries, they essentially used intermediaries for their warfare. Indirect rule (see also ch. 8) was *the* functional principle of the time. And, as Tilly pointed out (1990: 104), indirect rule imposed serious limits upon the state's power. In retrospect it appears that kings first invested effort in bringing the civilian branch of government under their control, strengthening it in the process. And when warfare demanded human and financial resources a medieval king could not even have fathomed because of constant instability among the states in Europe—it became time to bring the military branch of the state under the king's authority.

The modernization of the military through the creation of standing armies started in states with a strong central power like Sweden and Prussia, quickly followed by France, Austria, and Russia. A standing army with a body of professional officers and trained soldiers, a network of fortifications, and the need for regular supplies required a streamlining of the states' finances and a reorganization of central administrative bodies. Indeed, in France for instance, public works' services originated in the military need for better roads and led to the creation of special technical schools (see also section 7.3). The centralization of state power in those countries curtailed the power of nobility and parliaments. This same nobility was offered new career opportunities through the standing army and growing bureaucracy (Pomian 1993: 116). The relationship between military and bureaucracy was especially strong in Prussia. In Tilly's words "...national standing armies, national states, and direct rule caused each other" (1990: 104). With the nationalization of military power in the eighteenth century most European states moved from a system of indirect to direct rule (Tilly 1990: 103).

Maintaining a standing army not only called for a regular flow of weapons and money but also for facilities for veterans and relatives. Health and education of young males became a governmental concern, "thus military reorganization entered a wedge for expansion of state activity into what had previously been local and private spheres" (Tilly 1990: 106). By the end of the eighteenth century the process of horizontal integration (Pomian 1993: 147), in which states positioned themselves in relation to others, was more or less complete. And by then the process of vertical integration, the resolution of conflicts between groups in society, could enter its last stage. For the state still rested on the Estates, it was a *Standenstaat*, even though royal power had succeeded in controlling both the civilian and military branches of government. This power, together with a relatively peaceful international arena (see ch. 10) enabled kings to turn their attention inward. European states shifted from reactive to proactive repression (Tilly 1990: 115), slowly extending the state sphere to assuming tasks that had been the sole responsibility of local government and private initiative. The very strength of state and government guaranteed that vertical integration, through the extension of the suffrage, could be realized without plunging society into disorder.

9.5 Nation and State in the Modern World

The integration of state and society in the nineteenth century under the appeal of nationalism will not be discussed here, since it goes far beyond the scope of this book. But it was nation-building that completed that process of identification of the citizen with the state as it began back in the thirteenth century. The effects of social and cultural unification in tasks, structure and size of government have been discussed in chapters 5–7. At the advent of the twentieth century, and even more so in the two decades following the Second World War, the state is the prime actor in home and international affairs. Yet, some predict that the state has been done for, rendered almost obsolete as a form of political organization in a world that is torn between segregational and integrational forces, between international and regional interests.

Internationalization has stripped the state of its distinguishing characteristic: sovereignty in the classical sense. Hoffmann has already pointed to a changing content of "sovereignty,"

> The nation-state today is new wine in old bottles, or in bottles that are sometimes only a mediocre imitation of the old; it is not the same old wine. What must be examined is not just the legal capacity of the sovereign state, but the *de facto* capacity at its disposal: granted the scope of its auhtority, how much of it can be used, and with what results? (Hoffmann 1966: 911)

In this respect Jackson and Rosberg (1982) made a useful distinction between *juridical* and *empirical statehood*, indicating an appearance of formal sovereignty in international law, while at the same time that sovereignty is, *de facto*, being dismantled. Whether the state has outlived itself in contemporary politics can not really be addressed without attention for the development of international relations (see next chapter).

9.6 Literature

The literature on state-making and nation-building is extensive. The studies by Bendix (1977), Tilly (1975), Deutsch and Foltz (1966), Eisenstadt and Rokkan (1973) have not lost their relevance. More recent are studies by Cohen and Toland (1988), Hall (1987) and Olson (1982). An excellent theoretical discussion of the concept of state both in its historical development and its contemporary meaning is provided by Dyson (1980). His study is all the more important because of the explicit comparative approach. Much literature is available about the development of the early state, although this falls outside the scope of this chapter (Claesen and Skalnik 1978, 1981; Claesen 1991; Eisenstadt 1986, 1988). A general introduction to the medieval state is provided by Strayer (1970), Tipton (1972), and Ullmann (1966). Introductions to state-making and nation-building in specific regions and countries of the world are numerous (see bibliography).

The development of the welfare state in Western nations, which contributed so much to the fusion of state and nation, is addressed in such general studies as Flora and Heidenheimer (1984) who provide a descriptive analysis and by De Swaan (1989), from the Elias's school, who discusses welfare state development in the theoretical framework of processes of collectivization. Several national studies about welfare state development are available.

The development of the notion of sovereignty in the Western world is handsomely traced by Hinsley (1966), a somewhat older but still very useful source of information. Bendix (1973) is also relevant in this respect. Mentioned several times already, the study of Berman (1983) is a must for anyone who wishes to understand the origins of Western law. At the same time it provides a stepping stone to further understanding of the influence of the church. The studies by Hill (1970) on church and state in the Middle Ages, by Tellenbach (1979) about church, state, and society at the time of the investiture struggle, provide other interesting introductions. But of course Tierney's studies (1967, 1980, 1982, 1988) are invaluable. Written in the classical historical style of *Kritische Filologie* he carefully analyzed the meaning of various concepts in the context of the formation of constitutional thought. The studies mentioned above also pay attention to the influence of church organization on government. Also numerous are the studies about the influence of the military on state-making. Vagt's study (1938) is among the first of these type of investigations. Roberts's (1955) study of the military revolution in the period 1560–1660 is useful although somewhat dated. Parker's more recent study (1988) covers a larger period (1500–1800). Without doubt Tilly's book (1990) presents the larger framework within which the meaning of the military build up can be understood.

References

Archer, Margareth S. 1979. *The Social Origins of Educational Systems.* Beverly Hills, CA: SAGE Publications.

Dyson, Kenneth H.F. 1980. *The State Tradition in Western Europe: A Study of Idea and Institution.* Oxford: Martin Robertson.

Hobbes, Thomas. 1968. *Leviathan,* edited by C.B. MacPherson. Aylesbury: Hzell Watson & Viney, Ltd.

Hoffmann, Stanley. 1966. "Obstinate or Obsolete? The Fate of the Nation-State and the Case of Western Europe." *Daedalus* 95 no.4: 862–915.

Hoyt, Robert S. 1966. *Europe in the Middle Ages,* 2d. ed. New York: Harcourt, Brace & World Inc.

Jackson, Robert H. and Carl G. Rosberg. 1982. "Why Africa's Weak States Persist: The Empirical and the Juridical in Statehood." *World Politics* 35 no.1: 1–24.

Locke, John. 1986. *Two Treatises of Government,* edited by W.S. Carpenter. London and Melbourne: Dent.

Machiavelli, Niccolò. 1986. *The Prince,* edited by George Bull. Bungay: Richard Clay Ltd.

Migdal, Joel S. 1988. *Strong Societies and Weak States. State-Society Relations and State Capabilities in the Third World.* Princeton, NJ: Princeton University Press.

Mill, John Stuart. 1983. *On Liberty,* edited by Gertrude Himmelfarb. Bungay: Richard Clay Ltd.

———.1984. *Utilitarianism, On Liberty, and Considerations on Representative Government,* edited by H.B. Acton. London and Mel bourne: Dent.

Pomian, Krzysztof. 1993. *Europa en de Europese Naties.* Amsterdam: Uitgeverij Wereldbibliotheek. Translated from *L'Europe et ses Nations.* Paris: Gallimard, 1990.

Rousseau, Jean-Jacques. 1986. *The Social Contract and Discourses* edited by G.D.H. Cole. London and Melbourne: Dent.

Southern, R.W. 1975. *The Making of the Middle Ages.* London: Hutchinson & Co.

"The State of the Nation-State." *The Economist* 22 December 1990, 73–76.

Strayer, Joseph R. 1966. "The Historical Experience of Nation-Building in Europe." In *Nation-Building,* edited by K.W. Deutsch and W.J. Foltz, 17–26. New York: Atherton Press.

Timsit, Gérard. 1976. "Modèles administratifs et pays en développement." *Revue International des Sciences Administratives* 42, no.4, 350–356.

Tocqueville, Alexis de. 1990. *Democracy in America*, edited by P. Bradley. New York: Vintage Books.

Weilenmann, Hermann. 1966. "The Interlocking of Nation and Personality Structure." In *Nation-Building* edited by K.W. Deutsch and W.J. Foltz, 33–35. New York: Atherton Press.

10

International Relations:
Between Universal Authority
and Balance of Power

Universal authority and balance of power cannot coexist. When different peoples accept the universal authority of one institution, *horizontal integration* (the establishment of relations with other nations/states) is of a rather unimportant nature. Certainly, independence plays a role but that is only a relative independence from neighbors, since all adhere to one higher, universal authority. When that universal authority crumbles for whatever reason, horizontal integration becomes the need to establish an absolute independence from neighbors. When universal authority *above* states is no longer acknowledged and looses its mediating function, a mediation system *between* states must be established. In the period that the foundations for modern government were laid, Europe was divided into many principalities and united in and regulated by the universal authority of the Pope and Holy Roman Emperor. We have seen that new authorities arose, seeking to establish sovereignty within their own territory (ch. 9). We have also seen how that simple model of government—king, council, and field agents— disappeared and was replaced by a more elaborate apparatus (chs. 6 and 7). That same new government took new tasks upon itself (ch. 5) and all in the name of independent and absolute authority.

Government systems are different from region to region, adapting to the unique balance of power between groups in each region. The structural and legal similarity of secular governments in Europe, ultimately guided by universal authority, was replaced by a diversified system in which governments developed their own ways and means of protecting independence. Each government fought for survival on two fronts. At home where central authority had to balance its interests with traditional social power groups (ch. 8) and abroad where central authority was required to maintain independence from other—equally expansionist—authorities. Civil war, rebellion, and interstate war were common in Europe between 1300–1700.

Understanding the development of government in Europe requires knowledge of what happened in the interstate arena. On which basis did the new sovereignties redefine international relations? First, in the world of ideas a body of international secular law emerged (section 10.1). Second, in the world of interstate relations a balance of power politics evolved (section 10.2). And third, an expansionist policy was pursued to generate revenue and establish geopolitical dominance (section 10.3) which in turn unleashed even more interstate rivalry. Both in Europe and abroad governments have relied on and have been confronted with the influence of nongovernmental organizations. Their importance for the development of government also requires some discussion (section 10.4). The traditional periodization of international relations that marks the Napoleonic era as a time of transition (Carr 1985; Holsti 1974) is up for revision. In terms of international relations a period of universal authority (1100–1300) was followed by a long period of balance of power politics (1300–1945/1989). And only recently governments' abilities to set aside rivalry and channel their might into an authority above the states, in order the preserve peace, has been put to the test. Does the world again have the opportunity to develop a truly universal authority, but now on a secular basis? (section 10.5).

This chapter is based on the references mentioned at the end of the chapter. Only when a specific thought is taken from one author will I mention that in brackets. However, there is so much more literature. I limit myself here to discussing the main issues insofar as they pertain to the development of government in Western nations.

10.1 From Pax Dei to Pax Gentium: A Body of International Law

After the fall of the western Roman Empire (A.D. 476), Europe literally lost touch with the world (see also section 10.2 below) and became a *free-for-all* territory. First from the East, then from the South and the North, *Europe* was invaded and raided. From the mid-eighth century, however, Europe slowly came back on its own feet. The Mores were halted at the Pyrenees and the Vikings appeased with large land possessions (Brittany, Sicily). The revival of the western Roman Empire during Charlemagne's reign was short-lived, but from Otto I

(936–973: the first Holy Roman Emperor) onward, and in conjunction with the church, stability returned. The imperial crown was assumed to be a universal secular authority (that was never really established) while the Papacy managed to establish such in the spiritual realm. The sword and the cross were a most powerful tandem holding and guarding universal authority, neither disturbed nor challenged by the petty strife among the minor lords. Such was their might that they successfully enforced a *Pax Dei*, a peace because of God's will basically concerning relations between individuals. The *Treuga Dei* (the Truce of God) referred to a period of peace when warlords were not supposed to fight. At first this encompassed only Saturday afternoon to Monday morning, but later came to encompass more days of the week. The Peace and Truce of God spread from France all over Western Europe (eleventh and twelfth centuries).

We have already seen that from the thirteenth century on states were nibbling away at the edges of universal authority and in the fourteenth and fifteenth century emerged as the new power factor. The Pope's role in establishing a settlement between Portugal and Spain in 1493 (section 10.2) can be regarded as the last twitch of a decaying system of international relations. The demise of universal authority was confirmed in the event of the 1648 negotiations for the Peace of Westphalia, conducted between states representatives. But, long before this scholars had already turned their attention to the problem of how to fill the vacuum following the end of universal authority.

International relations had been based on God and Nature, and so international *law* hovered *above* states. Divine and natural law were still important, but a body of positive, man-made, law had already developed within territories. Its complement between states had yet to be designed. It was no coincidence that the foundations of a body of international law, building on the work of medieval thinkers, were laid by the Spanish and the Italians who were among the first to recognize the need for stable relations in the European as well as the colonial theater. Scholars such as the Spanish theologians Francisco de Vitoria (1480–1546) and Francisco Suárez (1548–1617) and the Italian Albericus Gentili (1552–1608: author of *De jure belli libri tres*, 1598) emphasized how a state is a member of a universal society and can never be completely independent. And so international relations, too, were redefined in the positivist framework of customs and agreements. This outlook on international law quickly dispersed throughout Europe. Jean Bodin stressed the necessity of it given the existence of sovereign states independent from papal and imperial supremacy. Contemporaries did not think, though, in terms of filling a void. They were practical thinkers, seeking to provide certainty at a time of civil and interstate war both inside and outside Europe. Grotius's (1583–1645) *Mare Liberem* (1609) was written with a keen eye for Dutch trading interests and its competition with Spanish, Portuguese, English, and French trade. Unaware of it he founded the law of the sea that is enforced up to this day and has a bearing upon, for example, the Antarctic Treaty. His major work, *De jure belli ac pacis libri tres* (1625) is not so much a starting point of something new as it is the conclusion of the search for a custom and agreements based international law: *Justice does not only bind men, but also nations.*

While around the 1600s the theoretical foundations for absolute sovereignty were laid, and in practice the secular and spiritual spheres of power were separated, the theoretical justification for dissecting the spiritual from the secular in international relations had to be formulated. In that sense, building on Hugo Grotius, the German jurist Samuel von Pufendorf (1632–1694) separated law from theology. His *De jure naturae et gentium* (1672) established a new body of law: the law of nations. And this work was carried further in *Le droit des gens; ou, Principes de la loi naturelle, appliqués à la conduite et aux affaires des nations et des souverains* (1758) by the Swiss lawyer Emmerich de Vattel (1714–1767). His book has been called the first modern book of international law. Vattel viewed Europe as a political system, united in diversity and held together by their mutual interests and relations. It displayed an awareness that the international community lacked the legal sanctions, regarding the use of violence, that the state had developed. In his work the positive approach to law merged with the balance of power notion. It appears to be no coincidence that the Pufendorf and Vattel studies were published in the same period that a separation-of-power notion developed within the state (ch. 9).

Law bound states and nations, but also governments and citizens. The international *Pax Gentium* found a domestic complement in *The Rights of Man* (1791–1792) of Thomas Paine (1737–1809) advocating basic freedoms of the individual. In domestic politics the rights of man were translated into systems of representative government based on popular elections, and representative administration based on equal rights to access government both in terms of influencing it (interest groups) and of employment in the civil service (ch. 8). The rights of man would enter the international arena with the United Nations 1948 declaration. This concluded the development of international law from *among* states to one *above* states.

At this point it is impossible to say whether ideas about proper domestic government influenced ideas about international relations or *vice versa*. If anything, it was an intricate and delicate exchange born out of the states' need to balance between domestic and foreign powers.

10.2 From Cathedral Race to Armaments Race: Balance of Power and Spheres of Influence

During the period that a body of international secular law was developed, the economic power shifted from the Mediterranean to the Atlantic. Even though England and France were already regarded as important in terms of military power around 1400, as far as the economy was concerned they were no match for the Venetians and Genovese who had established trade relations with the far east, and the Genovese and Catalans who travelled into West Africa and the Indian Ocean. As all over Europe domestic trade came to be regulated by government (ch. 5), international trade could not be protected by government regulation. In lack of the papal and imperial umbrella, protection was sought in negotiated alliances. It is important to note that the prince

> lacked a specialized network of bureaucrats and diplomats who could undertake technical negotiations in international commerce before the sixteenth century. They were thus limited to ratifying agreements arranged by the city-representatives, who were really competent to negotiate them. (Blockmans 1978: 206)

It will be no surprise that early diplomacy owed its origins as much to the development of trade networks in Europe as to the protection of political and military interests. The diplomatic service of the city-state of Venice, for example, sprang from a commercial organization. Indeed, Italian city-states were the first to send out emissaries all over Europe, assigned to further and protect the cities' trade interests (Holsti 1974: 53–58, 175–176). This example was quickly copied. Unlike Charlemagne's *missi dominici* these "modern" diplomats travelled in pump and circumstance, the one mission even more magnificent than the other in dress, promises and what have you. And all this to display the wealth and power of the sovereign in whose authority they travelled.

The *cathedral race* was over. No more would cities compete for the favor of God through the construction of ever higher Gothic churches. Instead, states raced for each other's favors, and in case such was not honored they made sure they could use military threat. The mediation of the church was called upon for the last time when the Catholic Spanish and Portuguese crowns settled their colonial disputes in the Treaty of Tordesillas (1493) which divided the world into a Spanish and Portuguese sphere of influence. It was the first time in early modern history that *spheres of influence* were established through diplomacy. Some 150 years later the Peace of Westphalia (or, Treaty of Munster, 1648) was the first international conference on matters of state, negotiated by hundreds of diplomats, a new breed of officials. From then on international relations became the playground of Foreign Offices and their diplomats. The Peace of Westphalia also represented the first exercise in redrawing the map of Europe.

The eighteenth century was peaceful in comparison to preceding centuries, but ended in a period of revolution and reform. In the aftermath of this revolutionary period, international affairs were settled in the manner previously developed. At the June 1815 Conference of Vienna, the political map of Europe was once more redrawn, reestablishing the balance of power between Austria, Prussia, France, England, and Russia. Directly following the Vienna Congress, the Holy Alliance (September 1815) was created, the first supranational peace organization of the modern period. Both were used as foundation for a balance of power politics, known as the Concert of Europe, and strengthened when the principle of intervention to preserve peace was formulated in the Protocol of Troppau (1820). It was on this basis that Western powers intervened in the Crimean War (1853–1856).

The Protocol of Troppau also had global implications in the sense that it gave voice to the idea of *Europe for the Europeans*. And so, when the Holy Alliance attempted to intervene in and inhibit some of the Latin American liberation movements, U.S. President James Monroe countered effectively, declaring *America for the Americans* (1823, Monroe Doctrine). Again the world was divided into two major spheres of influence. In *splendid isolation* from the European continent (the echoes of which are also relevant in understanding British participation in the European Union [EU]), the British had opposed the intervention principle in Troppau. Great Britain sided with the United States and quickly acknowledged the new independent states. Britain appeared to have forgotten what had brought about the American Revolution, for Canning spoke: "I have created the new world to restore balance." Furthermore, the British had learned from the American Revolution as is apparent in the creation of the Commonwealth (mid-nineteenth century), emphasizing cooperation among nations, and in conferring the dominion status to white emigration colonies.

The unification of the Italian and German states into two states (1861 and 1871) upset the careful balance maintained by the Concert of Europe. Bismarck instigated a politics of alliances which, at first, united imperial Europe (Russia, Austria, Germany) but, in the longer run, proved to be feeble. Alliances were not lasting, but shifting. The German empire embarked upon a continental block policy, strengthening its colonial and military power so that it could match—if not be superior to—Great Britain. The German naval construction program can be considered the first major armaments race. It became more and more difficult to maintain a balance of power politics, for the five powers in Europe no longer acted as one and various small regional crisis in the 1890–1910 period increased an atmosphere of crisis. Both in Europe and the colonies the situation was unstable, heightening a sense of insecurity. The assassination in Sarajevo (1914) was the proverbial drop in the bucket already filled to the full.

Immediately following the Great War the political will to establish some international forum was large and skillfully played upon by U.S. President Woodrow Wilson. The League of Nations and other international organizations were created with a view of furthering world peace. Despite all good intentions the League failed to meet its objective, partially because some of the major powers (U.S., U.S.S.R.) did not join, and partially because the nationalism that had resulted in the Great War flared up again, both in economic (tariff barriers) as well as in political-military terms. Various international conferences were convened to address the issue of how to maintain a balance of power, but to no avail. The first international conferences on disarmament were held in 1932–1933. The wingless force of the League became painfully clear when it could not play a role, mediating or leading, in the prevention of Japanese, Italian, and German expansionist politics which ultimately led to the Second World War.

This war provided the opportunity for a fresh start. The League was recast into the United Nations that from the outset addressed other issues besides military and political issues, such as agriculture, health, and development. International relations became simplified as well. There were no longer several major powers, but a bipolar world evolved where the shots were called by the United States and the Soviet Union. In this bipolar world new alliances were wrought. During the 1950s the various regions of the world became covered with a patchwork of military, political, and economic alliances, often related to one of the two spheres of influence. However, several of the New States allied into a neutral cooperation (Bandung Conference, 1955). The United Nations' ability to mediate was often put to the test and criticized, but, in retrospect, could not properly function in a world still caught in balance of power politics.

Even in the early-1980s few would have foreseen the sudden end to this, although—again in retrospect—the signs were there (Poland's Solidarity, 1981; Gorbachev's *glasnost* and *perestroika*, 1985). It was not until 1989, with the clearance of that symbol of division, the Berlin wall, that the world suddenly faced a whole new arena that it is still struggling to come to terms with. Global issues such as terrorism, arms control, environmental management already existed. In this respect, 1989 represented no change. Nor did 1989 represent change in terms of the actors in the internationalized world. In this sense, too, there was continuity (see section 10.4). But with bipolarism gone the issue of universal authority, or international sovereignty (Baker and Bivin Raadschelders 1990b), became all the more pressing. In terms of international relations the establishment of a universal authority invested with supranational sanctions may be necessary. Together with the organizational challenges involved in addressing both global and regional issues (Baker and Bivin Raadschelders 1990a) individual governments face a formidable task, a task which will be carried far into the twenty-first century.

10.3 The Expansion of Western European States: Colonization and Decolonization

Expansion is not exclusive to Europe. As Naroll (1966: 329) remarked: "It is only when we carefully study comparative history that we perceive in earlier centuries the existence of multiple international systems, each linked together, as ours is, by direct trade and diplomatic relations and governed by common concepts of morality." In the ancient world imperialism was synonymous with the acquisition of control over the civilized world. The Greeks had colonies, and it frequently happened that they seceded from their mother town. The Romans managed to create the largest empire in Western antiquity. Roman colonization, though, took place in areas where governments had already been in place. Through colonization a network of trade relations was created that stretched from southern and eastern Europe and North

Africa, via the Middle East, Central Asia and India to China. Greeks, Phoenicians, and Arabs traded among one another and with India. The Persians traded in the area known as the fertile crescent. The town of Merv in the Persian Empire was the starting point of the famous silk route that ran north of the Himalayas into China. More important, however, were trade relations on sea. The world consisted of three regions: Asia, Africa, and Europe. When unity in Western Europe dissolved (A.D. 300–500), trade relations between Europe and other areas in the world disappeared.

Under the rule of Charlemagne (764–814) a revival of trade occurred, but only for a short period of time. It would not be until the consolidation of the Holy Roman Empire that a new trade network could be established. During the Middle Ages colonies in the Greek manner were created by the Vikings, the Arabs, and the Italians. In 1259 German trade towns created a union that was formalized in 1358 and became known as the Hanseatic League. The league dominated trade in northwestern Europe. In the south of Europe, Italian cities started to dominate the Mediterranean and Levantine trade. Venice controlled the trade in herbs and spices; silk trade came under the influence of the Genovese. Genoa profited greatly from the new order and peace established by the Mongols in central Asia (Genghis Khan, 1206–1227). Gradually trade caravans penetrated further and further into Asia. Most notable and known is the journey of Marco Polo (1254–1324), who started on a journey to the Far East in 1271 and finally arrived in China in 1275. In the meantime, trade relations had come into existence with African states in the north and northeast of Africa (colonized by Islamic countries). The expansion of the Arab people was primarily based on religious motives: the Islamization of the world.

China and Europe had a great need for spices; trade routes were dominated by Arabian and Indian merchants. Meanwhile Portugal had started to explore Africa's western coast. In terms of European expansion this heralded a new phase: trade relations shifted from the Mediterranean to the Atlantic.

Conditions for Western European Expansion

Was Western European expansion unexpected? Some think it was, but in the eyes of contemporaries it was not unexpected at all. Each next step appeared to be a continuation of what had become common. In geopolitical terms however, the expansion was relatively unexpected.

Around the 1400s Europe did not seem destined for empire, and presented no match for Islamic states such as Mamluc Egypt or Negro Mali, nor for the Aztec and Inca empires in the Americas, or the Ottoman, Moghul, and Chinese Empires in Asia Minor and Major. Indeed, the most important cultural centers of the world could be found elsewhere (from a European point of view: in the periphery). Still, the question as to how unexpected Western European expansion was should be answered negatively for several reasons.

Under feudal rule and leadership of Pope and Emperor Europe had become a fairly stable region since the late-eleventh century. The *Pax Dei* and *Treuga Dei* were lived up to. Ever since the late-eleventh-century lords in Europe had their eyes on the Middle East, geared to the extermination of Islam, but also to canalize internal aggression outwardly. The European population was growing from the middle of the eleventh century onward. The old Roman roads were renovated and new roads were built. Also in the eleventh century, cities started growing in the northwest but especially in the south of Europe. As economic and military power increased, demand for better equipment generated further technological development: mills, gunpowder, the development of new and faster ships, new navigation techniques and instruments. Besides all this the Europeans had a natural inclination for exploration, as compared, for instance, to Japan which was much more an autarchic society. Western Europe was innovative. West European expansion started as a continuation of the expulsion of Islam from Europe (the Spanish *reconquista*). Besides this, Portuguese and Spanish traders were interested in a direct link with the gold and slave markets of West Africa.

The First Imperial Age, 1419–1760

In general, the first period of colonization can be divided into two parts. During the first part (1419–1550) the Portuguese and the Spaniards took the initiative, and so we can speak of a Mediterranean phase. During the second part (1550–1760) the Dutch, English, and French states became dominant and this could be called the Atlantic phase.

The Portuguese came first. Henry the Sailor (1396–1460) instituted the first sailors' school of the world and made plans to sail around the west coast of Africa in order to fight the Islam and to establish direct trade relations with the gold and slave markets already mentioned. They had a *pied-à-terre* in the Atlantic: in 1419 they had discovered and occupied the Madeiras. The same thing happened with the Azores

(1431) and Cape Verde (1445). In 1448 the Portuguese opened the first trade factory on the Atlantic west coast: Arguin. Many would follow, like the well-known Elmina in 1482 (later taken over by the Dutch). In a period of one-and-a-half centuries, many such trade factories would be established along the west coast, as far south as Luanda.

The Portuguese did not limit their interest to West Africa. Bartholomew Diaz sailed around the Cape of Good Hope in 1487; Vasco da Gama sailed to Insulinde in 1498; Cabral discovered Brazil in 1500; between 1505–1515 the Portuguese created a trade empire with factories on Goa, Ceylon, Malaya, and the Indonesian archipelago. All in all, Portuguese expansion looked east. Not surprisingly, for the Indonesian isles would prove to be the richest prize.

The Spaniards started in the late-sixteenth century. The Moors had just been expelled from Granada (1492) when Isabel of Castilla financed an expedition that was to search for a western sea route to Indonesia. The expedition was commanded by Christopher Columbus. He "discovered" America in 1492, and undertook four more journeys to the West Indies until 1504. Other expeditions followed. Amerigo Vespucci sailed the coasts of Middle and South America several times to reconnaissance the coastline of the new continent (1499–1502). During the years 1519–1521 the Aztec empire was subdued by Hernando Cortez. Pizzarro managed to conquer the Inca empire in the years 1531–1532. Colombia was conquered between 1535–1538. In the 1540s, the Spaniards also invaded North America. Spanish expansion therefore was mainly westward oriented.

It was not without reason that the Portuguese looked east and the Spaniards west. Pope Alexander VI had mediated the division of the world into two parts, a Portuguese colonial empire and a Spanish one (Treaty of Tordesillas [1493]). The dividing line was some 370 miles east of the Azores (straight through Brazil). In the middle of the sixteenth century Portugal and Spain were the superpowers of the world. At the same time the western border-states in Europe came to prominence. The middle of Europe rapidly lost significance, divided as it was among many principalities. At first the Dutch, French, and English were involved in ocean trade as merchants (1555: the guild of the Merchant Adventurers) or as pirates. In the second half of the 16th century, however, their governments became involved. And it is during this period that the *Europeanization* of the world started.

Common for the Portuguese-Spanish type of colonization was the creation of trade factories and the division of the colonial territory in administrative districts. The Spanish territory in South America for instance was divided in four vice-royalties (New Spain, 1525; Peru, 1542; New Granada, 1717–1740; Rio de la Plata, 1776). The viceroy acted as representative of the crown, but his powers were checked by a council (the Spanish Council of the Indies, created in 1523; the Portuguese Council of India, 1604). To regulate and maintain trade as well as to prevent fraud, both states created a special government department for colonial affairs (the Spanish *Casa de la Contratacíon*, 1503; the Portuguese *Casa da India*, 1505–1506). A viceroy governed with his own exchequer, judiciary, and chancery. Each vice-royalty was subdivided in captain-generalships, districts and urban and rural communities. The Portuguese territory in Brazil constituted one viceroyalty divided into four captain-generalships. Also characteristic was the fact that the Spanish and Portuguese settlers mingled with the indigenous population.

States in northwestern Europe had not been sitting idly by. From circles of the Merchant Adventurers, the English Muscovy (1554), Levantine (1581), and East India Companies (1600) were created. The Dutch followed suit with the creation of the East India Company of 1602 and the West India Company in 1621. These companies were created for reasons of glory and gold, and for the destruction of Portuguese-Spanish hegemony. Religious motives were no longer of interest. While the Treaty of Tordesillas established a status quo, such a system did not exist between England, France, and the Dutch Republic. Indeed, they carried their differences into the colonies. The Dutch fought the Spaniards and Portuguese wherever they could (Spain and Portugal were united in a personal union, 1580–1640). Notorious is the capture of the Spanish silver fleet by Dutch admiral Piet Heyn in 1625, an act of piracy but "legitimized" by the fact that Spain and the Dutch Republic were at war. In 1624 the Dutch conquered part of Portuguese Brazil. Dutch rule there would last until 1654 when they lost it to the English. The Dutch also acquired Curaçao, Surinam, and the Indonesian isle of Java. The French-English rivalry was mainly concentrated in North America. Both countries were active in the eastern part of territories presently known as Canada and the United States. In a colonial war, France was finally defeated (1754–1763) and North America became predominantly Anglo-Saxon. The English also occupied Senegal (formerly French) and Florida (formerly Spanish).

The way in which these three nations colonized territories differed from the Portuguese-Spanish trade factory occupation under state rule.

In South America, India and Indonesia the chartered company type of occupation dominated: autonomous companies based on private initiative administered the area with support from the state. In North America, and later Australia, a type dominated in which the imported population considered themselves to be equal to the people of the motherland, hence an occupation pattern which differed. The English wanted land for farms and plantations and expelled the original population from its land. Labor force was supplied by negroes. A mingling, such as had taken place in the Portuguese-Spanish territories, hardly occurred. However, these *white* colonies were governed, or better, came to be governed, in a rather centralized way by their respective mother countries. From 1678 on, French colonies were brought under military rule under a crown-appointed governor who was aided by civilian *intendants* (as in the mother country: ch. 7). In the English territories colonization was left to those who wanted to pursue it. For a while the New England colonies more or less governed themselves. English royal governors had "...no more than a skeletal bureaucracy..." (Scammel 1989: 164). By the time England wanted to assert its authority more persistently (Navigation Act, 1651) it was too late. English authority proved to be more fragile than any of its fellow sovereigns overseas. Against this background it is not surprising to see that the first movement for independence occurred in North America.

There is one thing the administrations in the various colonies had in common. In need of money, all mother countries who *settled* instead of only traded, came to use colonial office as a means of income in the course of the seventeenth century. Colonial office offered tremendous opportunities to those adventurous and eager enough to acquire wealth, and so gave tremendous opportunities to governments trying to establish new loyalties through the sale of office and tax farming. In Europe and the colonies both the sale of office and tax farming were widespread phenomena.

The First Decolonization, 1760–1830

The North American population considered themselves to be on equal footing with the motherland, and the colonial elite resented the paternalism with which the motherland governed the colonies (Boston Tea Party, 1773). The call for independence became increasingly louder. I will not speak of the American War of Independence (1776–1779) in detail. The outcome is well-known, but Great Britain did learn an important lesson: if you grant a colony a certain amount of autonomy, it may not want to secede from the commonwealth. Between 1867 and 1920 several British colonies received the dominion status.

The independence movements in the South American territories drew their inspiration from two sources. It was spiritually inspired by the Free Masonry movement that spread rapidly across the continent in the second half of the eighteenth century. Freemasons pointed to the fact that the colonies were exploited on behalf of the motherland's economies. The American and French revolutions provided a second source of inspiration. And when Napoleon invaded Spain and Portugal in 1808, the South American colonies seized the opportunity to declare independence: Argentina (1810), Venezuela (1811), Paraguay (1811), Brazil (1815), Chili (1818), Great Colombia (1819; split into Ecuador, Venezuela, and Colombia in 1830), Mexico (1821), Bolivia (1825), Uruguay (1828). The fact that Simon Bolívar had spent some time in France was of import as well. His ideas on democratic government inspire Latin American nations up to this day. Independence was also declared by several Central American countries. With the exception of Brazil, all countries gained sovereignty after extremely violent revolutions. Independence was followed by civil wars. Notwithstanding the fact that each country adopted a constitution, fighting between classes, races, and parties continued. In political terms these civil wars can be characterized as wars between unitarians and federalists, constant change of revolution and counter-revolution, anarchy, and military dictatorship. Many of the old South American aristocracy emigrated back to the mother country.

The Napoleonic era gave new opportunities to Great Britain. The French and the Dutch were driven from their possessions in India and South Africa. At the time of the Congress of Vienna, Great Britain ruled the seven seas as the undisputed most powerful country of the world.

The Second Imperial Age, 1830–1914

For this period we need to distinguish between developments in South America on the one hand and Africa and Asia on the other. As mentioned above many South American countries experienced almost ongoing civil wars (1830–1890). There was some European intervention. England seized the Falkland Isles (1833) off the coast of Argentina. The French, English, and Spanish governments intervened in the Mexican Civil War (1858–1861) which culminated in the proclamation of the Mexican Empire under French rule (1861). This would only last for two years, since the French had to withdraw under pressure of the United States (the Monroe Doctrine). Central America became the backyard of the United States, and they intervened several times in internal affairs (1890–1930, 1960–present: Nicaragua, Haiti, Dominican Republic, Cuba, Panama, El Salvador).

European colonialism changed in the nineteenth century under the influence of industrialization. Two periods can be recognized. The first period is characterized by the opening up of the world for Europe and especially for British trade (1830–1860). Several countries were forced to open their borders: Turkey and Egypt (1838), Persia (1841), China (1842), and Japan (1858). In the second period, a large-scale political and economic division of the world took place (1880–1914). In one sense it was peculiar to see that Europeans, and especially the English, developed a mood for empire building, since liberalism was the dominant political theory of the mid-nineteenth century. In the eyes of diehard liberals, colonization was a residue of mercantilism, the trade-capitalism sponsored and supported by the state. Colonization was no longer needed, they reasoned, since free trade had been realized. Why this discontinuity with the liberal past? There are two groups of theories about this: Eurocentric theories, and periphery theories.

In the Eurocentric theories, we find economic and political theories. The economic theories stress either trade-imperialism or capital-imperialism. The trade-imperialism theory emphasizes the need to find new colonies to safeguard trade (protectionism), and discover and exploit new natural resources. The capital-imperialism theory emphasizes the need to find new areas for investment, so that European surplus-capital had a profitable outlet. Governments go into less stable areas for cheap labor and they create the right conditions by annexing territory. From a political point of view some stress the *imperialism of the rulers*, required because of the new balance of power in Europe (the unification of Germany and Italy). Others focus on the so-called *imperialism of the masses,* claiming that imperialism provided an outlet for nationalism.

Those who adhere to periphery-theories claim that Eurocentric explanations of imperialism fall short of recognizing some characteristic features of internal developments in colonies. In their view, imperialism was an answer to problems caused by the intensified contact between Europe and the rest of the world. When the status quo was threatened in an area (through the expansion of another colonial country; or through resistance of the local population against colonial rule, as was the case in North Africa and Southeast Asia) the colonial powers entered into formal colonization.

In addition to the Eurocentric and periphery approaches, we must not forget the influence of developments in philosophy and political economy. Colonial powers expected to gain independence from worldwide competition, independence from economic crises in other countries, and a stabilization of the standard of life. From a Malthusian perspective the risk of overpopulation in Europe was experienced as extremely threatening for the European standard of life. In the second half of the nineteenth century the so-called *Volk-ohne-Raum* ideas gained prominence. The rise of new states such as Italy and Germany strengthened the idea that only great peoples with a lust for power (Nietzsche) who were prepared to struggle for survival (Darwin) were destined to rule over inferior, colored people (racism is a nineteenth-century invention). At the end of the nineteenth century this attitude received a somewhat positive slant in Rudyard Kipling's "the white man's burden," the moral duty of the whites to civilize the colored underdeveloped world. In the Netherlands this culminated into the so-called ethical policy in the Indonesian archipelago (Eymeret 1973).

The second phase of colonization differed from the first one in two respects. All colonial powers created subservient states with a governmental structure derived from the motherland. In this period colonial states became governed through apolitical administrations wherein a system of indirect rule dominated, more so in English and Dutch territories than in the French (Van den Doel 1994: 24, 451–452). In addition, the entire world was brought under the influence of Europe. For the first time the interior of Africa was colonized. France advanced into territories in northwest Africa, Madagascar, and Indochina. Great Britain acquired a series of countries from Egypt to South Africa in an almost unbroken line (German East Africa broke their chain), and they expanded into India, Burma, and Malaysia. The Belgians penetrated the Congo Basin, while Italy occupied Libya and Somalia.

With the advantage of hindsight it is evident that these enormous empires were very fragile. None of the colonial powers were capable of administering such massive areas adequately. No one, however, would have believed this at the end of the nineteenth century.

The development of infrastructures (railways, harbors, schools, hospitals), the economic exploitation of the colonies (plantations, industries, markets), together with the disturbance and extermination of ancient local traditions (to a degree far larger than in the first imperial age), not only created new desires, but also resentment and open hatred. This provided the fertile soil for the second period of decolonization.

The Second Decolonization, 1945–1975

On the eve of the Second World War, the colonial empires were still virtually intact. Only parts of the German and Ottoman empires had gone into the hands of England and France, as mandate-governed countries. Would it have been possible to foresee the changes soon to come? Indeed, here and there one could see a hesitant but persistent growth of nationalism (as in Indonesia). Yet, none of the colonial powers could have foreseen what was about to happen, this is because of three aspects of the postwar decolonization: the war itself, scope and speed. First, the war. The Japanese attack of colonies in Asia was successful and showed the weakness of the colonial empires of France and England. The psychological influence of their success was as great as in 1905, when the first Asian power (again Japan) managed to defeat a European power (Russia). Second, the scope. The second phase of decolonization encompassed the whole world. Asia came first (1945–1954), then Africa (1957–1964), and finally an aftermath in Africa (Angola, Mozambique in 1975) and South America (Surinam, 1975). Third, the speed. None of the colonial governments had expected such a speedy downfall of their power. They were not at all prepared.

A monocausal explanation of decolonization is impossible, if not undesirable. Some scholars stress factors such as a *rational calculus of profit and loss*, the loss of will to govern other countries, or the decreasing inequality in the balance of power. Others emphasize the fact that European ideas on freedom and equality had taken root in the non-Western world: declaration of human rights, the idea of self-determination, the idea of class-struggle. The Japanese occupation in Asia certainly offered ample opportunity to wrestle free from colonial suppression. After the war the colonial powers were not able to reinstitute their might. Nationalist movements had gained momentum (Indonesia) and enjoyed international support (United States, United Nations). The balance of power in the world had definitely changed. European hegemony, already challenged after the First World War, was a thing of the past. The United States and the Soviet Union were at the helm. The Third World was dragged into the Cold War: the Russian "visit diplomacy" vis-à-vis the American intervention to prevent the spread of communism (Korea, Vietnam), and (after 1961) American development aid (Peace Corps).

As stated, the colonial powers did not leave voluntarily. France was entangled in combat in Indochina and defeated at Dien Bien Phu (1954). The Dutch were forced to leave Indonesia after U.S. and UN opposition to the so-called police actions. The English left India after years of civil disobedience (Gandhi). The nationalist movements were the strongest where a large white settler society existed and/or substantial European investments were at stake (Belgian Congo, now Zaire; Algeria). The struggle for independence was most violent in Algeria, Rhodesia (Zimbabwe), Kenya, Angola, Mozambique, and Guinea Bissau.

The second phase of the postwar decolonization was heralded at the Conference of Bandung (1955) when twenty-nine Afro-Asian countries declared themselves against colonialism. The Suez War of 1956 generated strong nationalism in Africa. The Gold Coast (Ghana) was the first country to gain independence (1957), but political emancipation did not lead to economic emancipation and independence. It is in this sense that the Ghanaian president Kwame Nkrumah spoke of neocolonialism for the first time (1965).

The history after independence has been one of instability. To fight corruption several military coup d'états were successfully undertaken: Egypt (1952), Pakistan (1958), Ghana (1966), Indonesia (1967), Uganda (1971). The New States tended toward authoritarian forms of government: sometimes a military dictatorship under the leadership of kings (Ethiopia, Arabia) and politicians who were educated in the west (Nehru, Bourguiba), but also army officers (Nasser), nationalistic leaders (Nkrumah, Sukarno), and trained communists (Ho Chi Min). The occurrence of regional, tribal, and religious conflict fed the political instability (Ibo's in Nigeria and Biafra). The fact that the standard of living in many countries of the Third World is around or below subsistence level does not add to stability (famine in the Sahel, Ethiopia, Bangladesh).

Most New States have adopted the government structure of the former mother countries. In countries with a British background, the *district officer* is a key official, and municipal councils were created with limited influence. There is no strict separation of the legislative and executive bodies. In countries with a French background one will find a strongly centralized structure in which the provincial governors (*prefect*) and local mayors enjoy great discretionary powers. The influence of the state is still large, but nongovernmental actors have become increasingly important. (Anyone studying developments in the Third World should incorporate the enormous growth of multinational corporations.)

In any event the institutional development of the New States is influenced by Western-based political systems. Recently, however, institutional development in the New States increasingly includes notions of indigenousness. In the search for indigenous institutions governments will have to be aware of what kind of system they want to work with. In this respect three types of political systems have been distinguished (Cleaves 1980: 282–285). *Open systems* are characterized by large autonomous influences, agencies, and so forth. The distinction between public and private is blurred (Colombia, Peru), and governmental policy is in line with the needs of the dominant group. In a *closed system* the idea dominates that the state knows what is best for the people. There is a sharp cleft between central elite and local population (Brazil), and the state uses negative sanctions. Finally, in *intermediary systems* one may find less concentration of power at the center, more vertical political structures (party systems), and lively corporatist and/or societal structures (tribe, army, church, village). Classes and privileged groups behave according to what is typical for open systems (Mexico).

10.4 From State-Centric to Transnational Relations

For much of Europe's administrative history international relations were perceived in a state-centric perspective. The Peace of Westphalia constituted what had already been in the pipeline. International relations were high politics, affairs of the state. There were, however, other actors in the international arena, most notably the Hanseatic League, and later, the various trade companies for the colonies, operating with the silent or explicit approval of their governments. The Hanseatic League, however, was truly transnational as was the Fugger banking institution, while the seventeenth-century East and West India Companies were national trade corporations (Koch 1993: 138). It was not until the mid-nineteenth century that intergovernmental (Wallace and Singer 1970), multinational, and supranational organizations emerged in large scale.

International organization is a generic concept, encompassing intergovernmental relations (between governments), supranational relations (above governments) and multinational relations (between and above nongovernmental actors) (see table 10.1 for examples).

TABLE 10.1
Types of International Associations

	Purpose	Legal expression	Level	Members
UN	Peace	Treaty	Intergovernmental	States
IMF	Aid	Statute	Intergovernmental	States
EU	Union	Treaty	Supranational*	States
OAS	Alliance	Treaty	Intergovernmental	States
Red Cross	Aid	Statute	Multinational	Nations
Jews	Independence	Commitment	Multinational	Individuals
Greenpeace	Preservation	Statute	Multinational	Individuals
Shell	Monopoly	Statute	Multinational	Corporations
OPEC	Monopoly	Treaty	Multinational	Corporations

* Depending on point of view. For a unitarian the supranational aspects dominate, while a federalist would emphasize the intergovernmental aspects.

Literature on the meaning of international organizations for politics and policies in the global system is substantial and it would be futile in this context to attempt a complete discussion. Studies have been published about intergovernmental organizations (IGOs) and intergovernmental conferences (e.g., Haas 1958; Daltrop 1991; Jurrjens and Sizoo 1984). The growth rate of IGOs has been enormous (figure 10.1 below) (Wallace and Singer 1970).

The importance of nongovernmental actors is underlined in as many studies (e.g., Mansbach et al. 1976) and in the fact that within the International Institute of Administrative Sciences a working group on NGOs has been active. Relevant for this book, however, is the matter of the effect of internationalization on the development of government, though I allow myself to be impressionistic.

Basically the distinction between public and private—a legal construct, never a model of reality—has visibly lost meaning in a world where governments are but one among many actors in the international arena which have an impact on public policy. The influence of multinational corporations on economic policy is as large as that of its historical predecessors, the colonial trade companies. The influence of multinational associations on, for instance, environmental policy cannot be disregarded. What is more, international politics is no longer privy to governments, with nongovernmental national actors—often united multinationally—communicating directly with supranational bodies and with other governments. International relations have be-

FIGURE 10.1
Number of Nations and IGOs in the International System
in Successive Periods 1815–1960

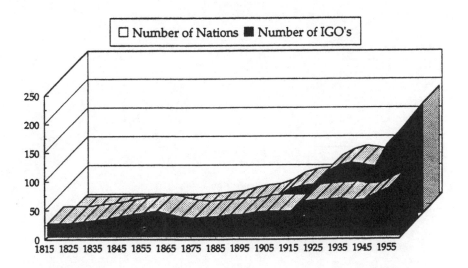

Source: Wallace and Singer, 1970: 277.

come transnational relations. Foreign affairs no longer have a distinct public and private sphere with a state-centric and a multinational pattern. Rosenau argues that a state-centric and a multicentric structure coexist in, what he calls, a bifurcated world structure (Rosenau 1992: 20). Given the degree of intertwinement between state and other nongovernmental actors it could be argued that a pattern of transnational interaction is now reality (figure 10.2).

The impact of this development on the structure and functioning of individual governments can hardly be overstated. International organizations, of whatever nature, pressure national governments to concur, for instance, with such general issues as human rights and with such specific issues as transposition of international regulations into national legislation. After all, international sovereignty does not (yet)

FIGURE 10.2
Patterns of State-centric, Multinational, and Transnational Interaction

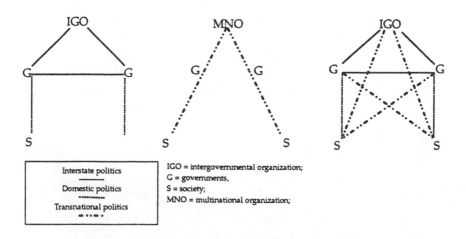

Interstate politics _____	IGO = intergovernmental organization;
Domestic politics •------•	G = governments,
Transnational politics ●••●•	S = society;
	MNO = multinational organization;

Source: Keohane and Nye 1971: 333–334

exist, and intergovernmental and supranational organizations still depend very much on the cooperation of the national states. Governments have also taken on new tasks, like in the field of environmental policy. By now we live in a world where almost every national public and private organization is a member of some international organization, or at least monitors closely the events that may have a bearing on their own situation. The international perspective also serves as a lever for achieving national goals. It is in this light that Hoffman (1966: 909) and later Milward (1993) argued that the creation of the European Community (EC), now the European Union, did not herald an age of supranationalism, but was rather an attempt to preserve traditional values and interests, such as the *state* and agriculture. It is also in this light that problems of metropolitan governance are now interpreted.

The economic competitiveness of the region in Europe provides a case for settling national problems of administrative organization at regional level (Hendriks et al. 1994; Jones and Keating 1995). Indeed the importance of subnational regions for the execution of supranational policy requires that thinking move beyond such ideologies as subsidiarity, and pays attention to the grubby details of organization and division of labor according to criteria of scale and accessibility (Van Braam and Raadschelders 1993). All the more so since states are increasingly aware of the power of subnational regions (Daltrop 1991: 119). The fact that the balance of power has lost meaning brings this transnational perspective even more to the forefront, all the more because it is clear that governments alone can no longer hope—in fact it is futile to try—to solve public problems by themselves.

10.5 Between Internationalization and Regionalization: A Secular Universal Authority?

Approaching the end of a (Western?) millennium, the world is as dynamic as ever and political leaders face challenges beyond the boundaries of the national state. After the demise of universal authority, states in Europe struggled among one another to assert their independence and enlarge their territorial sphere of influence. In this struggle ad hoc alliances were formed, shifting according to the need of the day. Once boundaries had been more or less established in Europe, the various states went elsewhere for profit, for settlement, but always for glory. Both in Europe as well as abroad, a balance-of-power politics was pursued in which the world was divided into spheres of influence—not that these were respected. Colonial possessions regularly changed hands and in this respect, Europe exported its regional differences. Starting in 1648, and actually materializing in the early-nineteenth century, the balance-of-power politics conducted by states as warlords was complemented by international diplomacy by states as peace seekers. In the twentieth century this culminated into the creation of some economic alliances (EU, Comecon, NAFTA, EFTA), beside the military and political alliances. The necessity of old-style military alliances has declined, but the importance of political and economic unions has not. These alliances can be found in world regions that have geographic, cultural, economic, and political ties. Several of these are multipurpose organizations, engaging in activities of a political, economic, military, and social nature. Examples are the Organization of American States (OAS), the League of Arab States, and the Association of Southeast Asian Nations (ASEAN) (Bennett 1991: 222–223). Functional regional organizations are the largest group, based on economic, political, and social cooperation (EU, Benelux, EFTA, OECD) (Bennett 1991: 238–239).

With the end of a bipolar system the world stands at a threshold: are we able to create a universal authority, assuming that such is necessary? (See table 10.2.) Regional organizations may have an important role to play in preventing regional conflict through principles of strict nonintervention in the internal affairs of member states, peaceful settlement of differences, and respect of territorial integrity. This is based on developing a mutual outlook on foreign policy, the creation of goodwill, and a sense of community. Sometimes an international organization is needed to help create and maintain internal stability. It appears that with the United Nations Transitional Authority in Cambodia (1992–1993), the UN is deploying international civil servants beside a military presence to help a country's administration in preparing a stable environment for free and fair elections (Goulding 1993; Steensma 1994). Such activity of the UN is not based on universal sovereignty, but its involvement is accepted and thus legitimate. Research on the possibilities of an international civil authority for peacemaking and keeping is still in its infancy (Leurdijk 1993). However, more and more people consider the creation of a United Nations Standing Army Force (UNSAF) (Rostow 1993), which would constitute a new-style military alliance. The UN is nowadays more involved in internal (civil) conflicts than it is in international wars, for which it was originally designed. A UNSAF may help to contain refugee flows, one of the spillover effects of internal strife, because the influx of refugees in surrounding or faraway regions may threaten security and stability in those regions. Canada, Denmark, France, and the Netherlands are among the countries that advocate a UNSAF.

The effects of internationalization are, curiously enough, most felt at the regional level, that is the various regions within the states. Consciously or not people react to what they see happening. The window to the world is wider than ever before (CNN). Are governments and administrations converging into larger units? Elias's model of state formation seems to suggest so (see chs. 4 and 9), but there is an important countercurrent. No matter how transnational public policy has become, the basic geographical orientation of the individual is still regional. The consequences of transnational public policy are evalu-

TABLE 10.2
Types of Intergovernmental Relations

	Purpose	Legal Expression	Level
Alliance	Economic/military	Treaty	Interstate
Balance of Power	Military/political	Mutual acceptance	Interstate
Commonwealth	Economic/military	Commitment/treaty	Interstate
Union	Various	Treaty	Supranational
Universal Authority	Peace	Law	International

ated in the context of the need of the region. Given the demographic, physical-geographic, and economic differences between regions, the policies pursued ought to be framework policies, the details of which are to be filled in according to the need of the region. Another counter-current is the existence of regional cultures within states with marked linguistic (Frisians and Dutch in the Netherlands, Walloons and Flemish in Belgium) and/or socio-cultural identities. Regional movements in Europe even united in multinational organizations such as the Bureau of Unrepresented Nations (1977) and the Free European Alliance (1978) (Daltrop 1991: 119). In some cases these regional cultures have become secessionist movements (Basques, Serbs).

Europe in the Middle Ages was a Europe of the regions. The regional identification may have submerged in the march of the state, but must always have been there, given the fact that they rise to importance again (Harvie 1994: 419–421). Not only in Europe but everywhere, the states' boundaries created on a drawing table are perceived as artificial. From an administrative point of view the region is rehabilitated as the level where policies are executed. The principle, or even ideology, of subsidiarity (see ch. 8) underlies this. Administrative structure and functioning still needs to adapt to this new world of international and regional levels. If the world is now united in diversity it needs a universal authority, and this can only be negotiated by the states. The state created an international political world and played an important role in redistributing welfare within their territories and in the process strengthened the regions, the regions from which states and governments in the Western world came forth some 800 years ago.

Almost thirty years ago Deutsch argued that "...with the awakening to political activity of an increasingly larger proportion of mankind, environmental pressures and the potential pressure of foreign-input messages will grow in most countries in the world" (Deutsch 1966:

16). His observation has proven to be correct, especially when looking at such international activities as instigated by the Club of Rome (1972) and the Bruntland Committee (1986). His words, however, acquire a specific meaning in the current context of searching for a new world order that has to deal with the fact that *foreign-input messages* sometimes cannot be presented without the use of force. Deutsch also argued that the impact of internationalization may become visible some thirty years after certain internationalizing events (1966: 26). In the 1966 bipolar world no one could have predicted the changes from 1989 onward. And so we may have to wait another thirty years to see what decisions of the 1989–1994 period significantly influenced further internationalization. It will be interesting to see to what extent an international authority can be created and maintained.

References

Armstrong, David, Lorna Lloyd, and John Redmond. 1996. *From Versailles to Maastricht: International Organisation in the Twentieth Century.* London: MacMillan Press Ltd.

Baker, Randall and Julie Bivin Raadschelders. 1990a. "Reshaping the Old Order: the European Community, the United States, and the New Century." *International Review of Administrative Sciences* 56, no.2: 285–303.

Baker, Randall and Julie Bivin Raadschelders. 1990b. "The Public Administration of International Sovereignty." *Australian Journal of Public Administration* 49, no.1: 75–81.

Bennett, A.L. 1991. *International Organizations.* Prentice-Hall International, Inc.

Bos, J.M.M. van den. 1991. *Dutch EC Policy-making: A Model-guided Approach to Coordination and Negotiation.* Amsterdam: Thesis Publishers.

Braam, A. van and Jos C.N. Raadschelders. 1993. "Europe and Its Regions: An Administrative Structure for Public Service Delivery." In *International Perspectives on Regional Development and Regional Organization,* edited by John L. Mikesell, 181–199. Bloomington, IN: School of Public and Environmental Affairs, Indiana University.

Carr, Edward. 1985. "States and Nationalism: The Nation in European History." In *States and Societies,* 3d ed., David Held, et al. Oxford: Oxford University Press, 181–194. Taken from E.H. Carr. *Nationalism and After,* 1945.

Cleaves, Peter S. 1980. "Implementation Amidst Scarcity and Apathy: Political Power and Policy Design." In *Politics and Policy Implementation in the Third World,* edited by Merilee S. Grindle, 281–303. Princeton, NJ: Princeton University Press.

Daltrop, Anne. 1991. *Political Realities: Politics and the European Community,* 8th ed. London and New York: Longman.

Deutsch, Karl W. 1966. "External Influences on the Internal Behavior of States." In *Approaches to Comparative and International Politics,* edited by R. Barry Farrell. Evanston, IL: Northwestern University Press, 5–26.

Fieldhouse, D.K. 1984. *Economics and Empire, 1830–1914.* London: MacMillan.

Goulding, M. 1993. "The Evolution of United Nations Peacekeeping." In *International Affairs* 69, no.3, 451–464.

Haas, Ernst B. 1958. *The Unity of Europe: Political, Social and Economic Forces 1950–1957.* Stanford, CA: Stanford University Press.

Harvie, Christopher. 1994. "Historical Perspectives on European Regionalism." In *Die Politik der dritten Ebene: Regionen im Europa der Union,* edited by Udo Bullman, 419–428. Baden-Baden: Nomos Verlagsgesellschaft.

Hendriks, Frank, J.C.N. Raadschelders, and T.A.J. Toonen. 1994."Provincial Repositioning in the Netherlands: Some Models and the Impact of European Integration." In *Die Politik der dritten Ebene: Regionen im Prozess der EG-integration,* edited by Udo Bullman, 147–160. Baden-Baden: Nomos Verlagsgesellschaft.

Hoffmann, Stanley. 1966. "Obstinate or Obsolete? The Fate of the Nation-State and the Case of Western Europe." *Daedalus* 95, no.4, 862–915.

Holsti, K.J. 1974. *International Politics: A Framework for Analysis,* 2d ed. London: Prentice-Hall International, Inc.

Jones, Barry and Micheal Keating, eds. 1995. *The European Union and the Regions.* Oxford: Clarendon Press.

Jurrjens, R. and J. Sizoo. 1984. *CSCE Decision Making: The Madrid Experience.* Den Haag: Martinus Nijhoff.

Keohane, R.O. and J.S. Nye. 1971. "Transnational Relations and World Politics." *International Organization* 25, no.4: 331–340.

Koch, Koen. 1993. "Beyond the 'New Paradigmatism': Some Traditional Thoughts about State-formation, Integration, World Polity and War." In *Over Staat en Statenvorming,* 137–156. Leiden: DSWO Press, 137–156.

Leurdijk, Dick. 1993. "Options for a Civil Authority of the UN." *Internationale Spectator* 47, no.11: 662–672.

Mansbach, Richard W., Yale H. Ferguson, and Donald E. Lampert. 1976. *The Web of World Politics: Non-State Actors in the Global System.* Englewood Cliffs, NJ: Prentice-Hall.

Naroll, Raoul. 1966. "Scientific Comparative Politics and International Relations." In *Approaches to Comparative and International Politics,* edited by R. Barry Farell, 329–337. Evanston, IL: Northwestern University Press.

Rochester, J. Martin. 1986. "The Rise and Fall of International Organization as a Field of Study." *International Organization* 40, no.4: 777–813.

Rosenau, J.N. 1992. *The United Nations in a Turbulent World.* Boulder, CO: Lynne Rienner Publishers, Inc.

Rostow, E.V. 1993. "Should the UN Charter Article 43 Be Raised From the Dead?" *Global Affairs* 8, no.1: 109–124.

Scammel, G.V. 1989. *The First Imperial Age: European Overseas Expansion, c. 1400–1715.* London: Harper Collins Academic.

Shaw, Michael. 1986. *International Law.* Cambridge: Grotius Publications Limited.

Steensma, Hans. 1994. *Blauwe boorden voor de vrede: Politiek-bestuurlijke aspecten van de VN-operatie in Cambodja.* Unpublished Masters Thesis, University of Leiden.

Wallace, Michael and J. David Singer. 1970. "Intergovernmental Organizations in the Global System, 1815–1964." *International Organization* 24, no.2: 239–287.

Wayne, C., W.C. McWilliams, and H. Piotrowski. 1990. *The World since 1945: A History of International Relations.* 2d ed. Boulder, CO: Lynne Rienner/London: Adamantine Press.

11

Past Lessons, Current Trends, and Future Challenges: Administrative History for a Changing World

At a trivial level of observation it appears that the solutions to problems of governance have always been the same: property, territory, and function are defined, and interaction is regulated. As we begin to look into how we define and regulate, a wonderful diversity unfolds. It then becomes clear that an array of possibilities exist from which we can choose.

In this book I have attempted to explore a field of inquiry that is both interesting and useful. In order to get my bearings on the present and to develop ideas about future challenges to governance, I had to start with the past. Developments in the past can be addressed in the distant composure of the scholar. Understanding of the present and assessing challenges in the future represents, at best, an intelligible judgement. In this chapter I address the position of administrative history in contemporary administrative science and will frequently refer to earlier chapters.

The development of administrative history as a field of research within administrative science has been decelerated because of three reasons. The first reason I mentioned in the introduction to this book: an emphasis of postwar administrative scientists on the present and the future. The second reason is that for a long time, administrative science was embedded in administrative law and political science, and research questions pertaining to the past reflected a legal/political interest. As I hope to have shown throughout this book, administrative history as part of the discipline of administrative science can develop and has developed quite a different set of questions and approaches. The third is that public administration has sometimes been regarded as the poor relative of business administration. There is little room for historical inquiry when "public" and "private" management methods are not distinguished from each other.

In this chapter, I pull the main lines of argument of this book together. I look again into the meaning of administrative history for contemporary society. I addressed this question in chapter 1, but in rather abstract phrases. It is now possible to be much more concrete. First I look into what the study of administrative history implies and position it within the field of research. In section 11.2, I briefly discuss the position of public administration vis-à-vis business administration in a historical context. In section 11.3, I describe what current developments have taken place in administrative history. Administrative scientists are looking increasingly into the past. This is not surprising given that administrative science has once again become a full-fledged discipline, looking for both intellectual roots and valuable insights. In this section I discuss what type of research is characteristic for administrative history.

Secondly, I present a middle-range theory concerning the growth of government. In doing so I reverse my line of argument in the previous chapters by starting with the context (chs. 8–10) and then moving into the effects (chs. 5–7) (section 11.4). Thus we can understand why government has become the largest single actor in any state system, with the largest possible clientele (and entire citizenry), with the largest possible range of wishes and demands it seeks to meet, and with the largest body of employees. Governments' greatest challenge these days is the reconstruction of the welfare state. This makes necessary a summary overview of the development of the welfare state (section 11.5), as well as an assessment of what challenges lie ahead (section 11.6). It is all the more important since the rescue of the welfare state is supposed to be a government responsibility. Whatever the reasons, we have come to rely upon governments' capability for much more than the simple protection of life, liberty, and property. And because of this, governments have come to look for expert counsel.

11.1 Expert Counsel on Public and Private: Public Administration and Business Administration in Perspective

Given governments' contemporary monopoly in guarding the framework for internal and external stability of society, there is a constant demand by government officials for expertise. Practitioners have to deal with the pressure to speedily present reforms that will work. They have found specialists who are eager to supply, administrative scientists among others. The specialist, though, walks a fine line between being a scholar and being an advisor. At the worst the "advisor" may come with "quick-and-dirty" solutions; at best the advisor presents an intellectual appraisal of pros and cons of certain options. The politician is left with the responsibility of making a choice in such a manner that what is advantageous to some will not be (too) detrimental to others (the Pareto optimum). The true scholar is bound to balanced reasoning and cannot present one-sided choices for absence of a black-and-white reality.

In the past it was argued that problems of governance could be solved by applying a simple set of management principles borrowed from business administration. The major flaw in this approach was that government was not recognized as representing something entirely different than business. The general management functions are alike for public and private organizations, but the differences are much more important (Allison 1982: 15–22). Thus the idea that everything will improve as long as government reforms according to principles of business administration is simplistic of not infantile.

Business administration has had profound influence on public administration, especially so in the United States. Given that in the last five decades, American administrative science evolved into the touchstone for administrative science in other countries, it is necessary to reflect somewhat on the nature of administrative science. Contemporary public administration is a relation of political science (England), business administration (United States) or of administrative law (France, Germany, Italy). The "roots" in the Netherlands are both in political science and law. Reforms in (local) government were the result of corrupt administration (United States), or of growth of local government (continental Europe). The reforms in state and local government in the United States between 1900–1940 have been justified in terms of enhancing efficiency. "Apply business management principles and all will come round with government" became a panacea, enthusiastically followed. The *National Performance Review* of U.S. Vice President Al Gore et al. (National Performance Review [NPR]) testified to this influence:

> From the 1930s through the 1960s, we built large, top-down, centralized bureaucracies to do the public's business. They were patterned after the corporate structures of the age.... (NPR, 1993: 3)

Fortunately the NPR also recognized that these management philosophies had been developed for the private sector, and as such hold little problem-solving promise for today's challenges of governance (NPR, 1993: 8). But both in North America and Europe the renewal of administrative science started from local government reform, attempting to create a more useful academic input.

In light of history, business management was only briefly (1900–1960) an example to public management, and not "through the ages" as the National Performance Review claims (1993: 8). Until the major codification efforts at the turn of the 1800s, there existed no clear demarcation between public and private (ch. 7). Trade was (at best) organized in guilds and was always regulated by government. Of the "national" trade companies in the seventeenth and eighteenth centuries, several were "private" (for instance the Dutch East and West India Companies) but they could not have functioned without the "benevolent" supervision of government. In fact, it is inconceivable that there was such a thing as private management in a mercantilist economy. Not only were large "colonizing" companies government controlled or regulated but through guilds, small-scale trade and manufacturing were controlled as well. Public and private were very much intertwined, financially, organizationally, and in terms of the people who pulled the strings. Governments invested in trade companies. Top functionaries often held positions both in government and in trade. What is more, both government and private organizations were overrun with corruption, fraud, and nepotism (ch. 10).

The rapid financial successes of industrialization almost succeeded in making some in the twentieth century believe that the standard for public administration ought to be business administration, disregarding such obvious phenomena characteristic of government as division of power, multiple inputs, immeasurable outputs, and lack of a clear measurable motive such as the profit motive in business. Those who argued that the business ideology is not the yardstick for evaluating government performance were many (e.g., Miller 1984: 13–14; Lane 1994). In the welfare states and even in the developing countries public administration is no longer defined in terms of efficiency for maximum profit but in terms of efficacy, accountability, and performance for maximum welfare.

Before industrialization everything was public and private at the same time. This was certainly the case in the Middle Ages. A distinction between the royal and the state household became apparent only toward the end of that period. In the early modern period business was contracted out in some cases (the trade companies) and tolerated by government. It was only through the Lockean notion of property being either public or private that the foundation was prepared for business administration as a scholarly pursuit. But business administration would never have developed if governments had not retracted their mercantilist policies, which is what happened between 1810–1870. Indeed, in the awakening of the mercantilist state (1600–1700) public administration quickly became an independent discipline (Rutgers 1993), two centuries before business administration. Administrative science from the 1800s onward was forced into the corner by the 1800s because of a laissez-faire ideology.

I have demonstrated in chapters 5–7 how the nineteenth century represents a change of values about and a change in government tasks. In chapter 1, I briefly described how public administration withdrew into constitutional law. In chapters 2 and 8–10, I have shown how governments in the nineteenth century became more responsive to the inherent tensions between ideas about and facts of governance. Government officials in the first half of the nineteenth century could only have concluded that government had to withdraw from many sectors in society given the profound impact of the Free Trade Movement (Kindleberger 1987: 102–103), the deep desire to dismantle the Old Regimes, and the negative perception of bureaucracy (ch. 7). Government, they thought, should only provide the constitutional framework within which the "private" sector could flourish. It should only guard public order and safety and so the "nightwatch state" was created.

In retrospect the idea of laissez-faire was short-lived. It was in the modern democracy in the making, emphasizing equality for all, that governments would again intervene in the private sector. The rise of specific interest groups in the second half of the nineteenth century confronted government (ch. 8) with an interesting dilemma. Could it regulate for the common good in such a manner that the pursuit of the private good was not endangered? The compromise was found in the welfare state, wherein to a smaller or larger extent government found itself in a mediating and/or negotiating role between private initiative (business) and organized interest (labor unions, environmental groups). Government in that role faced a new challenge: learning how to mediate between public and private interests instead of controlling. In a mediating role government cannot escape from disappointing one or another group. As a matter of fact government is much under fire both by business as well as by the citizen. In such a situation it becomes difficult not to look at the glaring "successes" of business administration, or not to be guided by Francis Bacon's "utility-criterion." In the search for usable knowledge, caution is demanded, a caution advocated by, for instance, Lindblom and Cohen (1979). The needs of the day, however, can be so pressing that there seems to be little room for caution and reflection.

Modern administrative science (and so administrative history) has indeed developed from political science and administrative law; it also developed at the same time as business administration did.

11.2 Current Trends in Administrative History

There is evidence throughout this book that public administration is no longer defined by business administration, (constitutional) history, administrative law, or political science. It has defined its own frame of reference. As became clear in chapter 2, administrative history does not quite belong to the core of the discipline of public administration. The number of articles concerning administrative history has slightly increased over the past twenty years. The change in emphasis is more striking, however, when one looks at monographs.

Within the postwar social sciences the history of government was the playing ground of political scientists and political theorists. For two decades after the Second World War the history of political systems was the dominating theme (e.g., Eisenstadt 1958, 1963 and Wittfogel 1957). Themes characteristic of political theory are the development of citizenship, of civic traditions, and of the relationship between citizen and his government. Modern political science developed a historical interest earlier than public administration did.

The Gladden (1972) and Jacoby (1973) studies mark a change to more attention for the development of government itself, of its bureaucracy, of its civil service, of its policy-making, and so forth. The publication of these two studies demonstrated that public administration (and so administrative history) added its own set of questions to those of administrative law, political science, and history. The bibliography in this book testifies to an increase in the attention for the development of government. Numerous monographs have been published in the past twenty years on the history of particular public organizations, particular periods, as well as on the development of national administrations over time. Scholars from different disciplinary backgrounds have come to cooperate in the effort to achieve better understanding of administrative history. Examples can be found throughout the preceding chapters. The collection of longitudinal data from primary sources about the development of government itself (administrative history proper, ch. 1; see also chs. 5–7) is required groundwork.

Firstly, this is needed to get an idea about degrees of continuity, diversity, and change in a national and in a comparative perspective. On the basis of such data we can improve our knowledge about patterns in the development of government. Secondly, this groundwork is needed because only then can we relate the development of government to its context of political participation and representation, state-making and nation-building, international relations (chs. 8–10) not to mention demographic development, economic development, technological development, developments in the physical environment, and so forth. I agree with Wallace and Singer (1970: 285) that data-collection is not an end in itself. It has an instrumental value for it opens up new research opportunities and provides a more solid basis to our knowledge about the interaction between the topic of research and its explanatory context. Thus I thoroughly disagree with the implications of the remark that "The mere accumulation of time series data on selected social indicators provides little more than descriptive data..." (Anderson 1973: 286). Although this is true in itself it disregards the fact that knowledge starts with data, and only when we have accumulated these we can begin understanding what these data tell us.

Administrative history is no longer the odd hobby of some dispersed scholars. Our time has witnessed several fundamental changes in the environment of government. What is the impact, on government and society, of changes—from a bipolar to a multipolar world, from a managed to an accountable and legitimate government, from an accepting to a demanding citizen, and from a public-versus-private to a public-and-private domain? The impact of changes may not be clear to us until some time has passed. We need distance in time before we can filter out events important and unimportant. However, the urgency displayed in texts concerning reform in government has increased in the previous decade. This requires that we somehow develop an interpretation of what happens in our own time, and this interpretation is without meaning if we have no inkling as to how and why the present situation developed.

The observation that

Historical analysis has little relevance to the present.... What is done is done. Only the present counts and making the future better counts even more. (Caiden 1987: 7) appears to be out of touch with developments in administrative science in the past decades, if not outright simplistic. The authors of the Blacksburg Manifesto stated that

> public administration has been dismayingly ahistoric and both ignorant and indifferent to its origins.... this casualness toward the founding of our field is a terrible mistake on our part. (Wamsley et al. 1990: 23)

However, a historical angle to the study of public administration as a discipline is not enough. In reference to Selznick (1957) Wamsley argues that an institution is best understood when looking into its history and into the way it was influenced by the social environment (Wamsley 1990: 121; 1996: 371). While administrative history in Europe starts to pick up again in the 1970s, it now appears that in the last decade it also strikes root in the United States (Miewald 1994).

An interpretation of the present will hold no promise to guide us, unless we know the limits and opportunities defined in the past. As early as 1962, Barrington Moore, Jr. argued that social science can best show "...the range of possible alternatives and the potentiality for effective action..." (in Lindblom and Cohen, 1979: 76). The notion of "path dependency," coined by Krasner (1988: 67), is very popular now in the social sciences. It captures our attention more than the historians' reference to the simultaneous forces of continuity, diversity, and change (ch. 5).

> where you can get to depends and where you're coming from, and some destinations you simply cannot get to from here. (Putnam 1993: 179)

Path dependency is just another way of saying that the past holds the key to the future. In view of the limits of causal analysis and with an urgent need "...to understand how history smooths out some paths and closes others off" (Putnam 1993: 181), it is clear that administrative history is an indispensable element of administrative science. There are two ways to support this claim. First, we can look into publications and research networks. Second, we can show that knowledge of the past enhances our understanding of the present (following sections). The increase in articles and—much more so—of books, on the development of government has already been mentioned. When Waldo wondered why there was no History of Government Journal yet (ch. 2), he could not have known about this *Yearbook of European Administrative History* since it had not yet attracted a wide audience. It has become common that studies about a contemporary issue (whether empirical studies or handbooks) include a historical perspective. This is notable in the works of administrative scientists like Gawthrop, Page, Stillman, Waldo, and Wright. The emphasis on institutional analysis in recent years is even more promising. Whether this type of analysis is called "historical political economy" (Maier 1987: 1–20) or "path-dependent" analysis (Krasner 1988) does not really matter, for in both approaches it is argued that institutional development is a major explanatory variable for understanding our contemporary predicaments. Institutional development becomes more common in research projects. The analysis of the long-term development of institutions for common-pool resource management (initiated by the Workshop in Political Theory and Policy Analysis, Indiana University, Bloomington, IN) is just one example. The Local Governance Research Programme that was launched in 1992 in Great Britain (funded by the Economic and Social Research Council) is another example, since one of its projects concerns the history of the development of local governance (Logopol 1994). Scholars of various background have institutionalized cooperative networks with a specific interest for theory and history. The *Public Administration Theory Network* is one, the working group on History of Administration of the *International Institute of Administrative Sciences* is another (ch. 1). I admit that these are just a few examples, but I hope that through this book, more research projects, publications, and networks are brought to my attention.

Administrative history can only flourish when scholars from various backgrounds bring their expertise into research projects and learn from one another in the effort to acquire a more complete understanding.

11. 3 A Middle-Range Theory about the Development of Government

In order to understand events in the world that surrounds us, people break reality down into manageable portions. Scholars do so in an explicated manner, through defining the realm of their attention, the concepts they use to describe "their" portion of reality, and presenting the theories from which they depart (ch. 3). Throughout this book I have paid attention to concepts and theories from the social and historical sciences, and presented my theories about portions of administrative history (chs. 5–8 and 10). At this point it is appropriate to present an analytic-descriptive theory based on the preceding chapters.

The development of government can be most completely understood against the background of the interdependent complexities of various developments in its environment. On a macroscale, researchers suspect and suggest explanatory links between the environment and their object of research. In-depth studies of the development of government (or an aspect thereof) in one region or locality may result in a more rigorously analyzed interaction between object and environment. However, what can be done on a microscale cannot be done on a macroscale and vice versa (ch. 3). Reality in its entire complexity is only accessible either through broad generalizations or through detailed studies limited in time and space. In this section I present a macroscale theory of the development of government with a middle-range scope. Tilly's theory of the interplay between capital and coercion and its impact on state formation is an admirable example of such a theory.

The development of government in the Western world since the late Middle Ages is one of growth and refinement. The growth of public tasks both in terms of breadth and depth, organizational differentiation both externally (the number of government departments and agencies) and internally (the number of subdivisions within one department or agency), and the increasing number of public functionaries and especially the civil servants, all testify to an increasing role of government. The High Middle Ages and the period of the Atlantic Revolutions represent the major periods of change, both in terms of ideas as well as actions. In its various manifestations, the growth of government is the product of the interplay between state-making and nation-building over a period of, say, 900 years (1050–1950).

My thesis is that in the Western world, the process of state-making dominated for centuries, and in due course was balanced by the process of nation-building. Only once state and nation were balanced, could a welfare state be created. The welfare state is the near-perfect fusion between state (protection of the territory) and nation (protection of the people). In the process, it forges central and local government.

Constant strife for territory was a characteristic of early state-making in the Western world. The ruler had to establish his claim to authority both to outside (neighboring states) and inside forces (regional princes). He had to allow elite representation, for it was forced upon him. At the same time he attempted to enlarge an independent power base through the creation of government departments (ch. 6) populated by servants loyal only to him (ch. 7). At the central level, government was preoccupied with tasks of a military, judicial, and financial

FIGURE 11.1
The Interplay of State-Making and Nation-Building

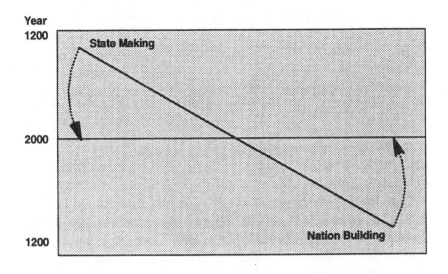

nature. At the local level, government persistently broadened its scope of activity with economic and social tasks (ch. 5). A major consequence of state-making was that international relations became balance-of-power politics, with sovereignty invested in the person of a secular ruler. Aquinas's views represented a backward look on the world, while those of Salisbury foreshadowed what was to come (ch. 9).

Balance-of-power politics would not be restricted to the core area, for from the fifteenth century onward it was "exported" to other parts of the world (ch. 10). Amidst the turmoil brought about by external strife (Italy), civil war (France), and colonization (Spain and Portugal) the idea of sovereignty became related to the abstraction of the state. Machiavelli's ideas made sense to the quarreling Italian city-states, but he still argued in favor of the medieval theory that "king = sovereign = state." A century later Bodin separated the ruler from sovereignty and state and advocated state sovereignty so as to avoid civil war. The question of how to avoid civil war also concerned Hobbes, and he pleaded for absolutism. His solution to anarchy was Machiavellian, befitting the times but of little use in the centuries to come.

It is important to realize that colonization forced the expansion of central governments into entrepreneurial endeavors, either directly or indirectly (ch. 10). Financing both colonization and the conduct of war in the European theater called for enormous amounts of revenue. Indirect and extraordinary taxes burdened the population (ch. 5). The balancing of the needs of state with those of the citizen was prepared for in several ways. Locke defined public and private property, Montesquieu created a notion of checks and balances, Rousseau developed a romantic idea about participatory democracy, Condorcet described a welfare state for which J.S. Mill provided the capstone.

At the local level, government slowly expanded its services, especially in the fields of education and health (ch. 5). The old notion of welfare which was based on charity was replaced by the idea of welfare as a minimum provision to which citizens were entitled (ch. 8). From then on, nation-building would become more important. The process of state-making was concluded as soon as external boundaries were established and accepted. Only then could central governments' attention shift full force to strengthening the internal cohesion of society.

In state-making the prime concern is carving out a territory and establishing external legitimacy, while in nation-building the emphasis is on creating provisions for the people within the territory—thus establishing internal legitimacy through community building.

England is generally believed to be the first state that became a nation, a "national state" (seventeenth century). Other countries followed. For a state to become a nation, the state had to utilize a growing sense of community among the people for its own purposes (establishing legitimate power) through providing services for its own citizenry. Characteristic of the change toward a true national state from the end of the nineteenth century onward is universal suffrage, government as mediator, an intertwining of central and local government, entrepreneurial tasks at local level, direct taxes and social security, enormous expansion of public tasks and public expenditure, and an increase in the number of public servants. Civil servants served not so much the state as the public. They sought to define their new role in relation to politics through detailed regulation of their legal position (ch. 7). The idea of the neutral public servant was severely put to the test in the twentieth century. If the civil servant was indeed neutral both to the public and to politics, it ought to serve no matter what party or person was in power. In totalitarian regimes, however, the public servant regressed into being a state servant and sometimes even a personal servant. John of Salisbury's idea that a tyrant can be denounced, has relevance for the twentieth century when wondering at which point a civil servant should no longer follow the guidelines of politics (Von Borch 1954).

In the early period of state-making, bureaucratization was manifest in increased administrative activity, refinement of rules and procedures, the development of specialized offices, and the hiring of subordinates who were knowledgeable (dimensions 1, 2, 3, 10, and 12 of the ideal type, see appendix 6.1). This had already happened in the High Middle Ages. With the growth of state power and thus of the number of people employed, the hierarchical organization of offices, the use of written documents, and contractual agreements increased (seventeenth and eighteenth centuries; dimensions 4, 5, and 13). Once the separation of public and private was no longer an idea, government came to supply the means of office (an office, paper, ink), public office could no longer be inherited or sold, and procedures for rational discipline and control were developed (formal hierarchy, defined and indivisible competence, staff and line: the first half of the nineteenth century; dimensions 6, 7, 8, 9, 11, and 14). The separation of public and private was complete once the civil servant had secured tenure, was fully compensated for his/her effort (adequate salary linked to rank and seniority, career opportunities, pension) and was protected against political whim (dimensions 15–20).

The main trends of the development of government are presented in figure 11.2. Neither in the discussion above nor in figure 11.2 are causal links assumed, for the simple reason that I cannot believe such is possible. What becomes clear, however, is that certain ideas and certain events came about at the same time. This is neither a coincidence nor a consciously adopted strategy. It just happened, and any explanation would be a violation of reality. Relevant for our own time is the advent of the welfare state, and so I shall summarize what I have presented in previous chapters.

11.4 The Construction of the Welfare State

In the early modern world, roughly from 1500–1800, central and local government in the Western world had a fairly clear idea about their responsibilities. The defense of the territory, and sometimes the

FIGURE 11.2
Institutional Development of Ideas

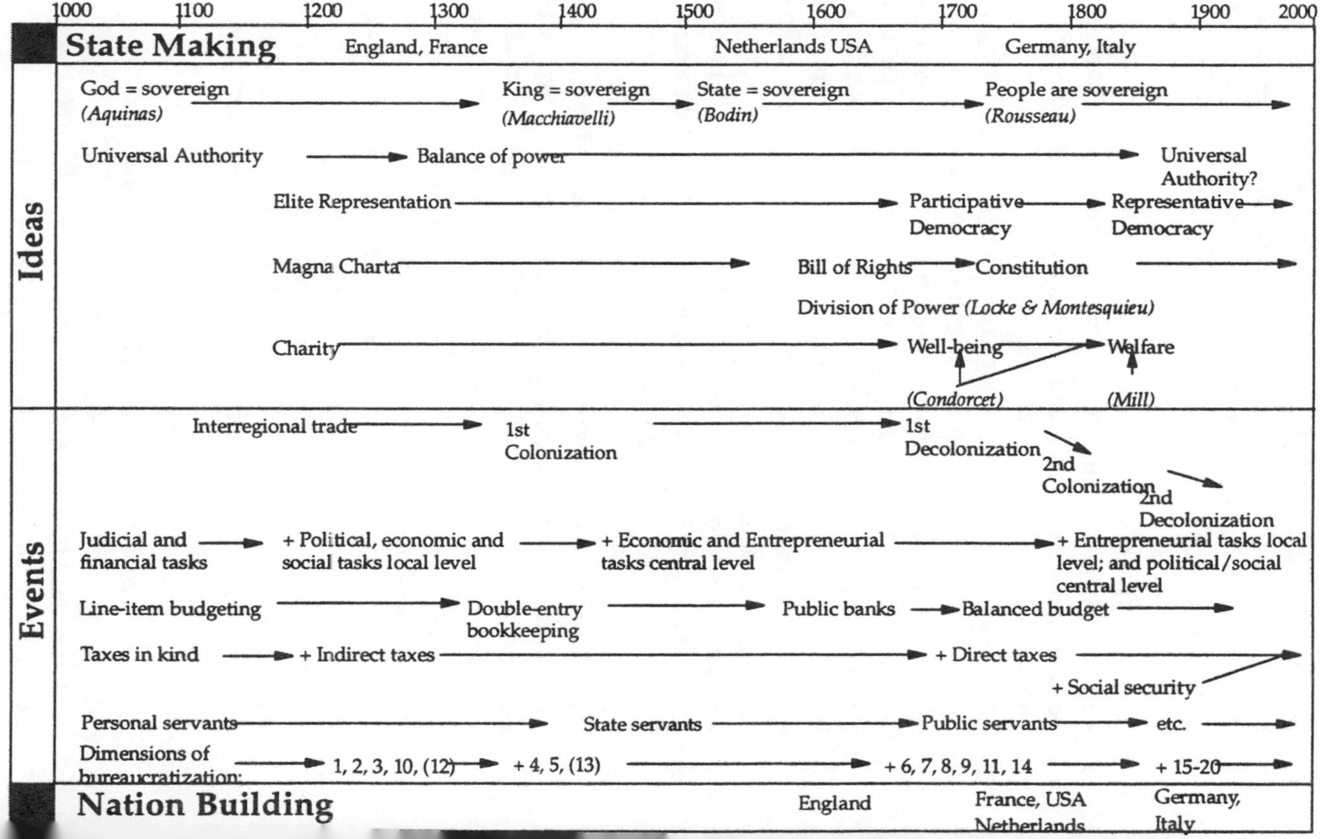

Timeline scale (top): 1000 — 1100 — 1200 — 1300 — 1400 — 1500 — 1600 — 1700 — 1800 — 1900 — 2000

State Making

Country markers along timeline:
England, France — Netherlands USA — Germany, Italy

Ideas:

- God = sovereign (Aquinas) → King = sovereign (Macchiavelli) → State = sovereign (Bodin) → People are sovereign (Rousseau) → Universal Authority?
- Universal Authority → Balance of power
- Elite Representation → Participative Democracy → Representative Democracy
- Magna Charta → Bill of Rights → Constitution
- Division of Power (Locke & Montesquieu)
- Charity → Well-being (Condorcet) → Welfare (Mill)

Events:

- Interregional trade → 1st Colonization → 1st Decolonization → 2nd Colonization → 2nd Decolonization
- Judicial and financial tasks → + Political, economic and social tasks local level → + Economic and Entrepreneurial tasks central level → + Entrepreneurial tasks local level; and political/social central level
- Line-item budgeting → Double-entry bookkeeping → Public banks → Balanced budget
- Taxes in kind → + Indirect taxes → + Direct taxes → + Social security
- Personal servants → State servants → Public servants → etc.
- Dimensions of bureaucratization: 1, 2, 3, 10, (12) → + 4, 5, (13) → + 6, 7, 8, 9, 11, 14 → + 15–20

Country markers along bottom timeline:
England — France, USA Netherlands — Germany, Italy

Nation Building

expansion of it, was mainly the concern of central government. The welfare of the citizen fell to local government which since the late Middle Ages had assumed tasks hitherto provided by the church and other communal organizations such as guilds. The maintenance of internal public order and safety, police and justice, was a shared responsibility. The central state's policy was outward oriented and its resources used for warfare. The territory was governed through indirect rule, as Tilly called it, using powerful intermediaries from among the clergy, urban oligarchy, landlords, and professional warriors who enjoyed significant autonomy in governance at regional and local level (ch. 8). Local government policy was mainly inwardly oriented—development of the local economy being the main goal—and the citizen being highly involved through compulsory and voluntary civic duty.

That division of labor disappeared (ch. 8). The Enlightenment and the Atlantic Revolutions generated a mentality change, mainly representing a change of ideas about governance and welfare. A century later the creation of the early welfare state changed the roles of local and central government in society.

The age of the Enlightenment and the Atlantic Revolutions had seen the birth of, for instance, Montesquieu's division of power, of Rousseau's *volonté generale*, and of the "Rights of Man" by Thomas Paine. These ideas constituted a farewell to the consequences of Hobbes's choice for either anarchy or absolutism, and strengthened the Lockean notion that individual property ought to be protected against the almighty state (ch. 9). The "invisible hand" of the English customs officer Adam Smith provided the cornerstone of the laissez-faire state to which many Western states in the nineteenth century adhered as is visible in a decline of government tasks. This was the end of mercantilism, but would it be the end of government intervention in economy and society through detailed regulation?

Amidst the turmoil of the French, American, and Dutch revolutions, and the rather peaceful, but just as significant changes in English government, few acted upon Condorcet's ideas about welfare for all (ch. 8), although this befitted the times. Establishing welfare and well-being (*eudaimonia*) for the citizenry (the greatest welfare for the greatest number) needed some thought first and, in time, would only partially be realized in the welfare state.

The laissez-faire or "nightwatchman state" was short-lived. As the nineteenth century progressed it became apparent that the combined and intertwined forces of industrialization, urbanization, demographic growth, deteriorating housing conditions, and epidemics needed a more fundamental solution than private philanthropy (charity) could offer. In addition to these urban and economic developments, the technological development constituted a second set of major changes. Newspapers became accessible to larger groups of people. Train, telegraph, and later telephone, brought people closer together. Local interest groups amalgamated into national organizations (labor unions, political parties, professional groups). Technology helped to create a sense of community. The bottom-up demand for better public services compelled both central and local governments to rely more and more on full-time personnel instead of "volunteers" (ch. 7). Central governments' policies became internally oriented, as is shown in a series of acts concerning public welfare, and public expenditure increased accordingly.

The combined effects of the advent of nationalism and of interest-groups made it impossible for the state to be concerned only with the international arena. Attention to internal stability was required as well. Indeed, some argue that the advent of the welfare state can be understood as the price the elite was willing to pay for social stability. Whether this or a more humanitarian explanation for the advent of the welfare state is accurate, is not at issue here. The fact remains that the welfare state could only be paid for on the basis of surplus production and efficient tax collection which in turn made redistributive policies a viable option.

To understand how this came about, we again need to turn to the late-eighteenth century, for it was then that the idea surfaced that government expenditure ought to be related to anticipated resources. The concept of a balanced budget was widely accepted in the first half of the nineteenth century (ch. 5). In relation to this, centralized organizational structures were created to improve tax collection. There was yet another change in the field of public finance. For ages indirect taxes had been a major source of revenue. They were also a primary cause of internal unrest for they disproportionately burdened the lower income groups. Naturally, another problem for government was that the volume of taxes collected was difficult to predict. This too changed since direct taxes, such as income tax (whose volume can be assessed prior to expenditure) made an efficient reallocation of resources possible.

In 1799 England was the first country to introduce an income tax even though it was quickly abandoned. Most Western governments introduced income taxes between 1860 and 1910. This too increased the interdependence between central and local government. Another

indispensable source of revenue for the welfare state was found in social insurance. Between 1880–1940 many Western countries witnessed
the enactment of a variety of social insurances. Together the income
tax and social insurances financed the welfare state (ch. 5). After the
Second World War government spending increased even more, and
instigated a revival of indirect taxes.

Increased revenue and efficient organization made the distribution
of welfare possible to an ever-increasing extent. The general trend has
been one in which welfare provisions moved from being a private and
local initiative to being a public and global matter (ch. 7). Indeed, the
state had come to intervene in economy and society and in economies
and societies at a scale unheard of during the mercantilist age. And as
a result of increasing quality and quantity of services, the organizational structure of government diversified enormously, and the number of personnel employed increased exponentially. In order to keep it
all working, increasing standardization of organization and hierarchy,
of procedures, of relations between citizens and government officials,
occurred. This is the process of bureaucratization and it is a consequence of societal developments whether of a physical, economic, social, or political nature.

Understanding bureaucracy requires an understanding of the society in which it is embedded. Bureaucratization is a general trend, but
bureaucracy was tailored to fit various national needs. Changes in bureaucracy implies changes in society. The early-twentieth-century reforms were inspired by the need to provide better services in a more
efficient way. Late-twentieth-century reforms are inspired by a slightly
different need: a good package of services for a reasonable price. The
difference is that in the early-twentieth century, the welfare state was
being built, while in the late-twentieth century, it needs to be trimmed.

11.5 The Welfare State under Siege:
A Global Perspective on Regional Issues

An optimist would say that the welfare state remains one of the greatest achievements of Western government, while the pessimist might
argue that the value of the welfare state has passed. At no time in history has a redistribution of resources taken place at such a scale in
order to serve such a large amount of people. The build up of the welfare state took about sixty years, 1890–1950, give or take a few years.
The heyday of the welfare state did not last more than twenty-five

years when worldwide economic decline began to nibble away at the edges of economic prosperity. Western governments have met the limits of their ability to provide welfare for all. In fact, no matter how hard government tries, it can no longer deny that welfare is not synonymous with well-being. A wave of reform is spreading throughout the Western world. Reform of the structure, the functioning, and the size of the civil service, reform of relations between employers and employees, budget cuts, and reform of the welfare state. All of these point to one underlying issue: an urgent need to redefine the role of government and of the citizen in society. To put it differently,

> If there is a crisis of the welfare state (paralleling the impasse of social democracy) it may be this that the very circumstances which make for a *depoliticization* of welfare provisions themselves require a willingness to *repoliticize* issues of welfare. (Pierson 1991: 219)

This is a huge task in itself but is an even greater challenge in the face of the changes in the global socio-political environment. Redefining the foundations of the welfare state would be relatively easy if it were a regional—that is, Western—issue only. Of the five crisis in nation-building distinguished by Lipset the first four can more or less be overcome. But the fifth and last crisis of welfare redistribution will never be solved, Lipset argued, simply because society changes (Lipset 1963: 5; see also Lipset 1990). And as we shall see now it changes because of a global intertwinement. Accepted and depoliticized issues such as a certain level of welfare provisions may be up for repoliticization if the environment so requires.

Redefining the Welfare State

For a number of reasons Western nation-states are confronted with an urgent need to redefine the basis of the welfare state. I can only present a tentative list of reasons—I am sure there are more.

One obvious reason is demographic development. The population is growing mainly due to greatly improved living conditions and astonishing advances in medical science. One of the consequences is that the population pyramid becomes unbalanced. The working part of the population is decreasing relative to the larger part of the population dependent upon entitlements. In some countries the financial support individuals are entitled to in cases of unemployment, inability to work because of a physical or mental handicap or age, is higher (the

Netherlands, Sweden) than in other countries (Great Britain, the United States). The extent to which government is able to support does depend upon the employed, but at the same time government cannot withdraw overnight from earlier policies and promises on which its population has come to rely.

Another obvious reason is public debt. In many Western countries public expenditure is rising sharply and being prefinanced through loans. In countries like the Netherlands and the United States, a substantial part of the revenue is necessary to pay off the interest, but what about the principal? So far, the solution of governments has been to reorganize, either through the creation of new types of organizational structures, or through downsizing personnel. It seems that severe cutbacks in welfare provisions can no longer be avoided, but politicians have a difficult task convincing the electorate that harsh measures in the short term need to be taken in order to maintain a satisfactory but, maybe, lower standard of living in the long run.

Reorganizing structure and downsizing are related to another feature of our times that imposes formidable impediments to any attempt to reconstitute, or should I say downsize, the welfare state. Given that governments operate in a society wherein many actors have learned to voice their demands, it is a tremendous task to deal with "...competing, overlapping, inconsistent, and expensive demands for new programs and expenditures..." (ch. 8) without eliminating earlier commitments. The crisis of citizen confidence in governments' problem-solving capabilities is, as some argue, visible in a breakdown of civic culture, of dwindling citizen participation. Glaring in the face of this perception are the numerous examples of citizens organized for the public interest in the Western world. Indeed, the number of interest groups has increased enormously in the twentieth century. But still, the negative and stereotypical ideas about governments' capabilities are a powerful adversary on the road to fundamental changes. After all, people act and react to perception more quickly than they start searching for facts.

I could also argue that during the 1760–1820 period the idea of civic duty was replaced by a notion of civil rights, first interpreted in terms of equality before the law, but in the course of the nineteenth century becoming synonymous with equal chances for the citizen. And, indeed, we have gone far beyond what John Stuart Mill called social liberalism wherein the state provides for those who cannot provide for themselves. This deterioration of the notion of civic duty (whether conscripted or compulsory) was noticed remarkably early by Tocqueville. When he spoke of "...democracy loosening social ties..." (ch. 8) he had in mind what happened to the families who moved from the poverty-stricken rural areas to the labor promising urban settlements where they had no other support but from their family and later from government. Tocqueville did not see himself as a prophet, but I can picture him nodding approvingly while reading Jacoby's remark about people willing to benefit from union membership as long as no sacrifice was required (ch. 8).

Did democracy loosen social ties? Did the responsibility for communal welfare successfully transfer to government and interest groups? Maybe modern democracy and welfare state created a lazy citizen or, at least, a citizen who is uncomfortable with the notion of duty. In most Western countries people do not find it difficult to point out who the abusers of the provisions of the welfare system are. And again, it does not matter whether these individuals or groups really exploit the welfare state or not, it is a perception that clouds judgement. We first need to establish how many people receive welfare provisions for good reasons and how many people abuse the system. Then we are dealing with facts, and only then we can assess the degree to which the welfare state needs to be refounded.

Yet another, but less obvious reason, for redefining the welfare state can be found in the advent of regionalism. The welfare state is a national state's creation that does not necessarily take regional differences into account. Promoting social and economic cohesion through the development of structural programs for backward regions in the European Union indicates more attention for the regions. The fairly recent emphasis on subsidiarity in the implementation of European Union policies provides another testimony to upcoming regionalism. After all, subsidiarity allows for diversity. Different regions have different needs. Regionalism is also apparent in the call for more autonomy for communities that share a linguistic and sociocultural identity within states different from the dominant culture.

A Global Perspective on the Welfare State

Redefining the welfare state is necessary if we want to maintain something of the standard of living we have grown accustomed to. It is pursued, however, in a state-centric framework that no longer applies. The transnational model of international relations is a more adequate representation of today's international and national arenas with multiple actors and multiple interests (ch. 10). The time when international relations were high politics is now behind us. The international political system which slowly developed and was confirmed in the Peace of Westphalia (1648) was based on a balance of power maintained through negotiations or war, if necessary. Maintaining a balance of power through diplomacy and through redrawing the map of the world is characteristic of nineteenth-century international relations. The West not only exported the state to the rest of the world, but also its ideas about human rights, equality, and the right to self-determination. The decolonization in the 1945–1975 period and the 1989 changes in Eastern Europe testify to the prolonged impact of these Western ideas.

Few of those who witnessed these changes as adults, however, could have foreseen what the New States and the former communist countries inherited. These territories were defined by artificial boundaries cutting across tribal areas and/or encompassing a variety of cultures. The impact of these negotiated boundaries, no doubt fitting the rationale of the time, on social stability in the newly independent states was and remains enormous; one need only look at events in many African states and in former Yugoslavia and what could happen in the Middle East (the Kurds, for instance) and in the Indian subcontinent.

What the New States and the Eastern European states also inherited was an administration modeled after the former mother countries respectively the Soviet Union. It is only in the 1980s that a search started, if one can call it that, for indigenous and democratic institutions. Who is to populate these institutions is subject to vehement and bloody civil unrest. The consequences of regionalism based on a sense of togetherness is more visible in the East and the South of the world than in the West. To be sure, in a bipolar world the forces of people's dissatisfaction could be more or less contained, and could not be unleashed. But with this gone, internationalization and regionalization together produce a highly unpredictable environment. There is a point when euphoria about change is replaced by the grim reality that the day-to-day standard of living is much slower to respond. Wrestling away from colonial or communist rule did not bring about immediate improvement in society and economy. People are becoming impatient.

To put it bluntly, maintaining the welfare state seems a rather piddling issue in the face of regional unrest and pressure on the environment. But the international community does not yet have a universal authority to enforce peace. In fact, international organizations are frequently used as a lever for achieving national goals. Hoffman's 1966 thesis that the European Community was created to protect and enhance national interests applies to all nation-states participating in one or more international bodies. National states are still inwardly oriented.

11.6 Many Pessimists, Few Optimists

Individual states are pressured to comply with basic human rights, are asked to limit whaling, are shown figures of what deforestation may do to the atmosphere. And I haven't even mentioned the political and strategic impact of population growth, disease, soil erosion, water depletion, air pollution, and possibly rising sea levels. More than two decades ago the Club of Rome report generated major unrest with the future state of the world (Meadows et al. 1972). It is interesting that in their list of symptoms and diseases that characterized the world's problems, they identified a disturbed environment, uncertainty about population growth, uncontrolled urban growth, a crisis of habits, estrangement among the young, a growing number of people who did not acknowledge the major value systems in society, and...bureaucratization. The analysis focused on the interrelated influence of population growth, food production, industrialization, depletion of natural resources, and pollution on the world system, but there was no attention paid to this other "disease" called bureaucracy. The Club of Rome report provided an analysis of the environmental pressures as they would develop within a bipolar political world system. Their conclusions were as pessimistic as those of other and older pessimists. Pessimism sometimes appears to be the dominant human condition. Critics of the report, however, pointed out human resourcefulness throughout the ages. They argued that doomsday thinking is usually based upon the assumptions that technology is stagnant, new resources will not be discovered, and no substitutes will be found for once-plentiful resources. Population growth tests the regenerative capacity of the environment, but the real problem is one of timing. How soon will we discover new technologies that can be put to practice? In the meantime we have to rely on temporary measures.

In absolute terms we may pour substantial amounts of money into the underdeveloped world, but it is only a drop in the bucket. We can rally our populations behind a good cause, the representatives of the media can wallow in the idea that broadcasts of Rwandan atrocities have caused many to donate a dollar, a pound, a guilder—but can we maintain a welfare state at an even lower level, in the face of a continuing need for aid and a more fundamental solution to world problems? Is not the ultimate test of the welfare state its success in truly redistributing welfare to the rest of the world—thus building a minimum *welfare status* for all?

Following the logic of people like Edward Gibbon, Oswald Spengler, Arnold Toynbee, and Paul Kennedy about the rise and fall of empires and great powers, or of Michael Wood in his BBC series on the origins of civilization—the West has had its day.

It is, however, not easy to remain optimistic when reputable authors present a millenarian outlook towards the future. In the *Atlantic Monthly* of February 1994 Robert D. Kaplan painted a most gruesome picture of what may await us, drawing upon a variety of publications (Benedict Anderson, Martin van Creveld, Joel Garreau, Thomas F. Homer-Dixon, Samuel P. Huntington, James Kurth, Michael Mandelbaum, and William I. Thompson among others) and his own experience. First Kaplan sketches the world order as it is or will quickly become:

> Part of the globe is inhabited by Hegel's and Fukuyama's Last Man, healthy, well fed, and pampered by technology. The other, larger part is inhabited by Hobbes' First Man, condemned to a life that is "poor, nasty, brutish, and short. Although both parts will be threatened by environmental stress, the Last Man will be able to master it; the First Man will not. (Kaplan 1994: 60)

Will the Last Man be able to master environmental stress? And, to quote Kaplan again, to what extent will "…environmental scarcity…inflame existing hatreds and affect power relationships…" (1994: 70)? These are intriguing questions, all the more because he writes:

> Whatever the laws, refugees find a way to crash official borders, bringing their passions with them, meaning that Europe and the United States will be weakened by cultural disputes. (1994: 62)

Can we keep, both literally and metaphorically, the underdeveloped world out of our welfare state? The refugee problem has assumed global proportions. Refugees not only bounce from one country to another within a region, they increasingly look toward the West and its "horns of plenty." In fact, national governments may consciously *encourage* emigration so as to put pressure on Western governments for support (Cuba, for instance). Kaplan continues:

the end of the Cold War will bring on a cruel process of natural selection among existing states. (1994: 70).

Unfortunately in the post-Cold War world, war may once again be the only outlet for frustration. What kind of war? Who will fight whom? Will fiction become reality—mirroring that futuristic movie of some years ago about a North African Mahdi on a long march? He assembles a massive following and leads them to the Strait of Gibraltar; they try to cross but are met by gunfire. Fortress Europe. If we are to believe Kaplan, will we see an evolving world map marked by moving centers of power—similar to the Middle Ages (1994: 75). Will the state as it exists today be able to rechannel regional unrest into more profitable avenues of activity? Or will it experience the following:

> Future wars will be those of communal survival, aggravated or, in many cases, caused by environmental scarcity. These wars will be subnational, meaning that it will be hard for states and local governments to protect their own citizens physically. This is how many states will ultimately die. As state power fades—*and with it the states' ability to help weaker groups within society, not to mention other states* (emphasis added)—peoples and cultures around the world will be thrown back upon their own strengths and weaknesses, with fewer equalizing mechanisms to protect them. Whereas the distant future will probably see the emergence of a racially hybrid, globalized man, the coming decades will see us more aware of our differences than of our similarities. To the average person, political values will mean less, personal security more. (Kaplan 1994: 74)

What will happen to the welfare state? How much shall we focus on our individual and short-term needs instead of on collective, long-term needs? Kaplan's outlook on the world to come is pessimistic, to say the least. He is the archetypical doomsday thinker of the late-twentieth century. His analysis is all the more powerful because he not only addresses environmental issues, but he puts them in perspective—taking into consideration the changes in the international political arena. Just as the pessimistic environmentalists conveniently overlook human creativity, Kaplan forgets the resilience of the political world order.

The idea of true international sovereignty in the form of a world government is not realistic in the contemporary situation. There is, however, international cooperation and determination to mediate international and national affairs. In fact, mediation is even accepted (such as UNTAC, ch. 10). Insofar as the political situation is threatened due to physical reasons, there have been attempts to alleviate the worst consequences. We possess the technical knowledge to alleviate pressures on our environment, illustrated, for instance, by the Indonesian government's rain forest protection program.

Citizens, politicians, and civil servants have to be more realistic about what they can expect from one another; they must be more patient for the results. Never was there a citizen, a politician, or a civil servant able to obliterate the impact of the past. In terms of societal development it has been attempted many times through subtle measures, brutal force, or horrendous physical and mental torture. It is this collective memory that wreaked havoc both in the developed and the underdeveloped world. In many regions throughout history this collective memory justified *lex tallionis* (an eye for an eye) over time.

The idea of retribution, however, has acquired a new dimension in our own time. Ever since the Nuremberg trials, people can demand revenge in the international legal sense. Crimes against humanity are a new phenomenon; they are certainly an infringement upon state sovereignty, however it is defined. From a global perspective, though, this can be looked upon as an example of a Western-centric approach to global problems.

In terms of government development, the impact of the past is even harder to change, not because government is resistant to change, but because society does not change overnight. Government and bureaucracy, in their present manifestation, are ultimately the product of what the citizenry wanted. And so, trimming bureaucracy means trimming public services and making political choices.

In the international political environment people will have to acknowledge the impact of the past. At the same time they should not advocate retribution or dominance of one part or another. Western nations must take the opportunity to right past wrongs. It is up to formerly oppressed peoples to look at the past as experience and not hold contemporary generations in Western nations responsible for what their oppressive forefathers did. It is cheap and easy for a national leader with charisma to hurl a society into chaos—it takes courage not to abuse the past. In a speech for the South African Parliament on 15 August 1994 President Nelson Mandela proved to be the living example of an individual who could distance himself from personal experience and look at what is needed. He wants to dismantle the last vestiges of Apartheid, but calls for national unity. He knows what black against black, black against white, and rich against poor may do to his country: a civil war that could destroy whatever foundation there is for a new society. Mandela is beyond the concerns of Bodin and Hobbes. National unity calls for sharing. International peace and international welfare call for the same.

11.7 Bureaucracy Is a Consequence Not a Cause

Administrative history, as the combined knowledge of various disciplines, helps us describe what has happened with government through the accumulation of data, helps us understand why it happened through analysis of developments in the environment, and may contribute to a useful assessment of the future challenges governments and citizens face. Data and understanding is what the scholar can provide—the assessment of future challenges is at best an intelligible judgement and most certainly a testimony to the limits of human intellect.

From the perspective of administrative history in the broader sense, the usefulness of looking into the past is evident when we are able to serve the present by using the past as experience and warning, and not as burden, debt, or source for revenge. Only then can we create a better future. And so, the ultimate usefulness of administrative history in the broader sense may well be gaining insight into why we want to dissociate ourselves from the past.

In the perspective of administrative history proper, this book has shown how the contemporary structure and functioning of government and bureaucracy are the consequences of political choices made in response to societal change. "Treating" bureaucracy is fighting the symptom, not the cause.

References

Allison, Graham T., Jr. 1982. "Public and Private Management: Are They Fundamentally Alike in All Unimportant Aspects?" In *Current Issues in Public Administration*, edited by Frederick S. Lane, 13–33. New York: St.Martin's Press.

Anderson, James G. 1973. "Causal Models and Social Indicators: Toward the Development of Social Systems Models." *American Sociological Review* 38, no.3: 285–301.

Caiden, Gerald et al., eds. 1983. *American Public Administration: A Bibliographical Guide to the Literature*. New York: Garland Publishers.

Gore, Al. 1993. *From Red Tape to Results: Creating a Government that Works Better and Costs Less.* Report of the National Performance Review New York: Times Books.

Kaplan, Robert D. "The Coming Anarchy." *The Atlantic Monthly* (February 1994): 44–76.

Kindleberger, Charles P. 1987. "The Rise of Free Trade in Western Europe." In *International Political Economy: Perspectives on Global Power and Wealth*, edited by Jeffrey A. Frieden and David A. Lake, 85–104. New York: St. Martin's Press.

Krasner, Stephen D. 1988. "Sovereignty: An Institutional Perspective." *Comparative Political Studies* 21, no.1: 66–94.

Lane, Jan-Erik. 1994. "Will Public Management Drive Out Public Administration?" *Asian Journal of Public Administration* 16, no.2: 139–151.

Lindblom, Charles E. and David K. Cohen. 1979. *Usable Knowledge: Social Science and Social Problem Solving*. New Haven, CT: Yale University Press.

Lipset, Seymour Martin. 1963. *Political Man: The Social Bases of Politics*. Garden City, NY: Doubleday/Anchor.

Lipset, Seymour Martin and Stein Rokkan. 1990. "Cleavage Structures, Party Systems, and Voter Alignments." In *The West-European Party System*, edited by Peter Mair, 111–128. Oxford: Oxford University Press.

Logopol 27 (June 1994): 14. (Newsletter for the workgroup on local government and politics of the European Consortium for Political Research.

Maier, Charles S. 1987. *In Search of Stability: Explorations in Historical Political Economy*. Cambridge: Cambridge University Press.

Meadows, Dennis L., Donella H. Meadows, Joergen Randers, and William Behrens. 1972. *The Limits to Growth: A Report for the Club of Rome Project on the Predicament of Mankind*. New York: Universe Books.

Miller, Trudi C., ed. 1984. *Public Sector Performance: A Conceptual Turning Point*. Baltimore, MD: Johns Hopkins University Press.

Pierson, Christopher. 1991. *Beyond the Welfare State? The New Political Economy of Welfare*. Cambridge: Polity Press.

Putnam, Robert D. 1993. *Making Democracy Work: Civic Traditions in Modern Italy*. Princeton, NJ: Princeton University Press.

Rutgers, M.R. 1994. "Can the Study of Public Administration Do Without a Concept of the State? Reflections on The Work of Lorenz von Stein." *Administratrion & Society* 26, no.3: 395–412.

Waldo, Dwight. 1982. "Public Administration Toward Year 2000: The Framing Phenomena." In *Current Issues in Public Administration*, edited by Frederick S. Lane, 499–512. New York: St.Martin's Press, 499–512.

Wamsley, Gary L. 1990. "Introduction." In *Refounding Public Administration,* edited by Gary L. Wamsley et al. Newbury Park, CA: SAGE Publications, 19–29.

———. 1990. "The Agency Perspective: Public Administration as Agential Leaders." In *Refounding Public Administration*, edited by Gary L. Wamsley et al., 114–162. Newbury Park, CA: SAGE Publications.

———. 1996. "A Public Philosophy and Ontological Disclosure as the Basis for Normatively Grounded Theorizing in Public Administration." In *Refounding Democratic Public Administration: Modern Paradoxes, Postmodern Challenges*, edited by Gary L. Wamsley and James F. Wolf. Thousand Oaks, CA: SAGE Publicatons, 351–401.

Wiarda, Howard J. 1985. "Future Directions in Comparative Politics." In *New Directions in Comparative Politics*, edited by Howard J. Wiarda 203–211. Boulder, CO: Westview Press.

Part Four

Bibliography of Administrative History

12

Some Notes on Selection and Classification

Every bibliography and discussion of a particular body of knowledge will fall short of expectations. Thus Strayer displayed disappointment in the range of literature used by Gladden. Huddleston's bibliography on administrative history is part of a bibliography on comparative public administration and thus could only cover the highlights (Huddleston 1984: ch. 3). The bibliography presented here has been compiled during the span of a decade, and in no way claims to be complete. Sometimes it was fortunate to have a bibliography at hand. Thus several references have been taken from Eisenstadt and Rokkan (1973), Gladden, (1972), Kamenka (1989), and Tilly (1975). Many titles were found in national studies of administrative history. Finally, articles proved to be an important source, especially those that provide an overview of the state of the art of administrative history in a particular country (see ch. 1).

In order to achieve some degree of completeness, certain restrictions had to be made in the choice of references here. Once I started collecting literature the sheer number of references required selection on several grounds.

First, as I argued in chapter 1, administrative history is not a discipline, but a topic within a range of disciplines. We can find examples of administrative history at least in the studies of public administration, history, political science, law (especially in legal history), historical sociology, and anthropology. Literature has been selected that fits the definitions of administrative history proper and broader as defined in chapter 1.

Second, this restriction clearly still leaves us with too much literature. Therefore I have limited myself to references in the fields of public administration, political science, and history. They have only been included if the title indicates dominant attention for government and administration. It goes without saying that in historical literature the reader will find much information on government in a particular era. For these I refer to handbooks of ancient history, medieval history, and early modern and modern history, as well as to general histories of a country. Arnold J. Toynbee's *A Study of History* (Abridgement of volumes 1–10 by D.C. Somervell (New York: Oxford University Press, 1947–1957) (N.B.: originally vols. 1–12 published by Oxford Press between 1934–1961) merits attention for its extensive discussion of government and administration throughout the centuries (see also Gladden 1976). Literature from the field of legal history has only been included when it is of a general and introductory nature. Publications dealing with legal *and* administrative history combined have been included. This is the case especially with Austrian and German literature (*Verfassungs- und Verwaltungsgeschichte*) as well as in French literature (*Histoire des institutions*). During the nineteenth century the study of public administration in these countries became part of the study of law, and thus administrative history became part of legal history. Given the influence that French and German experiences in government and administration had on the Western world, mentioning these studies is justified.

A third restriction comes from this second one. Since most of the literature in the social sciences on administrative history concerns the early modern and modern period (1500 to the present) that is the period I have focused on. For a broader perspective some of the major early state studies are included (Claesen 1970, 1980, 1991; Claesen and Skalnik 1978, 1981; Claesen and Van de Velde 1987; Eisenstadt et al. 1988). Insofar as Europe is concerned ancient and medieval government has attracted much less attention in the social sciences. Given the importance of these periods for administrative development in Europe a separate section is included on ancient and medieval government. The reader will find much more in historical literature.

The fourth restriction is that mostly twentieth-century literature is included. The high points of administrative history in the nineteenth century, though, are among the titles collected here.

The structure of the bibliography is a simple one. It opens with references about the field of administrative history, most of which have been discussed in the first chapter. This is followed by a section with general works on administrative history. This section contains references that could not be included in any of the other sections. Given the regional emphasis in most sections, this general section contains many comparative studies.

After these two sections there is a straightforward listing of literature according to continent: Africa, Asia, Australia, Europe, Latin America, and North America. Each of these sections opens with general, sometimes comparative, literature and is then followed by a listing of national studies. I realize that the literature mentioned for Africa, Asia, and Latin America might not at all reflect the range of studies that have been conducted there. In fact, this book might be very Eurocentric in content, as a consequence of the literature I have been able to digest. In the case of colonial empire literature concerning the relationship between mother country and colony, references are only listed under the name of the former colony. Articles or books that provide a comparison between some countries, are listed under those countries mentioned (as is the case especially with comparative studies on France, Germany, Great Britain, and Russia, for instance).

Books and articles can also be classified according to their national and comparative nature and their general or specific nature. Thus Gladden's *History of Public Administration* is a general and comparative study, as is Heady's chapter on the origin of administration. In several countries national studies have been published, such as those presented in chapter 4. It is clear that national studies on a specific topic dominate. We can easily find literature on the development of government departments and on specific policy areas such as poor relief, police, and so forth. Comparative studies on specific issues are much less available. Dominant are those studies on the civil service, although some comparative studies have been done on public finance and expenditure and public policy, for instance.

Each chapter ends with a section that identifies the major authors and publications in the topic discussed in that chapter. Chapters 1 and 2 introduce the leading scholars in the field of administrative history. Authors and publications important to a specific aspect of administrative history are discussed in the following chapters. I have therefore refrained from providing a short introduction to the major authors and publications in this bibliography.

Bibliography of Administrative History

The Field of Administrative History

Benjamin, R. 1982. "The Historical Nature of Social Science Knowledge: The Case of Comparative Political Inquiry." In *Strategies of Political Inquiry*, edited by E. Ostrom. Beverly Hills, CA: SAGE Publications.

Caiden, Gerald E. 1963. The Study of Australian Administrative History. Paper presented at the 1963 Conference of the Australasian Political Studies Association.

Caldwell, Lynton K. 1955. "The Relevance of Administrative History." *Revue Internationale des Sciences Administratives* 21, no.3: 453–466.

Dahl, Robert A. 1961. "The Behavioral Approach in Political Science: Epitaph for a Monument to a Successful Protest." *American Political Science Review* 55, no.4: 763–772.

Erikson, Kai T. 1973. "Sociology and the Historical Perspective." In *Applied Historical Studies: An Introductory Reader*, edited by Michael Drake, 13–30. London: Methuen & Co.

Fesler, James T. 1982. "The Presence of the Administrative Past." In *American Public Administration: Patterns of the Past*, 1–27. Washington D.C.: American Society for Public Administration.

Gladden, E.N. 1972. "Public Administration and History." *International Review of Administrative Sciences* 37, no.4: 379–384.

———. 1976. "Toynbee on Public Administration." *Revue International des Sciences Administratives* 42, no.4: 338–348.

Heyen, Erik-Volkmar. 1984. "Une histoire comparée, problème et perspective." In *Cahiers de l'histoire de l'administration*, no. 1 edited by André Molitor. Brussels: International Institute of Administrative Sciences.

Hoffmann, Wolfgang. 1966. "Zielsettzungen und Arbeitsweise der Verwaltungsgeschichte im Rahmen der Verwaltungswissenschaften." In *Verwaltungsgeschichte: Aufgaben, Zielsetzungen, Beispiele*, edited by Rudolf von Morsey. Speyer: Schriftenreihe der Hochschule Speyer.

———. 1975. "Erkenntnisprobleme moderner Verwaltungsgeschichte. Geschichtschreibung mit pragmatischer Absicht." In *Die Verwaltung*.

Huddleston, Mark W. 1984. "Administrative History." In *Comparative Public Administration: An Annotated Bibliography*. London: Garland Publishers.

Hume, L.J. 1980. "Administrative History." *Australian Journal of Public Administration* 39, nos. 3–4: 422–436.

————. 1981. "Administrative History." In *Understanding Public Administration*, edited by G.R. Curnow and R.L. Wettenhall, 160–174. Sydney: Allen and Unwin.

Jensen, Richard. 1969. "History and the Political Scientist." In *Politics and the Social Sciences*, edited by Seymour Martin Lipset, 1–28. London: Oxford University Press.

Lee, J.M. 1974. *Approaches to the Study of Public Administration, Part 4: The Historical Approach*. Milton Keynes: The Open University Press.

Mansfield, Harvey C. 1951. "The Uses of History." *Public Administration Review* 11, no.4: 51–57.

Mazrui, Ali A. 1968. "From Social Darwinism to Current Theories of Modernization: A Tradition of Analysis." *World Politics* 21, no.1: 69–83.

Molitor, André. 1983. "The History of Administration." *International Review of Administrative Sciences* 49, no.1: 1–3.

————, ed. 1984. Untitled. In *Cahiers de l'histoire de l'administration*, no.1. Brussels: International Institute of Administrative Sciences.

Nash, G.D. 1969. *Perspectives on Administration: The Vistas of History*. Berkeley and Los Angeles: Institute of Governmental Studies, University of California.

Nisbet, Robert A. 1969. *Social Change and History*. New York: Oxford University Press.

Raadschelders, J.C.N. 1994. "Administrative History: Contents, Meaning, and Usefulness." *International Review of the Administrative Sciences* 60, no.1: 117–129.

————. 1995. "The Use of Models in Administrative History: A Reply to Thuillier." In *The Influences of the Napoleonic "Model" of Administration on the Administrative Organization of Other Countries*, edited by Bernd Wunder. *Cahiers de l'histoire de l'administration*, no.4. Brussels: International Institute of Administrative Sciences.

Rugge, Fabio. 1993. "Eine Wissenschaft ohne Vergangenheit—eine Geschichte ohne Zukunft? Ein kleiner Streifung durch verwaltungswissenschaftliche Zeitschriften." *Jahrbuch für Europäische Verwaltungsgeschichte* 5: 369–380.

Starosciak, Jerzy. 1975. "Le caractère interdisciplinaire des recherches sur l'administration." *Revue International des Sciences Administratives* 41, no.1: 57–60.

Stolleis, Michael. 1989. "Bemerkungen zur Aktuellen Situation der 'Verwaltungsgeschichte.'" In *Institutions and Bureaucrats in the History of Administration*, edited by Seppo Tiihonen, 25–30. Helsinki: Government Printing Centre.

Tiihonen, Seppo. 1989. "Bureaucracy as a Problem and a Study Object." In *Institutions and Bureaucrats in the History of Administration*, 103–161. Helsinki: Government Printing Centre.

Waldo, Dwight. 1956. "Perspectives of History." In *Perspectives on Administration*, 50–76. Birmingham, AL: University of Alabama Press.

Wettenhall, R.L. 1967. "The Neglect of Administrative History." In *Papers and Proceedings of the Tasmanian Historical Research Association* 24, no.1: 2–20.

———. 1968. "History and Public Administration." *Papers and Proceedings of the Tasmanian Historical Research Association* 16, no.3: 95–107. In a slightly shorter version also published in *Public Policy and Administration: A Reader*, edited by R.N. Spann and G.R. Curnow, 216–223. Sydney: Wiley, 1975.

General Studies in Administrative History

Achterberg, N. 1979. "Strukturen der Geschichte der Verwaltung." *Die öffentliche Verwaltung* 32, no.16: 577–585.

Almond, Gabriel, Scott Flanagan, and Robert Mundt, eds. 1973. *Crisis, Choice, and Change: Historical Studies of Political Development.* Boston: Little Brown.

Alt, J.E. 1983. "The Evolution of Tax Structures." *Public Choice* 41, no.1: 181–222.

Ardant, Gabriel. 1971. *Histoire de l'impôt (Les grandes études historiques).* Paris: Fayard.

———. 1975. "Financial Policy and Economic Infrastructure of Modern States in Nations." In *The Formation of National States in Western Europe*, edited by Charles Tilly. Princeton, NJ: Princeton University Press.

Ashford, Douglas E. 1992. "Historical Contexts and Policy Studies." In *History and Context in Comparative Public Policy*, edited by Douglas E. Ashford, 27–37. Pittsburgh, PA : University of Pittsburgh Press.

Bendix, Reinhard. 1973. *Kings or People: Power and the Mandate to Rule.* Berkeley and Los Angeles: University of California Press.

———. 1977. *Nation-Building and Citizenship.* Berkeley and Los Angeles, CA: University of California Press.

Blickle, P. 1986. "Communalism, Parliamentarism, Republicanism." In *Parliaments, Estates and Representation* 6, no.1: 1–13.

Blockmans, W.P. and H. van Nuffel, eds. 1986. *Staat en religie in de 15e en 16e eeuw.* Brussels: van Nuffel.

Blockmans, Wim. 1990. "Beheersen en overtuigen: Reflecties bij nieuwe visies op staatsvorming." *Tijdschrift voor Sociale Geschiedenis* 16, no.1: 18–30.

Boogman, J.C. and G.N. van der Plaa, eds. 1980. *Federalism: History and current significance of a form of government.* The Hague: Martinus Nijhoff.

Brodtrick, Otto. 1981. "Bureaucracy through the Ages." *Optimum* 12, no.3: 5–15.

Brown, Nathan. 1990. "Brigands and State-Building." *Comparative Studies in Society and History* 32, no.2: 258–281.

Bruce, M. 1961. *The Coming of the Welfare State*. London: Batsford.

Carneiro, R.L. 1970. "A Theory of the Origin of the State." *Science* 69: 733–738.

———. 1981. "The Chiefdom, Precursor of the State." In *The Transition to Statehood in the New World*, edited by G.D. Jones and R.R. Kantz. Cambridge: Cambridge University Press.

———. 1987. "Cross-currents in the Theory of State Formation." *American Ethnologist* 14: 756–770.

Cassese, Sabino and Jill Pellew, eds. 1987. "The Introduction of Merit Systems in Various Bureaucracies: A Comparative Account." In *The merit system*, 12–23. *Cahier d'Histoire de l'Administration*, no.2. Brussels: International Institute of Administrative Sciences.

Castles, F.G., ed. 1989. *The Comparative History of Public Policy*. Cambridge: Polity Press.

Chapman, Brian. 1970. "Historical Introduction." In *The Profession of Government*. 4th ed., 10–44. London: Unwin University Books.

Chapman, R. 1984. *Administrative Leadership*. London: Allen & Unwin.

Claesen, H.J.M. 1970. *Van vorsten en volken: Een beschrijvende en functioneel-vergelijkende studie van de staatsorganisatie van vijf schriftloze vorstendommen*. Ph.D. thesis, University of Amsterdam, Amsterdam.

Claesen, H.J.M. and P. Skalnik, eds. 1978. *The Early State*. The Hague: Mouton Publishers.

Claesen, H.J.M. 1980. "Van incidentele aanvoerder tot beroepsbestuurder. Een overzicht van ontstaan en ontwikkeling van de politieke organisatie tot en met het ontstaan van de vroege staat." *Acta Politica* 15, no.1: 39–60.

Claesen, H.J.M. and P. Skalnik, eds. 1981. *The Study of the State*. Paris: Mouton Publishers.

Claesen, H.J.M. and P. van de Velde, eds. 1987. *Early State Dynamics*. In Studies in Human Society, vol. 2. Leiden: Brill.

Claesen, H.J.M. 1991. *Verdwenen koninkrijken en verloren beschavingen: opkomst en ondergang van de Vroege Staat*. Assen: Van Gorcum.

Cohen, R. and J.D. Toland. 1988. *State Formation and Political Legitimacy*. New Brunswick, NJ: Transaction Publishers.

Crossman, R.H.S. 1969. *Government and the Governed: A History of Political Ideas and Political Practice*. London: Chatto & Windus.

Delaney, W. 1962–1963. "The Development and Decline of Patrimonial and Bureaucratic Administrations." *Administrative Science Quarterly* 7, no.4: 458–501.

Duganne, Aug. J.H. 1860. *A History of Governments: Showing the Progress of Civil Society and the Structure of Ancient and Modern States*. New York: Robert M. de Witt.

Eisenstadt, S.N. 1958. *The Comparative Analysis of Historical Political Systems*. New York: Committee on Comparative Politics of the Social Science Research Council.

————. 1958. "Bureaucracy and Bureaucratization: A Trend Report and Bibliography." *Current Sociology* 7: 99–165.

————. 1963. *The Political Systems of Empires: The Rise and Fall of the Historical Bureaucratic Societies*. New York: Free Press.

————. 1965. *Essays in Comparative Institutions*. New York: John Wiley.

————. 1970. "Problems of Emerging Bureaucracies in Developing Areas and New States." In *Comparative Perspectives on Formal Organizations*, Henry A. Lansberger, 215–230. Boston: Little Brown and Company.

————. 1973. *Building States and Nations*, vols. 1–2, edited by S. N. Eisenstadt. Beverly Hills, CA: SAGE Publications.

————. 1980. "Comparative Analysis in State Formation in Historical Contexts." In *International Social Science Journal* 32, no.4: 624–654.

————, ed. 1986. *The Origin and Diversity of Axial-Age Civilizations*. Albany, NY: SUNY Press.

Eisenstadt, S.N. and A. Shachar. 1987. *Society, Culture, and Urbanization*. Beverly Hills, CA: SAGE Publications.

Flanigan, William H. and Edwin Fogelman. 1970–1971. "Patterns of Political Violence in Comparative Historical Perspective." In *Comparative Politics* 3, no.1: 1–20.

Flora, Peter. 1974. *Modernisierungsforschung: Zur empirischen Analyse der gesellschaftlichen Entwicklung*. Opladen: Westdeutscher Verlag.

Flora, P. and A.J. Heidenheimer, eds. 1984. *The Development of Welfare States in Europe and America*. New Brunswick, NJ: Transaction Publishers.

Geertz, Clifford, ed. 1963. *Old Societies and New States*. New York: Free Press.

Gladden, E.N. 1972. *A History of Public Administration*. 2 vols. London: Frank Cass.

Greenfeld, Liah. 1992. *Nationalism: Five Roads to Modernity*. Cambridge, MA: Harvard University Press.

Gurr, T.R. 1974. "Persistence and Change in Political Systems, 1800–1971." *American Political Science Review* 58, no.4: 1482–1504.

Hall, J.A., ed. 1987. *States in History*. 2d ed. Oxford: Basil Blackwell.

Heady, F. 1991. "Historical Antecedents of National Administrative Systems." In *Public Administration: A Comparative Perspective*, 5th ed., 150–187. Basel: Marcel Dekker Inc.

Heater, Derek. 1990. *Citizenship: The Civic Ideal in World History, Politics and Education*. London: Longman.

Hechter, Michael and William Brustein. 1980. "Regional Modes of Production and Patterns of State Formation in Europe." *American Journal of Sociology* 85, no.5: 1061–1094.

Held, David. 1985. "Introduction: Central Perspectives on the Modern State. In *States and Societies*, 3d ed., edited by David Held et al., 1–55. Oxford: Basil Blackwell and The Open University.

Heper, Metin. 1985. "The State and Public Bureaucracies: A Comparative and Historical Perspective." *Comparative Studies in Society and History* 27, no.1: 86–110.

Hinsley, F.H. 1966. *Sovereignty*. New York: Basis Books Inc.

Historical Research. 1986. Special issue on "Multiple kingdoms and federal states" 62, no. 148.

Hitch, Charles J. 1970. "Cost Effectiveness." In *The Administrative Process and Democratic Theory,* edited by Louis C. Gawthrop, 287–297. Boston, MA: Houghton Mifflin Company.

Huntington, Samuel P. 1968. *Political Order in Changing Societies*. New Haven, CT: Yale University Press.

Jacoby, Henry. 1973. *The Bureaucratization of the World.* Berkeley and Los Angeles: University of California Press.

Jaggers, Keith. 1992. "War-Making and State-Making in Europe and the Americas." *Comparative Political Studies* 25, no.1: 25–62.

Johnson, A.W. and T.K. Earle. 1987. *The Evolution of Human Societies. From Foraging Group to Agrarian State.* Stanford, CA: Stanford University Press.

Kamenka, Eugene. 1989. *Bureaucracy.* Oxford: Basil Blackwell.

Köhler, P.A., F. Zacher, and M. Partington. 1982. *The Evolution of Social Insurance.* London: Frances Pinter.

Konstas, Helen. 1957–1958. "Max Weber's Two Conceptions of Bureaucracy." *American Journal of Sociology* 63, no.4: 400–409.

Krasner, Stephen D. 1984. "Approaches to the State: Alternative conceptions and Historical Dynamics." *Comparative Politics* 16, no.2: 223–246.

Kraus, W. 1980. "Die herrschenden Diener: 4000 Jahre Beamtentum und die heutige Aktualität." *Europäische Rundschau* 8, no.3: 89–98.

Lane, Jan-Erik and Svante Ersson. 1990. *Comparative Political Economy.* London: Pinter Publishers.

Lohmann, Roger A. 1992. "The Evolution of the Commons in Western Civilization." In *The Commons: New Perspectives on Nonprofit Organizations and Voluntary Action,* 83–126. San Francisco, CA: Jossey-Bass Publishers, 83–126.

Meyer, Marshall W. and M. Craig Brown. 1977. "The Process of Bureaucratization." *American Journal of Sociology* 83, no.2: 364–385.

Meyer, M.W., W. Stevenson, and S. Webster. 1985. *Limits to Bureaucratic Growth.* Berlin and New York: Walter de Gruyter.

Mitchell, B.R. 1980. *European Historical Statistics, 1750–1975.* New York: Facts on File.

Mommsen, Wolfgang J. 1974. *The Age of Bureaucracy: Perspectives on the Political Sociology of Max Weber.* Oxford: Basil Blackwell.

Morselli, Emanuele. 1951. "On the Historiography of Thought on Public Finance." *Public Finance* 6, no.1: 53–79.

Moore, Jr., Barrington. 1966. *Social Origins of Dictatorship and Democracy: Lord and Peasant in the Making of the Modern World.* Boston, MA: Beacon Press.

Mousnier, Roland. 1982. *La Monarchie absolue en Europe du 5e siècle à nos jours*. Paris: PUF.

Olson, Mancur. 1982. *The Rise and Decline of Nations: Economic Growth, Stagflation, and Social Rigidities*. New Haven, CT.: Yale University Press.

Ostrom, Elinor. 1990. *Governing the Commons: The Evolution of Institutions for Collective Action*. Cambridge: Cambridge University Press.

Page, Edward C. 1995. "Patterns and Diversity in European State Development." In *Governing the New Europe*, edited by Jack Hayward and Edward C. Page, 9–43. Cambridge: Polity Press.

Parker, Geoffrey. 1988. *The Military Revolution: Military Innovation and the Rise of the West, 1500–1800*. Cambridge: Cambridge University Press.

Peters, B. Guy. 1991. "The Development of Tax Systems." In *The Politics of Taxation: A Comparative Perspective*. Cambridge and Oxford: Blackwell.

Poggi, Gianfranco. 1978. *The Development of the Modern State: A Socio logical Introduction*. Stanford, CA: Stanford University Press.

Pryor, F.L. 1968. *Public Expenditures in Communist and Capitalist Nations*. London: George Allen and Unwin Ltd.

Raadschelders, J.C.N. 1995. "Rediscovering Citizenship. Historical and Contemporary Reflections." *Public Administration* (UK) 73 no.4: 611–625.

Raadschelders, J.C.N. and M.R. Rutgers. 1996. "A History of Civil Service Systems." In *Civil Service Systems in Comparative Perspective*, edited by A.J.G.M. Bekke, J.L. Perry and Th. A.J. Toonen, 67–99. Bloomington, IN: Indiana University Press.

Roberts, Michael. 1955. *The Military Revolution 1560–1660*. Belfast: Marjory Boyd.

Rokkan, S. 1970. *Citizens, Elections, Parties: Approaches to the comparative study of the processes of development*. Oslo: Universitetsforlaget.

Roorda, D.J. and A.H. Huusen. 1977. "Das Heft in der Hand und Geld im Kasten. Historische beschouwingen over vroeg-moderne overheidsbureaucratie in Europa." *Tijdschrift voor Geschiedenis* 90, nos.3–4: 303–325.

Rose, Richard. 1976. "On the Priorities of Government: A Developmental Analysis of Public Policies." *European Journal of Political Research* 4, no.3: 247–289.

———. 1984. *Understanding Big Government: The Program Approach*. Beverly Hills, CA: SAGE Publications.

———, ed. 1987. *Public Employment in Western Nations*. 2d ed. Cambridge: Cambridge University Press.

Rostow, Walt W. 1971. *Politics and the Stages of Growth*. Cambridge: Cambridge University Press.

Rozman, Gilbert. 1978. Urban Networks and Historical Stages. *Journal of Interdisciplinary History* 9, no.1: 65–91.

Rustow, Dankwart A. and Kenneth Paul Erickson. 1991. *Comparative Political Dynamics: Global Research Perspectives*. New York: Harper Collins Publishers.

Rutgers, M.R. 1993. "Wortels van de bestuurskunde." In *Tussen Fragmentatie en Integratie: Bestuurskunde als kennisintegrerende wetenschap*, 49–104. Delft: Eburon.

Schwartz, Richard D. and James C. Miller. 1964–1965. "Legal Evolution and Social Complexity." *American Journal of Sociology* 70, no.2: 159–169.

Seligman, Edwin R.A. 1931. *Essays in Taxation*. 10th ed. New York: The MacMillan Company.

————. [1911] 1970. *The Income Tax: A Study of the History, Theory and Practice of the Income Tax at Home and Abroad*. New York: A.M. Kelley.

Silberman, Bernard S. 1993. *Cages of Reason: The Rise of the Rational State in France, Japan, The United States, and Great Britain*. Chicago, IL: The University of Chicago Press.

Skocpol, Theda, ed. 1984. *Vision and Method in Historical Sociology*. Cambridge: Cambridge University Press.

Spender, J.A. 1983. *The Government of Mankind*. Cassell.

Strayer, Joseph R. 1975. "The Development of Bureaucracies." *Comparative Studies in Sociology and History* 17, no.4: 504–509.

Swaan, A. de. 1988. In *Care of the State: Health Care, Education and Welfare in Europe and the USA in the Modern Era*. Cambridge: Polity Press; also published in Dutch (Amsterdam, 1989).

Taylor, Charles Lewis, ed. 1983. *Why Governments Grow: Measuring Public Sector Size*. Beverly Hills, CA: SAGE Publications.

Theoretische Geschiedenis. 1991. Special issue on "Souvereiniteit: Lotgevallen van een Begrip" 18, no.4.

Toynbee, Arnold Joseph. 1947–1957. *A Study of History*. Abridgement of volumes I–X by D.C. Somervell. New York: Oxford University Press.

Vor, Marc Peter Henri de. 1992. *The Growth of Government: Economic History, Transaction Costs and Property Rights*. Ph.D. thesis, Catholic University of Brabant, Tilburg, the Netherlands.

Webber, Carolyn and Aaron Wildavsky. 1986. *A History of Taxation and Expenditure in the Western World*. New York: Simon and Schuster.

Weber, Max. 1980. *Wirtschaft und Gesellschaft: Grundrisz zur Verstehenden Soziologie*, edited by J. Winckelman. 5th ed. Tübingen: J.C.B. Mohr.

Weilenmann, Hermann. 1966. "The Interlocking of Nation and Personality Structure." In *Nation-Building*, edited by K.W. Deutsch and W.J. Foltz, 33–55. New York: Atherton Press.

Werthman, M.S., and M. Dalby, eds. 1971. *Bureaucracy in Historical Perspective*. Glenview, IL: Scott Foresman.

White, L., C. Bland, W.R. Sharp, and F.M. Marx. 1935. *Civil Service Abroad*. New York: McGraw-Hill.

Wickwar, W. Hardy. 1970. *The Political Theory of Local Government*. Columbia, SC: University of South Carolina Press.

Wittfogel, Karl A. 1957. *Oriental Despotism: A Comparative Study of Total Power*. New Haven, CT: Yale University Press.

Woolf, Stuart. 1989. "Statistics and the Modern State." In *Comparative Studies in Society and History* 31, no.3: 588–604.

Yoffee, N. and G.L. Cowgill. 1988. *The Collapse of Ancient States and Civilizations*. Tucson, AZ: University of Arizona Press.

AFRICA

General Works

Burke, F.G. 1969. "Public Administration in Africa: the Legacy of Inherited Colonial Institutions." *Journal of Comparative Administration* 1, no.3: 345–378.

Claesen, H.J.M. and P. Geschiere. 1984. *Staatsvorming in Afrika*. Meppel: Boom. (Also in *Sociologische Gids* 31, no.4: 298–387).

Cohen, William B. 1971. *Rulers of Empire: The French Colonial Service in Africa*. Stanford, CA: Stanford University Press.

Connah, G. 1987. *African Civilizations, Precolonial Cities, and States in Tropical Africa*. Cambridge: Cambridge University Press.

Davidson, Basil. 1992. *The Black Man's Burden: Africa and the Curse of the Nation-State*. New York: Times Books.

Eisenstadt, S.N., Michael Abitbol, and Naomi Chazan. 1988. "State Formation in Africa, Conclusions." In *The Early State in African Perspective: Culture, Power and Division of Labor*, 168–200. Leiden: Brill, Studies in Human Society, vol.3.

Fleming, William G. 1966. "Authority, Efficiency, and Role Stress: Problems in the Development of East African Bureaucracies." *Administrative Science Quarterly* 11, no.3: 386–404.

Gifford, Prosser and W. Roger Louis, eds. 1967. *Britain and Germany in Africa. Imperial Rivalry and Colonial Rule*. New Haven, CT: Yale University Press.

———. 1982. *The Transfer of Power in Africa: Decolonization, 1940–1960*. New Haven, CT.: Yale University Press.

Hartmann, L.M. 1957. "Imperial Africa and Italy: Administration." In *The Cambridge Medieval History*. Vol. 2. Cambridge: Cambridge University Press.

Kasfir, Nelson. 1976. *The Shrinking Political Arena: Participation and Ethnicity in African Politics, with a Case Study of Uganda*. Berkeley and Los Angeles: University of California Press.

Kasfir, Nelson. 1983. "Introduction: Relating Class to State in Africa." *The Journal of Commonwealth & Comparative Politics* 21, no.3: 1–22.

Kottak, C.Ph. 1972. "Ecological Variables in the Origin and Evolution of the African States." *Comparative Studies in Society and History* 14, no.2: 351–380.

Lonsdale, John. 1981. "States and Social Processes in Africa: A Historiographical Study." *African Studies Review* 24, nos.2–3: 139–225.

Markovitz, Irving Leonard. 1976. "Bureaucratic Development and Economic Growth." *The Journal of Modern African Studies* 14, no.2: 183–200.

Rothchild, Donald and Naomi Chazan. 1988. *The Precarious Balance: State and Society in Africa.* Boulder, CO.: Westview Press.

Saul, John. 1979. *The State and Revolution in Eastern Africa.* New York: Monthly Review Press.

Schapera, I. 1965. *Government and Politics in Tribal Societies.* New York: Schocken Books.

Skalnik, P. 1983. "Questioning the Concept of the State in Indigenous Africa." *Social Dynamics* 9, no.2: 11–18.

———. 1987. "On the Inadequacy of the Concept of the 'Traditional State'" (illustrated with ethnographic material on Namin, Ghana). *Journal of Legal Pluralism* 25/26: 301–325.

Egypt

Björkman, Walther. 1928. "Beiträge zur Geschichte der Staatskanzlei im islamischen Ägypten." *Abhandlungen aus dem Gebiet der Auslandskunde* 28. Hamburg: Hamburg University.

Breasted, James Henry, ed. 1906–1907. *Ancient Records of Egypt.* Chicago, IL: University of Chicago Press.

Edgerton, William F. 1947. "The Government and the Governed in the Egyptian Empire." *Journal of Near Eastern Studies* 6, no.3: 152–160.

Gyles, Mary F. 1959. *Pharaonic Policies and Administration, 663 to 323 B.C..* Chapell Hill, NC: University of North Carolina Press.

Hayes, W.C. 1953. "Notes on the Government of Egypt in the Late Middle Kingdom." *Journal of Near Eastern Studies* 12, no.1: 31–39.

Hellek, W. 1954. *Untersuchungen zu den Beamtentiteln des Ägyptischen alten Reiches.* Glückstadt.

Hunter, F. Robert. 1984. *Egypt Under the Khedives, 1805–1879: From Household Government to Modern Bureaucracy.* Pittsburg, PA: University of Pittsburg Press.

Kees, H. 1933. "Beiträge zur altägyptischen Provincialverwaltung unter der Geschichte des Feudalismus." In *Nachrichten von der Gesellschaft der Wissenschaften zu Göttingen, Philosophisch-Historischen Klasse.* Vol. 3, 579–598. Berlin: Weidman.

———. 1934. "Zur Innenpolitik der Saitendynastie." In *Nachrichten von der Gesellschaft der Wissenschaften zu Göttingen, Philosophisch-Historischen Klasse.* Vol. 1, 95–106.

Maspero, M.G. 1890. "La carrière administrative de deux hauts fonctionnaires égyptiens vers la fin de la IIIème dynastie." *Journal Asiatique*, 8th series, vol 15: 269–428.

Wallace, Sherman Le Roy. 1938. *Taxation in Egypt.* Princeton, NJ: Princeton University Press.

Welles, Bradford. 1949. "Ptolemaic Administration in Egypt." In *Journal of Juristic Papyrology* 3, no.1: 21–48.

Ethiopia

Asmerom, Haile Kiros. 1978. *Emergence, Expansion, and Decline of Patrimonial Bureaucracy in Ethiopia, 1907–1974: an Attempt at Historical Interpretation.* Amsterdam: University of Amsterdam.

Dahomey

Herskovits, M.J. 1967. *Dahomey: An Ancient West African Kingdom.* 2d ed. New York: J.J. Augustin.

Ghana

Lewin, T.J. 1978. *Asante before the British: The Prempean Years, 1875–1900.* Lawrence, KS: The Regents Press of Kansas.
Kooperman, L. and S. Rosenberg. 1977. "The British Administrative Legacy in Kenya and Ghana." *International Review of Administrative Sciences* 43, no.3: 267–272.
McCarthy, M. 1983. *Social Change and the Growth of British Power in the Gold Coast, The Fante States 1807–1874.* Lanham: University Press of America.
Oheno-Darko. I.E. 1977. *Government and Politics in Ghana, 1850–1972.* Akrokerri: Akrokerri College.
Wilks, Ivor. 1975. *Asante in the Nineteenth Century.* Cambridge: Cambridge University Press.

Kenya

Berman, B. 1976. "Bureaucracy and Incumbent Violence: Colonial Administration and the Origins of the 'Mau-Mau' Emergency in Kenya." *British Journal of Political Science* 6, no.2: 143–175.
Kooperman, L. and S. Rosenberg. 1977. "The British Administrative Legacy in Kenya and Ghana." *International Review of Administrative Sciences* 43, no.3: 267–272.

Nigeria

Nicolson, I. 1969. *The Administration of Nigeria 1900–1960: Men, Methods and Myths.* Oxford: Clarendon Press.
Perham, Margery. 1937. *Native Administration in Nigeria.* New York: Oxford University Press.
Smith, M.G. 1960. *Government in Zazzau.* London: Oxford University Press.

Smith, B.C. 1972. "Field Administration and Political Change: the Case of Northern Nigeria." *Administrative Science Quarterly* 17, no.1: 99–109.

Sudan

Collins, R. 1972. "The Sudan Political Service: a Portrait of the 'Imperia-Lists.'" *African Affairs* 71, no.284: 293–303.
Tymouski, M. 1987. "The Early State and after in Precolonial West Sudan." In *Early State Dynamics*, edited by H.J.M. Claesen and P. van der Velde, 54–69. Leiden: Brill.

Tanzania

Willis, Roy. 1981. *A State in the Making.* Bloomington, IN: University of Indiana Press.

Uganda

Apter, David E. 1961. *The Political Kingdom in Uganda: A Study in Bureaucratic Nationalism.* Princeton, NJ: Princeton University Press.
Fallers, Lloyd A. 1956. *Bantu Bureaucracy: A Study of Integration and Conflict in the Political Institutions of an East African People.* Cambridge: Heffer & Sons.

Zaire

Young, Crawford and Thomas Turner. 1985. *The Rise and Decline of the Zairean State.* Madison, WI: University of Wisconsin Press.

ASIA AND PACIFIC OCEAN

General Works

Aberle, David F. 1957. *Chakan and Duger Mongol bureaucratic administration: 1912–1945.* New Haven, CT: HRAF Press.
Braibanti, R., ed. 1966. *Asian Bureaucratic Systems Emergent from the British Imperial Tradition: Burma, Ceylon, India, Malaysia, Nepal, Pakistan.* Durham, NC: Duke University Press.
Evers, Hans-Dieter. 1987. "The Bureaucratization of Southeast Asia." In *Comparative Studies on Society and History* 29, no.4: 666–685.
Golay, Frank H. 1976. "Southeast Asia: The 'Colonial Drain' Revisited." In *Southeast Asian History and Historiography*, edited by C.D. Cowan and O.W. Wolters. Ithaca, NY: Cornell University Press.

Hall, K.R. 1985. *Maritime Trade and State Development in Early Southeast Asia.* Honolulu, HI: University of Hawai Press.

Keddie, Nikki R. 1991. "The Revolt of Islam and Its Roots." In *Comparative Political Dynamics. Global Research Perspectives*, edited by Dankwart A. Rustow and Kenneth Paul Erickson, 292–308. New York: Harper Collins Publishers.

Krader, Lawrence. 1958. "Feudalism and the Tartar Polity of the Middle Ages." *Comparative Studies in Society and History* 1, no.1: 76–99.

Mommsen, W.J. and J.A. de Moor, eds. 1992. *European Expansion and Law: The Encounter of European and Indigenous Law in Nineteenth- and Twentieth-Century Africa and Asia.* Oxford and New York: Berg.

Pack, Melvin Deloy. 1981. *The Administrative Structure of the Palace at Mari (ca. 1800–1750 B.C.).* Ann Arbor, MI: University Microfilms International.

Quah, John S.T. 1978. "The Origins of Public Bureaucracies in the ASEAN countries." *Indian Journal of Public Administration* 24, no.2: 400–429.

Tinker, Hugh. 1966. "Structure of the British Imperial Heritage." In *Asian Bureaucratic Systems Emergent from the British Imperial Tradition: Burma, Ceylon, India, Malaysia, Nepal, Pakistan*, edited by R. Braibanti, 23–86. Durham, NC: Duke University Press.

Burma

Furnival, John S. 1948. *Colonial Policy and Practice: A Comparative Study of Burma and Netherlands India.* Cambridge: Cambridge University Press.

Pye, Lucian W. 1962. *Politics, Personality, and Nation-building: Burma's Search for Identity.* New Haven, CT: Yale University Press.

Ceylon (Sri Lanka)

Tambiah, S.J. 1955. "Ethnic representation in Ceylon's Higher Administrative Services, 1870–1946." *University of Ceylon Review* 13, no.1: 113–134.

Hovy, L. 1991. *Ceylonees plakkaatboek: Plakkaten en andere wetten uitgevaardigd door het Nederlands bestuur op Ceylon, 1638–1796.* Hilversum: Verloren.

China

Balasz, Etienne. 1957. "Chinesische Geschichstwerke als Wegweiser zur Praxis der Bürokratie." *Saeculum: Jahrbuch für Universalgeschichte* 8: 210–223.

———. 1959. "La pérennité de la société bureaucratique en Chine." *International Symposium on History of Eastern and Western Cultural Contacts.* Tokyo, 31–39.

————. 1964. *Chinese Civilization and Bureaucracy: Variations on a Theme*. New Haven, CT: Yale University Press. Translated by H.M. Wright. Edited by Arthur F. Wright.

Berkelbach van der Sprenkel and P.N. Otto. 1958. *The Chinese Civil Service: The Nineteenth Century*. Canberra: University of Canberra Press.

Bielenstein, Hans. 1980. *The Bureaucracy of Han Times*. Cambridge: Cambridge University Press.

Bünger, K. 1947. "Über die Verantwortlichkeit der Beamten nach klassischem chinesischem Recht." *Studia Serica* 6: 159–191.

Chi, C.T. 1963. *Key Economic Areas in Chinese History, as Revealed in the Development of Public Works for Water Control*. London: Allen & Unwin.

Chia, C.Y. 1956. "The Church-State Conflict in the T'ang Dynasty." In *Chinese Social History*, edited by E.T. Zen and J. de Francis, 197–207. Washington D.C.: American Council of Learned Societies.

Creel, Herrlee G. 1964. "The Beginnings of Bureaucracy in China: The Origins of the Hsien." *Journal of Asian Studies* 22, no.2: 155–84.

————. 1970. *The Origins of Statecraft in China*. Vol 1. Chicago, IL: University of Chicago Press.

————. [1970] 1982. "On the Origin of *Wu-Wei*." In *What is Taoism? and Other Studies in Chinese Cultural History*, 48–76. Chicago: University of Chicago Press. Reprint, Midway.

————. [1970] 1982. "The Meaning of *Hsing-ming*." In *What is Taoism? and Other Studies in Chinese Cultural History*, 79–91. Chicago : University of Chicago Press. Reprint, Midway.

————. [1970] 1982. "The *Fa-chia*: 'Legalists' or 'Administrators'? In *What is Taoism? and Other Studies in Chinese Cultural History* 92–100. Chicago: University of Chicago Press. Reprint, Midway.

Davis, Richard L. 1986. *Court and Family in Sung China, 960–1279: Bureaucratic Success and Kinship Fortunes for the Shik of Ming-Chou*. Durham, NC: Duke University Press.

Duara, Prasenjit. 1987. "State Involution: A Study of Local Finances in North China 1911–1935." *Comparative Studies in Society and History* 29, no.1: 132–161.

Eberhard, W. 1948. "Some Sociological Remarks on the Systems of Provincial Administration during the Period of the Five Dynasties." *Studia Serica*, supplementary volume, 1–18.

Eberhard, W. 1951. "Remarks on the Bureaucracy in North China during the Tenth Century." *Oriens* 4, no.2: 280–299.

Fairbank, John K., ed. 1957. *Chinese Thought and Institutions*. Chicago, IL: University of Chicago Press.

Franke, H. 1940. "Dschan Mong-fü: Das Leben eines chinesischen Staatsmannes, Gelehrten und Künstlers unter der Mongolenherrschaft." *Sinica* 15: 25–46.

Franke, O. 1931. "Der Bericht Wang An Shih's von 1058 über Reform des Beamtentums." In *Sitzungsberichte der preussischen Akademie der Wissenschaften, Historisch-philosophischen Klasse*, 218–242.

Franke, Wolfgang. 1960. *The Reform and Abolition of the Traditional Chinese Examination System*. Cambridge, MA (mimeograph).

Gale, E.M. 1929. "Historical Evidences Relating to Early Chinese Public Finance." *Proceedings of the Pacific Coast Branch, American Historical Association*, 48–62.

Han, Y.S. 1946. "The Chinese Civil Service Yesterday and Today." *Pacific Historical Review* 15, no.2: 158–170.

Herson, Lawrence J.R. 1982. "China's Imperial Bureaucracy: It's Direction and Control." In *American Public Administration: Patterns of the Past*, edited by James W. Fesler, 41–56. Washington D.C.: American Society for Public Administration.

Ho, K.L.A. 1952. "The Grand Council in the Ch'ing Dynasty." *Far Eastern Quarterly* 11, no.2: 167–182.

Holzman, D. 1957. "Les débuts du système médiévale choix et de classement des fonctionnaires." In *Mélanges de l'institut des hautes études chinoises*, 387–414. Paris: Institut des Hautes Études Chinoises.

Hsieh, P.C. 1925. *The Government of China, 1644–1911*. Baltimore, MD: Johns Hopkins University Press.

Hsu, Cho-Yun. 1965. "The Changing Relationship between Local Society and the Central Political Power in the Former Han: 206 B.C–A.D.8." *Comparative Studies in Society and History* 7, no.4: 358–370.

Hucker, Charles O. 1958. "Governmental Organization of the Ming Dynasty." *Historical Journal of Asian Studies* 21, no.1: 1–67.

———. 1966. *The Censorial System of Ming China*. Stanford, CA: Stanford University Press.

Kracke, Edward A., Jr. 1947. "Family vs. Merit in Chinese Civil Service Examinations under the Empire." *Harvard Journal of Asiatic Studies* 10, no.2: 103–123.

———. 1953. *Civil Service in Early Sung China 960–1067*. Cambridge, MA: Harvard University Press.

Leung, Man-Kam. 1977. *Juan Yuan (1764–1849): The Life, Works and Career of a Chinese Scholar-Bureaucrat*. Ph.D. thesis, University of Hawaii, Honolulu, Hawaii.

Liang, F.C. 1956. "Local Tax Collectors in the Ming Dynasty." In *Chinese Social History* edited by E.T. Zen and J. de Francis, 271–281. Washington D.C.: Americal Council of Learned Societies.

Liu, James T.C. 1959. "Some Classifications of Bureaucrats in Chinese Historiography." In *Confucianism in Action*, edited by D.S. Nivison and A.F. Wright, 165–181. Stanford, CA: Stanford University Press.

———. 1959. *Reform in Sung China: Wang An-Shih (1021–1086) and His New Policies*. Cambridge, MA: Harvard University Press.

Loewe, Michael. 1967. *Records of Han Administration.* Cambridge: Cambridge University Press.

Marsh, Robert. 1962. "The Venality of Provincial Office in China and in Comparative Perspective." *Comparative Studies in Society and History* 4, no.4: 454–466.

Metzger, Thomas A. 1973. *The Internal Organization of Ching Bureaucracy: Legal, Normative, and Communication Aspects.* Cambridge, MA: Harvard University Press.

Michael, Franz. 1942. *The Origin of Manchu Rule in China: Frontier and Bureaucracy as Interacting Forces in the Chinese Empire.* Baltimore, MD: Johns Hopkins Press.

Mu, Ch'ien. 1982. *Traditional Government in Imperial China: A Critical Analysis.* Translated by Chün-tu Hsüen and George O. Totten. Hong Kong: Chinese University Press.

Sariti, Anthony William. 1970. *The Political Thought of Ssu-ma Kuang: Bureaucratic Absolutism in the Northern Sung.* Ph.D. diss. Georgetown University, Washington, D.C.

Shryok, J.K. 1932. *The Origin and Development of the State Cult of Confucius.* N.p.: Century Co..

Skocpol, Theda. 1985. "States and Revolutions: France, Russia and China." In *States and Societies.* 3d ed., edited by David Held, 151–169. Oxford: Basil Blackwell/ Open University.

Teng, Ssu-yü. 1943. "Chinese Influence on the Western Examination System." *Historical Harvard Journal of Asiatic Studies* 7, no.2: 267–312.

Twitchett, D. 1956. "The Government of T'ang in the Early Eighth Century." *Bulletin of the School of Oriental and African Studies* 18, no.2: 322–330.

Walker, R.L. 1947. "The Control System of the Chinese Government." *Far Eastern Quarterly* 7, no.1: 2–21.

Wang, Yü-ch'üan. 1949. "An Outline of the Central Government of the Former Han Dynasty." *Harvard Journal of Asiatic Studies* 12, no.1: 134–185.

Wei-Ming, Tu. 1976. *Centrality and Commonality: An Essay on Chung-Yung,* Monograph no.3 of the Society for Asian and Comparative Philosophy. Honolulu, HI: The University Press of Hawaii.

Williamson, H.R. 1935–1937. *Wang-An-Shih, a Chinese Statesman and Educationalist of the Sung Dynasty.* London: Probsthain.

Wittfogel, Karl August. 1947. "Public Office in the Liao Dynasty and the Chinese Examination System." *Harvard Journal of Asiatic Studies* 10, no.1: 13–40.

Hawaii

Handy, E.S. Craighill. 1933. "Government and Society." *Ancient Hawaiian Civilizations.* Honolulu: n.p., 31–42.

India

Altekar, A.S. 1958. *State and Government in Ancient India.* 3d ed. Delhi: Motilal Banarsidass.

Ambedkar, B.R. 1925. *The Evolution of Provincial Finance in British India: A Study in the Provincial Decentralization of Imperial Finance.* London: P.S. King & Son, Ltd.

Bardhan, Pranab. 1984. *The Political Economy of Development in India.* Oxford: Blackwell.

Beaglehole, T.H. 1977. "From Rulers to Servants: The ICS and the British Demission of Power in India." *Modern Asian Studies* 11: 237–255.

Blunt, Edward. 1937. *The ICS: The Indian Civil Service.* London: Faber & Faber.

Booth, Anne. 1986. "The Colonial Legacy and its Impact on Post-Independence Planning in India and Indonesia." *Itenerario* 10, no.1: 1–30.

Coen, Terence Creagh. 1971. *The Indian Political Service: A Study in Indirect Rule.* London: Chatto & Windus.

Cohn, Bernard S. 1966. "Recruitment and Training of British Civil Servants in India, 1600–1860." In *Asian Bureaucratic Systems Emergent from the British Imperial Tradition: Burma, Ceylon, India, Malaysia, Nepal, Pakistan,* edited by R. Braibanti, 87–140. Durham, NC: Duke University Press.

Bristow, Sir Robert. 1959. *Cochin Saga: a History of Foreign Government and Business Adventures in Kerala, South India, by Arabs, Romans, Venetians, Dutch, and British.* London: Cassell.

Derrett, J. Duncan M. 1961. "The Administration of Hindu Law by the British." *Comparative Studies in Society and History* 4, no.1: 10–52.

Ewing, A. 1984. "The Indian Civil Service 1919–1924: Service Discontent and the Response in London and New Delhi." *Modern Asian Studies* 18, no.1; 33–53.

Fasseur, C. and D.H.A. Kolff. 1986. "Some Remarks on the Development of Colonial Bureaucracies in India and Indonesia." *Itenerario* 10, no.1: 31–46.

Ghosal, Akshoy Kumar. 1944. *The Civil Service in India Under the East India Company: A Study in Administrative Development.* Calcutta: University of Calcutta.

Griffin, Lepel Henry. 1977. *The Rajas of the Punjab: Being the History of the Principal States in the Punjab and their Political Relations with the British Government.* New Delhi: Manu.

Handa, Ram Lal. 1927. *A History of the Development of the Judiciary in the Punjab (1846–1884).* Lahore: Punjab Government Records Office Publication Series 2.

Hasan, Ibn. [1936] 1967. *The Central Structure of the Mughal Empire.* Lahore: Pakistan Branche Oxford University Press).

Houben, V.J.H. 1987. "Native States in India and Indonesia: the Nineteenth Century." *Itinerario* 11: 107–134.

Houben, V.J.H. and D.H.A. Kolff. 1988. "Between Empire Building and State Formation: Official Elites in Java and Mughal India." *Itinerario* 12: 165–194.

Hunt, Roland and John Harrison. 1980. *The District Officer in India 1930–1947.* London: n.p.

Kapur, Daya Krishna. 1928. *A History of the Development of the Judiciary in the Punjab (1884–1926).* Lahore: Punjab Government Records Office Publication Series.

Lovett, Sir H. Verney. 1934. "District Administration in Bengal, 1858–1918." In *The Cambridge Shorter History of India*, edited by H.H. Doddwell. Cambridge: University Press.

Lybyer, A.H. 1913. "The Government of the Mogul Empire." In *The Government of the Ottomon Empire,* appendix 4. Cambridge, MA: Harvard Universtiy Press.

Mason, Philip [Philip Woodruff, pseud.]. [1953] 1985. *The Men Who Ruled India.* London: Jonathan Cape.

Matthai, John. 1915. *Village Government in British India.* London: T. Fischer Unwin.

Misra, B.B. 1970. *The Administrative History of India, 1834–1947: General Administration.* London: Oxford University Press.

———. 1977. *The Bureaucracy in India: An Historical Analysis of Development up to 1947.* New Delhi: Oxford University Press.

Mishra, Hare Krishna. 1989. *Bureaucracy under the Mughals* A.D. *1516 to* A.D. *1707.* New Delhi: Amar Prakashan.

Mookerji, A. 1920. *Local Government in Ancient India.* Oxford: Clarendon Press.

Mookerji, R.K. 1919. *Local Government in Ancient India.* Oxford: Clarendon Press.

Moreland. 1957. "The Revenue System of the Mughul Empire." In *The Cambridge History of India, IV. The Mughul Period*, edited by Sir Richard Brun, 449–475. New Delhi: S. Chand.

Mukerji, S.N. 1966. *History of Education in India.* Baroda.

O'Mally, L.S.S. 1965. *The Indian Civil Service, 1601–1930.* 2d ed. London: Frank Cass and Co. Ltd.

Prasad, Beni. 1928. *Theory of Government in Ancient India.* Allahabad: Indian Press.

Puri, B.N. 1968. *History of Indian Administration.* Choupatty: Bharatyin Vidya Bhavan.

Robb, P.G. 1976. *The Government of India and Reform: Polcies toward Politics and the Constitution 1916–1921.* Oxford: Oxford University Press.

Sakkar, J. 1921. *Mughal Administration.* Calcutta: Sarskar.

Shamasastry, R. 1961. *Kautilya, Artha-sástra.* Mysore: Mysire Printing and Publishing House.

Sharma, R.S. 1968. "Usury in Early Medieval India (A.D.400–1200)." *Comparative Studies in Society and History,* 8: 56–77.

Sinha, H.N. [1935] 1963. *The Development of Indian Polity*. Ph.D. diss. Bombay: n.p.

Smith, Vincent A. 1926. *Akbar, the Great Mogul, 1542–1605*. 2d ed. Dehli: S. Chand. & Co.

Spangenberg, Bradford. 1976. *British Bureaucracy in India: Status, Policy and the I.C.S. in the Late-Nineteenth Century.* Columbia, MO: South Asia Books.

Srivastava, Dharma Bhanu 1979. *The Province of Agra: Its History and Administration*. New Delhi: Concept.

Zwart, Frank de. 1992. *Mobiele bureaucratie: Manipulaties met overplaatsingen van ambtenaren in India*. Amsterdam: Thesis Publishers.

Indonesia

Benda, Harry J. 1966. "The Pattern of Administrative Reforms in the Closing Years of Dutch Rule in Indonesia." *The Journal of Asian Studies*, 25: 589–605.

Booth, Anne. 1986. "The Colonial Legacy and its Impact on Post-Independence Planning in India and Indonesia." *Itinerario* 10, no.1: 1–30.

Day, Clive. 1904. *The Policy and Administration of the Dutch in Java*. New York: MacMillan.

Doel, H.W. van den. 1994. *De Stille Macht: Het Europese binnenlands bestuur op Java en Madoera, 1808–1942*. Amsterdam: Bert Bakker.

Eymeret, Joel. 1973. "L'administration Napoleonienne en Indonesie." *Revue française d'histoire d'outre-mer* 218, no.1: 27–44.

Fasseur, C. and D.H.A. Kolff. 1986. "Some Remarks on the Development of Colonial Bureaucracies in India and Indonesia." *Itinerario* 10, no.1: 31–46.

Fasseur, C. 1993. *De Indologen: Ambtenaren voor de Oost 1825–1950*. Amsterdam: Bert Bakker.

Furnival, John S. 1948. *Colonial Policy and Practice: A Comparative Study of Burma and Netherlands India*. Cambridge: Cambridge University Press.

Geertz, Clifford. 1981. *Negara: The Theater State in Nineteenth Century Bali*. Princeton, NJ: Princeton University Press.

Moertono, Soemarsaid. 1968. *State and Statecraft in Old Java: A Study of the Later Mataram Period, Sixteenth to Nineteenth Century*. Ithaca, NY: Cornell University Press.

Otto, J.M. 1991. "Een Minahasser in Bandoeng: Indonesische oppositie in de koloniale gemeente." In *Excursies in Celebes*, edited by H.A. Poeze. Leiden: University of Leiden, 185–215.

Siagian, Sondang Paian. 1965. *The Development and Problems of Indigenous Bureaucratic Leadership in Indonesia*. Ph.D. thesis, Indiana University, Bloomington, IN.

Sutherland, Heather. 1973. *Pangreh Pradja: Java's Indigenous Administrative Corps and its Role in the Last Decades of Dutch Colonial Rule*. New Haven, CT: Yale University Press.

————. 1979. *The Making of a Bureaucratic Elite: The Colonial Transformation of the Javanese Priyayi*. Singapore: Heinemann.

Wal, S.L. van der. 1963. *Het Onderwijsbeleid in Nederlands-Indië 1900–1940*. Groningen: Wolters.

Iran

Amedroz, H.F. 1913. "Abbasid Administration in Its Decay." *Journal of the Royal Asiatic Society* 25, no.3: 823–842.

Deimel, Anton. 1932. "Beamter." In *Reallexicon der Assyriologie,* vol.1, edited by Erich Ebeling and Bruno Meissner, 441–444.

————. 1932. "Die Beamten zur Zeit der ersten Dynastie von Babylon." In *Reallexicon der Assyriologie* vol.1, edited by Erich Ebeling and Bruno Meissner, 444–451.

Samadi, S.B. 1955. "Some Aspects of the Theory of the State and Administration under the Abbasids." *Islamic Culture* 29, no.1: 120–150.

Savory, R.M. 1960. "The Principal Offices of the Safawid State during the Reign of Isma'il I." *Bulletin of the School for Oriental and African Studies*, no.1: 91–105.

Japan

Akita, George. 1976. *Foundations of Constitutional Government in Modern Japan: 1868–1900*. Cambridge, MA: Harvard University Press.

Asakawa, Kanichi. 1911. "Notes on Village Government in Japan after 1600, II." *Journal of the American Oriental Society* 31: 151–216.

————. 1928. *Japan, from the Japanese Government History*. New York: P.F. Collier & Son Company.

————. 1963. *The Early Institutional Life of Japan: A Study in the Reform of 645 A.D.* New York: Paragon Book Reprint Corp.

Bailey, Jackson. 1965. "The Origin and Nature of the Genro." In *Studies on Asia*, edited by Robert K. Sakai. Lincoln, NE: University of Nebraska Press, 129–141.

Bowen, Roger W. 1980. *Rebellion and Democracy in Meiji Japan: A Study of Commoners in the Popular Rights Movement*. Berkeley and Los Angeles: University of California Press.

Dowdy, E. 1972. *Japanese Bureaucracy: Its Development and Modernization*. Melbourne: Cheshire Press.

Hall, John Whitney. 1961. *Government and Local Power in Japan, 500–1700: A Study Based on Bizen Province*. Princeton, NJ: Princeton University Press.

Hall, John Whitney and Marius B. Jansen, eds. 1968. *Studies in the Institutional History of Early Modern Japan*. Princeton, NJ: Princeton University Press.

Hall, John Whitney and Jeffrey P. Mass, eds. 1974. *Medieval Japan: Essays in Institutional History.* New Haven, CT: Yale University Press.

Iwata, Masakazu. 1964. *Okubo Toshimichi: The Bismarck of Japan.* Berkeley and Los Angeles: University of California Press.

McLaren, W.W. 1914. *Japanese Government Documents. Transactions of the Asiatic Society of Japan.* First series, part 1. Tokyo: Asiatic Society of Japan.

Miller, Richard J. 1979. *Japan's First Bureaucracy: A Study of Eighth-century Government.* East Asia papers, no.9. Ithaca, NY: Cornell University Press.

Okada, Tadao. 1965. "The Unchanging Bureaucracy." *Japan Quarterly* 12, no.2: 169–176.

Ooms, Herman. 1975. *Charismatic Bureaucrat: A Political Biography of Matsudaira Sadanotu, 1758–1829.* Chicago and London: University of Chicago Press.

Osamu, Wakita. 1982. "The Emergence of the State in Sixteenth Century Japan: From Oda to Tokugawa." *Journal of Japanese Studies* 8, no.2: 343–367.

Silberman, Bernard S. 1967. "Bureaucratic Development and the Structure of Decision-Making in the Meiji Period: The Case of the Genro." *Journal of Asian Studies* 27, no.1: 81–94. (Reprinted 1968. Edited by R. Graham and W. Downey. *Quantitative History.* Homewood, IL: Dorsey Press).

———.1970. "Bureaucratic Development and the Structure of Decision-Making in Japan: 1868–1925." *Journal of Asian Studies* 29, no.2: 347–362.

———. 1973. "Ringi-sei—Traditional Values or Organizational Imperatives in the Japanese Upper Civil Service: 1868–1945. *Journal of Asian Studies* 32, no.2: 251–264.

———. 1976. "Bureaucratization of the Meiji State: The Problem of Succession in the Meiji Restoration, 1868–1900." *Journal of Asian Studies* 35, no.3: 421–430.

———. 1978. "Bureaucratic Development and Bureaucratization: The Case of Japan. *Social Science History* 2, no.4: 385–398.

———. 1993. "Japan." In *Cages of Reason: The Rise of the Rational State in France, Japan, The United States, and Great Britain* 159–222. Chicago: The University of Chicago Press.

Totman, Conrad. 1967. *Politics in the Tokugawa Bakufu 1600–1843.* Cambridge, MA: Harvard University Press.

Troost, Kristina Kade. 1990. *Common Property and Community Formation: Self-Governing Villages in Late Medieval Japan, 1300–1600.* Ph.D. diss. Department of History, Harvard University, Cambridge, MA.

Tsuji, Kiyoaki. 1982. "Public Administration in Japan: History and problems." *International Review of the Administrative Sciences* 47, no.2: 119–124.

Wilson, Robert. 1957. *Genesis of the Meiji Government in Japan, 1868–1871.* Berkeley, MA: University of California Press.

Malaysia

Emerson, Rupert. 1937. *Malaysia: A Study in Direct and Indirect Rule*. New York: MacMillan.

Gullick, J.M. 1958. *Indigenous Political Systems of Western Malaya*. London: London School of Economics, monographs on social anthropology.

———. 1992. *Rulers and Residents: Influence and Power in the Malay States 1870–1920*. Oxford: Oxford University Press.

Khasnor, Johan. 1984. *The Emergence of the Modern Malay Administrative Elite*. Oxford: Oxford University Press.

Means, Gordon P. 1968–1969. "The Role of Islam in the Political Development of Malaysia." *Comparative Politics* 1, no.2: 264–284.

Ness, Gayl D. 1970. "The Malayan Bureaucracy and its Occupational Communities: A Comment on James de Vere Allen's 'Malayan Civil Service, 1874–1941.'" *Comparative Studies in Society and History* 12, no.2: 179–186.

Parmer, J. Norman. 1960. *Colonial Labor Policy and Administration: A History of Labor in the Rubber Plantation Industry in Malaya c.1910–1941*. New York: Monograph of the Association for Asian Studies, no.9.

Tilman, Robert O. 1964. *Bureaucratic Transition in Malaya*. Durham, NC: Duke University Press.

Vere Allen, A.J. de. 1970. "The Malayan Civil Service 1874–1941: Colonial Bureaucracy/Malayan Elite." In *Comparative Studies in Society and History*, 12, no.2, 149–178.

Nepal

Pradhan, P. 1973. "The Nepalese Bureaucracy: A Historical Perspective." *Philippine Journal of Public Administration* 17, no.2: 178–196.

Philippines

Corpuz, Onofre D. 1957. *The Bureaucracy in the Philippines*. Manila: Institute of Public Administration, University of the Philippines.

Jenista, Frank L. 1974. "Problems of the Colonial Civil Service: An Illustration from the Career of Manuel L. Quezon." *Southeast Asia* 3, no.3: 809–829.

Phelan, John Leddy. 1959. "Free versus Compulsory Labor: Mexico and the Philippines 1540–1648." *Comparative Studies in Society and History* 1, no.2: 189–201.

———. 1960. "Authority and Flexibility in the Spanish Imperial Bureaucracy." *Administrative Science Quarterly* 5, no.1: 47–65.

Zafra, Nicolas. 1963. "The Residencia in the Colonial Administrative System in the Philippines." *Philippine Historical Bulletin* 7, no.1: 14–33.

Singapore

Kathirithamby-Wells, J. 1969. "Early Singapore and the Inception of a British Administrative Tradition in the Straits Settlements (1819–1832)." *Journal of the Malaysian Branch of the Royal Asiatic Society* 42, no.2.

Seah, Chee-Meow. 1971. *Bureaucratic Evolution and Political Change in an Emerging Nation: A Case Study of Singapore.* Ph.D. thesis, Victoria University of Manchester, Manchester, England.

Thailand

Quaritch Wales, H.G. 1934. *Ancient Siamese Government and Administration.* London: Bernard Quaritch Ltd.

Yemen

Dresch, Paul. 1989. *Tribes, Government, and History of Yemen.* Oxford: Clarendon Press.

Australia

Bibliography of Australian Public Administrative History. *Public Administration* (Sydney, 1964) 23, no.2: 181–182.

Bibliography of Administrative History. Melbourne: Victorian Regional Group of the Royal Institute of Public Administration, 1966.

Burroughs, P. 1967. *Britain and Australia 1831–1955: A Study in Imperial Relations and Crown Lands Administration.* Oxford: Clarendon Press.

Curnow, Ross and Hilary Golde. 1995. "Australia: 'Napoléonisme sans doctrines?' In *The Influences of the Napoleonic "Model" of Administration on the Administrative Organization of Other Countries*, edited by Bernd Wunder, 77–96. Brussels: Cahiers de l'Histoire de l'Administration, no.4. International Institute of Administrative Sciences.

Deane, R.P. 1963. *The Establishment of the Department of Trade.* Canberra: Australian National University.

Dickey, B. 1974. "Responsible Government in New South Wales: The Transfer of Power in a Colony of Settlement." *Journal of the Royal Australian Historical Society* 60, no.4: 217–242.

Dickey, B. 1979. "The Evolution of Care for Destitute Children in New South Wales, 1875–1901." *Journal of Australian Studies* 4, no.1: 38–57.

Eddy, J.J. 1969. *Britain and the Australian Colonies, 1818–1831: The Technique of Government.* Oxford: Clarendon Press.

Finn, Paul D. 1987. *Law and Government in Colonial Australia.* Melbourne and New York: Oxford University Press.

Hawker, G.N. 1979. "An Investigation of the Civil Service: the South Australian Royal Commission of 1888–1891." *Journal of the Royal Australian Historical Society* 55, no.1: 46–58.

Hyslop, R. 1973. *Australian Naval Administration 1900–1939.* Melbourne: Hawthorn Press.

Kewley, T.H. 1973. *Social Security in Australia, 1900–1972.* Sydney: Sydney University Press.

Knight, K.W. 1971. "Patronage and the 1894 Royal Commission of Inquiry into the New South Wales Public Service." *Australian Journal of Politics and History* 7, no.2: 166–185.

Knight, K.W. and K.W. Wiltshire. 1973. *The Growth of Public Services in Australia.* Sydney: Committee for Economic Development of Australia.

Larcombe, F.A. 1978. *A History of Local Government in New South Wales (1831–1978).* Vols. 1–3. Sydney: Sydney University Press.

La Nauze, J.A. 1949. "The Collection of Customs in Australia: A Note on Administration." *Historical Studies in Australia and New Zealand* 4, no.13: 25–33.

MacIntyre, S. and R. Mitchell, eds. 1989. *Foundations of Arbitration: The Origins and Effects of State Compulsory Arbitration, 1890–1914.* Melbourne: Oxford University Press.

McMartin, Arthur. 1958. "The Payment of Officials in Early Australia." *Public Administration* (Sydney) 17, no.1: 45–80.

———. 1958. "The Treasury of New South Wales, 1786–1836." *Public Administration* (Sydney) 17, no.3: 213–228.

———. 1959. "Aspects of Patronage in Australia, 1786–1836." *Public Administration* (Sydney) 18, no.4: 326–340.

Scott, R.D. and R.L. Wettenhall. 1980. "Public Administration as a Teaching and Research Field." *Australian Journal of Public Administration* 39, no.3–4: 478–497.

Wettenhall, R.L. 1973. "The Ministerial Department: British Origins and Australian Adaptations." *Public Administration* (Sydney) 32, no.3: 233–250.

———. 1976. "Modes of Ministerialization, Part 1: Towards a Typology—the Australian Experience." *Public Administration* 54, no.1: 1–20.

———. 1976. "Modes of Ministerialization, Part 2: From Colony to the State in the Twentieth Century." *Public Administration* 54, no.4: 425–451.

———. 1977. "Commonwealth Statutory Authorities: Patterns of Growth." *Australian Journal of Public Administration* 36, no.4: 357–366.

EUROPE

Ancient Government until A.D. 500

Alford, C. Fred. 1989. "Selection by Lot in Ancient Athens." In *Pathways to*

Power: Selecting Rulers in Pluralist Democracies, edited by Mattei Dogan, 219–238. Boulder, CO: Westview Press.

Arnold, W.T. 1906. *The Roman System of Provincial Administration to the Accession of Constantine the Great*, revised ed. by E.S. Shuckburgh. Oxford: B.H. Blackwell.

Barker, Ernest. 1956. *From Alexander to Constantine: Passages and Documents Illustrating the History of Social and Political Ideas 336 B.C.–A.D. 337*. Oxford: Clarendon Press.

Beyer, William C. 1959. "The Civil Service of the Ancient World." *Public Administration Review* 19, no.4: 243–249.

Burn, A.R. 1952. *The Government of the Roman Empire from Augustus to the Antonines*. London: English Universities Press.

Carradine, Ian, ed. 1987. *Coinage and Administration: The Athenian and Persian empires*. Ninth Oxford Symposium on Coinage and Monetary History, Oxford, England.

Goffart, Walter. 1972. "From Roman Taxation to Medieval Seigneurie: Three Notes." *Speculum: A Journal of Mediaeval Studies* 47, no.2: 165–187; no.3, 373–394.

Harper, George McLean. 1928. "Village Administration in the Roman Provinces of Syria." *Yale Classical Studies* 1: 103–168.

Hofmeyer, J.H. [1927] 1967. "Civil Service in Ancient Times: The Story of its Evolution." *Public Administration* 5, no.1: 76–93. Reprint in *Readings in Comparative Public Administration*, edited by Nimrod Raphaeli, 69–91. Boston, MA: Allyn & Bacon.

Jones, A.H.M. 1949. "The Civil Service (Clerical and Subclerical Grades)." In *Journal of Roman Studies* 39: 38–55.

————. 1960. *Studies in Roman Government*. Oxford: Blackwell.

Jones, Henry Stuart. 1920. *Fresh Light on Roman Bureaucracy.* Oxford: Clarendon Press.

Larsen, J.A.O. 1955. *Representative Government in Greek and Roman History*. Berkeley and Los Angeles: University of California Press.

Last, Hugh. 1936. "The Principate and the Administration." In *The Cambridge Ancient History*, vol 11, edited by S.A. Cook, F.E. Adcock, and M.P. Charlesworth, 393–434. Cambridge: University Press.

Loewenstein, Karl. 1973. *The Governance of Rome*. The Hague: Nijhoff.

Mattingly, H. 1910. *The Imperial Civil Service of Rome*. Cambridge: Cambridge University Press.

Mommsen, Theodor. 1968. *The Provinces of the Roman Empire: the European Provinces*. Chicago, IL: University of Chicago Press.

Nigro, Felix A. 1960. "Ancient Greece and 'Modern' Administration." *Personnel Administration* 23, no.1: 11–19.

Runciman, W.G. 1982. "Origins of States: The Case of Archaic Greece." *Comparative Studies in Society and History* 24, no.2: 351–377.

Schomann, G.F. 1880. *The Antiquities of Greece: The State*. London: Rivingtons.

Snyder, David P. 1969. "The Gracchi Horse: A Study in Pre-Raphaelite Management." *Public Administration Review* 29, no.1: 65–71.

Stevenson, G.H. 1934. "The Imperial Administration." In *The Cambridge Ancient History*, volume 10, edited by S.A. Cook, F.E. Adcock, and M.P. Charlesworth, 182–217.

———. 1939. *Roman Provincial Administration till the Age of the Antonines.* New York: G.E. Stechert & Co. and Oxford: Basil Blackwell.

Medieval Government, A.D. *500–1500*

General Works

Berman, H.J. 1983. *Law and Revolution: The Formation of the Western Legal Tradition.* Cambridge: Cambridge University Press.

Blockmans, W. P. 1978. "A Typology of Representative Institutions in Late Medieval Europe." *Journal of Medieval History* 4, no.2: 189–215.

Caenegem, R.C. van. 1967. *De Instellingen van de Middeleeuwen: Geschiedenis van de westerse staatsinstellingen van de Ve tot de XVe eeuw.* Ghent: Wetenschappelijke Uitgeverij en Boekhandel.

Coulborn, Rushton. 1956. *Feudalism in History.* Princeton, NJ: Princeton University Press.

Durliat, Jean 1990. *Les finances publiques de Diocletien aux Carolingiens (284–889).* Sigmaringen: Jan Thorbecke, Beihefte zu francia, no.21.

Grapperhaus, Ferdinand H.M. 1984. "Some Remarks on the Development of Taxation in Western Europe up to the Sixteenth Century." *Publication du centre européen d'études bourguignonnes* 24: 1–9.

Hill, Bennett D., ed. 1970. *Church and State in the Middle Ages.* New York: John Wiley and Sons.

Jusselien, M. 1922. "La Chancellerie de Charles le Chauve." *Le Moyen Age,* 33: 1–91.

Kantorowicz, E.H. 1957. *The King's Two Bodies: A Study of Medieval Political Theology.* Princeton, NJ: Princeton University Press.

Kieser, Alfred. 1989. "Organizational, Institutional, and Societal Evolution: Medieval Craft Guilds and the Genesis of Formal Organizations." *Adminstrative Science Quarterly* 34, no.4: 540–564.

Miller, Maureen. 1983. "From Ancient to Modern Organization: The Church as Conduit and Creator." *Administration and Society* 15: 275–293.

Stephenson, Carl. 1967. "The Origin and Nature of the Taille." In *Mediaeval Institutions, Selected Essays by Carl Stephenson,* 41–103. Ithaca, NY: Cornell University Press.

———. 1967. "Taxation and Representation in the Middle Ages." In *Mediaeval Institutions, Selected Essays by Carl Stephenson,* 104–125. Ithaca, NY: Cornell University Press.

Strayer, Joseph R. 1966. The Historical Experience in Nation-Building in

Europe. In *Nation-Building*, edited by K.W. Deutsch and W.J. Foltz, 17–26. New York: Atherton Press.

————. 1970. *On the Mediaeval Origins of the Modern State*. Princeton, NJ.: Princeton University Press.

————. 1970. *Medieval Statecraft and the Perspectives of History*. Princeton, NJ: Princeton University Press.

Tellenbach, Gerd. 1939. *Church, State, and Christian Society at the time of the Investiture Contest*. Translated by R.F. Bennett. Atlantic Highlands, N.J.: Humanities Press and Brighton: Harvester.

Tierney, Brian. 1967. *The Crisis of Church and State 1050–1300*. Englewood Cliffs, NJ: Prentice-Hall.

————. 1979. *Church Law and Constitutional Thought in the Middle Ages*. London: Variorum Reprints.

Tierney, Brian and Peter Linehan, eds. 1980. *Authority and Power: Studies on Medieval Law and Government*. Cambridge: Cambridge University Press.

Tierney, Brian. 1982. *Religion, Law, and the Growth of Constitutional Thought, 1150–1650*. Cambridge: Cambridge University Press.

Tierney, Brian. 1988. *Origins of Papal Infallibility, 1150–1350: A Study on the Concepts of Infallibility, Sovereignty, and Tradition in the Middle Ages*. 2d ed. Leiden: E.J. Brill.

Tipton, C.L., ed. 1972. *Nationalism in the Middle Ages*. New York: Holt, Rinehart & Winston.

Ullmann, Walter. 1966. *Principles of Government and Politics in the Middle Ages*. 2d ed. London: Methuen.

Ullmann, Walter. 1969. *The Carolingian Renaissance and the Idea of Kingship*. London: Methuen.

Byzantine Empire

Andréadès, A. 1921. "La vénalité des offices, est-elle d'origine byzantine?" In *Revue historique de droit français et étranger* 45: 232–241.

————. 1926. "Le recrutement des fonctionnaires et les universités dans l'empire byzantin." In *Mélanges de droit romain dédiés a Georges Cornil*. Paris, 17–40.

Boak, A.E.R. and J. Dunlap. 1924. *Two Studies in Later Roman and Byzantine Administration*. New York: Macmillan.

Bréhier, Louis. 1949. *Les Institutions de l'Empire Byzantin: L'Evolution de l'humanité*. Paris: Michel.

Bury, John Bagnell. [1911] 1958. *The Imperial Administrative System in the Ninth Century*. London: H. Frowde and New York: B. Franklin.

Carney, T.F. 1971. *Bureaucracy in Traditional Society: Romano-Byzantine Bureaucracies Viewed from Within*. Lawrence, Kansas: Coronado Press.

Charanis, Peter. 1961. "The Transfer of Population as a Policy in the Byzantine Empire." *Comparative Studies in Society and History* 3, no.2: 140–154.

Dendias, M. 1939. "Études sur le gouvernement et l'administration en Byzance." In *Actes du cinquième congrès international d'études byzantines.* Rome, 122–145.

Diehl, Charles. 1936. "The Government and Administration of the Byzantine Empire." In *The Cambridge Medieval History,* vol. 4, edited by H.M. Gwatkin and J.P. Whitney, 726–744. Cambridge: Cambridge University Press.

Dölger, Franz. 1927. *Beiträge zur Geschichte der byzantinischen Finanzverwaltung besonders des 10. und 11. Jahrhunderts.* In Series Byzantinisches Archiv, no. 8. München: Beck.

Dunlap, James E. 1924. *Two Studies in Later Roman and Byzantine Administration.* New York and London: MacMillan and Co.

Franzius, Enno. 1967. *History of the Byzantine Empire: Mother of Nations.* New York: Funk & Wagnalls.

Guilland, Rodolphe. 1946. "Études sur l'histoire administrative de Byzance." In *Byzantina-Metabyzantina,* no. 1: 165–179.

———. 1947. "Études sur l'histoire administrative de l'empire byzantin: Le Césarat." *Orientalia Christiana Periodica* 13, no.1: 168–194.

———. 1949. "Études sur l'histoire administrative de l'empire byzantin: Le Grand Connétable." *Byzantion,* no. 19: 99–111.

———. 1952. "Vénalité et favoritisme à Byzance." In *Revue des études Byzantines,* no.10: 35–46.

Liebeschuetz, J.H.W.G. 1990. *Barbarians and Bishops: Army, Church, and State in the Age of Arcadius and Chrysoston.* Oxford: Clarendon Press.

Rouillard, G. 1928. *L'administration civile de l'Egypte byzantine.* Paris.

Runciman, Steven. 1977. *The Byzantine Theocracy.* Cambridge: Cambridge University Press.

France

Fesler, James W. 1962. "French Field Administration: The Beginnings." In *Comparative Studies in Society and History* 5, no.1: 76–111.

Haskins, Charles H. 1918. *Norman Institutions.* Cambridge: Cambridge University Press.

Lot, Ferdinand and Robert Fawtier. 1957–1958. *Histoire des Institutions Françaises au Moyen Age.* Paris: Presses Universitaires de France.

Luchaire, Achille. 1883. *Histoire des Institutions Monarchiques de la France sous les Premiers Capétiens (987–1180).* Paris: Imprimerie National.

Michel, Robert. 1910. *L'Administration Royale dans la Sénéchaussée de Beaucaire au Temps de Saint Louis.* Paris: Societé de L'Ecole des Chartes.

Strayer, Joseph R. 1932. *The Administration of Normandy under Saint Louis.* Cambridge: The Mediaeval Academy of America.

―――. 1970. *Les Gens de justice du Languedoc sous Philippe le Bel.*
Toulouse: Etudes d'histoire meriodinale, no.5.
―――. 1976. *The Royal Domain in the Baillage of Rouen.* London: Variorum.

Germany

Brackmann, A. 1961. "The Beginnings of the National State in Medieval
Germany and the Norman Monarchies." In *Medieval Germany 991–1250,*
vol. 2, edited by G. Barraclough, 281–299. Oxford: Basil Blackwell.
Cohn, Henry J. 1965. *The Government of the Rhine Palatinate in the fifteenth
century.* London: Oxford University Press.
Willoweit, D. 1983. "Die Entwicklung und Verwaltung des spätmittelal-
terlichen Landesherrschaft." In *Deutsche Verwaltungsgeschichte I: Von
Spätmittelalter bis zum Ende des Reiches,* edited by K.G.A. Jeserich et al.,
118–130. Stuttgart: Deutsche Verlags-Austalt.

Great Britain

Brown, A.L. 1987. *The Governance of Late Medieval England, 1272–1461.*
London: Arnold.
Cam, Helen Maud. 1963. *Liberties and Communities in Medieval England:
Collected Studies in Local Administration and Topography.* New York:
Barnes and Noble.
Chrimes, S.B. 1966. *An Introduction to the Administrative History of Medi-
aeval England.* 3d ed. Oxford: Basil Blackwell.
Clanchy, M.T. 1979. *From Memory to Written Record: England, 1066–1347.*
Cambridge, MA: Harvard University Press.
Critchley, T.A. 1967. *A History of Police in England and Wales, 900–1066.*
London: Constable.
Hogan, M.J. 1979. "The Administration of Early Medieval England, with
Special Reference to Northumberland." *Public Administration* (Sydney)
38, no.3.
Jewell, Helen M. 1972. *English Local Administration in the Middle Ages.*
New York: Barnes & Noble Import Division, Harper & Row Publishers.
Loyn, H.R. 1984. *The Governance of Anglo-Saxon England, 500–1087.* Lon-
don: Arnold.
Lyon, Bryce. 1980. *A Constitutional and Legal History of Medieval England.*
2d ed. New York: W.W. Norton & Co..
Morris, William A. 1972. *The Medieval English Sheriff to 1300.* Manchester:
University Press.
Otway-Ruthven, J. 1936. The King's Secretary in the Fifteenth Century. In
Transactions of the Royal Historical Society, 4th ser., vol. 19: 81–100.
―――. 1939. *The King's Secretary and the Signet Office of the XV Century.*
Cambridge.

Poole, Austin Lane. 1951. *From Doomesday Book to Magna Charta, 1087–1226*. Oxford: Clarendon Press.

Tout, Thomas Frederick. 1909. *The Empire and the Papacy, 918–1273*. 5th ed. London: Rivingtons.

———. 1916. *The English Civil Service in the Fourteenth Century*. Manchester: The University Press and New York: Longmans, Green and Co.

———. 1924. *Some Conflicting Tendencies in English Administrative History During the Fourteenth Century*. New York: Longmans, Green and Co.

———. 1932–1934. "The Beginnings of a Modern Capital: London and Westminster in the Fourteenth Century." In *The Collected Papers of Thomas Frederick Tout*, vol. 3, 249–275. Manchester: Manchester University Press.

———. 1952. "The Emergence of a Bureaucracy." In *Reader in Bureaucracy.*, edited by Robert K. Merton. Glencoe, IL: The Free Press.

———. 1967. *Chapters in the Administrative History of Mediaeval England; the Wardrobe, the Chamber, and the Small Seals*. 2d ed. Manchester: The University Press.

Warren, W.L. 1987. *The Governance of Norman and Angevin England, 1986–1272*. London: Arnold.

West, Francis. 1966. *The Justiciarship in England 1066–1232*. Cambridge Studies in Medieval Life and Thought, vol. 12. London: Cambridge University Press.

Willard, James and William Morris, eds. 1940–1950. *The English Government at Work, 1327–1336*. Cambridge: The Mediaeval Academy of America.

Italy

Becker, Marvin. 1960. "Some Popular Aspects of Oligarchical, Dictatorial and Signorie in Florence 1282–1382." In *Comparative Studies in Society and History*, 2, no.4, 421–439.

Maarongio, Antonio. 1966. "A Model State in the Middle Ages: The Norman and Swabian Kingdom of Sicily." In *Comparative Studies in Society and History* 6, no.3: 307–320.

Rubenstein, Nicolai. 1966. *The Government of Florence under the Medici, 1434 up to 1494*. Oxford: Oxford University Press.

The Low Countries (Belgium and the Netherlands)

Arend, O. van den. 1939. *Zeven lokale baljuwschappen in Holland*. Hilversum: Verloren.

Blockmans, W.P. and R. van Uytven. 1969. "Constitutions and their Application in the Netherlands during the Middle Ages." In *Belgisch Tijdschrift voor Filologie en Geschiedenis* 47: 399–424.

Boer, D.E.H. de, E.H.P. Cordfunke, and F.W.N. Hugenholz, eds. 1991. *Holland in wording: De ontstaansgeschiedenis van het graafschap Holland tot het begin van de vijftiende eeuw.* Hilversum: Verloren.

Bos-Rops, J.A.M.Y. 1993. *Graven op zoek naar geld: De inkomsten van de graven van Holland en Zeeland.* Hilversum: Verloren.

Caenegem, R.C. van. 1971. "Considérations critiques sur l'ordnonnance comtale flamande connue sous le nom 'd'Ordonnance sur les baillis.'" In *Studia Historica Gandensia*, no.102: 133–152. Ghent: Universiteit van Gent.

Camps, H.P.H. 1989. *De stadrechten van graaf Willem II van Holland: Een diplomatische, tekstkritische en historische studie.* Hilversum: Verloren.

Coenen, J.M.A. 1986. *Graaf en grafelijkheid, een onderzoek naar de graven van Holland en hun omgeving in der dertiende eeuw.* Ph.D diss., University of Utrecht, Utrecht, the Netherlands.

Dolfing, B. 1993. "Vroegste ontwikkelingen in het waterschap." In *Waterschappen in Nederland: Een bestuurskundige verkenning van de institutionele ontwikkeling*, edited by J.C.N. Raadschelders and Th.A.J. Toonen, 61–80. Hilversum: Verloren.

Eibrink-Jansen, E.A.M. 1927. *De opkomst van de vroedschap in enkele Hollandse steden.* Haarlem: Amicitia.

Gosses, I.H. 1917. *De rechterlijke organisatie van Zeeland in de middeleeuwen.* Groningen/'s-Gravenhage: J.B. Wolters.

Kan, F.J.W. van. 1988. *Sleutels tot de macht: De ontwikkeling van het Leidse patriciaat tot 1420.* Hilversum: Verloren.

Linden, H. van der. 1982. "Een nieuwe overheidsinstelling: het waterschap circa 1100–1400." In H.P.H. Jansen et al., *Algemene Geschiedenis der Nederlanden* vol. 3: 60–76. Bussum: Unieboek.

Maes, L.Th. 1977. "Ambtenarij en bureaucratisering in regering en gewesten van de Zuidelijke Nederlanden in de 13e–15e eeuw." In *Tijdschrift voor Geschiedenis* 90, no.3–4: 350–357.

Marsilje, J.W. 1985. *Het financiële beleid van Leiden in de laat-Beierse en Bourgondische periode.* Hilversum: Verloren.

Nowé, H. 1929. *Les baillis comtaux de Flandre, des origines a la fin du XIVe siecle.* Brussels: n.p.

Ossewaarde, F. 1989. "Het Haags baljuwsambt 1586–1795: hatelijk ambt of principael officie?" In *Jaarboek van die Haghe* 19, 19–45.

Peteghem, Paul P.J.L. van. 1987. *Centralisation aux anciens Pays-Bas: Le droit de patronage laïque, 1394–1598.*

———. 1990. *De Raad van Vlaanderen en staatsvorming onder Karel V (1515–1555): een publiekrechtelijk onderzoek naar centralisatiestreven in de XVII provincien.* Nijmegen: Gerard Noodt Instituut.

Pirenne, Henri [1913] 1963. *Early Democracies in the Low Countries.* New York: Harper and Row.

Postma, C. 1989. *Het hoogheemraadschap van Delfland in de middeleeuwen, 1290–1589.* Hilversum: Verloren.

Prevenier, W. 1972. "Ambtenaren in stad en land in de Nederlanden: Socio-professionele evoluties, veertiende tot zeventiende eeuw." In *Bijdragen en Mededelingen betreffende de Geschiedenis der Nederlanden*, no. 87: 44–59. An updated version in English (1974): "Officials in Town and Country-side in the Low Countries: Social and Professional Developments from the Fourteenth to the Sixteenth Century." In *Acta Historiae Neerlandicae*, VII.

Rompaey, J. van. 1967. "Het grafelijk baljuwsambt in Vlaanderen tijdens de Bourgondische periode." In *Verhandelingen van de Koninklijke Vlaamse Academie voor Wetenschappen, Letteren en Schone Kunsten van België*, Klasse der Letteren, verhandeling no. 62. Brussels: n.p.

Schepper, Hugo de and Jean-Marie Cauchies. 1993. "Justicie, gracie en wetgeving: Juridische instrumenten van de landsheerlijke macht in de Nederlanden, 1200–1600." In *Beleid en bestuur in de oude Nederlanden: Liber Amicorum Prof. dr. M. Baelde*, 127–182. Ghent: Vakgroep Nieuwe Geschiedenis.

Uyttebrouck, A. 1975. *Le gouvernement du duché de Brabant au bas moyen âge 1355–1430*. Brussels: Université libre de Bruxelles.

Verkerk, C.L. 1982. *Coulissen van de macht: Een sociaal-institutionele studie betreffende de samenstelling van het bestuur van Arnhem in de middeleeuwen en een bijdrage tot de studie van stedelijke elitevorming*. Hilversum: Verloren.

Verloren van Themaat, L.M., ed. 1983. *Oude Dordtse lijfrenten: Stedelijke financiering in de vijftiende eeuw*. Hilversum: Verloren.

Spain

Powers, James F. 1988. *A Society Organized for War: The Iberian Municipal Militias in the Central Middle Ages, 1000–1284*. Berkeley and Los Angeles: University of California Press.

Early Modern and Modern Government

General Works

Anderson, Perry. 1978. *Passages from Antiquity to Feudalism*. London: NLB.

———. 1979. *Lineages of the Absolutist State*. London: NLB.

———. 1985. "The Absolutist States of Western Europe." In *States and Societies*, 3d ed. edited by David Held et al., 137–150. Oxford: Basil Blackwell.

Armstrong, J.A. 1972. "Old Regime Governors: Bureaucratic and Patrimonial Attributes." In *Comparative Studies in Sociology and History* 16, no.1: 2–29.

———. 1973. *The European Administrative Elite*. Princeton, NJ: Princeton University Press.

Barker, Ernest. 1944. *The Development of Public Services in Western Europe 1660–1930*. London: Oxford University Press.

Blockmans, Wim P. 1994. "Voracious States and Obstructing Cities: An Aspect of State Formation in Preindustrial Europe." In *Cities and the Rise of States in Europe, A.D. 1000 to 1800*, edited by Charles Tilly and Wim P. Blockmans, 218–250. Boulder, CO: Westview Press.

Blondel, Jean. 1977. "Types of Government Leadership in Atlantic Countries." *European Journal of Political Research* 5, no.1: 33–51.

Caenegem, R.C. van. 1977. *Over koningen en bureaucraten: Oorsprong en ontwikkeling van de hedendaagse staatsinstellingen*. Amsterdam and Brussels: Elsevier.

Carr, Edward. 1985. "States and Nationalism: The Nation in European History." In *States and Societies* 3d ed., edited by David Held et al., 181–194. Oxford: Blackwell/The Open University.

Crowley. 1971. "Long Savings in the Role of Government: An Analysis of Wars and Government Expenditure in Western Europe since the Eleventh Century." *Public Finance* 26, no.1: 25–43.

Dogan, M., ed. 1975. *The Mandarins of Western Europe: the Political Role of Top Civil Servants*. London: SAGE Publications.

Elias, N. 1982. *The Civilizing Process*. Part 2. New York and Oxford: Uricon Books, Blackwell.

Finer, Herman. 1975. "State and Nation-Building in Europe: The Role of the Military." In *The Formation of National States in Western Europe*, edited by Charles Tilly, 84–163. Princeton, NJ: Princeton University Press.

Fischer, W., P. Lundgreen. 1975. "The Recruitment and Training of Administrative and Technical Personnel." In *The Formation of National States in Western Europe*, edited by Charles Tilly, 456–561. Princeton, NJ: Princeton University Press.

Flora, P., ed. 1983. *State, Economy, and Society in Western Europe 1815–1975: A Data Handbook*. Frankfurt am Main: Campus Verlag.

Friedrich, C.J. 1963. *Man and His Government: an Empirical Theory of Politics*. New York: McGraw Hill.

Grapperhaus, Ferdinand H.M. 1993. *De pelgrimstocht naar het draagkrachtbeginsel: Belastingheffing in West-Europa tussen 800–1800*. Zutphen: Walburg Pers/Kluwer.

Griffiths, G. 1968. *Representative Government in Western Europe in the 16th century: Commentary and Documents for the Study of Comparative Constitutional History*. Oxford: Clarendon Press.

Grimm, D. 1986. "The Modern State: Continental Traditions." In *Guidance, Control, and Evaluation in the Public Sector*, edited by F.X. Kaufmann, G. Majone, and V. Ostrom, 89–109. Berlin: Walter de Gruyter & Co.

Grunow, D. 1968. "Development of the Public Sector: Trends and Issues." In *Guidance, Control, and Evaluation in the Public Sector* edited by F.X. Kaufmann, G. Majone, and V. Ostrom, 25–58. Berlin: Walter de Gruyter & Co.

Hechter, Michael and William Brustein. 1984. "Regional Modes of Production and Patterns of State Formation in Western Europe." *American Journal of Sociology* 89, no.6: 1346–1374.

Heidenheimer, Arnold. 1973. "The Politics of Public Education, Health, and Welfare in the USA and Western Europe: How Growth and Reform Potentials Have Differed." *British Journal of Political Science* 3, no.3: 315–340.

Hintze, Otto. 1962. *Soziologie und Geschichte, Staat und Verfassung*, edited by Gerhard Oestreich. Göttingen: Vandenhoeck & Ruprecht.

Heyen, E.V., ed. 1989–1993. *Jahrbuch für Europäische Verwaltungsgeschichte*. Baden-Baden: Nomos Verlagsgesellschaft.

    Vol.1. 1989. "Formation und Transformation des Verwaltungswissens in Frankreich und Deutschland" (18./19.Jh.).

    Vol.2. 1990. "Konfrontation und Assimilation nationalen Verwaltungsrechts in Europa" (19./20.Jh);

    Vol.3. 1991. "Beamtensyndikalismus in Frankreich, Deutschland und Italien";

    Vol.4. 1992. "Die Anfänge der Verwaltung der Europäischen Gemeinschaft."

    Vol.5. 1993. "Bürokratisierung und Professionalisierung der Sozialpolitik in Europa (1870–1980)."

    Vol.6. 1994. "Bilder der Verwaltung. Memorien, Karikaturen, Romane, Architektur."

    Vol.7 1995. "Öffentlichte Verwaltung und Wirtschaftskrise."

Immergut, Ellen M. 1992. *Health Politics: Interests and Institutions in Western Europe*. Cambridge: Cambridge University Press.

King, A. 1973. "Ideas, Institutions and the Policies of Governments: a Comparative Analysis: Parts 1 and 2." *British Journal of Political Science* 3, no.3: 291–313.

———. 1973. "Ideas, Institutions and the Policies of Governments: A Comparative Analysis: Part Three." *British Journal of Political Science*, 3, no.4: 409–423.

Landes, D.S. 1981. "The Foundations of European Expansion and Dominion: an Equilibrium Model." *Itinerario* 5, no.1: 46–61.

Lichbach, M.I. 1984. *Regime Change and the Coherence of European Governments* 21, no.1. Denver, CO: Monograph series in World Affairs, University of Denver.

Milward, Alan S. 1992. *The European Rescue of the Nation-State*. London: Routledge.

Page, Edward C. 1990. "The Political Origins of Self-Government and Bureaucracy: Otto Hintze's Conceptual Map of Europe." *Political Studies*, 38, no.1: 39–55.

Raeff, Marc. 1975. "The Well-ordered Police State and the Development of Modern Society in Seventeenth and Eighteenth Century Europe." *American Historical Review* 80, no.4: 1221–1243.

Rose, Richard. 1976. "On the Priorities of Government: A Developmental Analysis of Public Policies." *European Journal of Political Research* 4, no.1: 247–289.

Tarschys, Daniel. 1975. "The Growth of Public Expenditures: Nine Modes of Explanation." *Scandinavian Political Studies* 10: 9–31.

Tierney, Brian. 1965. "The Prince is Not Bound by the Laws: Accursius and the origins of the Modern State." In *Comparative Studies in Society and History* 5, no.4: 378–400.

Theory and Society 18, no. 4. 1988. Special issue on "Cities and States in Europe 1000–1800."

Tilly, Charles, ed. 1975. *The Formation of National States in Western Europe.* Princeton, NJ: Princeton University Press.

———. 1989. Cities and States in Europe, 1000–1800. *Theory and Society* 18, no.4: 563–584.

———. 1990. *Coercion, Capital, and European States* A.D. *990–1990.* Cambridge: Blackwell.

———. 1994. "Entanglements of European Cities and States." In *Cities and the Rise of States in Europe,* A.D. *1000 to 1800,* edited by Charles Tilly and Wim P. Blockmans, 1–27. Boulder, CO: Westview Press.

Torstendahl, R. 1991. *Bureaucratization in Northwestern Europe 1880–1985. Domination and Governance.* London: Routledge & Kegan Paul.

Vagts, Alfred. [1937] 1967. *A History of Militarism: Civilian and Military.* New York: Free Press.

Williams, E.N. 1970. *The Ancien Régime in Europe: Government and Society in the Major States, 1648–1789.* London: The Bodley Head.

Wunder, Bernd, ed. 1995. *The Influences of the Napoleonic "Model" of Administration on the Administrative Organization of Other Countries.* Brussels: International Institute of Administrative Sciences, Cahier d'Histoire de l'Administration, no.4.

Austria

Bacher, Roman. 1990. *Der Tiroler Provinziallandtag von 1848 im Rahmen der allgemeinen österreichischen Verfassungsentwicklung.* Juridicial diss., University of Innsbruck, Innsbruck, Austria.

Beidtel, I. 1968. *Geschichte der österreichische Staatsverwaltung, 1749–1848.* Frankfurt am Main: Sauer & Auvermann.

Bundsmann, Anton. 1961. *Die Entwicklung der politischen Verwaltung im Tirol und Voralberg seit Maria Theresia bis 1918.* Dornbirn: Vorariberger Verlagsanstalt.

Brauneder, Wilhelm. 1995. "The Structure of General Administration in the Habsburg Monarchy during the Time of Emperor Napoleon I." In *The Influences of the Napoleonic "Model" of Administration on the Administrative Organization of Other Countries,* edited by Bernd Wunder,

97–113. Brussels: International Institute of Administrative Sciences, Cahier d'Histoire de l'Administration, no.4.

Dhondt, Luc. 1977. "Staatsveiligheidsmodel en bureaucratisering onder Maria-Theresia en Jozef II (1740–1780)." *Tijdschrift voor Geschiedenis* 90, nos. 3–4: 423–438.

————. 1977. "Van Ancien Régime naar 'moderne' bureaucratie: De hervorming van het vorstelijk bestuursapparaat in 1787." *Tijdschrift voor Geschiedenis* 90, nos. 3–4: 439–456.

Hellbling, E.C. 1974. *Osterreichische Verfassungs- und Verwaltungsgeschichte von 1500 bis 1955*. 2d ed. Vienna: Springer.

Hintze, O. 1901. "Der österreichische und der preussische Beamtenstaat im 17. und 18. Jahrhundert." In *Historisches Zeitschrift* neuefolge, no. 50: 401–444.

MacHardy, Karin J. 1992. "The Rise of Absolutism and Noble Rebellion in Early Modern Hapsburg, Austria 1570–1620." *Comparative Studies in Society and History* 34, no.3: 407–438.

Müller, Wolfgang. 1992. "Austrian Governmental Institutions: Do They Matter?" In *West-European Politics* 15, no.1: 99–131.

Mell, A. 1929. *Grundrisz der Verfassungs—und Verwaltungsgeschichte des Landes Steiermark.*

Schulze, R. 1985. "Verwaltungsgeschichtsschreibung in Deutschland und Osterreich." *Die Verwaltung* 18, no.3: 351–374.

Schwartz, H.F. 1943. *The Imperial Privy Council in the Seventeenth Century.* Cambridge: Cambridge University Press.

Sommer, Luise. 1920. *Die österreichische Kameralisten.* Vienna: Carl Königen.

Belgium (including the Austrian Netherlands)

Baelde, M. 1965. *De Collaterale Raden onder Karel V en Filips II (1531–1578): Bijdrage tot de geschiedenis van de centrale instellingen in de zestiende eeuw.* Brussels: Koninklijke Vlaamse Academie voor Wetenschappen.

————. 1971. "Financial Policy and the Evolution of the Demesne in the Netherlands under Charles V and Philip II (1530–1560)." In *Government in Reformation Europe (1520–1560)*, edited by H.J. Cohn. London: MacMillan.

België, Het openbaar initiatief van de gemeenten. Historische grondslagen (Ancien Régime). 1984 Brussels: Gemeentekrediet.

België, Het openbaar initiatief van de gemeenten in 1795–1940. 1986 Brussels: Gemeentekrediet.

Buyten, L. van. 1965. "De achttiende-eeuwse inmengingspolitiek van de Centrale Besturen in de Brabantse steden." In *Mededelingen van de Geschied- en Oudheidkundige Kring voor Leuven en omgeving* 5, no.1: 49–79.

————. 1977. "Bureaucratie en bureaucratisering in de lokale besturen der

Zuidelijke Nederlanden, 16e tot 18e eeuw." *Tijdschrift voor Geschiedenis* 90, no.3–4: 503–523.

Depré, R. 1978. "Groei van de ambtenarij getoetst aan voorbeelden in België." *Bestuurswetenschappen* 32, no.3: 163–183.

Gillisen, J et al. 1975. *De besluitvorming vroeger en nu.* Brussels: Algemeen Rÿksarchief.

Hansotte, G. 1986. *Les institutions politiques et judiciaires de la principauté de Liège aux temps moderne.* Brussels: Credit Communal.

Peteghem, Paul van. 1993. "'Politie' in Brugge, Gent, Maastricht en Nijmegen: Een bijdrage tot vergelijkende institutionele stadsgeschiedenis in de Nederlanden." In *Beleid en bestuur in de oude Nederlanden: Liber Americorum Prof. dr. M. Baelde,* edited by Hugo Soly and René Vermeir, 461–476. Ghent: Vakgroep Nieuwe Geschiedenis.

Schepper, Hugo de and Geoffrey Parker. 1979. "The Decision-Making Process in the Government of the Catholic Netherlands under the Archdukes 1596–1621." In *Spain and the Netherlands 1559–1659,* edited by G. Parker, 164–176 and 258–266. London: Fontana.

Schepper, Hugo de, ed. 1977. *Bronnen voor de geschiedenis van de instellingen in België.* Brussels: Algemeen Rijksarchief en Rijksarchief in de Provinciën.

———. 1977. "Vorstelijke ambtenarij en bureaukratisering in regering en gewesten van 's Konings Nederlanden, 16de–17de eeuw." *Tijdschrift voor Geschiedenis* 90, no.3–4: 358–377.

Wilwerth, Claude. 1995. "Les influences du modèle napoléonien sur l'organisation administrative de la Belgique." In *The Influences of the Napoleonic "Model" of Administration on the Administrative Organization of Other Countries,* edited by Bernd Wunder. Brussels: International Institute of Administrative Sciences, Cahier d'Histoire de l'Administration, no.4: 115–134.

Czechoslovakia

Maly, Karel. 1993. "Zur Lage der Verwaltungsgeschichtsschreibung in de Tschechoslowakei nach 1989." *Jahrbuch für Europäische Verwaltungsgeschichte* 5: 363–368.

Denmark

Blomquist, Helle and Per Ingesman, eds. 1993. *Forvaltningshistorisk antologi.* Copenhagen: Jurist-of Oekonomforbundets Forlag.

Bogason, Peter. 1991–1992. "Strong or Weak State? The Case of Danish Agricultural Export Policy, 1849–1906." *Comparative Politics* 24, no.2: 219–227.

Dombernowsky, Lotte. 1983. *Lensbesiddern som amtmand: Studier i administration af fynske grevskaber og baronier 1671–1849.*

Dübeck, Inger, and Ditlev Tamm. 1991. "The History of Danish Public Administration: Actual Problems and New Tendencies." *Jahrbuch für Europäische Verwaltungsgeschichte* 3: 311–326.

Frandsen, Karl-Erik, ed. 1984. *Atlas over Danmarks administrative inddeling efter 1660.* 2 vols. Copenhagen: Folkemängdeu; Kongeriget Danmark.

Hammerich, Kai. [1848] 1921. "Overgangen fra kollegeum til ministerium." In *Der Danske Centraladministration,* edited by Aage Sachs, 395–509. Copenhagen: Pios.

Jensen, Niels. 1973. *Oversigt over centraladministrationens udviklung siden 1848.* Copenhagen: Munksgaarel.

Jörgensen, Frank and Morten Westrup. 1982. *Dansk central administration i tiden indtil 1848.*

Jörgensen, Harald. 1985. *Lokaladministration i Danmark: Oprindelse og historisk udvikling indtil 1970 en oversigt.*

Knudsen, Tim. 1991. "State Building in Scandinavia: Denmark in a Nordic Context." In *Welfare Administration in Denmark,* edited by Tim Knudsen, 9–105. Copenhagen: Institute of Political Science.

———. 1995. *Dansk statsbygning.* Copenhagen: Jurist-of Oekonomforbundets Forlag.

Levine, Daniel. 1978. "Conservatism and Tradition in Danish Social Welfare Legislation 1830–1933: A Comparative View." In *Comparative Studies in Society and History* 20: 54–69.

Pedersen, E. Ladewig. 1983. "War, Finance and the Growth of Absolutism. Some Aspects of the European Integration of Seventeenth-century Denmark. In *Europe and Scandinavia: Aspects of the Process of Integration in the Seventeenth century,* edited by Göran Rystad. Lund: University of Lund.

Petersen, Niels. 1960. "Oversigt over centraladministrationens udvikling siden 1848." *Administrationsudvalget af 1960* 2, no. 320: 68–80.

Petersen, Niels. 1973. "Oversigt over centraladministrationens udvikling siden 1848." In *Den offentlige forvaltning i Danmark,* edited by Jörgen Nue-Möller, 87–257. n.p.

Sachs, Aage, ed. 1921. *Den danske Centraladministration* (Udgivet i anledning af den danske Kancellibynings 200 ärs dag). Copenhagen: Pios.

Tillotson, Amanda R. 1988–1989. "Open States and Open Economies (Denmark's Contribution to a Statist Theory of Development)." *Comparative Politics* 21, no.3: 339–354.

Waaben, Ebba. 1948. "Trock of embedsstandens stilling 1848–1948." In *Centraladministrationen 1848–1948.* Copenhagen: n.p.

Finland

Anckar, Dag. 1981. "The History of the Finnish Parliament." *European Journal of Political Research* 9, no.2: 209–214.

Kalleinen, Kristiina. 1994. *The generalgubernatorstvo of Finland 1823–1861* (in Finnish). Helsinki: Government Printing Centre, Studies in Administrative History, 12.

Marshev, Vadim. 1989. "On the History of Public Administration in Finland." In *Institutions and Bureaucrats: Studies on Administrative History*, edited by Seppo Tiihonen, 15–24. Helsinki: Government Printing Centre.

Murto, Eero. 1994. *The Prime Minister: the Role of the Prime Minister in Finland from Independence in 1917 to 1993* (in Finnish). Helsinki: Government Printing Centre, Studies in Administrative History, 13.

Nousianinen, Jaako. 1988. "Bureaucratic Tradition, Semi-Presidential Rule and Parliamentary Government: the Case of Finland." *European Journal of Political Research* 16, no.2: 229–249.

Pohls, Maritta. 1994. *From Families to Civil Servants Posts: Civil Servants of the Finnish Postal Service, 1864–1899* (in Finnish). Helsinki: Government Printing Centre, Studies in Administrative History, 15.

Savolainen, Raimo. 1994. *Finnish Senators and Favoritism Practised by the Russian Emperor in 1809–1892* (in Finnish). Helsinki: Government Printing Centre, Studies in Administrative History, 14.

Schweitzer, Robert. 1996. *The Rise and Fall of the Russo-Finnish Relations. The History of the "Second" Committee on Finnish Affairs in St. Petersburg (1857–1891)*. Helsinki: Government Printing Centre, Studies in Administrative History, 23.

Selovuori, Jorma, Lotta Saastamoinen, Tuomas Parkkari, and Timo Moilanen. 1995. *Information on Civil Service 1809–1984: Statistics of Administrative History I* (in Finnish). Helsinki: Painatuskeskus.

Selovuori, Jorma and Tuomas Parkkari. 1995. *Catalogue on Civil Servants: Statistics of Administrative History II* (in Finnish). Helsinki: Painatuskeskus.

Selovuori, Jorma. 1996. *Studies on Administrative History in Finland*. Helsinki: Government Printing Centre, Studies in Administrative History, 24.

Tiihonen, Seppo and Paula Tiihonen. 1984. *The History of Administration in Finland* (in Finnish). Helsinki: Valtion Painatuskeskus.

Tiihonen, Seppo, ed. 1989. *Institutions and Bureaucrats*. Studies on Administrative History. Publications of the Commission on the History of Central Administration in Finland, 1.

———. 1994. *Authority*: Part I *The European Model*. Part II *Sweden and Russia* (in Finnish). Helsinki: Government Printing Office.

———. 1995. "Creation of the Finnish Administrative System under the impact of European Administrative Models." In *The Influences of the Napoleonic "Model" of Administration on the Administrative Organization of Other Countries*, edited by Bernd Wunder. Brussels: International Institute of Administrative Sciences, Cahier d'Histoire de l'Administration, no.4, 241–259.

———. 1995. "Literaturhinweise zur finnischen Verwaltungsgeschichte." In *Jahrbuch für Europäische Verwaltungsgeschichte* 7: 349–357.

Torke, Hans-Joachim. 1989. "Administration and Bureaucracy in Nineteenth-Century Russia: The Empire and the Finnish Case." In *Institutions and Bureaucrats*, edited by Seppo Tiihonen. Studies on Administrative History. Publications of the Commission on the History of Central Administration in Finland, 1: 31–42.

Westerlund, Lars. 1993. *Provincial Administration in Finland: Prefects, Central Government and Politics, 1808–1992* (in Finnish). Helsinki: Government Printing Office, Studies in Administrative History, 8.

France

Antoine, Michel. 1970. *Le Conseil du Roi sous le règne de Louis XV*. Geneva: Librarie Droz.

Antoine, Michel and Pierre Barral et al. 1975. *Origine et histoire des cabinets minstres en France*. Geneva: Librairie Droz.

Arbois de Jubainville, H. de. 1880. *L'Administration des Intendants, d'après les archives de l'Aube*. Paris: H. Champion Libraire.

Ardant, G. 1972. *Histoire de l'impôt*. Les Grandes Etudes historiques. Paris: Fayard.

Ardashev, Pavel. 1909. *Les Intendants de Provence sous Louis XVI*. Paris: Librairie Félix Alcan.

Armstrong, J.A. 1972. "Old Regime Administrative Elites in France, Prussia and Russia." *Revue International des sciences administratives* 38, no.1: 21–40.

Aulard, Alphonse François Victor. 1913. "La centralisation Napoléonienne: les préfets." In *Études et leçons sur la révolution française*, edited by Alphonse F.V. Aulard, 7. Paris: Librairie Félix Alcan.

Baecque, Francis de, et.al. 1976. *Les Directeurs de ministère en France (XIXe–XXe siècles)*. Geneva: Librairie Droz.

Baldwin, John. 1991. *Philippe Auguste et son gouvernement*. Paris: Fayard.

Beaucorps, Charles de. 1911. "Une Province sous Louis XIV: l'Administration des Intendants d'Orléans: De Creil, Jubert de Bouville et de la Baudonnaye (1686–1713)." *Mémoires de la Société Archéologique et Historique de l'Orléanais* 33: 37–500.

Beaud, O. 1988. "Bureaucratie et syndicalisme: Histoire de la formation des associations professionelles des fonctionnaires civils des ministères (1870–1914)." *Revue Administrative* 41, no.4: 309–322.

Behrens, C.B.A. 1985. *Society, Government, and the Enlightenment: the Experiences of Eighteenth-Century France and Prussia*. London: Thames & Hudson Ltd.

Bezard, Yvonne. 1932. *Fonctionnaires Maritimes et Coloniaux sous Louis XIV: Les Bégon*. Paris: Editions Albin Michel.

Bluche, François. 1959. "L'Origine sociale des secrétaires d'Etat de Louis XIV (1661–1715)." *XVIIe Siècle* 42–43, no.1: 8–22.

————. 1966. "Les Magistrats de la Cour des Monnaies de Paris au XVIIIe siècle, 1715–1790." *Belles Lettres: Annales littéraires de l'université de Besancon*, no.81.

————. 1966. "Les Magistrats du grand conseil au XVIIIe siècle, 1690–1791." *Belles Lettres: Annales littéraires de l'université de Besancon*, 82.

Boislisle, A. de. 1884. *Les Conceils du Roi sous Louis XIV*. Paris: Libraire Hachette.

Boissonade, P. 1897. *La police municipale à Potiers au XVIIIe siècle*. Poitiers: Blais & Roy.

Bonney, Richard. 1978. *Political Change in France under Richelieu and Mazarin 1624–1661*. Oxford: Oxford University Press.

————. 1981. *The King's Debts: Finance and Politics in France 1589–1661*. Oxford: Clarendon Press.

Bordes, Maurice. 1957. *D'Etigny et l'administration de l'intendance d'Auch (1751–1767)*. Auch: Cocharaux.

————. 1960. "Les Intendants de Louis XV." *Revue Historique* 84, no.223: 45–62.

————. 1961. "Les Intendants Eclairés de la Fin de l'Ancien Régime." *Revue d'Histoire Economique et Sociale* 39, no.1: 57–83.

————. 1972. *L'administration provinciale et municipale en France au XVIIIe siècle*. Paris.

Bosher, J. 1964. "The Premiers Commis des Finances in the Reign of Louis XVI." *French Historical Studies* 3, no.3: 475–494.

————. 1970. *French Finances 1770–1795—From Business to Bureaucracy*. Cambridge: Studies in Early Modern History.

————, ed. 1973. *French Government and Society 1500–1850: Essays in Memory of Alfred Cobban*. London: Athlone Press.

Buisson, H. 1958. *La Police: Son Histoire*.

Burdeau, F. 1989. *Histoire de l'administration française du XVIIIe au XXe siècles*. Paris: Editions Montchrestien- EJA.

Cameron, I.A. 1977. "The Police of Eighteenth-Century France." *European Sociological Review* 7, no.1: 467–476.

Caritey, J. 1959. "Pour un histoire des ministères du XIXe Siècle." *Revue Administrative*, no. 78: 216–219.

Chapman, Brian. 1955. *The Prefects and Provincial France*. London: n.p.

Chenot, B., et al. 1975. *Histoire de l'administration française depuis 1800: Problèmes et méthodes*. Geneva: Librarie Droz.

Chéruel, A. 1855. *Histoire de l'Administration Monarchique en France depuis l'Avénement de Philippe-Auguste jusqu'à la Mort de Louis XIV*. Paris: Dezobry, E. Magdeleine et Cie.

————. 1880. *Dictionnaire historique des institutions, moeurs et coutumes de la France*. 5th ed. Paris: Hachette & Cie.

Chevallier, J.J. 1967. *Histoire des institutions et des régimes politiques de la France moderne 1789–1958*. 3d ed. Paris: Dalloz Sirey.

————. 1970. *L'Elaboration historique du principe de séparation de la juridiction administrative et de l'administrative active.* Paris: Librairie Generale de Droit et de Jurisprudence.

Church, Clive H. 1963. *The Organization and Personnel of French Central Government under the Directory.* Ph.D. thesis, University of London.

————. 1967. "The Social Basis of the French Central Bureaucracy under the Directory, 1795–1799." *Past and Present* 36, no.1: 59–71.

————. 1974. "Bibliographie pour l'histoire administrative: Travaux de langue anglaise sur la France." *Bulletin de l'Institute Internationale d'Administration Publique* 30: 369–384.

————. 1974. "Du Nouveau sur les origines de la Constitution de 1793." *Revue Historique de Droit Francais et étranger* 52, no.4: 594–627.

————. 1981. *Revolution and Red Tape: The French Ministerial Bureaucracy 1770–1850.* Oxford: Clarendon Press.

Clinquart, Jean. 1983. *L'Administration des douanes en France de la Révolution de 1848 à la Commune (1848–1871).* Neuilly-sur-Seine: ed. Assocation pour l'histoire de l'administration des douanes.

————. 1989. *L'Administration des douanes en France sous la Révolution.* Paris: ed. Association pour l'histoire de l'administration des douanes.

Coulaudon, Aimée. 1932. *Chazerat: Dernier Intendant de la Généralité de Riom et Province d'Auvergne (1774–1789).* Ph. D. diss., University of Paris, Faculté de Droit, Jouve et Cie.

Dawson, G. 1969. *L'Evolution des structures de l'administration locale déconcentrée en France, l'exemple du Departement du Pas-de-Calais et de la region du Nord.* Paris: Librairie Generale de Droit et de Jurisprudence.

Dogan, Mattei. 1989. "Career Pathways to the Cabinet in France, 1870–1986." In *Pathways to Power: Selecting Rulers in Pluralist Democracies*, edited by Mattei Dogan, 19–44. Boulder, CO: Westview Press.

Doucet, R. 1948. *Les Institutions de la France au XVIe siècle.* Paris: Doucet.

Dumas, F. 1894. *La Généralité de Tours au XVIIIe Siècle: Administration de l'Intendant du Cluzel (1766–1783).* Tours: L. Pericat Libraire.

Durand-Barthez, P. 1973. *Histoire des structures du Ministère de la Justice 1789–1945.* Paris: Presses Universitaires de France.

Duval, Louis. 1891. *Les Intendants d'Alençon au XVIIe Siècle et les Memoires de J.B. de Pomereu.* Alençon: Librairie Loyer-Fontaine.

Ellul, Jacques. 1962. *Histoire des institutions de L'époque Franque à la Révolution.* Paris: Presses Universités.

Fischer, W. 1977. "Rekrutierung und Ausbildung für den modernen Staat: Beamte, Offiziere und Techniker in England, Frankreich und Preuszen in der frühen Neuzeit." In *Studien zum Beginn der modernen Welt*, by R. Koselleck. Stuttgart: Klett-Cotta.

Ford, Franklin L. 1953. *Robe and Sword: The Regrouping of the French Aristocracy after Louis XIV.* Cambridge: Cambridge University Press.

Fougère, Louis, et al. 1972. *Histoire de l'Administration*. Paris: Institut Française des Sciences Administratives, cahiers no. 7.

Fréville, Henri 1953. *L'Intendance de Bretagne (1689–1790): Essai sur l'histoire d'une intendance en pays d'états aus XVIIIe siècle*. Ph. D. diss. University of Paris, Faculté de Lettres. Rennes: Olihon, Editeur.

Fritschy, W. 1990. "Taxation in Britain, France and The Netherlands in the Eighteenth Century." *Economic and Social History in the Netherlands* 2: 57–79.

Gillis, A.R. 1989. "Crime and State Surveillance in Nineteenth Century France." *American Journal of Sociology* 95, no.2: 307–341.

Godard, Charles. 1901. *Les pouvoirs des Intendants sous Louis XIV, Particulièrement dans les Pays d'Elections de 1661 à 1715*. Ph.D. diss. University of Paris, Faculté de Lettres.

Godechot, J. 1951. "L'Origine des institutions francaise de l'époque révolutionnaire." *Revue internationale d'histoire politique et constitutionnelle* 1, no.1: 92–99.

———. 1968. *Les Institutions de la France sous la Révolution et l'Empire*. 2d ed. Paris.

Gousset. P. 1961. "L'Evolution historique de l'administration centrale du commerce et de l'industrie." *Revue Administrative* 80, no.1: 132–137.

Gruder, Vivian R. 1968. *The Royal Provincial Intendants: A Governing Elite in Eighteenth Century France*. Ithaca, NY: Cornell University Press.

Hanley, S. 1989. "Engendering the State: Family Formation and State Building in Early Modern France." *French Historical Studies* 16, no.1: 4–27.

Hanotaux, Gabriel. 1884. *Origines de l'Institution des Intendants des Provinces*. Paris: Champion Libraire.

Harding, Robert R. 1978. *Anatomy of a Power Elite: The Provincial Governors of Early Modern France*. New Haven, CT: Yale University Press.

Harrison, M. 1990. "The French Constitution Council: A Study in Institutional Change." *Political Studies* 38, no.4: 603–619.

d'Hauterive, Ernest. 1943. *Napoléon et sa Police*. Paris: n.p.

Histoire de l'administration française depuis 1800. Problèmes et méthodes 1975. Geneva.

Hoock, Jochen. 1989. "Economie politique, statistique et réforme administrative en France et en Allemagne dans la deuxième moitié du 18e siècle." *Jahrbuch für Europäische Verwaltungsgeschichte* 1: 33–46.

Kesler, Jean-Francois. 1964. "Les Ancièn Elèves de l'Ecole Nationale d'Administration." *Revue Francaise de Science Politique* 14, no.2: 243–267.

Kessler, Marie-Christine. 1977. "Historique du système de formation et de recrutement des hauts fonctionnaires." *Revue Française d'Administration Publique* 1: 9–52.

———. 1978. "Recruitment and Training of Higher Civil Servants in France: The Ecole Nationale d'Administration." *European Journal of Political Research* 6, no.1: 31–52.

King, James E. [1949] 1972. *Science and Rationalism in the Government of Louis XIV 1661–1683.* New York: Octagon Books.

Le Clerc, Bernard and Vincent Wright. 1973. *Les Préfets du Second Empire.* Paris: Cahiers de la Fondation des Sciences Politiques.

Le Clère, Marcel. 1964. *Histoire de la Police.* Paris: Presses Universitaires de France.

Legendre, P. 1968. *Histoire de l'administration de 1750 à nos jours.* Paris: Thémis.

———. 1972. "Le Régime Historique des bureaucraties occidentales. Remarques sur le cas français." *Revue Internationale des Sciences Administratives,* 38, no.4: 361–378.

Leguin, C.A. 1966. "An Anti-Clerical Bureaucrat in Eighteenth Century France-J.M. Roland." *Catholic Historical Review* 51, no.4: 487–542.

Lhéritier, Michel. 1920. *L'Intendant Tourny (1695–1760).* Paris: Librairie Félix Alcan.

Ligou, Daniel. 1960. "A propos de la révolution municipale." *Revue d'histoire économique et sociale* 38, no.2: 146–177.

Livet, Georges. 1948. *Deux siècles d'Alsace française 1648–1789–1848.* Strasbourg/Paris: n.p.

———. 1956. *L'Intendance d'Alsace sous Louis XIV, 1648–1715.* Paris: Société d'Edition "Les Belles Lettres."

Major, J.R. 1960. *Representative Institutions in Renaissance France 1421–1559.* Madison, WI: University of Wisconsin Press.

Marchand, J. 1889. *Un Intendant sous Louis XIV: Etude sur l'Administration de Lebret en Provence (1687–1704).* Paris: Librairie Hachette.

Markoff, John. 1975. "Governmental Bureaucratization: General Processes and an Anomalous Case." *Comparative Studies in Society and History* 17 no.4: 479–503.

Mathias, P and P. O'Brien. 1976. "Taxation in Britain and France, 1715–1810: A Comparison of the Social and Economic Incidence of Taxes Collected for Central Governments." *Journal of European Economic History* 5, no.3: 601–650.

Mead, G.J. de C. 1954. *The Administrative Noblesse of France during the Eighteenth Century.* London: London University Press.

Monin, H. 1884. *Essai sur l'Histoire Administrative du Languedoc pendant l'Intendance de Basville (1685–1719).* Paris: Librairie Hachette.

Monnier, François. 1991. "Les historiens face au droit et à l'administration d'ancien régime." *Jahrbuch für Europäische Verwaltungsgeschichte* 3: 327–334.

———. 1995. "Remarques sur l'administation française d'ancien régime: l'émergence de la spécificité administrative française." In *The Influences of the Napoleonic "Model" of Administration on the Administrative Organization of Other Countries,* edited by Bernd Wunder. Brussels: International Institute of Administrative Sciences, Cahier d'Histoire de l'Administration, no.4, 35–55.

Montyon, Auget de. 1812. *Particularités et Observations sur les Ministres des Finances de France les plus Célèbres depuis 1660 jusqu'en 1791*. Paris: Le Norman, Imprimeur-Libraire.

Mousnier, R. 1947. "Le conseil du roi de la mort de Henri V au governement personnel de Louis XIV." In *Études d'histoire moderne et contemporaine* 1: 29–67.

Mousnier, R. [1948] 1971. *La vénalité des offices sous Henri IV et Louis XIII*. Paris: Presses Universitaires de France.

Nienhaus, Ursula D. 1987. "Technological Change, the Welfare State, Gender, and Real Women: Female Clerical Workers in the Postal Services in Germany, France, and England 1860–1945." In *Internationale wissenschaftliche Korrespondenz zur Geschichte der deutschen Arbeiterbewegung* 2: 223–231.

O'Reilly, E. 1881. *Mémoires sur la Vie Publique et Privée de Claude Pellot, Conseiller, Maitres des Requetes, Intendant et Premier Président du Parlement de Normandie (1619–83)*. Paris: H. Champion.

Osborne, T.R. 1983. *A Grande Ecole for the Grand Corps: The Recruitment and Training of the French Administrative Elite in the Nineteenth century*. Boulder, CO: The Westview Press

Pagès, Georges. 1932. "Essai sur l'Evolution des Institutions Administratives en France du Commencement du XVIe Siècle à la Fin du XVIIe." *Revue d'histoire moderne* 7, no.1: 8–57, 113–137.

———. 1932. "La Vénalité des Offices dans l'Ancienne France." *Revue Historique*, no. 169 (january-june): 477–95.

Paravicini, W. and K.F. Werner, eds. 1980. *Histoire comparée de l'administration (IVe–XVIIIe siècles)*, Actes du XIVe colloque Franco-Allemand. München: Artemis.

Petot, Jean. 1958. *Histoire de l'administration des Ponts et Chaussées 1599–1815*. Paris: Librairie Marcel Rivière.

Pierre, Henry. 1950. *Histoire des Préfets: Cent Cinquante Ans d'Administration Provinciale 1800–1950*. Paris: Nouvelles Editions Latines.

Ponteil, Felix. 1956. *Napoléon et l'organisation autoritaire de la France*. Paris: n.p.

———. 1966. *Les Institutions de la France de 1814 à 1870*. Paris: Presses Universitaires de France.

Poullet, P. 1907. *Les Institutions francaises 1795–1815*.

Poutier, C. 1960. "L'Evolution des structures ministérielles de 1800 à 1944." In *Thése Droit*. Paris: [Presses Universités?].

Ravitch, N. 1966. *Sword and Mitre, Government and Episcopate in France and England in the Age of Aristocracy*. The Hague/Paris: Mouton.

Richardson, N. 1966. *The French Prefectoral Corps, 1814–1830*. Cambridge: Cambridge University Press.

Ricommard, J. 1933. *La Lieutenance Générale de Police à Troyes au XVIIIe Siècle, 1700–1790*. Diss., University of Paris, Faculté de Lettres.

Ricommard, J. 1937. "Les Subdélégués des Intendants jusqu'à Leur Erection en Titre d'Office." *Revue d'Histoire Moderne* 12, no.6: 338–407.

Root, Hilton L. 1991. "The Redistributive Role of Government Economic Regulation in Old Regime France and England." *Comparative Studies in Society and History* 33, no.2: 338–369.

Sagnac, Philippe. 1939. "Louis XIV et Son Administration." *Revue d'Histoire Politique et Constitutionnelle* 3, no.1: 23–47.

Salmon, J.H.M. 1967. "Venality of Office and Popular Sedition in the Seventeenth Century France." *Past and Present* 37 (July): 21–43.

Samoyault, Jean-Pierre. 1971. *Les bureaux du Secrétariat d'Etat des affaires étrangères sous Louis XV.* Paris: Pédone.

Sautel, G. 1982. *Histoire des institutions publiques depuis le Révolution francaise: administration, justice, finance.* 5th ed. Paris: Dalloz Sirey.

Savant, Jean. 1958. *Les Préfets de Napoléon.* Paris: Hachette.

Schmale, Wolfgang. 1992. "Neuere Forschungen zur Verwaltungsgeschichte der Landgemeinden in Frankreich und Deutschland vor der Industrialisierung." *Jahrbuch für Europäische Verwaltungsgeschichte* 4: 343–363.

Serres, Borelli de. 1895–1900. *Recherches sur Divers Services Publics du XIII au XVII Siècle.* Paris: [Société de l'histoire de Paris?].

Sharp, Walter Rice. 1931. *The French Civil Service: Bureaucracy in Transition.* New York: MacMillan Co.

Silberman, Bernard S. 1993. "France." In *Cages of Reason: The Rise of the Rational State in France, Japan, The United States, and Great Britain,* 89–156. Chicago, IL: The University of Chicago Press.

Siwek-Pouydesseau, J. 1969. *Le corps préfectoral sous la Troisième et la Quatrième République.* Paris: Colin.

Skocpol, Theda. 1985. "States and Revolutions: France, Russia and China. In *States and Societies* 3d ed., edited by David Held et al., 151–169. Oxford: Blackwell/The Open University.

Sturgill, C.C. 1971. "The Relationship of French General Officers to the Civil Government of France, 1715–1730." In *Transactions of the Conference Group for Social and Administrative History,* 1: 38–52. Madison, WI: University of Wisconsin Press.

Tersen, H. 1913. *Origines et évolution du Ministère de l'Interieur.* Montpellier: n.p.

Thuillier, Guy and Jean Tulard. 1974. "Pour une histoire des Directeurs de Ministère en France au XIXe et XXe Siècles." *Revue internationale des sciences administratives* 40, no.3: 227–229.

Thuillier, Guy. 1980. *Bureaucratie et Bureaucrates en France au XIXe siècle.* Geneva: Librarie Droz.

Thuillier, Guy and Jean Tulard. 1982. *Histoire de l'administration francaise, volume 2 1870–1958.* Paris: Cours de l'Institut d'études Politiques.

———. 1983. "L'histoire de l'administration en France." *International Review of the Administrative Sciences* 49, no.1: 13–16.

Vignes, Joseph Bernard Maurice. 1961. *Histoire des doctrines sur l'impot en France*. Paris: Librairie général de droit et de jurisprudence.

Viollet, P. [1890] 1966. *Histoire des Institutions Politiques et Administratives de la France*. Aalen: Scientia.

Whitcomb, E.A. 1974. "Napoleon's Prefects." *American Historical Review* 125, no.4: 1089–1118.

Wishnia, J. 1978. *French Fonctionnaires: the Development of Class Consciousness and Unionization (1884–1926)*. Ph.D. diss., State University of New York at Stonybrook.

Wolfe, Martin. 1966. "French Views of Wealth and Taxes from the Middle Ages to the Old Regime." *Journal of Economic History* 26, no.4: 466–483.

Wolfe, Martin. 1972. *The Fiscal System of Renaissance France*. New Haven, CT: Yale University Press.

Wright, Vincent. 1976. "L'Ecole Nationale d'Administration de 1848 à 1849: un échec révélateur." *Revue Historique* 100, no. 260: 21–42.

———. 1976. "Les Directeurs et secretaire generaux des administrations centrales sous le second empire." In *Les Directeurs de Ministère en France (XIXe–XXe siècles)*, Francis de Baecque, 38–50. Geneva: Librairie Droz.

———. 1977. "Les épurations administratives de 1848 à 1895." In Paul Gerbod et al., *Les épurations administratives: XIXe–XXe siècles*. Geneva: Librairie Droz.

———. 1990. "The History of French Mayors: Lessons and Problems." In *Jahrbuch für Europäische Verwaltungsgeschichte* 2: 269–280.

Zeller, G. 1948. *Les institutions de la France au XVIième siècle*. Paris: n.p.

Germany

Agena, Carl-August. 1972. *Der Amtmann im 17. und 18. Jahrhundert: Ein Beitrag zur Geschichte des Richter-und Beamtentums*. Ph.D.thesis, Göttingen.

Applegate, Celia. 1990. *A Nation of Provincials: The German Idea of Heimat*. Los Angeles: n.p.

Armstrong, J.A. 1972. "Old Regime Administrative Elites in France, Prussia and Russia." *Revue International des Sciences Administratives* 38, no.1: 21–40.

Behrens, C.B.A. 1985. *Society, Government, and the Enlightenment: the Experiences of Eighteenth-Century France and Prussia*. London: Thames & Hudson.

Bödeker, H.E. 1989. "'Verwaltung,' 'Regierung' und 'Polizei' in deutschen Wörterbüchern und Lexika des 18, Jahrhunderts." *Jahrbuch für Europäische Verwaltungsgeschichte* 1: 15–32.

Boynton, G. and G. Loewenberg. 1975. "The Decay of Support for Monarchy and the Hitler Regime in the Federal Republic of Germany." *British Journal of Political Science* 4, no.4: 453–488.

Borch, H. 1954. *Obrigkeit und Widerstand: Zur politischen Soziologie des Beamtentums.* Tübingen: Mohr (Siebeck).

Bowen, Ralph H. 1950. "The Roles of Government and Private Enterprise in German Industrial Growth, 1870–1914." *Journal of Economic History* 10, Supplement, 68–81.

Brandenburg, Mark. 1967. *Regierung und Verwaltung: Gesammelte Abhandlungen zur Staats-, Rechts- und Sozialgeschichte Preussens,* edited by Gerhard Oestreich. Göttingen: Vandenhoeck & Ruprecht.

Braun, Rudolph. 1975. "Taxation, Sociopolitical Structure and State-Building: Great Britain and Brandenburg-Prussia." In *The Formation of National States in Western Europe,* edited by Charles Tilly, 243–327. Princeton, NJ: Princeton University Press.

Caplan, Jane. 1977. "The Politics of Administration: the Reich Interior Ministry and the German Civil Service, 1933–1943." *The Historical Journal* 20, no.3: 707–736.

Carsten, F.L. 1950. "The Great Elector and the Foundation of the Hohenzollern Despotism." *English Historical Review* 65, no.2: 175–202.

Cullity, P. 1967. "The Growth of Governmental Employment in Germany 1882–1959." *Zeitschrift für die gesamte Staatswissenschaft* 123, no.2: 201–217.

Derlien, Hans-Ulrich. 1989. "A Longitudinal Study of the West German Federal Elite: Methodology and Findings of Two Recent Reports." In *Institutions and Bureaucrats in the History of Administration,* by Seppo Tiihonen, 3–14. Helsinki: Government Printing Centre.

Derlien, Hans-Ulrich. 1991. "Historical Legacy and Recent Developments in the German Higher Civil Service." *International Review of the Administrative Sciences* 57, no.3: 385–401.

Dominicus, Alexander. 1929. "Die deutsche Verwaltung in Elsasz-Lothringen 1871–1918." *Elsasz-Lothringes Jarhbuch* 8: 311–329.

Dorn, Walter. 1931–1932. "The Prussian Bureaucracy in the Eighteenth Century." *Political Science Quarterly* 46, no.3: 403–423,47/no.2: 75–94, 259–273.

———. 1940. *Competition for Empire, 1740–1763.* New York: Harper & Bros.

Dorwart, Reinhold August. 1953. *The Administrative Reforms of Frederick William I of Prussia.* Cambridge, MA: Harvard University Press.

———. 1971. *The Prussian Welfare State before 1740.* Cambridge, MA: Harvard University Press.

Fenske, Hans. 1985. *Bürokratie in Deutschland: Vom späten Kaiserreich bis zur Gegenwart.* Berlin: n.p.

Fischer, W. 1977. "Rekrutierung und Ausbildung für den modernen Staat: Beamte, Offiziere und Techniker in England, Frankreich und Preuszen in der frühen Neuzeit." In R. Koselleck, *Studien zum Beginn der modernen Welt,* by R. Kosselleck. Stuttgart: Klett-Cotta.

Ford, Guy Stanton. 1922. *Stein and the Era of Reform in Prussia, 1807–1815.* Princeton, NJ: Princeton University Press.

Frank, Elke. 1966. "The Role of Bureaucracy in Transition." *Journal of Politics* 28, no.4: 725–753.

Franz, Günther, ed. 1972. *Beamtentum und Pfarrerstand, 1400–1800.* Limburg an der Lahn: Starke.

Friedrich, Carl J. 1930. "The German Civil Service and the Prussian Civil Service." In *The Civil Service in the Modern State,* edited by L.D. White. Chicago, IL: University of Chicago Press.

Gelpke, Franz. 1902. *Die geschichtliche Entwicklung des Landrathsamtes der preussischen Monarchie.* Berlin: C. Heymann.

Gillis, John R. 1968. "Aristocracy and Bureaucracy in Nineteenth-century Prussia." *Past and Present* 41 (December): 105–129.

———. 1971. *The Prussian Bureaucracy in Crisis, 1840–1860: Origins of an Administrative Ethos.* Stanford, CA: Stanford University Press.

Goldschmidt, Friedrich and Paul Goldschmidt. 1881. *Das Leben des Staatsrath Kunth.* Berlin: Julius Springer.

Hartung, Fritz. 1961. "Studien zur Geschichte der preussischen Verwaltung (1942–1948)." In *Staatsbildende Kräfte der Neuzeit: Gesammelte Aufsätze,* 178–344. Berlin: Duncker & Humblot.

Hattenhauer, H. 1978. *Geschichte des Beamtentums.* Vol 1. In *Handbuch des öffentlichen dienstes,* by W. Weise. Köln/Berlin/Bonn/München: C. Heymann Verlag KG.

Heffter, Heinrich. 1950. *Die deutsche Selbstverwaltung im 19. Jahrhundert. Geschichte der Ideen und Institutionen.* Stuttgart: K.F. Koehler.

Heinrich, Henning and K.G.A. Jeserich. 1992. *Verwaltungsgeschichte Ostdeutschlands 1815–1945.*

Heinzen, Karl. 1854. *Die Preussische Büreaukratie.* Darmstadt: Carl Wilhelm Leske.

Henning, H. 1984. *Die deutsche Beamtenschaft im 19. Jahrhundert: Zwischen Stand und Beruf.* Stuttgart: Steiner.

Heyen, Erk Volkmar. 1984. *Wissenschaft und Recht der Verwaltung seit dem Ancien Régime: Europäische Ansichten.* Frankfurt am Main: Klostermann.

Heyen, Erk Volkmar and Mathias Rautenberg. 1994. "Verwaltungsgeschichte der DDR: Hinweise su Literaturstand und Archivlage." *Jahrbuch für Europäische Verwaltungsgeschichte* 6: 299–318.

———. 1995. "Deutsche Verwaltungsgeschichte aus der Sicht von DDR-Archivaren: Zum wissenschaftlichen Profil unveröffentliche Diplomarbeiten." *Jahrbuch für Europäische Verwaltungsgeschichte* 7: 359–372.

Hintze, Otto. [1901] 1962. "Der österreichische und der preussische Beamtenstaat im 17. und 18. Jahrhundert." *Historisches Zeitschrift,* neuefolge, 50: 401–444. Reprinted in *Staat und Verfassung: Gesammelte Abhandlungen zur allgemeinen Verfassungsgeschichte.* Göttingen: Vandenhoeck & Ruprecht.

————. 1908. "Die Entstehung der modernen Staatsministerien." In *Historische Zeitschrift* 100: 53–111. Münich and Berlin: Cotta.

————. [1910] 1962. "Der Commissarius und seine Bedeutung in der allgemeinen Verwaltungsgeschichte: Eine Vergleichende Studie." In *Staat und verfassung: Gesammelte Abhandlungen zur allgemeinen Verfassungsgeschichte*, edited by Gerhard Oestrich, 242–274. Göttingen: Vandenhoeck & Ruprecht.

————. [1932] 1962. "Die Entstehung des modernen Staatsleben." In *Staat und verfassung: Gesammelte Abhandlungen zur allgemeinen Verfassungsgeschichte*, edited by Gerhard Oestrich, 497–502. Göttingen: Vandenhoeck & Ruprecht.

————. [1908] 1967. "Der preussische Militär- und Beamtenstaat im 18. Jahrhundert." In *Regierung und Verwaltung; Gesammelte Abhandlungen zur Staats-, Rechts- und Sozialgeschichte Preussens*, edited by Gerhard Oestrich, 419–428. Göttingen: Vandenhoeck & Ruprecht.

————. [1915] 1967. "Der Ursprung des preussischen Landratsamts in der Mark Brandenburg." In *Regierung und Verwaltung; Gesammelte Abhandlungen zur Staats-, Rechts- und Sozialgeschichte Preussens*, edited by Gerhard Oestrich, 164–203. Göttingen: Vandenhoeck & Ruprecht.

Hintze, Otto and Gustav Schmoller. 1901. *Die Behördenorganisation und die allgemeine Staatsverwaltung Preussens im 18. Jahrhundert*. Berlin: B. Parey; Acta Borussica. Denkmäler der Preussischen Staatsverwaltung im 18. Jahrhundert.

Hoock, Jochen. 1989. "Economie politique, statistique et réforme administrative en France et en Allemagne dans la deuxième moitié du 18e siècle." In *Jahrbuch für Europäische Verwaltungsgeschichte* 1: 33–46.

Hubatsch, Walther. 1973. *Friedrich der Grosse und die preussische Verwaltung*. Köln and Berlin: n.p.

————. 1975. *Grundriss zur deutschen Verwaltuugsgeschichhe 1015–1945*. Marburg and Lahn: Gohann-Gottfried-Herder-Institut.

Jacob, Herbert. 1963. *Field Administration in Germany, 1871–1959*. New Haven, CT: Yale University Press.

————. 1963. *German Administration since Bismarck: Central Authority versus Local Autonomy*. New Haven, CT: Yale University Press.

Janowski, Manfred. 1968. *Prussian Policy and the Development of the Ruhr Mining Region, 1766–1865*. Ph.D. diss. University of Wisconsin, Madison WI.

Jeserich, K.G.A. 1978. "Gedanken zu einer 'Deutschen Verwaltungsgeschichte.'" *Die öffentliche Verwaltung* 31, no.10: 360–363.

Jeserich, K.G.A., H. Pohl, and G.C. von Unruh. 1983–1988. *Deutsche Verwaltungsgeschichte*. Stuttgart: Deutsche Verlags-Anstalt.

Jeserich, K.G.A. and H. Neuhaus. 1991. *Persönlichkeiten der Verwaltung: Biographien zur deutschen Verwaltungsgeschichte 1648–1945*. Stuttgart and Berlin: Deutsche Verlags-Anstalt.

Johnson, H.C. 1975. *Frederick the Great and His Officials*. New Haven, CT: Yale University Press.

Knemeyer, F.L. 1970. *Regierungs- und Verwaltungsreformen in Deutschland zu Beginn des 19. Jahrhunderts*. Köln.

Kube, Horst. 1939. *Die Geschichtliche Entwicklung der Stellung des preussischen Oberpräsidenten*. Würzburg: Konrad Triltsch.

Kübler, Horst. 1976. *Besoldung und Lebenshaltung der unmittelbaren preuzsischen Staatsbeamten im 19. Jahrhundert*. Neurenberg.

Kunz, Andreas. 1990. "The State as Employer in Germany: From Paternalism to Public Policy." In *The State and Social Change in Germany 1880–1980*, edited by W.R. Lee and Eve Rosenschaft, 34–60. New York: St. Martin's Press.

Lee, Loyd E. 1980. *The Politics of Harmony: Civil Service, Liberalism and Social Reform in Baden, 1800–1850*. Newark, DE: University of Delaware Press.

Lehmann, Max. 1902–1905. *Freiherr vom Stein*. Leipzig: S. Hirzel.

Liebel, Helen P. 1965. *Enlightened Bureaucracy versus Eenlightened Despotism in Baden, 1750–1792*. Philadelphia, PA: Transactions of the American Philosophical Society, New Series 55, no.5.

Lotz, Albert. 1914. *Geschichte des deutschen Beamtentums*. Berlin: R. von Decker Verlag.

Marchet, Gustav. 1966. *Studien über die entwicklung der Verwaltungslehre in Deutschland von der zweiten Hälfte des 17. bis zum ende des 18. Jahrhunderts*. Frankfurt: Sauer und Auvermann.

Marx, Fritz Morstein. 1982. "German Administration and the Speyer Academy." In James W. Fesler, *American Public Administration: Patterns of the Past*. Washington D.C.: American Society for Public Administration, 57–68.

Meler, E. von. 1898–1899. *Hannoverische Verfassunge und Verwaltungsgeschichte 1680–1866*.

Mohnhaupt, H. 1989. "Vorstufen der Wissenschaften von 'Verwaltung' und 'Verwaltungsrecht' an der Universität Göttingen (1750–1830)." In *Jahrbuch für europäische Verwaltungsgeschichte* 1: 73–104.

Möller, W. 1929. *Das Preuszische Beamten- und Besoldungswesen von 1870–1928: mit ausgewählten Quellen zur nationalsozialistischen Beamtenpolitik*. Frankfurt: Schriftreihe der Vierteljahrshefte für Zeitgeschichte.

Mommsen, Hans. 1966. *Beamtentum im Dritten Reich: mit ausgewählten Quellen zur nationalsozialistischen Beamtenpolitik*. Stuttgart: n.p.

Mommsen, Wolfgang J. and W. Mock, eds. 1981. *The Emergence of the Welfare State in Britain and Germany 1850–1950*. London: Croom Helm.

Muncy, Lysbeth W. 1944. *The Junker in the Prussian Administration under William II, 1888–1914*. Providence and Rhode Island: Brown University Press.

———. 1947. "The Junkers and the Prussian Administration from 1918 to 1939." *Review of Politics* 9, no.4: 482–501.

Müthling, H. 1966. *Die Geschichte der deutschen Selbstverwaltung*. Köln: W. Kohlhammer Verlag.

Nienhaus, Ursula D. 1987. "Technological Change, the Welfare State, Gender and Real Women: Female Clerical Workers in the Postal Services in Germany, France and England 1860–1945." *Internationale wissenschaftliche Korrespondenz zur Geschichte der deutschen Arbeiterbewegung* 2: 223–231.

Parry, Geraint. 1963. "Enlightened Government and its Critics in the Eighteenth Century Germany." *Historical Journal* 6, no.2: 178–192.

Raeff, Marc. 1983. *The Well-Ordered Police State: Social and Institutional Change through Law in the Germanies and Russia, 1600–1800.* New Haven, CT: Yale University Press.

Rejewski, Harro J. 1973. *Die Pflicht zur politische Treue im preuzsischen Beamtenrecht 1850–1918.* Berlin: Duncker & Humblot.

Ritter, Gerhard A., ed. 1973. *Vom Wohlfahrtsausschutzs zum Wohlfahrtsstaat.* Cologne.

Rohmer, Friedrich. 1848. *Deutschlands alte und neue Bureaukratie.* Munich: Kaiser.

Rosenberg, Hans. 1943. "The Rise of the Junkers in Brandenburg-Prussia, 1410–1653. *American Historical Review* 49, no.1: 1–22/ no.2: 228–242.

———. 1958. *Bureaucracy, Aristocracy and Autocracy: the Prussian Experience 1660–1815.* Boston, MA: Beacon Press.

Rugge, F. 1990. "Deutsche Lehren der lokalen Selbstverwaltung und deren Einflusz auf die italienische Literatur (1870–1914)." In *Deutsche Rechtswissenschaft und Staatslehre im Spiegel der italienische Rechtskultur während der zweiten Hälfte des 19. Jahrhunderts,* by R.Schulze c.s. Berlin, 311–328.

Rutgers, M.R. 1990. "Lorenz von Stein als grondlegger van de bestuurskunde." *Bestuurswetenschappen* 44, no.4: 286–300.

Schmale, Wolfgang. 1992. "Neuere Forschungen zur Verwaltungsgeschichte der Landgemeinden in Frankreich und Deutschland vor der Industrialisierung." *Jahrbuch für Europäische Verwaltungsgeschichte* 4: 343–363.

Schmidt, Richard. 1932. *Die Bürokratisierung des modernen England und ihre Bedeutung für das heutige deutsche Behördensystem.* Leipzig: V.S. Hirzel.

Schmoller, Gustav. 1870. "Der preussische Beamtenstand unter Friedrich Wilhelm I." *Preussische Jahrbücher* 27: 148–72, 253–70, 538–55.

———. 1894. "Über Behördenorganisation, Amtswesen und Beamtentum im allgemeinen und speziell in Deutschland und Preussen bis zum Jahre 1713." In *Acta Borussica, Behördenorganisation,* I, 15–143.

———. 1909. "Historische Betrachtungen über Staatenbildung und Finanzentwicklung." *Jahrbuch für Gesetzgebung, Verwaltung, und Volkswirtschaft im Deutschen Reich* 33, no.1: 1–64.

———. 1921. *Preussische Verfassungs-, Verwaltungs- und Finanzgeschichte.* Berlin: Reimar Hobbing.

Schulze, R. 1985. "Verwaltungsgeschichtsschreibung in Deutschland und Osterreich." *Die Verwaltung* 18, no.3: 351–374.

Seeley, Sir John Robert. 1968. *Life and Times of Stein: or, Germany and Prussia in the Napoleonic Age.* New York: Greenwood Press.

Small, Albion. 1909. *The Cameralists: The Pioneers of German Social Polity.* Chicago, IL: The University of Chicago Press.

Spittler, G. 1980. "Abstraktes Wissen als Herrschaftsbasis: Zur Entstehungsgeschichte bürokratischer Herrschaft im Bauernstaat Preuszen." In *Kölner Zeitschrift für Soziologie und Sozialpsychologie* 32, no.3: 574–604.

Süle, Tibor. 1986. "Kommunalen Handels- und Verwaltungshochschulen in der deutschen Beamtenausbildung und Fortbildung 1879–1918." *Die Verwaltung* 19, no.4: 475–500.

———. 1988. *Preuzsische Bürokratietradition: Zur entwicklung von Verwaltung und Beamtenschaft in Deutschland 1871–1918.* Göttingen.

Supple, Barry. 1985. "States and Industrialization: Britain and Germany in the Nineteenth Century." In *States and Societies.* 3d ed, edited by David Held, 170–180. Oxford: Blackwell/The Open University.

Ule, Carl Hermann. 1961. *Die Entwicklung des offentlichen Dienstes.* Cologne: Carl Heymanns Verlag.

Weis, E. 1973. "Der Einflusz der Französischen Revolution und des Empire auf die Reformen in den süddeutschen Staaten." *Beihefte zu Francia* 1, no.1: 569–583. München: Artemis.

———. 1974. "Absolute Monarchie und Reform im Deutschland des späten 18. und frühen 19. Jahrhunderts." In *Geschichte in der Gesellschaft: Festschrift K. Bos*, 436–461. Stuttgart: F. Prinz.

Wunder, Bernd. 1978. *Privilegierung und Disziplinierung: Die Entstehung des Berufsbeamtentums in Bayern und Würtemberg (1780–1825).* München/Wien: Oldenbourg.

———. 1984. "Die Reform der Beamtenschaft in den Rheinbundstaaten." In *Reformen im rheinbündischen Deutschland*, edited by E. Weiss, 181–194. München.

———. 1986. *Geschichte der Bürokratie in Deutschland.* Frankfurt am Main: Suhrkamp.

———. 1989. "La bureaucratie d'Etat en France et en Allemagne: Rôle et structure." In *La Révolution, la France et l'Allemagne*, edited by H. Berding et al., 115–147. Paris: Editions de la Maison des Sciences de l'Homme.

———. 1995. "L'influence du modèle napoléonien sur l'administration allemande." In *The Influences of the Napoleonic "Model" of Administration on the Administrative Organization of Other Countries.* Brussels: International Institute of Administrative Sciences, Cahier d'Histoire de l'Administration, no.4, 59–75.

Great Britain

Anderson, M.A. 1956. *Edmund Hammond, Permanent Under-Secretary for Foreign Affairs, 1854–1873.* London: unpublished Ph.D. thesis.

Anderson, Olive. 1965. "The Janus Face of Mid-Nineteenth-Century English Radicalism: The Administrative Reform Association of 1855." *Victorian Studies* 8, no.3: 231–242.

———. 1974. "The Administrative Reform Association, 1855–1857." In *Pressure from Without in Early Victorian England*, edited by Patricia Hollis, 262–288. London: Arnold.

Ashford, Douglas E. 1974. "The Effects of Central Finance on the British Local Government System." *British Journal of Political Science* 4, no.3: 305–322.

Ashton, Robert. 1956. "Revenue Farming under the Early Stuarts." In *Economic History Review* 8, no.3: 310–321.

Aylmer, G.E. 1959. "Office Holding as a Factor in English History, 1625–1642." *History* 44, no.2: 228–240.

———. 1961. *The King's Servants: The Civil Service of Charles I 1625–1642*. New York: Columbia University Press.

———. 1973. *The State's Servants: The Civil Service of the English Republic 1649–1660*. London: Routledge & Kegan Paul.

Barnes, Thomas Garden. 1961. *Somerset, 1625–1640: A County's Government During the "Personal Rule"*. Cambridge, MA: Harvard University Press.

Baxter, Stephen Bartow. 1957. *The Development of the Treasury 1660–1702*. Cambridge, MA: Harvard University Press.

Beard, C.A. 1904. *The Office of Justice of the Peace in England: its Origin and Development*. New York: MacMillan.

Bell, H.E. 1953. *An Introduction to the History and Records of the Court of Wards and Liveries*. Cambridge: The University Press.

Bellamy, Christine. 1988. *"Administering Central-Local Relations, 1871–1919: the Local Government Board in its Fiscal and Cultural Context."* Manchester: Manchester University Press.

Binney, J.E.D. 1958. *British Public Finance and Administration, 1774–1792*. Oxford: Clarendon Press.

Blakeley, Brian. 1972. *The Colonial Office 1868–1892*. Durham, NC: Duke University Press.

Borand, J. 1974. *Local Government Reform in England 1888–1974*. London: Croom Helm Ltd.

Braun, Rudolph. 1975. "Taxation, Sociopolitical Structure and State-Building: Great-Britain and Brandenburg-Prussia." In *The Formation of National States in Western Europe* edited by Charles Tilly, 243–327. Princeton, NJ: Princeton University Press.

Brebner, J.B. 1948. "Laissez-faire and State Intervention in Nineteenth-Century Britain." *Journal of Economic History*, 8th Supplement, 59–73.

Cell, John W. 1970. *British Colonial Administration in the Mid-Nineteenth Century*. New Haven, CT: Yale University Press.

Chester, Daniel Norman. 1981. *The English Administrative System 1780–1870*. Oxford: Clarendon Press.

Clark, D.M. 1936–1937. "The Office of Secretary to the Treasury in the Eighteenth Century." *American Historical Review* 62, no.1: 30–38.

Clifton, Gloria. 1985. *Professionalism, Patronage and Public Service in Victorian London: The Staff of the Metropolitan Board of Works 1856–1889.* London: Athlone Press.

Cohen, Emmeline W. 1941. *The Growth of the British Civil Service 1780–1939.* London: George Allen & Unwin.

Coleman, Christopher and David Starkey, eds. 1986. *Revolution Reassessed: Revisions in the History of Tudor Government and Administration.* Oxford: Clarendon Press.

Cooper, J.P. 1960. "Differences between English and Continental Governments in the Early Seventeenth Century." In *Britain and the Netherlands*, edited by J.S. Bromley and E.H. Kossman. London: Chatto & Windus.

Craig, Sir John. 1955. *A History of Red Tape: An Account of the Origin and Development of the Civil Service.* London: MacDonald & Evans Ltd.

Cromwell, Valerie. 1966. Interpretations of Nineteenth-Century Administration: An Analysis. *Victorian Studies* 9, no.3: 245–255.

Cromwell, Valerie and Zara S. Steiner. 1972. "The Foreign Office before 1914: A Study in Resistance." In *Studies in the Growth of Nineteenth-Century Government*, edited by Gillian Sutherland, 167–194. London: Routledge & Kegan Paul.

Cromwell, Valerie, et al. 1978. *Aspects of Government in Nineteenth Century Britain.* Dublin: Irish University Press.

Cross, Claire, David Loades, and J.J. Scarisbrick, eds. 1988. *Law and Government under the Tudors: Essays Presented to Sir Geoffrey Elton.* Cambridge: Cambridge University Press.

Davis, Ralph. 1966. "The Rise of Protection in England, 1689–1786." *Economic History Review* 19, no.2: 306–317.

Dibble, Vernon K. 1965. "The Organization of Traditional Authority: English County Government, 1558–1640." In *Handbook of Organizations*, edited by James G. March, 879–909. Chicago, IL: Rand McNally.

Dickson, Peter George Muir. 1967. *The Financial Revolution in England: A Study in the Development of Public Credit 1688–1756.* London: St. Martin's Press.

Dietz, Frederick C. 1964. *English Public Finance 1485–1641, I. English Government Finance 1485–1558, II. English Public Finance 1558–1641, III.* 2d ed. London: Frank Cass & Co Ltd.

————. 1967. "English Public Finance and the National State in the Sixteenth Century." In *Facts and Factors in Economic History: Articles by Former Students of Edwin Francis Gay.* Cambridge, MA: Harvard University Press.

Donajgrodzki, A.P. 1972. "New Roles for Old: The Northcote-Trevelyan Report and the Clerks of the Home Office, 1822–1848." In *Studies in the Growth of Nineteenth-Century Government*, edited by Gillian Sutherland, 82–109. London: Routledge & Kegan Paul.

Dowell, Stephen. 1965. *A History of Taxation and Taxes in England from the Earliest Times to the Present Day.* 3d ed. London: Frank Cass & Co Ltd.

Eaton, Dorman B. 1880. *Civil Service in Great Britain: A History of Abuses and Reforms and their Bearing upon American Politics.* New York: Harper and Brothers.

Elton, G.R. 1962. *The Tudor Revolution in Government: Administrative Changes in the Reign of Henry VIII.* Cambridge: Cambridge University Press.

Emden, Cecil S. 1956. *The People and the Constitution: Being a History of the Development of the People's Influence in British Government.* London: Oxford University Press.

Emmerson, Harold. 1956. *The Ministry of Works.* London: Putnam's Sons.

Fiddes, George V. 1926. *The Dominions and Colonial Offices.* London: Putnam's Sons.

Finer, S.E. 1952. "Patronage and the Public Service." In *Public Administration* 30, no.4: 329–360.

Fischer, W. 1977. "Rekrutierung und Ausbildung für den modernen Staat: Beamte, Offiziere und Techniker in England, Frankreich und Preuszen in der frühen Neuzeit." In *Studien zum Beginn der modernen Welt,* by R. Koselleck. Stuttgart: Klett-Cotta.

Fraser, Peter. 1960. "The Growth of Ministerial Control in the Nineteenth-Century House of Commons." *English Historical Review* 74, no.296: 444–463.

Fritschy, W. 1990. "Taxation in Britain, France and The Netherlands in the Eighteenth Century." *Economic and Social History in the Netherlands* 2: 57–79.

Fry, Geoffrey Kingdon. 1969. *Statesman in Disguise: The Changing Role of the Administrative Class of the British Home Civil Service, 1853–1966.* London: MacMillan and New York: Humanities Press.

Gleason, John Howes. 1969. *The Justices of the Peace in England, 1558–1640: A Later Eirenarcha.* Oxford: Clarendon Press.

Gordon, Hampden. 1935. *The War Office.* London.

Gretten, R.H. 1913. *The King's Government: A Study of the Growth of the Central Administration.* London: G. Bell and Sons, Ltd.

Hart, Jennifer. 1972. "The Genesis of the Northcote-Trevelyan Report." In *Studies in the Growth of Nineteenth-Century Government,* edited by Gillian Sutherland, 63–81. London: Routledge & Kegan Paul.

Heath, Thomas L. 1927. *The Treasury.* London.

Hennock, E. Peter. 1982. "Central/Local Government Relations in England: An Outline 1800–1950." *Urban History Yearbook,* 38–45.

Heussler, Robert. 1963. *Yesterday's Rulers: The Making of the British Colonial Service.* Syracuse, NY: Syracuse University Press.

Hoon, E.E. [1938] 1968. *The Organization of the British Customs System, 1696–1786.* New York: Newton Abbot, Devon.

Hughes, Edward. 1934. *Studies in Administration and Finance, 1558–1825, with Special Reference to the History of the Salt Tax in England.* Manchester: Manchester University Press.

———. 1949. "Sir Charles Trevelyan and Civil Service Reform, 1853–1855." *English Historical Review* 64: 53–88, 206–234.

———. 1954, 1955. Civil Service Reform 1853–1855. *Public Administration* 32, no.1: 17–51/33, no.3: 299–306.

Jeffries, Charles Joseph. 1956. *The Colonial Office.* London: Allen & Unwin and New York: Oxford University Press.

Johnson, N. 1985. "Change in the Civil Service: Retrospect and Prospect." *Public Administration* (UK) 63, no.4: 415–433.

Jones, Kathleen. 1991. *The Making of Social Policy in Britain 1830–1990.* London: The Athlone Press Ltd.

Jones, Ray. 1971. *The Nineteenth-Century Foreign Office: An Administrative History.* London: Weidenfeld & Nicholson.

Karraker, C.H. 1930. *The Seventeenth-Century Sheriff: a Comparative Study of the Sheriff in England and the Chesapeake Colonies, 1607–1689.* Chapel Hill, NC: University of North Carolina Press.

Kelsall, Roger K. 1955. *Higher Civil Servants in Britain from 1870 to the Present Day.* London: Routledge & Kegan Paul Ltd.

Kennedy, William. 1964. *English Taxation 1640–1799: An Essay on Policy and Opinion.* New York: A.M. Kelley.

Lee, J.M. 1963. *Social Leaders and Public Persons: A Study of County Government in Cheshire since 1888.* Oxford: Oxford University Press.

Llewellyn-Smith, Hubert. 1928. *The Board of Trade.* London.

Lowe, Rodney. 1984. "Bureaucracy Triumphant or Denied? The Expansion of the British Civil Service, 1919–1939." *Public Administration* 62, no.3: 291–310.

Lubenow, William C. 1971. *The Politics of Government Growth: Early Victorian Attitudes toward State Intervention, 1833–1848.* Hamden, CT: Archon Books.

Lucas, B.K. and P.G. Richards. 1978. *A History of Local Government in the Twentieth Century.* London: George Allen & Unwin.

MacDonagh, Oliver. 1958. "The Nineteenth-Century Revolution in Government: A Reappraisal." *The Historical Journal* 1, no.1: 52–67.

———. 1961. *A Pattern of Government Growth, 1800–1860: The Passenger Acts and Their Enforcement.* London: MacGibbon and Kee.

MacGregor, O.R. 1951. "Civil Servants and the Civil Service: 1850–1950." *Political Quarterly* 22, no.2, 154–163.

MacLeod, Roy M. 1968. *Treasury Control and Social Administration: A Study of Establishment Growth at the Local Government Board 1871–1905.* London.

———. 1973. "Statesmen Undisguised." *American Historical Review* 78, no.5: 1386–1406.

———, ed. 1982. *The Government of Victorian London, 1855–1889: the Metropolitan Board of Works, the Vestries, and the City Corporation.* Cambridge, MA: Harvard University Press, Belknap Press.

———, ed. 1988. *Government and Expertise: Specialists, Administrators and Professionals, 1860–1919.* Cambridge: Cambridge University Press.

Maine, Henry. 1893. *Lectures on the Early History of Institutions.* London: J. Murray.

Martindale, Hilda. 1938. *Women Servants of the State, 1870–1938.* London: Allen & Unwin.

Mathias, P and P. O'Brien. 1976. "Taxation in Britain and France, 1715–1810: A Comparison of the Social and Economic Incidence of Taxes Collected for Central Governments." *Journal of European Economic History* 5, no.3: 601–650.

McConville, Sean. 1981. *A History of English Prison Administration, 1750–1877.* London: Routledge & Kegan Paul Ltd.

Middleton, C.R. 1976. "The Emergence of Constitutional Bureaucracy in the British Foreign Office." *Public Administration* (UK) 53, no.4: 365–382.

Mommsen, Wolfgang J and W. Mock, eds. 1981. *The Emergence of the Welfare State in Britain and Germany 1850–1950.* London: Croom Helm Ltd.

Morgan, K.O. 1981. *Rebirth of a Nation: Wales 1880–1980.* Oxford: Clarendon Press; Cardiff: University of Wales Press.

Moses, Robert. 1914. *The Civil Service of Great Britain: Studies in History, Economics and Public Law.* New York: Columbia University Press.

Nelson, R.R. 1969. *The Home Office, 1782–1802.* Durham, NC: Duke University Press.

Newsam, Frank. 1954. *The Home Office.* London, n.p.

Newsholme, Arthur. 1925. *The Ministry of Health.* London.

Nienhaus, Ursula D. 1987. "Technological Change, the Welfare State, Gender and Real Women: Female Clerical Workers in the Postal Services in Germany, France and England 1860–1945." *Internationale wissenschaftliche Korrespondenz zur Geschichte der deutschen Arbeiterbewegung* 2: 223–231.

Parris, Henry. 1960. "A Civil Servant's Diary, 1841–1846." *Public Administration* 38, no.4: 369–380.

———. 1960. "The Nineteenth-Century Revolution in Government: A Reappraisal Reappraised." *The Historical Journal* 3, no.1: 17–37.

———. 1968. The Origins of the Permanent Civil Service 1780–1830. In *Public Administration* 46, no.2: 143–166.

———. 1969. *Constitutional Bureaucracy: The Development of British Central Administration since the Eighteenth Century.* London: George Allen & Unwin.

Peacock, A. and J. Wiseman. 1961. *The Growth of Public Expenditure in the United Kingdom.* Princeton, NJ: Princeton University Press.

Pellew, Jill. 1982. *The Home Office 1848–1914: From Clerks to Bureaucrats.* Rutherford, NJ: Fairleigh Dickinson University Press.

————. 1983. "Practitioners versus Theorists: Early Attitudes of British Higher Civil Servants towards their Profession." *International Review of Administrative Sciences* 49, no.1: 4–12.

————. 1991. "The Study of English Public Administration in the Nineteenth and Early Twentieth Centuries: a Bibliographic Account. *Jahrbuch für Europäische Verwaltungsgeschichte* 3: 299–310.

Pickthorn, K.W.M. 1967. *Early Tudor Government: Henry VII.* New York: Octagon Books Inc.

————. 1967. *Early Tudor Government: Henry VIII.* New York: Octagon Books Inc.

Plumb, J.H. 1956. *Sir Robert Walpole: The Making of a Statesman.* London: Cresset Press.

Prouty, Roger. 1957. *The Transformation of the Board of Trade, 1830–1855: A Study of Administrative Reorganization in the Heyday of Laissez Faire.* London: William Heinemann.

Ravitch, N. 1966. *Sword and Mitre, Government, and Episcopate in France and England in the Age of Aristocracy.* The Hague: Mouton.

Redlich, J, F. Hirst. 1970. *The History of Local Government in England.* London: MacMillan.

Reith, Charles. 1948. *A Short History of the British Police.* London: Oxford University Press.

Richards, Melville. 1969. *Welsh Administrative and Territorial Units, Medieval and Modern.* Cardiff: University of Wales Press.

Richardson, Walter C. 1952. *Tudor Chamber Administration 1485–1547.* Baton Rouge, LA: Louisiana State University Press.

————. 1953. *Stephen Vaughan, Financial Agent of Henry VIII; A Study of Financial Relations with the Low Countries.* Baton Rouge, LA: Louisiana State University Press.

————. 1961. *History of the Court of Augmentation, 1536–1554.* Baton Rouge, LA: Louisiana State University Press.

Roach, John. 1971. *Public Examinations in England: 1850–1900.* Cambridge: Cambridge University Press.

Roberts, David. 1958–1959. "Jeremy Bentham and the Victorian Administrative State." *Victorian Studies* 2, no.2: 193–210.

————. 1960. *Victorian Origins of the British Welfare State.* New Haven, CT: Yale University Press.

Root, Hilton L. 1991. "The Redistributive Role of Government Economic Regulation in Old Regime France and England." *Comparative Studies in Society and History* 33, no.2: 338–369.

Roper, M. 1977. "Public Records and the Policy Process in the Twentieth Century." *Public Administration* (UK) 55, no.3: 253–267.

Rosevaere, H. 1969. *The Treasury: The Evolution of a British Institution.* London: Allen Lane, the Penguin Press.

————. 1973. *The Treasury 1660–1870: The Foundation of Control—His-*

torical Studies and Documents. London: Allen Lane, the Penguin Press.

Sainty, J.C. 1972. *Treasury Officials: 1660–1870*. London: University of London, Athlone Press.

————. 1974. *Officials of the Board of Trade: 1660–1870*. London: University of London, Athlone Press.

————. 1975. *Home Office Officials, 1782–1870*. London: University of London, Athlone Press.

————. 1976. *Colonial Office Officials*. London: University of London, Institute of Historical Research.

Schmidt, Richard. 1927. *Die Bürokratisierung des modernen England und ihre Bedeutung für das heutige deutsche Behördensystem*. Leipzig: V.S. Hirzel.

Selby-Bigge, Lewis A. 1927. *The Board of Education*. London: Putnam's Sons.

Seton, Malcolm. 1926. *The India Office*. London: Putnam's Sons.

Sharp, Evelyn Adelaide. 1969. *The Ministry of Housing and Local Government*. London: George Allen & Unwin.

Silberman, Bernard S. 1993. "Great Britain." In *Cages of Reason: The Rise of the Rational State in France, Japan, The United States, and Great Britain*, 287–410. Chicago: The University of Chicago Press.

Skeel, Caroline Anne James. 1904. *The Council in the Marches of Wales: A Study in Local Government during the Sixteenth and Seventeenth Centuries*. London: H. Rees, Ltd.

Smellie, K.B. 1950. *A Hundred Years of English Government*. London: Gerald Duckworth and Co., Ltd..

————. 1973. *A History of Local Government*. London: George Allen & Unwin.

Smith, B.C. 1971. "Reform and Change in British Central Administration." *Political Studies* 19, no.2: 213–226.

Snelling, R.C. and T.J. Barron. 1972. The Colonial Office and its Permanent Officials, 1801–1914. In *Studies in the Growth of Nineteenth-Century Government*, edited by Gillian Sutherland, 139–166. London: Routledge & Kegan Paul.

Steiner, Zara S. 1969. *The Foreign Office and Foreign Policy 1898–1914*. London: Cambridge University Press.

Strang, Lord. 1955. *The Foreign Office*. London.

Supple, Barry. 1985. "States and Industrialization: Britain and Germany in the Nineteenth Century." In *States and Societies*, 3d ed., edited by David Held, 170–180. Oxford: Blackwell/The Open University.

Sutherland, Gillian. 1970. Recent Trends in Administrative History. *Victorian Studies* 13, no.4: 408–411.

————, ed. 1972. *Studies in the Growth of Nineteenth-Century Government*. London: Routledge & Kegan Paul.

Swart, K.W. 1949. *Sale of Offices in the Seventeenth Century*. Den Haag: Martinus Nijhoff.

Thane, Pat. 1991. *Foundations of the Welfare State.* 8th ed. London and New York: Longman.

The Civil Service: Vol.I, Report of the Committee 1966–1968 (i.e., The Fulton Report, also containing a reprint of *Report on the Organisation of the Permanent Civil Service,* 1854, the so-called Northcote-Trevelyan report).

Thomson, Mark A. 1932. *The Secretaries of State, 1681–1782.* Oxford: Clarendon Press.

Thomson, Gladys Scott. 1923. *Lord Lieutenants in the Sixteenth Century: A Study of Tudor Local Administration.* London: Longmans, Green.

Tilly, John and Gaselee Stephen. 1933. *The Foreign Office.* London.

Troup, Edward. 1925. *The Home Office.* London.

Veverka, Jindrich. 1963. The Growth of Government Expenditure in the United Kindom since 1790. *Scottish Journal of Political Economy* 10, no.1: 111–127.

Ward, W.R. 1955. "Some Eighteenth-Century Civil Servants." *English Historical Review* 70, no.1: 25–54.

Wernham, John R. 1966. *Before the Armada: The Growth of English Foreign Policy, 1485–1588.* London: Cape.

Wesseling, H.L. 1989. "British and Dutch Imperialism: A Comparison." *Itinerario* 13, no.1: 61–76.

Western, John R. 1965. *The English Militia in the Eighteenth Century.* London: Routledge & Kegan Paul.

Wheare, K.C. 1978. "Civil Service." In *Aspects of Government in Nineteenth Century Britain,* edited by P. and G. Ford, 5–40. Dublin: Irish Academic Press, Ltd.

Willcox, William Bradford. 1940. *Gloucestershire; A Study in Local Government, 1590–1640.* New Haven, CT: Yale University Press.

Williams, Henry. 1958. *The Council in the Marches of Wales under Elisabeth I.* Cardiff: University of Wales Press.

Willis, J. 1933. *The Parliamentary Powers of English Government Departments.* Cambridge, MA: Harvard University Press.

Wilson. F.M.G. 1968. *The Organization of British Central Government, 1914–1964.* London.

Winnifrith, John. 1960. "The Rt. Hon. Sir Alexander Spearman, Bart. (1793–1874): Gladstone's Invaluable Public Servant." *Public Administration* 38, no.3: 311–320.

Wright, Maurice. 1969. *Treasury Control of the Civil Service, 1854–1874.* New York: Oxford University Press.

Young, D.M. 1961. *The Colonial Office in the Early Nineteenth Century.* London: Longmans, Green (for the Royal Commonwealth Society).

Greece

Andronopoulos, B. and M. Mathioudakis. 1988. *Histoire administrative de la Grèce moderne (1821–1974)* (in Greek). Athens: n.p.

Moschopoulos, Denis. 1995. "L'influence du modèle napoléonien sur l'administration grecque." In *The Influences of the Napoleonic "Model" of Administration on the administrative organization of Other Countries*, edited by Bernd Wunder. Brussels: International Institute of Administrative Sciences, Cahier d'Histoire de l'Administration, no.4, 137–157.

Moschopoulos, Denis. 1995. "Les influences du modèle napoléonien d'administration dans les îles Ioniennes pendant la période de la domination française." In *The Influences of the Napoleonic "Model" of Administration on the Administrative Organization of Other Countries*, edited by Bernd Wunder. Brussels: International Institute of Administrative Sciences, Cahier d'Histoire de l'Administration, no.4, 161–178.

Ireland

Barrington, T.J. 1987. "Ireland: The Interplay of Territory and Function." *West European Politics* 10, no.4: 130–147.

Birrel, D. 1978. "The Northern Ireland Civil Service—From Devolution to Direct Rule." In *Public Administration* (UK) 56, no.3: 305–320.

Cohan, Alvin S. 1970. *Revolutionary and Non-Revolutionary Elites: The Irish Political Elite in Transition; 1919–1969*. Ph.D. thesis, University of Georgia, Athens, Georgia.

King, Desmond S. 1986. "The Public Sector Growth and State Autonomy in Western Europe: The Changing Role and Scope of the State in Ireland since 1950." *West European Politics* 9, no.1: 81–96.

McDowell, R.B. 1964. *The Irish Administration, 1801–1914*. London: Routledge & Kegan Paul.

McElligot, T.J. 1958. *Representative Government in Ireland: A Study of Dail Eireann 1919–1948*. London: Oxford University Press.

Norman, E.R. 1969. *The Catholic Church and Irish Politics in the Eighteen Sixties*. Irish History Series, 5. Dundalk: Dundalgan Press.

Robins, J.A. 1961. "The County in the Twentieth Century." *Administration* 9, no.1: 88–94.

Turpin, D. 1954. "The Local Government Service: Consolidating the Service." *Administration* 2: 81–94.

Whyte, John H. 1960. "The Influence of the Catholic Clergy on Elections in Nineteenth-Century Ireland." *The English Historical Review* 75, no.2: 239–259.

———. 1965. "Landlord Influence at Elections in Ireland, 1760–1885." *The English Historical Review* 80, no.4: 740–760.

———. 1971. *Church and State in Modern Ireland, 1923–1970*. London: Gill & MacMillan.

Italy

Aimo, Pierre. 1985. *L'Italia napoleonica: l'amministrazione come amministrazione dello Stato*. Milan.

————. 1992. "La 'Sciarpa Tricolore': sindaci e maires nell'Europa dell'-Ottocento." *Jahrbuch für Europäische Verwaltungsgeschichte* 4: 293–324.

————. 1995. "L'influence du modèle napoléonien sur l'administration italienne." In *The Influences of the Napoleonic "Model" of Administration on the Administrative Organization of Other Countries*, edited by Bernd Wunder, 181–195. Brussels: International Institute of Administrative Sciences, Cahier d'Histoire de l'Administration no.4.

Antonielli, L. 1983. *I prefetti dell'Italia napoleonica, Republica e Regno d'Italia*. Bologna: Mulino.

Brown, Alison. 1979. *Bartolomeo Scala, 1430–1497, Chancellor of Florence: The Humanist as Bureaucrat*. Princeton, NJ: Princeton University Press.

Cassese, S. 1983. "Il prefetto nella storia amministrativa." *Revista trimestrale di diritto pubblico* 33.

————, ed. *Ricerca sulla storia dell'amministrazione dello Stato 1861–1943*. (I Storia dei Ministeri, II Biografie dei funcionari).

Fried, Robert C. 1963. *The Italian Prefects*. New Haven, CT: Yale University Press.

Leonardi, Robert, Nanetti Y. Rafaella, and Robert P. Putnam. 1987. "Italy: Territorial Politics in the Post-War Years. The Case of Regional Reform." *West European Politics* 10, no.4, 88–107.

Litchfield, R. Burr. 1986. *Emergence of a Bureaucracy: the Florentine patricians, 1530–1790*. Princeton, NJ: Princeton University Press.

Randeraad, Nico. 1992. *Authority in Search of Liberty: The Prefects in Liberal Italy (1861–1895)*. Ph.D. diss., European University Institute, Florence.

Rotelli. 1972. *La Presidenza del Consiglio dei Ministri: Il problema del coordinamento dell'amministrazione centrale in Italia 1848–1948*. Milan.

Rugge, F. 1990. "Deutsche Lehren der lokalen Selbstverwaltung und deren Einflusz auf die italienische Literatur (1870–1914)." In *Deutsche Rechtswissenschaft und Staatslehre im Spiegel der italienische Rechtskultur während der zweiten Hälfte des 19. Jahrhunderts*, by R. Schulze et al., 311–328. Berlin: Duncher & Humblot.

Taradel, A. 1964. *Alcune caratteristiche dello sviluppo della burocrazia italiana dal 1861 ai nostri giorni*. Milan.

————. 1971. *Carriere e retribuzioni deglie impiegate dello Stato 1861–1968*. Milan.

————. 1971. *Gli organici delle carriere direttive delle amministrazioni centrali dello Stato dal 1853 al 1969*. Rome.

Netherlands

Alberts, W.J. 1969. *Geboorte en groei van de Nederlandse gemeente.* Alphen a/d AD Rijn: Samsom.

Alkemade, M.J.M. and J.C.N. Raadschelders. 1992. "Ontstaan en ontwikkeling van ministeries van algemeen bestuur 1798-heden." In *Ministeries van algemeen bestuur,* 2d ed., edited by J.N. Breunese and L.J. Roborgh 33–63. Leiden: SMD.

Bemelmans-Videc, M.L. 1984. *Economen in overheidsdienst 1945–1975; bijdragen van economen aan de vorming van het sociaal-economisch beleid.* Ph.D. diss., University of Leiden, Leiden.

Beth, J.C. 1907. *De departementen van algemeen bestuur, gedurende het tijdvak 1798–1908.* Groningen: Van der Kamp.

Blécourt, A.S. de 1902. *De ambachten van Rijnland, Delfland en Schieland: Een overzicht van wetgeving, bestuur en rechtspraak in deze landschappen.* Haarlem: V. Loosjes.

———. 1903. *De organisatie der gemeenten gedurende de jaren 1795–1851.* Haarlem: V. Loosjes.

———. 1912. *Ambacht en gemeente: De regeering van een Hollandsch dorp gedurende de 17e, 18e, en 19e eeuw.* Zutphen: Firma J.H.A. Wansleven & Zoon.

Boels, Henk. 1933. *Binnenlandse Zaken: Ontstaan en ontwikkeling van een departement in de Bataafse tijd, 1795–1806. Een reconstructie.* 's-Gravenhage: SDU Uitgeverij Koninginnegracht.

Braam, A. van. 1957. *Ambtenaren en bureaucratie in Nederland 1850–1950.* Zeist: Uitgeversmaatschappij W. de Haan.

———. 1977. "Bureaucratiseringsgraad van het plaatselijk bestuur van Westzaandam ten tijde van de Republiek." *Tijdschrift voor Geschiedenis,* 90, nos.3–4: 457–477.

Brainich von Brainich Felth, C.H. 1993. "Centralisatie en waterschapswetgeving." In *Waterschappen in Nederland: Een bestuurskundige verkenning van de institutionele ontwikkeling,* edited by J.C.N. Raadschelders, Th.A.J. Toonen, 107–131. Hilversum: Verloren.

Brasz, H.A. 1960. *Veranderingen in het Nederlandse communalisme: De gemeentebesturen als element in het Nederlandse stelsel van sociale beheersing.* Assen: Van Gorcum & Compagnie N.V.

Brauw, W.M. de. 1864. *De departementen van algemeen bestuur in Nederland sedert de omwenteling van 1795.* Utrecht: Kemink.

Breunese, J.N. 1982. "Twee eeuwen Nederlandse provincie." *Bestuur: Maandblad voor Overheidskunde* 1, no.1: 14–19.

———. 1983. "Wasdom der gemeenten: Geschiedenis en perspectief." *Bestuur: Maandblad voor Overheidskunde* 2, no.2: 6–11.

Carasso, L.C., J.M.P. Koopmans, J.C.N. Raadschelders, and I.F.J. Voermans (1995). "Organisatiedifferentiatie bij de rijksoverheid in historisch perspectief 1862–1992." *Bestuurswetenschappen* 48, no.6: 483–495.

Diederiks, H.A. 1977. "De collecteurs van de gemene landsmiddelen in Amsterdam en omstreken in de tweede helft van de 18e eeuw." *Tijdschrift voor Geschiedenis* 90, nos. 3–4: 484–502.

Dirksen, W. 1972. "Openbare financiën in Nederland van 1790 tot 1820; veranderingen bij de overgang van een republikeinse statenbond naar koninkrijk." *Pro Civitate Historische uitgaven* 8, no. 34: 85–131.

Dogan, Mattei and Maria Scheffer van der Veen. 1957–1958. "Le personnel ministériel hollandais 1848–1958." *L'Année Sociologique* no.2: 383–409.

Fockema-Andreae, S.J. 1961. *De Nederlandse staat onder de Republiek.* Amsterdam: KNAW.

Fockema-Andreae, S.J. and H. Hardenberg, eds. 1964. *500 Jaar Staten-Generaal in de Nederlanden: Van Statenvergadering tot Volksvertegenwoordiging.* Assen: Van Gorcum.

Fritschy, Wantje. 1985. "Overheidsfinanciën als uiting van het 'institutionele onvermogen' van de achttiende eeuwse Republiek." *Economisch- en Sociaal-Historisch Jaarboek* 48: 19–47.

―――. 1988. *De patriotten en de financiën van de Bataafse Republiek. Hollands krediet en de smalle marges voor een nieuw beleid (1795–1801).* Amsterdam.

―――. 1990. "Taxation in Britain, France and the Netherlands in the eighteenth century." *Economic and Social History in the Netherlands* 2: 57–79.

Fruin, R. and H.T. Colenbrander. 1992. *Geschiedenis der staatsinstellingen in Nederland tot den val der Republiek,* 2d ed. Den Haag: Nijhoff.

Gabriëls, A.J.C.M. 1990. *De Heren als dienaren en de dienaar als heer.* The Hague: Stichting Hollandse Historische Reeks.

Gelderen, M. van. 1991. *Op zoek naar de Republiek: Politiek denken tijdens de Nederlandse Opstand (1555–1590).* Hilversum: Verloren.

Gosman, J.G. 1989. "De ontwikkeling van een centrale bureaucratie in Nederland: Van de laatste jaren van de Republiek tot de Belgische afscheiding." *Bestuurswetenschappen* 43, no.1: 35–50.

Gosses, I.H. and N. Japikse. 1947. *Handboek tot de staatkundige geschiedenis van Nederland.* 3d ed. Den Haag: Nijhoff.

Grapperhaus, F.H.M. 1982. *Alva en de tiende penning.* Zutphen: Walburg Pers.

Haitsma Muller, E.O.G. 1989. *Het Nederlands gezicht van Machiavelli. Twee en een halve eeuw interpretatie 1550–1800.* Hilversum: Verloren.

Hart, Marjolein 't. 1989. In *Quest for Funds: Warfare and State Formation in the Netherlands,* 1620–1650. Ph.D. Diss., University of Leiden, Leiden.

―――. 1990. "Staatsvorming, Sociale Relaties en Oorlogsfinanciering in de Nederlandse Republiek." *Tijdschrift voor Sociale Geschiedenis* 16, no.1: 61–85.

Hemerijck, Anton. 1992. *The Historical Contingencies of Dutch Corporatism.* Ph.D. thesis, Balliol College, University of Oxford.

Hovy, L. 1991. *Ceylonees Plakkaatboek: Plakkaten en andere wetten uit-gevaardigd door het Nederlands bestuur op Ceylon, 1638–1796.* Hilversum: Verloren.

Hugenholtz, W.R. and H. Boels. 1977. "De griffie van de Staten-Generaal en van de Nationale Vergadering, 1780–1798." *Tijdschrift voor Geschiedenis* 90, no.3–4: 391–422.

Ijsselmuiden, P.G. van. 1988. *Binnenlandse Zaken: De ontwikkeling naar de moderne bureaucratie in Nederland.* Kampen: Kok.

Jacobs, B.C.M. 1986. *Justitie en politie in 's-Hertogenbosch voor 1629: De bestuursorganisatie van een Brabantse stad.* Assen/Maastricht: van Gorcum.

Janssens, J.W. 1992. *De commissaris van de Koningin: Historie en functioneren.* 's-Gravenhage: VNG-uitgeverij.

Kloosterman, W.L. 1993. "Het waterstaatsbeheer in de Bataafs-Franse tijd: 1795–1813." In *Waterschappen in Nederland: Een bestuurskundige verkenning van de institutionele ontwikkeling,* edited by J.C.N.Raadschelders and Th. A.J. Toonen, 93–106. Hilversum: Verloren.

Kocken, M.J.A.V. 1973. *Van stads- en plattelandsbestuur naar gemeentebestuur: Proeve van een geschiedenis van ontstaan en ontwikkeling van het Nederlands gemeentebestuur tot en met de Grondwet van 1851.* Den Haag: Mouton.

Koppenjan, J.F.M. 1993. *Management van de beleidsvorming: Een studie naar de totstandkoming van beleid op het terrein van het binnenlands bestuur.* Den Haag: VUGA.

Kossmann, E.H. 1960. *Politieke Theorie in het Zeventiende-eeuwse Nederland* KNAW, nieuwe reeks, 67, no.2. Amsterdam: N.V. Noord-Hollandsche Uitgevers Maatschappij.

Leeuwen, Marco H.D. van. 1990. Bijstand in Amsterdam ca. 1800–1850: Armenzorg als beheersings- en overlevingsstrategie. Ph.D. diss., University of Utrecht.

Margry, P.J. et al., eds. 1989. *Van Camere van der Reckeninge tot Algemene Rekenkamer.* 's-Gravenhage: Staatsdrukkerij.

Meer, F.M. van der and L.J. Roborgh. 1988. "Changing Patterns in Local and Central Government Employment: An Adaptation to a Post-Industrial Society 1945–1985." In *Public Infrastructure Redefined,* edited by L.J. Roborgh, R.R. Stough, and Th.A.J. Toonen, 161–178. Bloomington/Leiden/Rotterdam: Groen b.v.

Meer, F.M. van der and J.C.N. Raadschelders. 1988. "Urbane problematiek in Nederland." In *Bestuurswetenschappen* 41, no.7: 487–498.

———. 1992. "Administrative History in the Netherlands: State of the Art and Research Agenda." *Jahrbuch für Europäische Verwaltungsgeschichte* 4, 327–342.

Meer, F.M. van der, J.C.N. Raadschelders, L.J. Roborgh, and Th.A.J. Toonen. 1991. "Representativeness and Bureaucracy in the Netherlands." In *La*

Representativité de l'Administration Publique, by V. Wright, 193–224. Brussels: Cahier d'Histoire de l'Administration, no.3; International Institute of the Administrative Sciences.

Meer, F.M. van der and J.C.N. Raadschelders. 1993. "Waterschapspersoneel en waterschapsorganisatie 1900-heden." In *Waterschappen in Nederland: Een bestuurskundige verkenning van de institutionele ontwikkeling*, edited by J.C.N. Raadschelders and Th.A.J. Toonen, 31–45. Hilversum: Verloren.

———. 1995. "Between Restoration and Consolidation: The Napoleonic Model of Administration in the Netherlands 1795–1990." In *The Influences of the Napoleonic "Model" of Administration on the Administrative Organization of Other Countries*, edited by Bernd Wunder, 199–221. Brussels: International Institute of Administrative Sciences, Cahier d'Histoire de l'Administration no.4.

Meer, F.M. van der and L.J. Roborgh. 1993. *Ambtenaren in Nederland: Omvang, bureaucratisering en representativiteit van het ambtelijk apparaat*. Alphen aan den Rijn: Samsom H.D. Tjeenk Willink.

Postma, J.K.T. 1989. "De positie van de minister van Financiën in historisch perspectief." *Bestuur: Maandblad voor Overheidskunde* no.6: 194–198.

Raadschelders, J.C.N. 1984. "Bromsnor en de ordehandhaving: Het politieapparaat en de Nederlandse staatsorganisatie 1815–1900." In *Tijdschrift voor de Politie* 46: 551–556.

———. 1988. "Bureaucratisering in het gemeentelijk onderwijsbestel 1795–1980." In *Gemeenten en onderwijs* edited by A.M.L. van Wieringen, J. Ax, and S. Karsten, 177–188. Lisse: Swets & Zeitlinger.

———. 1988. "Coproduction in Historical Perspective: Initiative and Participation in Local Government." In *Public Infrastructure Redefined* edited by L.J. Roborgh, R.R. Stough and Th.A.J. Toonen, 265–280. Bloomington/Leiden/Rotterdam: Groen BV.

———. 1989. "Departementen in historisch en vergelijkend perspectief." In *Wetenschap over departementen: Theoretische confrontaties*, edited by J.L.M. Hakvoort and J.M. de Heer, 16–38. 's-Gravenhage: VUGA.

———. 1990. *Plaatselijke bestuurlijke ontwikkelingen 1600–1980: Een historisch-bestuurskundig onderzoek in vier Noord-Hollandse gemeenten*. 's-Gravenhage: VNG-uitgeverij.

———. 1992. *Lokale Bestuursgeschiedenis*. Zutphen: Walburg Pers.

Raadschelders, J.C.N. and Th.A.J. Toonen, eds. 1993. *Waterschappen in Nederland: Een bestuurskundige verkenning van de institutionele ontwikkeling*. Hilversum: Verloren.

Raadschelders, J.C.N. 1994. "Understanding the Development of Local Government: Theory and Evidence from the Dutch Case." *Administration & Society* 25, no.4: 410–443.

———. 1995. *De historische ontwikkeling van bureaucratie in Nederland (1795–1970)*. Compendium voor Politiek en Samenleving in Nederland. Houten: Bohn Stafleu Van Loghum.

Randeraad, N. 1994. "Ambtenaren in Nederland (1815–1915)." *Bijdragen en Mededelingen over de Geschiedenis van Nederland* 109, no.2: 209–236.

———. 1994. "Thorbecke en de inrichting van het lokale bestuur." *Tijdschrift voor Geschiedenis* 107, no.4: 537–558.

Roozendaal, Peter van. 1993. "Cabinets in the Netherlands 1918–1990: the Importance of Dominant and Central Parties." *European Journal of Political Research* 23, no.1: 35–55.

Rosenthal, U. 1990. "De oorlog vergeten: de overheidsorganisatie na 1945." In *Vijftig jaar na de inval. Geschiedschrijving en Tweede Wereldoorlog*, edited by J.P.B. Jonker et al., 125–139. 's-Gravenhage: SDU Uitgeverij.

Rijpperda Wierdsma, J.V. 1937. *Politie en justitie: een studie over Hollandschen staatsbouw tijdens de Republiek*. Zwolle: J.J. Tijl.

Schepper, Hugo de. 1981. *Raad van State 450 jaar*. 's-Gravenhage: Staatsuitgeverij.

Smit, J.G. 1977. "De ambtenaren van de centrale overheidsorganen der Republiek in het begin van de zeventiende eeuw." *Tijdschrift voor Geschiedenis* 90, no.3–4: 378–390.

Soest, J. van et al., eds. 1988. *De Hoge Raad der Nederlanden 1838–1988*. Zwolle: W.E.J. Tjeenk Willink.

Stuurman, S. 1993. *Verzuiling, kapitalisme en patriarchaat: aspecten van de ontwikkeling van de moderne staat in Nederland*. Nijmegen: SUN.

Swaan, A. de. 1988. *In Care of the State: Health Care, Education and Welfare in Europe and the USA in the Modern Era*. Cambridge: Polity Press; also published in Dutch, 1989, Amsterdam.

Swart, Koenraad Wolter. 1949. *Sale of Offices in the Seventeenth Century*. 's-Gravenhage: Nijhoff.

Toonen, Theo A.J. 1990. "The Unitary State as a System of Co-Governance: the Case of the Netherlands." *Public Administration* 68, no.4: 281–296.

Valk, A. van der. 1990. "Ruimtelijke planning 1850–1900, een les voor het heden." In *Bestuur: Maandblad voor Overheidskunde* no.4: 97–100.

Veldheer, Vic. 1987. "De positie van gemeenten in historisch perspectief." In *Gemeente, Burger, Klant*, edited by Theo Roes et al., 29–60. Rijswijk: Sociaal Cultureel Planbureau.

Veldheer, Vic. 1994. *Kantelend bestuur: Onderzoek naar de ontwikkeling van taken van het lokale bestuur in de periode 1851–1985*. Rijswijk: Sociaal Cultureel Planbureau.

Vries, O. 1977. "Geschapen tot ieders nut: Een verkennend onderzoek naar de Noordnederlandse ambtenaar in de tijd van het Ancien Régime." *Tijdschrift voor Geschiedenis* 90, nos.3–4: 328–349.

Waltmans, Henk. 1994. *Gemeentelijke herindelingen in Nederland: Van de Franse tijd tot heden*. Hoogezand: Uitgeverij Stubeg.

Wesseling, H.L. 1989. "British and Dutch Imperialism: A Comparison." *Itinerario* 13, no.1: 61–76.

Wolters, M. 1988. "Gemeentebeleid en ambtelijke organisatie: De historische ontwikkeling opnieuw bezien." *Beleidswetenschap* 2, no.2: 121–144.
————. 1989. "Beleidsprocessen in historisch perspectief: De verhouding
tussen Rijk en gemeenten." *Beleidswetenschap* 3, no.2: 58–69.

Norway

Amodt, R., ed. 1987. *Fra Lekmenn till profesjonelle kommuner*. Oslo: Kom-
muneforlaget.
Benum, Edgeir. 1979. *Den norske sentraladministrations historie, 1845–1884*.
Vol. 2. Oslo: Universitetsforlaget.
Debes, Jan. 1980. *Den norske sentraladministrations historie, 1940–1945*.
Vol.5. Oslo: Universitetsforlaget.
Donjem, H. 1969. *Rekrutteringen till departementene 1945–1965*. Ph.D. diss.,
University of Oslo, Oslo, Norway.
Maurseth, Per. 1979. *Den norske sentraladministrations historie, 1814–1844*.
Vol. 1. Oslo: Universitetsforlaget.
Nausdalslid, J. 1989. "Lokalstyret i historisk perspektiv." In *Kommunalstyring:
Innföring i kommunalkunnskap frå ein planlegginssynstad*, edited by J.
Nausdalslid. Oslo: Det Norske Samlaget.
Steffens, H.K. 1914. *Den Norske Centraladministration Historie 1814–1914*.
Kristiania: Stenersen.
Tönneson, Käre D. 1979. *Den norske sentraladministrations historie 1914–
1940*. Vol.4. Oslo: Universitetsforlaget.

Poland

Ajnenkiel, A., B. Lesnodorski, W. Rostocki. 1990. *Historia ustroju Polski
(1764–1939)* (History of political government in Poland). Warsaw: PWN.
Czaplinski, M. 1985. *Biurokracja niemieckiego imperium kolonialniego:
Charakterystyka urzednikow kolonialnych* (The Bureaucracy of the Ger-
man Colonial Empire: Characteristics of Colonial Functionaries). Wroclaw:
Ossolineum.
Izdebski, Hubert. 1990. "Histoire de l'administration en Pologne: Essai d'un
bilan." *Jahrbuch für Europäische Verwaltungsgeschichte* 2: 259–268.
Kutrzeba, S. 1917. *Historia ustroju Polski w zarysie* (Short History of Polish
Government). Lwow: University of Lwow.
Lysiak, Ludwik. 1972. "L'administration locale en Pologne au seuil de la IIe
République." In *Entwicklungsfragen der Verwaltung in Mitteleuropa* ed-
ited by A. Csizmadia. Pécs: University of Pécs.
Lysiak, Ludwik. 1979. "Le démembrement ou l'unité d'administration en
Pologne aux temp de la 2e République (1918–1939)." *Entwicklung der
städtischen und regionalen Verwaltung in den letzten 100 Jahren in Mittel-*

und Osteuropa 2: 103–121. Internationale Rechtshistorische Konferenz, 12–15 September 1977, Budapest, Hungary.

Malec, Jerzy. 1984. "La science de la police et son influence sur la réforme de l'administration publique au siècle des Lumières en Pologne." In *Wissenschaft und Recht der Verwaltung seit dem Ancien Régime. Europäische Ansichten*, edited by E.V. Heyen, 59–69. Frankfurt am Main: Klostermann.

———. 1986. *Polka mysl administracyjna XVIII wieku* (Polish Administrative Thought in the Eighteenth Century). Krakau.

———. 1990. "L'impact étranger sur l'administration locale du territoire polonais dans la première moitié du 19e siècle." *Jahrbuch für Europäische Verwaltungswissenschaft* 2: 21–32.

———. 1995. "Des influences du modèle Napoléonien sur l'organisation administrative de la Pologne au début du 10ème siècle." In *The Influences of the Napoleonic "Model" of Administration on the Administrative Organization of Other Countries*, edited by Bernd Wunder, 223–238. Brussels: International Institute of Administrative Sciences, Cahier d'Histoire de l'Administration no.4.

Pruszynski, Jan P. 1983. "Esquisse de l'histoire de l'administration en Pologne." *International Review of the Administrative Sciences* 49, no.1: 39–48.

Stelmach, M. 1981. *Kancelaria pruskich urzedow administracji panstowowej na przykladzie rejencji w latach 1808–1945 (The Chancery of the Prussian Authorities in State Government as Example of the Government in the Years 1808–1945)*. Szczecin: Voïvodie Archives.

Wiatr, Jerzy. 1988. *The Soldier and the Nation: The Role of the Military in Polish Politics, 1918–1985*. Boulder, CO: Westview Press.

Portugal

Hespanha, A.M. 1982. "Historiografia juridica e politica do Direito (Portugal 1900–1950)." In *A formacao de Portugal contemporaneo, 1900–1980*. Lisbon.

Russia

Amburger, Erik. 1966. *Geschichte der Behördenorganisation Russlands von Peter dem Grossen bis 1917*. Leiden: E.J. Brill.

Armstrong, J.A. 1972. "Old Regime Administrative Elites in France, Prussia and Russia." *Revue International des sciences administratives* 38, no.1: 21–40.

Giers, Nicholas Karlovich. 1962. *The Education of a Russian Statesman: The Memoirs of Nicholas Karlovich Giers*. Edited by Charles and Barbara Jelavich. Berkeley and Los Angeles: University of California Press.

Hans, Nicholas. 1964. *History of Russian Educational Policy (1701–1917)*. New York: Russell and Russell.

Hassell, James E. 1967. *The Vicissitudes of Russian Administrative Reform, 1762–1801.* Ph.D. thesis, Cornell University, Ithaca, NY.

Lantzeff, George V. 1983. *The Russian Colonial Administration: Its Origins and Development to the End of the 17th Century, With Special Reference to Siberia.* Unpublished Ph.D. diss., University of California, Berkeley, CA.

Lincoln, W. Bruce. 1972. "The Genesis of an Enlightened Bureaucracy in Russia, 1825–1856." *Jahrbücher für Geschichte Osteuropas* 20, no.3: 321–330.

Petersen, Claes. 1979. *Peter the Great's Administrative and Judicial Reforms: Swedish Antecedents and the Process of Reception.* Lund: Insitutet för Rättshistorisk Forskning.

Pintner, Walter M. 1970. "The Social Characteristics of the Early-Nineteenth-Century Russian Bureaucracy." *Slavic Review* 29, no.3: 429–43.

———. 1975. "The Russian Higher Civil Service on the Eve of the Great Reform." *Journal of Social History* 8, no.3: 55–68.

Pintner, Walter McKenzie and Don Karl Rowney, eds. 1980. *Russian Officialdom: The Bureaucratization of Russian Society from the Seventeenth to the Twentieth Century.* London: MacMillan.

Raeff, Marc. 1957. *Michael Speranski: Statesman of Imperial Russia, 1772–1839.* The Hague: Martinus Nijhoff.

———. 1957. "The Russian Autocracy and Its Officials." In *Russian Thought and Politics*, edited by Hugh McLean, Martin E. Malai and George Fischer, 77–91. Harvard Slavic Studies no.4. Cambridge: Cambridge University Press

———. 1966. *Plans for Political Reform in Imperial Russia, 1730–1905.* Russian Civilization Series. Englewood Cliffs, NJ: Prentice-Hall.

———. 1983. *The Well-Ordered Police State: Social and Institutional Change through Law in the Germanies and Russia, 1600–1800.* New Haven, CT: Yale University Press.

Rigby, T.H. 1972. "The Birth of Soviet Bureaucracy." *Politics* (Australia) 3, no.2.

Robbins, Richard G., Jr. 1987. *The Tsar's Viceroys: Russian Provincial Governers in the Last Years of the Empire.* Ithaca, NY: Cornell University Press.

Skocpol, Theda. 1985. "States and Revolutions: France, Russia and China." In *States and Societies*, edited David Held c.s. 151–169. 3d ed. Oxford: Blackwell/Open University.

Starr, S. Frederick. 1972. *Decentralization and Self-Government in Russia 1830–1870.* Princeton, NJ: Princeton University Press.

Torke, Hans Joachim. 1967. "Das russissche Beamtentum in der ersten Hälfte des 19. Jahrhunderts." *Forschungen zur Osteuropäische Geschichte* 13: 7–345.

———. 1989. "Administration and Bureaucracy in Nineteenth-Century Russia: The Empire and the Finnish Case." In *Institutions and Bureaucrats in the History of Administration*, edited by Seppo Tiihonen, 31–42. Helsinki: Government Printing Centre.

Weismann, Neil B. 1981. *Reform in Tsarist Russia: the State Bureaucracy and Local Government, 1900–1914.* New Brunswick, NJ: Rutgers University Press.

Whelan, Heide W. 1982. *Alexander III and the State Council: Bureaucracy and Counter-Reforms in the Late Imperial Russia.* New Brunswick, N.J.: Rutgers University Press.

Yaney, G.L. 1973. *The Systematization of Russian Government: Social Evolution and the Domestic Administration of Imperial Russia, 1711–1905.* Urbana, IL: University of Illinois Press.

Scandinavia

Blomstedt, Y., et al. 1985. *Administratsjon i Norden paa 1700-talet.* Oslo: Universitetsforlaget.

Ericsson, Birgitta, et al. 1982. *Stadsadministration i Norden paa 1700-talet.*

Gustafsson, Gunnel. 1980. "Modes and Effects of Local Government Mergers in the Scandinavian Countries." *West European Politics* 3, no.3: 339–357.

Klingman, D. 1980. "Economic Development and the Growth of Public Expenditure in Scandinavia." *Political Studies* 28, no.1: 20–42.

Knudsen, Tim and Bo Rothstein. 1994. "State-Building in Scandinavia." *Comparative Politics* 26 no.2: 203–220.

Meyer, P. 1960. "The Development of Public Administration in the Scandinavian Countries since 1945." *International Review of the Administrative Sciences* 26, no.2: 135–146.

Peters, B. and D. Klingman. 1977. "Patterns of Expenditure Development in Sweden, Norway and Denmark." *British Journal of Political Science* 7, no.3: 387–412.

Rystad, Göran, ed. 1983. *Europe and Scandinavia: Aspects of the Process of Integration in the Seventeenth Century.* Lund: University of Lund.

Spain

Carrasco Canals, Carlos. 1975. *La burocracia en la España del Siglo XIX.* Madrid: Instituto de Estudios de Administración Local.

García Madaría, José M. 1980. "Metodología del estudio de la Historia de la Administración pública espanola y aproximación a sus fuentes." *Revue International des Sciences Administratives* 46, no.1: 35–47.

Königsberger, H.G. 1951. *The Government of Sicily under Philip II of Spain: A Study in the Practice of Empire.* London: Staples.

Lapeyre, Henri. 1969. "L'Organisation municipale de la ville de Valence (Espagne) aux XVIe et XVIIe siècles." In *Ville de l'Europe méditerranéenne et de l'Europe occidentale du Moyen Age aux XIXe siècle.* Saint-Brieuc: Les Belles Lettres; Annales de la Faculté des Lettres et Sciences Humaines de Nice, nos.9–10.

Linz, Juan J. and Amando de Miguel. 1968. "La elite funcionarial Española ante la reforma administrativa." *Sociología de la administración pública Española, Anales de moral social y economica* 17. Madrid: Centro de Estudios Sociales de la Santa Cruz del Valle de los Caidos, 199–249.

Martin, José Louis. 1969. "Organisation municipal de la villa de Gata en el siglo XVI." In *Ville de l'Europe méditerranéenne et de l'Europe occidentale du Moyen Age aux XIXe siècle,* 101–111. Saint-Brieuc: Les Belles Lettres; Annales de la Faculté des Lettres et Sciences Humaines de Nice, nos.9–10.

Thompson, I.A.A. 1976. *War and Government in Habsburg Spain.* London: Athlone Press.

Sweden

Buchholz, Werner. 1979. "Staat und Ständegesellschaft in Schweden zur Zeit des Überganges vom Absolutismus sum Ständen parlamentismus 1718–1720." *Acta Universitatis Stockholmiensis* 27. Stockholm.

Carlsson, A.B. 1913. *Den svenska centralförvaltningen 1520–1809.* Stockholm.

Carlsson, Sten. 1949. *Ståndssamhälle och ståndpersoner 1700–1865.* Uppsala.

Castles, Francis. 1976. "Policy Innovation and Institutional Stability in Sweden." *British Journal of Political Science* 6, no.2: 203–216.

Elmroth, I. 1962. *Nyrekryteringen Till de Högre Ambetema 1720–1809.* Lund: Gleerup.

Höök, E. 1962. *Den offentliga sektorns expansion: En studie av de offentliga civila utgifternas utveekling ären 1913–58.* Uppsala: Almquvist & Wicksell.

Roberts, Michael. 1979. *The Swedish Imperial Experience, 1560–1718.* Cambridge: Cambridge University Press.

Tarschys, Daniel. 1975. "The Growth of Public Expenditures: Nine Modes of Explanation." *Scandinavian Political Studies* 10, no.1: 9–31.

———. 1978. *Den öffentlichen Revolution (Schweden 1600–1950).* Stockhold: Liber.

———. 1983. "Government Growth: The Case of Sweden, 1523–1983." *Studies in Public Policy* no.121. Strathclyde: University of Strathclyde, Center for the Study of Public Policy.

———. 1988. "Tributes, Tariffs, Taxes, and Trade: The Changing Sources of Government Revenue." *British Journal of Political Science* 18, no.1: 1–20.

Switzerland

Friedrich, Carl J. and Taylor Cole. 1932. *Responsible Bureaucracy: A Study of the Swiss Civil Service.* Cambridge: Harvard University Press.

Nawiaski, H. n.d. "Die grossen Entwicklungslinien der Personalwesens in der Schweiz." *Das Personalwesens der öffentlichen Verwaltung.* Einsiedeln: Veröffentlichungen der Schweizerischen Verwaltungskurse, Band XIX.

Turkey (including Ottoman Empire)

Aricanli, T. n.d. *The Role of the State in Social and Economic Transformation of the Ottoman Empire.* Cambridge, MA: Harvard University Press.

Davison, R. 1968. "The Advent of the Principle of Representation in the Government of the Ottoman Empire." In *Beginnings of Modernization in the Middle East: The Nineteenth Century,* edited by W.R. Polk and R.L. Chambers, 93–108. Chicago, IL: Chicago University Press.

Findley, C.V. 1980. *Bureaucratic Reform in the Ottoman Empire: The Sublime Porte 1789–1922.* Princeton, NJ: Princeton University Press.

Fleischer, Cornell H. 1986. *Bureaucrat and Intellectual in the Ottoman Empire: The Historian Mustafa Ali (1541–1600).* Princeton, NJ: Princeton University Press.

Gladden, E.N. 1937. "Administration of the Ottoman Empire under Suleiman." *Public Administration* 15, no.2: 187–193.

Heper, Metin. 1976. "Political Modernization as Reflected in Bureaucratic Change: The Turkish Bureaucracy and a 'Historical Bureaucratic Empire' Tradition." *International Journal of Middle Eastern Studies* 7, no.4, 507–521.

———. 1980. "Center and Periphery in the Ottoman Empire with Special Reference to the Nineteenth Century." *International Political Science Review* 1, no.1, 81–105.

Inalcik, H. 1977. "Centralization and Decentralization in Ottoman Administration." In *Studies in Eighteenth Century Islamic History,* edited by T. Naff and R. Owen, 27–52, 362–369. London and Amsterdam: Feffer & Simons.

Karpat, K.H. 1972. "The Transformation of the Ottoman State, 1789–1909." *International Journal of Middle East Studies* 3, no.3: 243–281.

Lybyer, Albert Howe. [1913] 1966. *The Government of the Ottoman Empire in the Time of Suleiman the Magnificent.* Cambridge, MA: Harvard University Press.

Rustow, Dankwart A. 1968. "Atatürk as Founder of a State." *Daedelus* 97, no.3: 793–828.

Shinder, J. 1978. "Early Ottoman Administration in the Wilderness: Some Limits on Comparison." *International Journal of Middle Eastern Studies* 9, no.4: 497–517.

Weiker, Walter F. 1968. "The Ottoman Bureaucracy: Modernization and Reform." *Administrative Science Quarterly* 13, no.3: 451–470.

Wright, Walter Livingston, Jr. 1935. *Ottoman Statecraft.* Princeton, NJ: Princeton University Press.

LATIN AMERICA

General Works

Altamira, R. 1939. "La décentralisation législative dans le régime colonial espagnol (XVIème–XVIIIème siècles)." *Bulletin du comité international des sciences historiques* 11: 165–190.

Borah, W. 1956. "Representative Institutions in the Spanish Empire in the Sixteenth Century-The New World." *The Americas* 12, no.3: 246–257.

Castañeda, N. 1955. "Spanish Medieval Institutions and Overseas Administration: The Prevalance of Medieval Concepts." *The Americas* 11, no.2: 115–129.

Chevalier, F. 1944. "Les municipalités indiennes en Nouvelle Espagne (1520–1860)." *Annuario de historio del derecho español* 15: 352–386.

Conrad, Geoffrey and Arthur A. Demarest. 1984. *Religion and Empire: The Dynamics of Inca and Aztec Expansionism.* Cambridge: Cambridge University Press.

Fisher, Lilian Estelle. [1926] 1967. *Viceregal Administration in the Spanish-American Colonies.* Reprint of Ph.D. diss. New York: Russell & Russell.

———. 1929. *The Intendant System in Spanish America.* Berkeley and Los Angeles: University of California Press.

———. 1963. "Colonial Government." In *Colonial Hispanic America*, edited by A. Curtis Wilgus. New York: Reiss.

Gallo, A.G. 1944. *Los orígenes de la administración governmental de la Indias.* Madrid: Instituto Francisco de Vitoria, University of Madrid.

Haring, C.H. 1918. "The Early Spanish Colonial Exchequer." *American Historical Review* 23, no.4: 779–796.

———. 1919. "Ledgers of the Royal Treasurers in Spanish America in the Sixteenth Century." *Hispanic American Historical Review* 2, no.2: 173–187.

———. 1947. *The Spanish Empire in America.* New York: Oxford University Press.

Heper, Metin. 1991. "Transitions to Democracy Reconsidered: A Historical Perspective." In *Comparative Political Dynamics: Global Research Perspectives*, edited by Dankwart A. Rustow and Kenneth Paul Erickson, 192–210. New York: Harper Collins Publishers.

Lynch, J. 1958. *Spanish Colonial Administration 1782–1810.* London: Athlone Press.

Parry, J.H. 1948. *The Audiencia of New Galicia in the Sixteenth Century: A Study in Spanish Colonial Government.* Cambridge: Cambridge University Press.

———. 1953. *The Sale of Public Offices in the Spanish Indies under the Habsburgs.* Berkeley and Los Angeles: University of California Press.

Phelan, John Leddy. 1960. "Authority and Flexibility in the Spanish Imperial Bureaucracy." *Administrative Science Quarterly* 5, no.1: 47–66.

————. 1967. *The Kingdom of Quito in the Seventeenth Century: Bureau-cratic Politics and the Spanish Empire.* Madison, WI: University of Wisconsin Press.

Roscher, W. 1944. *The Spanish Colonial System.* New York: G.E. Stechert.

Sarfatti, Magali. 1966. *Spanish Bureaucratic-Patrimonialism in America.* Politics of Modernization Series, no.1. Berkeley and Los Angeles: University of California Press.

Wiarda, Howard J., ed. 1974. *Politics and Social Change in Latin America: The Distinct Tradition.* Amherst, MA: University of Massachusetts Press.

————, ed. 1981. *Corporatism and National Development in Latin America.* Boulder, CO: Westview Press.

Argentina

Dana Montaño, Salvador M. 1975. "Rol del Estado y de la Administratición Pública: Evolución Histórica." *Revue International des Sciences Administrative* 41, no.1: 61–66.

Bolivia

Lofstrom, W. 1973. "From Colony to Republic: A Case Study in Bureaucratic Change." *Journal of Latin American Studies* 5, no.2: 177–197.

Brazil

De Carvalho, José Murilo. 1982. "Political Elites and State Building: The Case of Nineteenth-Century Brazil." *Comparative Studies in Society and History* 24, no.3: 378–399.

Manchester, A.K. 1972. "The Growth of Bureaucracy in Brazil, 1808–1821." *Journal of Latin American Studies* 4, no.1: 77–83.

Uricoechea, Fernando. 1980. *The Patrimonial Foundations of the Brazilian Bureaucratic State.* Berkeley and Los Angeles: University of California Press.

Jamaica

Metcalf, George. 1965. *Royal Government and Political Conflict in Jamaica.* London: Longmans.

Mexico

Bennett, Douglas and Kenneth Sharpe. 1979–1980. "The State as Banker and Entrepeneur (The Last Resort Character of the Mexican's State Intervention, 1917–1976)." *Comparative Politics* 12, no.2: 165–189.

Brumfiel, E.M. 1983. "Aztec State-Making: Ecology, Structure and the Origin of the State." *American Anthropologist* 85, no.1: 261–284.

Cárdenas, Luis García. 1983. "Historia de la Administración Pública en México." *International Review of the Administrative Sciences* 49, no.1: 17–38.

Phelan, John Leddy. 1959. "Free versus Compulsory Labor: Mexico and the Philippines 1540–1648." *Comparative Studies in Society and History* 1, no.2: 189–201.

Poitras, Guy E. 1973. "Welfare Bureaucracy and Clientele Politics in Mexico." *Administrative Science Quarterly* 18, no.1: 18–26.

Peru

Moore, J.P. 1954. *The Cabildo in Peru under the Habsburgs: A Study in the Origins and Powers of the Town-Council in the Vice-Royalty of Peru (1530–1700)*. Durham, NC: Duke University.

Stauper, F.M. 1927. "Church and State in Peru." *Hispanic American Historical Review* 7, no.4: 410–437.

Surinam

Meiden, G.W. van der. 1986. *Betwist bestuur: een eeuw strijd om de macht in Suriname 1651–1753*. Amsterdam: De Bataafsche Leeuw.

Schiltkamp, J.A. and T.Th. de Smidt, ed. 1973. *Plakaten, ordonnantiën en andere wetten uitgevaardigd in Suriname 1667–1816*. Amsterdam: Emmering.

Wieringen, A.G. van. 1912. *Geschiedenis der belastingen in de kolonie Suriname*. The Hague: Algemene Landsdrukkerij.

NORTH AMERICA

Canada

Bates, Stewart. 1939. *Financial History of Canadian Governments*. Ottawa: Royal Commission on Dominion-Provincial Relations.

Bird, Richard. 1970. *The Growth of Government Spending in Canada*. Toronto: Canadian Tax Foundation.

Foot, D.K. 1977. *Provincial Public Finance in Ontario: an Empirical Analysis of the Last Twenty-five Years*. Toronto: University of Toronto Press.

Gow, J.I. 1971. "Histoire Administrative du Québec et théorie administrative." *Revue Canadienne de Science Politique* 4, no.1: 141–145.

———. 1979. "L'administration québécoise de 1867 à 1900: un Etat en formation." *Canadian Journal of Political Science* 12, no.3: 555–620.

———. 1985. "One Hundred Years of Quebec Administrative History, 1867–1970." *Canadian Public Administration* 28, no.2: 244–288.

———. 1986. *Histoire de l'administration publique québécoise, 1867–1970.* Montreal: Les Presses de l'Université de Montréal and l'Institut d'administration publique du Canada.

Hodgetts, J.E. 1955. *Pioneer Public Service: An Administrative History of the United Canadas, 1841–1867.* Toronto: University of Toronto Press.

———. 1973. *Canadian Public Service: A Physiology of Government, 1867–1970.* Toronto: University of Toronto Press.

Mishler, William and David B. Campbell. 1977–1978. "The Healthy State: Legislative Responsiveness to Public Health Care Needs in Canada." *Comparative Politics* 10, no.4: 479–497.

United States of America

Andrews, Charles McLean. 1908. *British Committees, Commissions, and Councils of Trade and Plantations 1622–1675.* Baltimore, MD: The Johns Hopkins Press.

———. 1904. *Colonial Self-Government, 1652–1689.* New York: Harper & Bros.

Armstrong, Ellis L., ed. 1976. *History of Public works in the United States 1776–1976.* Chicago, IL: American Public Works Association.

Arnold, Peri. 1986. *Making the Managerial Presidency: Comprehensive Reorganization Planning, 1905–1980.* Princeton, NJ: Princeton University Press.

Aronson, Sidney H. 1964. *Status and Kinship in the Higher Civil Service.* Cambridge, MA: Harvard University Press.

Ashford, Douglas E. 1991. "History and Public Policy vs. History of Public Policy: Review of Francis G. Castles' *The Comparative History of Public Policy.*" *Public Administration Review* 51, no.4: 358–362.

Benson, George, Sumner Benson, Harold McClelland et al. 1965. *The American Property Tax: Its History, Administration, and Economic Impact.* Claremont, CA: Institute for Studies in Federalism, Lincoln School of Public Finance, Claremont's Men College.

Borcherding, Thomas E. 1977. "The Sources of Growth of Public Expenditures in the United States, 1902–1970." In *Budgets and Bureaucrats: The sources of Government Growth* edited by Thomas E. Borcherding. Durham, NC: Duke University Press.

Bradley, Ronald S. and Mayer N. Zald. 1965–1966. "From Commercial Elite to Political Administrator: The Recruitment of the Mayors of Chicago (1837–1965)." *American Journal of Sociology* 71, no.2: 153–167.

Caldeira, G. 1981. "The United States Supreme Court and Criminal Cases, 1935–1976: Alternative Models of Agenda Building." *British Journal of Political Science* 11, no.4: 449–470.

Caldwell, Lynton K. 1944. *The Administrative Theories of Hamilton and Jefferson: Their Contributions to Thought on Public Administration.* Chicago, IL: University of Chicago Press.

————. 1976. "Novus ordo Seclorum: The Heritage of American Public Administration." *Public Administration Review* 36, no.5: 476–488.

Callahan, Raymond E. 1962. *Education and the Cult of Efficiency: A Study of the Social Forces that Have Shaped the Administration of the Public Schools.* Chicago, IL: University of Chicago Press.

Chandler, Ralph Clark, ed. 1987. *A Centennial History of the American Administrative State.* New York: Free Press; London: Collier McMillan Publishers.

Civil Service, *History of the Federal Civil Service, 1798 to the Present* (official publ. Washington).

Coleman, James Karl. 1935. *State Administration in South Carolina.* New York: Columbia University Press; London: P.S. King and Son, Ltd..

Corwin, Edward Samuel. 1970. *The President, Office and Powers, 1787–1957: History and Analysis of Practice and Opinion.* New York: New York University Press; London: Oxford University Press, H. Milford.

Diamond, Sigmund. 1958. "From Organization to Society: Virginia in the Seventeenth Century." *American Journal of Sociology* 63, no.5: 457–475.

Dickerson, Oliver Morton. 1912. *American Colonial Government 1696–1765: A Study of the British Board of Trade in its Relation to the American Colonies, Political, Industrial, Administrative.* Cleveland, OH: The Arthur H. Clark Co.

Eaton, Dorman B. 1880. *Civil Service in Great Britain: A History of Abuses and Reforms and Their Bearing upon American Politics.* New York: Harper and Bros.

Fabricant, S. 1952. *The Trend of Government Activity in the United States since 1900.* New York: National Bureau of Economic Research, Inc.

Ferguson, Elmer James. 1961. *The Power of the Purse: A History of American Public Finance, 1776–1790.* Chapel Hill, NC: University of North Carolina Press.

Fesler, James W., ed. 1967. "The Heritage of the Eighteenth and Nineteenth Centuries." In *The 50 States and their Local Governments.* New York: Alfred A. Knopf Inc.

————, ed. 1982. *American Public Administration: Patterns of the Past.* Washington D.C.: American Society for Public Administration.

Formisano, Ronald P. 1974. "Differential-Participant Politics: The Early Republic Political Culture." *American Political Science Review* 68, no.2: 473–487.

Garnett, James L. 1980. *Reorganizing State Government. The Executive Branch,* Boulder, CO: Westview Press.

Garrard, J.A. 1976. "The History of Local Political Power—Some Suggestions for Analysis." *Political Studies* 25, no.2: 252–269.

Gawthrop, Louis C. 1987. "Toward an Ethical Convergence of Democratic Theory and Administrative Politics." In *A Centennial History of the American Administrative State* edited by Ralph Clark Chandler, 189–216. New York: The Free Press; London: Collier McMillan Publishers.

————. 1993. "The Ethical Foundations of American Public Administration." *International Journal of Public Administration* 16, no.2: 139–163.

Griffith, Ernest S. 1927. *The Modern Development of City Government in the United Kingdom and the United States.* London: Oxford University Press.

————. 1972. *History of American City Government: The Colonial Period.* New York: Praeger.

————. 1974. *A History of American City Governments: The Progressive Years and Their Aftermath.* New York: Praeger.

Hannan, Michael T. and John Freeman. 1987. "The Ecology of Organization Founding: American Labor Unions, 1836–1985." *American Journal of Sociology* 92, no.4: 910–943.

Hatch, Louis Clinton. 1904. *The Administration of the American Revolutionary Army.* New York: Longmans, Green and Co.

————. 1934. *A History of the Vice-Presidency of the United States.* Revised and edited by Earl L. Shoup. New York: The American Historical Society, Inc.

Heady, Ferrel. 1987. "Comparative Public Administration in the United States." In *A Centennial History of the American Administrative State*, edited by Ralph Clark Chandler, 477–508. New York: Free Press; London: Collier McMillan Publishers.

Heidenheimer, Arnold. 1973. "The Politics of Public Education, Health and Welfare in the United States and Western Europe: How Growth and Reform Potentials Have Differed." *British Journal of Political Science* 3, no.3: 315–340.

Hoogenboom, Ari. 1968. *Outlawing the Spoils: A History of the Civil Service Reform Movement, 1865–1883.* Urbana, IL: University of Illinois Press.

Hooks, Gregory. 1984. "The Rise of the Pentagon and the U.S. State Building: The Defense Program as Industrial Policy." *American Journal of Sociology* 89, no.6: 1346–1374.

Karraker, C.H. 1930. *The Seventeenth Century Sheriff: A Comparative Study of the Sheriff in England and the Chesapeake Colonies, 1607–1689.* Chapel Hill, NC: University of North Carolina Press.

Karl, Barry Dean. 1963. *Executive Reorganization and Reform in the New Deal: the Genesis of Administrative Management, 1900–1939.* Cambridge, MA: Harvard University Press.

————. 1976. "Public Administration and American History: A Century of Professionalism." *Public Administration Review* 36, no.5: 489–503.

Keller, Morton. 1979. *Affairs of State: Public Life in Late Nineteenth Century America.* Cambridge, MA: Harvard University Press.

Kettl, Donald. 1986. *Leadership at the Fed.* New Haven, CT: Yale University Press.

Lipset, Seymour Martin. 1963. *The First New Nation: The United States in Historical and Comparative Perspective.* New York: Basic Books.

Mansfield, Harvey Claflin. 1939. *The Comptroller General: A Study in the Law and Practice of Financial Administration.* New Haven, CT: Yale University Press; London: Oxford University Press, H. Milford.

Mansfield, Harvey Claflin. 1982. "Federal Executive Reorganization: Thirty Years of Experience." In *American Public Administration: Patterns of the Past,* edited by James W. Fesler, 215–235. Washington D.C.: American Society for Public Administration.

Maranto, Robert and David Schultz. 1991. *A Short History of the United States Civil Service.* Lanham, MD: University Press of America.

Martin, Daniel W. 1987. "Déjà Vu: French Antecedents of American Public Administration." *Public Administration Review* 47, no.3: 297–303.

———. 1988. "The Fading Legacy of Woodrow Wilson." *Public Administration Review* 48, no.2: 631–635.

McCaffery, Jerry L. 1987. The Development of Public Budgeting in the United States. In *A Centennial History of the American Administrative State,* edited by Ralph Clark Chandler, 345–377. New York: Free Press; London: Collier McMillan Publishers.

McCurdy, Howard E. 1987. "How Novelists View Public Administration." In *A Centennial History of the American Administrative State,* edited by Ralph Clark Chandler, 543–594. New York: Free Press; London: Collier McMillan Publishers.

McGraw, Thomas. 1985. *Prophets of Regulation: A History of Regulation in the United States.* Cambridge, MA: Harvard University Press.

McGruder, Frank Abbott. 1947. "County and Township Government" In *American Government: A Consideration of the Problems of Democracy,* 548–597. Boston, MA : Allyn and Bacon.

MacLeod, William Christie. 1924. *The Origin of the State Reconsidered in the Light of the Data of Aboriginal North America.* Philadelphia, PA:

MacMahon, Arthur W. and John D. Millett. 1939. *Federal Administrators: A Biographical Approach to the Problem of Departmental Management.* New York: Columbia University Press.

Merritt, Richard L. 1966. "Nation-Building in America: The Colonial Years." In *Nation-Building,* edited by K.W. Deutsch and W.J. Foltz, 56–72. New York: Atherton Press.

Meyer, John W., David Tyack, Joane Nagel, and Audri Gordon. 1979. "Public Education as Nation-Building in America: Enrollments and Bureaucratization in the American States, 1870–1930." *American Journal of Sociology* 85, no.3: 591–613.

Miewald, Robert D. 1984. "The Origins of Wilson's Thought: The German Tradition and the Organic State." In *Politics and Administration. Woodrow Wilson and American Public Administration,* edited by Jack Rabin and James S. Bowman, 17–30. New York and Basel: Marcel Dekker Inc.

———. 1994. "European Administrative History and American Public Administration." *Jahrbuch für Europäische Verwaltungsgeschichte* 6: 319–328.

Mohl, Raymond A. 1973. "Three Centuries of American Public Welfare: 1600–1932." *Current History* 65, no.383: 6–10, 38–39.

Morrow, William L. 1987. "The Pluralist Legacy in American Public Administration." In *A Centennial History of the American Administrative State*, edited by Ralph Clark Chandler, 161–188. New York: The Free Press; London: Collier McMillan Publishers.

Mosher, Frederick C. 1968. "The Evolution of American Civil Service Concepts." In *Democracy and the Public Service*, 53–98. London: Oxford University Press.

———. 1983. *Basic Documents of American Public Administration 1776–1950.* 2d ed. London: Holmes & Meier Publishers, Inc.

Munro, William Bennett. 1920. "The History of Local Government." In *The Government of the United States: National, State, and Local*, 535–571. New York: The MacMillan Company.

Nelson, Michael. 1982. "A Short, Ironic History of American National Bureaucracy." *The Journal of Politics* 44, no.3: 747–778.

Nelson, W.E. 1982. *The Roots of American Bureaucracy 1830–1900.* Cambridge, MA: Harvard University Press.

Neustadt, R.E. and E.R. May. 1986. *Thinking in Time: The Uses of History for Decsision-Makers.* New York: Free Press.

O'Toole, Lawrence J., Jr. 1987. "Doctrines and Developments: Separation of Powers, the Politics-Administrative Dichotomy and the Rise of the Administrative State." *Public Administration Review* 47, no.1: 17–23.

Peroff, K. and M. Podolak-Warren. 1979. "Does Spending on Defence Cut Spending on Health? A Time-Series Analysis of the U.S. Economy, 1929–1974." *British Journal of Political Science* 9, no.1: 21–39.

Riper, Paul van. 1958. *History of the United States Civil Service.* Evenston: Row, Peterson.

———. 1987. "The American Administrative State: Wilson and the Founders." In *A Centennial History of the American Administrative State*, edited by Ralph Clark Chandler, 3–36. New York: Free Press; London: Collier McMillan Publishers.

Rohr, John A. 1987. "The Administrative State and Constitutional Principle." In *A Centennial History of the American Administrative State*, edited by Ralph Clark Chandler, 113–159. New York: Free Press; London: Collier McMillan Publishers.

Rozman, G. 1978. "Urban Networks and Historical Stages." *Journal of Interdisciplinary History* 9, no.1: 65–91.

Sageser, A. Bower. 1935. *The First Two Decades of the Pendleton Act.* Lincoln.

Schiesl, Martin J. 1977. *The Politics of Efficiency: Municipal Administration and Reform in America 1880–1920.* Berkeley and Los Angeles: University of California Press.

Schneider, David M. 1938. *The History of Public Welfare in New York State, 1609–1866*. Chicago, IL: University of Chicago Press.

Shambaugh, Benjamin Franklin, ed. 1938. *Municipal Government and Administration in Iowa*. Iowa City, IA: State Historical Society of Iowa.

Sharp, Walter Rice. 1927. "Le développement de la bureaucratie aux Etats-Unis." *Revue des Sciences Politiques* 50, no.3: 393–415, 539–54.

Short, Lloyd Milton. 1923. *The Bureau of Navigation: Its History, Activities and Organization*. Baltimore, MD: The Johns Hopkins Press.

———. 1923. *The Development of National Administrative Organization in the United States*. Baltimore, MD: The Johns Hopkins Press.

Silberman, Bernard S. 1964. *Ministers of Modernization*. Tucson, AZ: University of Arizona Press.

———. 1993. "The United States." In *Cages of Reason: The Rise of the Rational State in France, Japan, The United States, and Great Britain*, 227–283. Chicago, IL: The University of Chicago Press, 227–283.

Skocpol, Theda and Margaret Somers. 1980. "The Uses of Comparative History in Macrosocial Inquiry." *Comparative Studies in Society and History* 22, no.2: 174–197.

Skocpol, Theda and John Ikenberry. 1983. "The Political Formation of the American Welfare State in Historical and Comparative Perspective." *Comparative Social Research* no. 6: 87–148.

Skowronek, Stephen. 1982. *Building a New American State: The Expansion of National Administrative Capacities, 1877–1920*. Cambridge: Cambridge University Press.

Starr, Paul. 1982. "Transformation in Defeat: The Changing Objectives of National Health Insurance, 1915–1980." *American Journal of Public Health* 72, no.1: 78–88.

Stewart, Frank Mann. 1929. *The National Civil Service Reform League: History, Activities, and Problems*. Austin, TX: The University of Texas.

———. 1950. *A Half-Century of Municipal Reform: The History of the National Municipal League*. Berkeley and Los Angeles: University of California Press.

Stillman, Richard J., II. 1982. "The Future of the American Constitution and the Administrative State After the Bicentennial: Some Reflections." *Public Administration Review* 48, no.4: 813–815.

———. 1990. "The Peculiar "Stateless" Origins of American Public Administration and Consequences for Government Today." *Public Administration Review* 50, no.2: 156–157.

———. [1987] 1991. "The Rise of U.S. Bureaucracy." In *The American Bureaucracy* 29–68. Chicago, IL: Nelson Hall. *Public Administration: Concepts and Cases*, 49–79.

Sutton, John R. 1990. "Bureaucrats and Entrepeneurs: Institutional Responses to Deviant Children in the U.S.A., 1890–1920s." *American Journal of Sociology* 95, no.6: 1367–1400.

Swaan, A. de. 1988. *In Care of the State: Health Care, Education, and Welfare in Europe and the USA in the Modern Era*. Cambridge: Polity Press. Also published in Dutch, Amsterdam: Bert Bakker, 1989.

Teaford, Jon C. 1984. *Unheralded Triumph: City Government in America, 1870–1900*. Baltimore, MD: Johns Hopkins University Press.

Tolbert, Pamela S. and Lynne G. Zucker. 1983. "Institutional Sources of Change in the Formal Structure of Organizations: The Diffusion of Civil Service Reform, 1880–1935." *Administrative Science Quarterly* 28, no.1: 22–39.

U.S. Bureau of the Census. 1960. *Historical Statistics of the United States: Colonial Times to 1957*. Washington D.C.: U.S. Government Printing Office.

U.S. Bureau of the Census. 1962. *Census of Governments* 6, no.4. Washington D.C.: U.S. Government Printing Office.

U.S. Bureau of the Census. 1964. *Historical Statistics on Governmental Finances and Employment*. Washington D.C.: U.S. Government Printing Office.

Waldo, Dwight. 1987. "Politics and Administration: On Thinking about a Complex Relationship." In *A Centennial History of the American Administrative State* edited by Ralph Clark Chandler, 89–112. New York: Free Press; London: Collier McMillan Publishers.

Wildavsky, Aaron. 1987. "On the Balance of Budgetary Cultures." In *A Centennial History of the American Administrative State*, edited by Raph Clark Candler, 379–413. New York: Free Press; London: Collier McMillan Publishers.

White, Leonard B. 1948. *The Federalists: A Study in Administrative History, 1789–1801*. New York: The Macmillan Co.

———. 1951. *The Jeffersonians: A Study in Administrative History, 1801–1829*. New York: The Macmillan Co.

———. 1954. *The Jacksonians: A Study in Administrative History, 1829–1861*. New York: The Macmillan Co.

———. 1958. *The Republican Era: 1869–1901: A Study in Administrative History*. New York: The Macmillan Co..

Whitnah, Donald R. 1961. *A History of the United States Weather Bureau*. Urbana, IL: University of Illinois Press.

———, ed. 1983. *Government Agencies*. n.p.

Wiebe, R.H. 1967. *The Search for Order, 1877–1920*. New York: Hill and Wang.

Williams, Irving G. 1956. *The Rise of the Vice Presidency*. Washington, D.C.: Public Affairs Press.

Wilmerding, Lucius. 1943. *The Spending Power: A History of the Efforts of Congress to Control Expenditures*. New Haven, CT: Yale University Press; London: Oxford University Press, H. Milford.

Wilson, James Q. 1975. "The Rise of the Bureaucratic State." *The Public Interest* 10, no.41: 77–103.

Wilson, Woodrow. 1889. *The State: Elements of Historical and Practical Politics.* Boston: D.C. Heath.

Wooddy, Carroll H. 1934. *The Growth of Federal Government, 1915–1932.* New York: McGraw-Hill.

Wren, Daniel A. 1972. *The Evolution of Management Thought.* New York: Ronald Press.

Wright, Deil S. 1990. "Federalism, Intergovernmental Relations, and Intergovernmental Management: Historical Reflections and Conceptual Comparisons." *Public Administration Review* 50, no.2: 168–178.

Index of Authors